MGB

DBY 582T

MGB

RESTORATION / PREPARATION / MAINTENANCE

JIM TYLER

Every effort has been made to ensure that the maintenance procedures described in this book are correct. The Author and Publishers accept no responsibility for any loss or injury arising from any of the procedures and activities described.

First published in 1992 by Osprey Publishing,
Reed Consumer Books, Michelin House,
81 Fulham Road, London SW3 6RB
Reprintrd spring 1995 and autumn 1997

A catalogue record for this book is available on request from the British Library.

ISBN 1-85532-190-4

Page design: Gwyn Lewis
Editors: Shaun Barrington, Mansur Darlington
Phototypeset by Tradespools Ltd., Frome, Somerset
Printed in Great Britain by
The Bath Press

HALF-TITLE *MGB V8 3-1/2 litre; competition engine can be overbored by the professionals to 4 litres or taken out even further.*

TITLE PAGE *1979 MGB Roadster. (Photo: Andrew Morland)*

CONTENTS

ACKNOWLEDGEMENTS

The author gratefully acknowledges the help and assistance given by many companies and individuals in the preparation of this book.

The author is fortunate in living in an area where the MGB is particularly well served for spares and restoration businesses. Many local companies and individuals have helped in the preparation of this book. Special thanks go to Graham, John and Bob (shop), Trevor and John (workshop) of the Bromsgrove MG Centre for their help and advice and for allowing the author access to their workshops. Whilst this book was being prepared, the MG Owner's Club Magazine reported that the business had been awarded the prestigious '5 Spanner' rating for their workshop, to add to their existing '5 Star Dealership' award. Both are richly deserved. Situated right next door to the Bromsgrove MG Centre, Peter Harper – professional restorer of MGBs – was very generous in sharing the benefit of his years of experience and for providing photographs taken in his workshop.

Pete and John of Motor Fayre in Kidderminster made a first-class job of fitting a V8 engine into a Heritage bodyshell and were a mine of information on the subject.

Worcester Windscreens came to the rescue and proved to a doubting author that it is possible to fit windscreen finishing trim to the GT! Another Worcester company, Worcester MG Centre (also known as Sandsome Walk Service Station) were generous in their advice and in allowing the author access to their workshops.

Graham Hickman and the staff of Rolling Road Auto-Tune Services (RATS) gave the benefit of their years of experience in performance preparation.

SIP Holdings provided the excellent HandyMig gasless MIG welder and the Tornado compressor which are used by the author. Sykes Pickavant were helpful in providing photographs of their renowned range of hand tools.

Two other MG specialist businesses gave valuable assistance. The staff of the Ron Hopkinson MG centre have always impressed the author with their willingness to advise callers and their intimate knowledge of the MGB spares business. The V8 Centre supplied much helpful documentation dealing with the fitting of the Rover V8 engine into the MGB.

Thanks also to Autodata for permission to reproduce the diagrams throughout.

Lastly but by no means least, many of the author's friends have, over the years, contributed to his understanding of the maintenance, repair and restoration of the MGB.

INTRODUCTION

The MGB's high survival rate is a testament to the quality of its manufacture, to the wide availability of spares and to the continuing dedication and enthusiasm of its owners. The introduction of Heritage Roadster and GT bodyshells, coupled with the superb MGB spares and professional restoration industries, mean that no 'B' need now deteriorate to such an extent that it cannot be rebuilt. The future of the car seems assured.

Yet the MGB remains (and, one hopes, always will remain) an economical classic sports car. The prices realised by all but the rarer variants make the 'B' an attractive alternative to second-hand examples of more recent, characterless, vehicles. Unfortunately, this affordability means that the values of MGBs can be far lower than their restoration costs, which discourages some owners from spending sufficient money on their cars to make them roadworthy and sound.

Many examples which have been offered for sale and which the author has examined over the years have at some stage been maintained, repaired or restored shoddily. These have either been in poor condition mechanically due to poor maintenance, have suffered very poor quality bodywork repair, or very often both!

This book is intended to help the MGB owner to identify and rectify mechanical and bodywork defects, and then to maintain the car in safe and roadworthy condition, at the lowest cost. It is not, however, a workshop manual nor is it a general guide to the arts of bodywork repair. It should be used in conjunction with a good workshop manual such as the Autodata MGB Workshop Manual and, if more in-depth information is required on bodywork or other techniques, the 'How To Restore' series published by Osprey Automotive.

This book is written to suit the viewpoint of the person who has limited knowledge of car mechanical and bodywork repair, and whose facilities might extend only to a single car garage and a small range of hand tools. Most of the tasks described in the book have been attempted personally by the author, emulating the circumstances in which the reader might typically operate. This has entailed working in basic conditions with a limited range of tools.

Many of the jobs covered in the book have been carried out on a 24-year-old example of the car, which has the usual complement of corroded body panels and seized nuts and bolts. This approach has highlighted many problems which are not usually mentioned in workshop manuals because they are not encountered on the more recent examples of cars which are often used during the compilation of such books. These are, none the less, problems which will beset the average DIY enthusiast working at home.

Certain tasks in the repair and restoration of the MGB can only be carried out satisfactorily in appropriately equipped workshops which are staffed by experienced professionals. Other tasks which might be attempted at home are far better undertaken professionally for a variety of reasons. It is only those tasks which can be undertaken safely and which will result in a safe car, and those which are not riddled with opportunities for things to go badly and (usually) expensively wrong, that are covered in the greatest detail.

Some tasks, such as reconditioning a major mechanical component or attempting to restore a completely rotten or badly distorted bodyshell, are today rendered wholly unnecessary by the wide availability and comparative low costs of complete assemblies. In both these instances, it can be far more economical to opt for an exchange reconditioned unit or a new bodyshell than to attempt a DIY repair.

Many of the components of the MGB are referred to by different names in different countries, and even within a single country it is by no means unusual to hear a component referred to by two or more different names. This is especially true of body panels, but also of many mechanical components. The author has used, as far as possible, the component names which appear in the British Leyland Parts Catalogue. Use of these recognised terms can help prevent misunderstandings from arising when you come to order spares. If you can obtain a copy, the factory parts catalogue will furnish you with the correct part numbers for any necessary spares, and allow you to check to your own satisfaction that you are ordering the correct part by its unique number.

Always have the full engine number, year of manufacture and details of the original destination market of your car to hand when ordering spares. It is surprisingly easy inadvertently to obtain a spare part for the wrong year or mark of MGB, and such errors usually only show up when you try to fit it.

MGB GTs at Beaulieu. (Photo: Andrew Morland)

1 • A SHORT HISTORY

The MGB was launched in Roadster (drophead) form in 1962 as the replacement for the pretty and much-loved but rather spartan and, in due course, dated MGA. Unlike the MGA, which had a separate chassis, the new car was of unitary construction and incorporated strong chassis-like members into the pressed-steel body.

Design work on a replacement for the MGA had started in earnest during 1960, based on earlier factory styling exercises in the late 1950s, which had resulted in a design very closely resembling the MGB. At this time the company possessed very limited production capabilities for the manufacture of the MGA's chassis, which was bought in component form and then assembled at the factory. The market for sports cars at the time was large and growing, and in order to meet this new demand, the production bottleneck caused by the MGA's chassis was dealt with simply by designing a replacement car which did not have a chassis.

The opening of a huge pressed-steel plant not too far from MG's Abingdon home made the move to unitary construction possible, and the path was cleared for the company to increase sports car output. Unitary construction had already been used successfully by the British Motor Corporation (BMC) on the Sprite (the car which arguably launched the whole concept of mass-produced, low-cost small sports cars). Almost every pressing on the new MG played a part in maintaining its rigidity, creating a very strong monocoque bodyshell whose longevity would only really be fully appreciated decades later.

For a drophead sports car of the period, the MGB offered relative comfort and ample room for the occupants. The clean styling was quite a departure from that of contemporary sports cars yet, unlike most other 'modernistic' cars of the time which were characterised by toned-down features drawn from American auto-styling (fins and lots of gaudy brightwork), it has never dated. The retention of the 'classic' MG grille plus leather seats and optional wire wheels helped win over the hearts of many MG diehards who might otherwise have rebelled against a car which was such a departure for the company.

The MGB was powered by the proven 'B' Series four-cylinder overhead valve engine, enlarged to 1800cc and delivering a reported 95bhp at the flywheel. With a top speed comfortably in excess of 100mph and a 0-60mph time of around 12.6 seconds, the car compared quite well with its competitors, of which some could accelerate far more quickly, some of which had a higher top speed, and a few of which both accelerated faster than the MGB and had a higher top speed, but always at a far higher price.

Very desirable optional extras for the car included wire wheels, an oil cooler, a front anti-roll bar and even the heater! A few months after the car went on sale a further option of the Laycock D-type overdrive which gave the car its renowned unstressed high-speed touring capability was also added.

The launch car was fitted with a three-bearing (18GA) engine which was thought by some to be prone to crank-whip (literally flexing of the crankshaft which could occur at very high revolutions and which has the potential to wreck mains and big end bearings in next to no time). The 18GA engine had been earmarked for the forthcoming Austin 1800 saloon, although the three-bearing unit was not considered smooth enough for a saloon car and the five-bearing 18GB was developed. This was fitted in the MGB from 1964, and the same basic unit, with minor alterations, was to remain with the car for the next sixteen years of production.

Cars still fitted with the three-bearing crank engine are now extremely rare but by no means unknown. The average road car would probably never be pushed to the point at which serious crank whip occurs.

In 1965 the MGB GT was launched. The 1959 styling exercises, which so greatly influenced the eventual design of the MGB, had included a fastback hard-top version, and scale models of the result show a strong resemblance to the eventual lines of the MGB GT, excepting that the windscreen height, and hence the roof line, were lower. After reportedly trying the same exercise with the MGB (and getting the same too-low roof line) the car was sent to Pininfarina and there acquired its perfectly proportioned hard-top. Looking for all the world like a miniature Aston Martin or E-Type Jaguar, the car could not fail.

The GT version of the MGB was given a warm reception by the motoring press. Early reports praised the looks of the car which made it into a real head-turner, and nearly every motoring journalist was impressed by the handling and performance. Many testers reported that the car felt 'tauter' than the roadster. Although in later years the car (in all its guises) was to be heavily criticised in the motoring press for its handling, by 1966 standards it was obviously more than satisfactory.

In 1967 the MGC arrived. Although outwardly very similar to the 'B', this 2912cc straight six-cylinder 'C' series engine derivative was, in fact, a very different car under the skin. The tall engine unit simply would not fit into the standard car with the huge cross-member which carried the standard front suspension in place, and so an alternative member and a torsion bar suspension system were developed. Even so, the bonnet needed a bulge and a further 'teardrop' to clear the rocker box cover and carburettor respectively! The torsion bar suspension consisted of a wide upper wishbone and a single link lower member which was connected to the torsion bar. The torsion bar ran to the main fixed chassis member, which was strengthened. The torsion bar was adjustable, which was fortunate, because the engine turned out to be rather heavier than the four-cylinder unit and so made the car sit lower at the front end. The bar could be adjusted to compensate. The front dampers were telescopic, whilst at the rear, lever arm dampers were retained.

The MGC was intended to replace the big Healey three-litre range but failed to win the hearts of Healey fans; being considerably more nose-heavy than the MGB and possessing raised ground clearance

LEFT *1969 MGB Roadster with much-maligned black grille.*

The Mk1 MGB GT was arguably one of the nicest looking cars of its time.

courtesy of the 15in wheels, the handling of the 'C suffered and the performance increase was not spectacular enough to compensate for this. Originally, the MGC was to have been marketed with both MG and Healey badges, although the latter arrangement never came to fruition.

The version of the 'C' series engine that was designed for the MGC developed slightly less power than the original, and had its main bearings increased in number from four to seven, which made it less willing to rev. Just under 9,000 MGCs were reportedly built, with around 35 per cent staying in the UK and most of the rest going to the USA. Needless to say, the 'C is now a rare and valuable car.

Also in 1967, the company introduced the Mark 2 MGB, most readily identified by the twin reversing lights. The main improvements were an all-synchro gearbox, and negative-earth electrical system with an alternator instead of the earlier positive-earth system and dynamo. USA cars suffered the indignity of being fitted with the first of a range of safety and emission control equipment to satisfy ever-tighter legislation which was one day to assist in the car's demise. Both the standard MGB and the MGC were available with an automatic gearbox from 1967.

The Mark 3 appeared in 1969 and attracted criticism from traditionalist MG enthusiasts because of its recessed black grille. Further exhaust emission equipment was fitted to USA export cars. For the first time the car had reclining seats. Numerous detail changes followed, including even more controls and safety equipment for USA cars.

Following the success of one Ken Costello in independently fitting the 'B' with the Rover V8 3.5-litre engine, British Leyland introduced their own version in 1973 in GT form only. Some 2,500 of these were manufactured until 1976. The car was not offered in MG's most successful market place, the USA. This may have partly been due to problems in meeting exhaust emission regulations but was more probably due to the fact that the limited numbers of engines available would have in turn limited the numbers of cars. It may have been felt that too many USA buyers would have cancelled their ordered MGBs and tried to obtain one of the far fewer V8s, costing the company huge numbers of sales of the standard model.

In 1974 drastic changes which had proven necessary for the USA were introduced across the range and further angered the home market purists. The most obvious and most criticised of these were the combined raising of ride height (which increased already considerable body roll levels) and huge black 'rubber' bumpers, which in reality consisted of heavy steel bumpers covered in black polyurethane. These were necessary to meet new USA crash collision legislation.

Emission laws were also tightened, and since the heavier GT was in a higher emission class than the Roadster and would have required extra emission control equipment to meet the criteria for vehicles in its weight class, British Leyland elected to take the GT out of the USA market. The GT need not, therefore, have been fitted with rubber bumpers and had its ride height raised, but presumably the extra expense of running two separate production lines persuaded the manufacturers to apply the 'improvements' across the range.

A limited edition 'Jubilee' model of 750 cars was manufactured in 1975 to mark MG's Fiftieth Anniversary, and the following year the car's body roll was tamed with a rear anti-roll bar plus a thicker bar at the front. The final 1000 cars were known as 'Limited Edition' and featured special brown (drophead) and silver (GT) paintwork and spoilers.

Production ended in October 1980.

Reams have been written by way of a post-mortem for the MGB to explain why so successful a car should have been taken out of production. There is no single reason for this, but a combination. The general situation within the BL group at the time was very complicated. Both MG and Triumph had for some time been developing new designs to replace the MGB and TR6 respectively, and whilst the MG design, the ADO21, was for an advanced mid-engined car which utilised the existing Maxi engine but which would have required great investment, Triumph designed the easy-to-build TR7. The TR7 was permitted to go ahead, whilst MG were left with no successor to the MGB.

It is interesting to reflect that the two most appealing of the 1990s small sports cars, the Mazda MX5 and the Toyota MR2, have so much in common with the MGB and ADO21 respectively. One can only speculate as to whether the UK would still produce the world's favourite sports cars had MG been allowed to continue at the expense of Triumph.

Nearer to that 'Black Monday' when the decision to close Abingdon was announced, the British Leyland group were trying to sell the relatively new Triumph TR7 in America and withdrew the MGB totally from its largest market. The company may have lacked the financial resources to develop new emission control equipment for the engines in both cars and may have had to settle for one or the other. It seems more likely that they simply did not wish to compete with themselves by having two two-seater ragtops in the same market place. The company also reportedly needed its financial resources for the development program of the Metro car.

The profitability of the MGB in the United States suffered with a change in the exchange rate. On the home market, in 1980 the MGB roadster sold for 10 per cent less than the price of the TR7 convertible, and as it is difficult to see any sign of higher quality to justify the extra cost of the TR7, the TR7 was probably by far the more profitable of the two to manufacture.

But the MGB refused to die then, as it still refuses to die today. As the 1990s begin it is the most popular sports car on the roads of the UK if not of the world.

MG RV8

The MGB story took possibly its most exciting twist in October 1992 when Rover Cars unveiled the beautiful MG RV8 at the British Motor Show. Based on the standard Heritage bodyshell but with flared wings giving the car lines reminiscent of those of the AC Cobra (the development car was code-named 'Adder' in deference to the Cobra), the RV8 aroused even more excitement than did the MGB at its launch.

Using the same Rover V8 unit which powered the Costello and factory V8s, but bored out to give a capacity of 3.9 litres, the car can accelerate from a standstill to 60 mph in around 6 seconds – half the length of time the average 'B takes! Top speed is listed at 135 mph, and the legal motorway limit of 70 mph (UK) is achieved at a whisker over 2,400 rpm in top gear. The tried and trusted 77mm 5-speed gearbox makes the most of the engine power.

Many people were surprised that the MG RV8 retained the live axle of the MGB rather than an independent rear suspension but, given that the car was strictly limited edition and that no more than 2,000 examples were to be made, this lack of

Although the RV8 did attract some criticism from sections of the motoring press, more enlightened reviewers who realised what the car was really about – an MGB for the 1990s rather than a 'supercar' – loved it. (Courtesy Rover Cars).

The MG RV8 was the motoring sensation of 1992, attracting more press and TV coverage than any other new car. Although based on the Heritage MGB bodyshell, the flared wings, fat tyres and general styling of the car give it a much more aggressive look than the standard MGB. (Courtesy Rover Cars).

development investment becomes easier to understand. However, some work was needed in order to allow drivers to keep the rear rubber in contact with tarmac on acceleration, and torque control arms were fitted to aid axle location, along with an anti-roll bar. More efficient telescopic dampers replaced the traditional lever-arm types, and a torque bias differential feeds power to wheels according to their traction.

The old front lever arm damper, which formed the upper suspension link on the MGB, was replaced with a telescopic damper and an upper wishbone. Subtle changes to the suspension geometry were incorporated to allow better use of the properties of modern tyres. Coupled with an all-new braking system, the on-road behaviour of the MG RV8 was a marked improvement on that of the MGB.

In keeping with the role of the RV8 as a high-speed tourer, the interior was – by MGB standards – sumptuous, with leather upholstery and burr elm veneer in abundance. The MG RV8 was erroneously perceived by many – most especially the motoring press – at its launch to be an attempt by Rover to create a 'supercar', whereas the truth of the matter was that the car was an MGB V8 for the 1990s, it was a limited edition celebration of the 30th anniversary of the most successful and best loved British sports car of all time.

LIVING WITH AN MGB

People buy MGBs for all manner of reasons. Some have always harboured secret desires for a classic British sports car and some – the author included – promised themselves many years ago (in their youth) that one day they would own a specific year and model of MGB. Some people buy MGBs thinking that they are fast cars, which is not really true nowadays when many quite ordinary small family cars will match the MGB's performance.

The fact emerges that many people buy the cars for sentimental reasons without firstly finding out whether the cars will do whatever they require of them. In other words, they have no idea of what life with an MGB will be like. This section of the book is intended to present the practicalities of MGB ownership.

It is difficult to know what yardstick to apply in order to assess and describe a car, when it has been out of production for many years yet is still used by tens of thousands of people as a sports car, a classic car and as daily transport. It would be patently unfair to try to compare it directly with any modern car, yet such comparisons are difficult to avoid and the old MGB – in common with several sports cars of the 1960s – actually does rather well! The car could, alternatively, be compared with a contemporary sports car such as the Triumph GT6 or one of the TR range, but handling and performance would depend to such an extent upon the relative conditions of the two individual old cars as to make the results fairly worthless.

The only fair and realistic way to assess the car is as a classic sports car which has the potential to offer practical and reliable transportation in today's world, which is, after all, what most first-time buyers seek from an MGB. In meeting these requirements, the car is by no means unique, but is unarguably the leading example of a very small select group. Whilst many classic sports cars can out-perform the MGB on the road or in terms of investment value, few alternatives can match the MGB for its combination of availability and cheapness of spares, longevity, strength, aesthetic appeal, practicality and performance.

One of the first attractions of MGB ownership to come to the attention of the new owner is the instant adoption into the great unofficial 'family' of MGB enthusiasts. Ninety-nine out of every hundred MGB drivers, it seems, wave or flash their lights whenever they see another MGB. If an owner is unlucky enough to suffer a breakdown then it would be a rare passing MGB driver who did not stop to offer assistance!

MGB ownership opens up organised social activities for those who care to seek out the nearest branch of either of the UK or several overseas owners' clubs. There are more regional and national level activities open to the MGB owner than there are for the driver of any other classic British sports car. More important than any of the above is the sheer joy of driving that solid classic sports car on the open road.

MGB VERSUS THE MODERN CAR

How practical a car, though, is the MGB as a dependable means of everyday transport? A mechanically good example is surprisingly practical. The comparatively simple technology of the MGB must actually reduce the chances of breakdowns when compared to (and this will be more marked in the future) well-used examples of the electronics-dependent engines of today. Electronic 'fail-safe' devices have been used on many motor cars since the 1970s, and each extra device as it ages and becomes less reliable is not a benefit but, simply, a liability because it is something else to go wrong!

For instance, a simple old-fashioned dashboard oil-pressure warning light or gauge might be replaced in the modern car with an electronic circuit which cuts out the ignition and disables the engine if a serious fault such as low oil pressure or massive overheating appears to develop in the engine. Thus, a fault in the fail-safe circuit itself (by no means unknown) in the modern car can leave the driver stranded with a perfectly healthy car which refuses to run. Furthermore, modern electronic components are not usually designed to be repairable, but if faulty they must often be replaced. There is little on the 'low technology' MGB which cannot be repaired, reconditioned or replaced with a widely-available spare, which is an important factor in saving the car from ever becoming totally obsolete for want of a spare part.

The day to day 'up front' running costs of the MGB are very often higher than those of more modern vehicles. The MGB requires more frequent and more time-consuming attention than the modern car, and due to the age of the engine likely to be fitted, consumables such as oil and filters cannot be changed too frequently. Against this, the MGB owner will not, unlike the owner of a new car, face the dilemma of whether to have the car serviced at an inflated price at the franchise garage (and get the service book stamped) or whether to find a cheaper servicing alternative and suffer the reduced residual value of a car without a stamped service book. Some franchise car garages charge as much for labour during an 'official' major service as MGB specialists do for a sill change!

Fuel consumption can vary between 22mpg and perhaps 27mpg, stretching to just over 30mpg on a long overdrive-assisted run (all dependent on the state of the individual car). By modern standards, this level of fuel consumption is high; certainly over 50 per cent more fuel will be used by the MGB than by the fuel-efficient cars of similar performance of the late 1980s.

The MGB wins hands down when it comes to the pricing and availability of spares. Firstly, the MGB owner has the option of buying non-guaranteed spares from a breakers yard, guaranteed reconditioned spares from MGB specialists, plus sundry brand new spares from the original manufacturers such as Lucas and SU, and even complete bodyshells! Furthermore, the prices which are charged for those spares will usually not exceed, and sometimes be far less than, the prices of spares for most modern vehicles, both of UK manufacture and imported. There are exceptions, though, and a few MGB spares are inexplicably exorbitantly priced.

In its overseas markets the foregoing comments may not be strictly accurate, because although the MGB will normally have a full supply of spares, there will be far fewer retail sources and the prices will be higher accordingly. In the main, spares sources will be specialist businesses offering the option of mail order trading for those owners unfortunate enough to be located a long distance from the nearest stockist.

Insurance costs for the MGB in the UK are maintained at very low levels by arrangements between the owners' clubs and insurance brokers. More, however, could be done in educating the insurers about the unusually low risk posed by the average MGB owner. First, a classic car is unlikely to be driven in a reckless manner because of its value. Secondly, a classic car is far more likely to be properly maintained in a roadworthy condition than an ageing example of a modern vehicle. Finally, the MGB is no longer to be considered a 'performance' vehicle, in fact it is slow in comparison with many modern cars which – inexplicably – fall into lower insurance groups.

Appreciation and depreciation

The greatest cost benefit offered by the MGB in comparison with the modern vehicle is its lack of depreciation. At the time of writing, a modern car which is purchased new and run for the average UK annual mileage of 11,000 miles will depreciate to scrap value (unless it becomes recognised as a classic) within a maximum of ten to twelve years. Look up the price of a new car and you will see that it does not cost as much to keep an MGB in good repair over a ten to twelve year period (and to pay for the extra petrol) as it does to bear the depreciation of a new car.

For the price of a new car it is possible to buy an MGB and restore it to superb (not concours) condition, giving in effect almost a 'new' MGB. After ten or so years, the restored MGB might have cost rather more to run than the modern vehicle (due to higher fuel consumption) but the MGB will be worth many times as much as the more modern car because, although both will initially depreciate, the MGB will begin at some stage to appreciate while the other car carries on depreciating. This appreciation in value has attracted many investors into the classic car scene, and at the time of writing values have peaked and some have collapsed following an unprecedented surge (those cars which showed the greatest rise in value also showed the greatest falls following the peak). If you are attracted to the classic car purely for reasons of investment, bear in mind that a classic car, like any other investment, can go down as well as up in value, markedly so if a temporary 'bubble' of surging values bursts!

Legislation and obsolescence

Lead in petrol was a great talking point of the late 1980s because of reported links between atmospheric lead levels and brain damage in children. The use of unleaded petrol was promoted as a consequence of this. Ozone layer damage also hit the headlines, and car manufacturers reluctantly responded with catalytic converters. At some time in the future (perhaps by the time you are reading this book) legislation is likely to be implemented to outlaw leaded petrol and to limit the emission of ozone-damaging gases, which could, at a stroke, remove from the roads many classic cars which could not comply with the new regulations.

The MGB is the least likely of classic sports cars to be legislated off the roads in this manner. So many examples of the car exist that huge profit potentials exist for the manufacture of accessories which will enable the car to comply with almost any requirements which might be made of it. Items such as cylinder heads able to withstand unleaded petrol, and catalytic converters have already been developed for the MGB. No matter what the legislative process throws at the motorist in the future, be it safety cages, collapsible steering columns, ABS braking systems or even ejector seats and parachutes, the MGB owner will almost certainly be able to comply. The only way in which the car could be legislated off the road would be a blanket ban on cars over a certain age, but the availability of brand-new bodyshells would still probably allow MGB owners to keep going when no other classic sports car was permitted on the road!

DRIVING THE MGB

A surprisingly high number of people seem to have a jaundiced view of the MGB's performance. They will earnestly inform you that the MGB is a slow car and that its handling is awful, yet, almost without exception, they will grudgingly admit to never having owned, and in many cases never having driven, the MGB! The source of these erroneous second-hand opinions is not too difficult to trace.

Throughout the 1960s the MGB was constantly praised for its performance and handling by the motoring press world-wide. In the early 1970s, however, a few journalists began to criticise the car in these two areas, drawing direct comparisons with the then latest examples of sports and performance cars (most of which have since passed largely into obscurity). As the decade wore on, the articles became evermore disparaging, not because the MGB had become a lesser car but probably because of the emergence of a new type of much more sensational writing style and, perhaps the fact that new and younger journalists were now writing, and writing about a car with which they had had no experience as a new and exciting vehicle.

The journalists of the 1970s and thereafter ignored the fact that the MGB had proven itself a very capable competition car across a wide range of events. In the hysteria which followed the Mini Cooper's 1964 Monte Carlo win, the fact that the MGB had won its GT class was overlooked by many, and probably forgotten by the time it became fashionable amongst journalists to deride the car. In the same year, the MGB took a class win and second place in the Austrian Alpine Rally. The previous year the car had also proven its potential on the track, taking class wins at Goodwood, Silverstone and Le Mans. Many class and outright wins on and off the track followed – too many to list here – to be crowned with an outright win in the 5000-plus kilometre Nürburgring 48-hour endurance event.

The MGB is still winning historic racing events and hill climbs. In 1990, Ron Gammons drove an MGB to second place in the Pirelli Classic Marathon, which recreates as closely as is practical the Monte Carlo of old. Despite being narrowly beaten by Paddy Hopkirk in a Mini Cooper 1275S, the MGB took second, third and fourth places, ahead of other Cooper 1275Ss, Morgan Plus Fours and other cars which are usually acknowledged as being faster than the MGB!

The modern MGB rally drivers are using cars which are probably far better set up than any of the works or privately-developed rally MGBs of the sixties, and one can only wonder at what successes the car might had enjoyed if the same sort of modifications had been available then. The Pirelli MGBs, incidentally, were prepared by Ron Gammons' company, Brown and Gammons.

The cars which won competitions years ago usually bore scant detailed resemblance to road-going versions. Suspensions were uprated or even redesigned, engines were tuned, blueprinted and sometimes replaced with far more powerful units. Which leads back to the widely held low opinion of the performance of the standard car.

The engine

The following relates to the standard 1800cc engine without emission control equipment.

The 1800cc 'B' series engine in standard tune is reckoned to produce around 84bhp at the flywheel (the widely published figure of 95bhp is today disputed by many), which equates to around 70-75bhp

Separated by more than a decade, the 1966 Mark 1 GT and the 1977 rubber bumper Roadster appear to be poles apart. Yet obvious differences in ride height, passenger comfort and instrumentation seem to fade away when the cars are compared on the road. The sensation of actually driving each of the two cars is remarkably similar, so that, whichever year, mark or type of MGB you choose, you will still be able to enjoy that tangible MGB 'experience'.

at the wheels (due to transmission losses). With an all-up weight ranging between 2030lb and 2400lb, only 3.5-4bhp per 100lb cannot be expected to give outstanding acceleration. As the MGB is in reality a 'sports touring' car rather than a pure sports car, the torque of the engine is probably of greater consideration than the power output, and in this respect the car is certainly not wanting.

The standard MGB delivers 110 foot pounds (ft lb) of torque at an leisurely 3000rpm. Torque is best thought of as brute force which allows you, for instance, to stay in overdriven top gear on hills which force drivers of cars with less torque to change down in order to raise the revs and hence the bhp. The engine is thus extremely tractable and ideal for use in a touring car.

Published 0-60mph performance figures can be quite misleading, in so far as they do not equate to what can be achieved on the road but describe a gearbox- and engine-wrecking thrash in ideal conditions. Also useless as a comparison between two different models, because of different gear ratios, but very revealing as to the actual road performance, are the 30-50mph, 40-60mph and etc figures, which show clearly how good the car is at overtaking other vehicles. In these the MGB does rather well in comparison with both contemporary sports cars and also with many modern vehicles.

To sum up the performance of the 1800cc MGB, it allows unstressed (and hence pleasurable) progress. It will happily cruise day in, day out at 70mph on motorways at a little over 3000rpm in overdrive top and will probably return fuel consumption figures around the 25 mpg mark. On more ordinary roads, progress is aided by the nicely balanced ratios of overdrive third and straight third; when coming up behind a slower vehicle, the car may be changed down from overdrive top to overdrive third and flicked out of overdrive as the overtaking manoeuvre begins to produce a satisfying and safe surge of power.

A properly set-up example of the engine is very smooth from its tickover of 600-700rpm right through the rev band up to the recommended 5500rpm ceiling. An example in excellent condition may be pushed beyond this if desired without the likelihood of instantaneous tragedy, although the practice cannot be recommended. Those cars which are fitted with emission controls may well suffer flat spots between 1000 and 1500 rpm.

Handling and roadholding

Even the most ardent admirer of the MGB will be forced to admit that modern vehicles handle far better than the standard MGB. The handling and roadholding which delighted users and journalists throughout the early 1960s was outclassed by that of many later cars, and not just sports cars but also quite ordinary family saloons.

The performance put up by the 'B comes down to two factors: the weight of the 'B' series engine and the degree of body roll suffered by the car in all its variants. The nose weight of the car tends to promote understeer as a corner is entered. The body roll allows the centre of gravity of the rear end of the car to begin to lift quite easily when into the corner. If the speed of the car and the tightness of the bend are sufficient then the traction of the rear wheels can reduce and allow the rear end of the car to come around sharply, changing the gentle and controllable understeer into oversteer. At all normal road speeds, however, the change from understeer to oversteer is very gentle and controllable.

Different variants of the MGB suffer these two problems to differing extents. The earliest Roadsters often lacked anti-roll bars (a front anti-roll bar was available as an optional extra) and so cornering suffered. Rear anti-roll bars were not standardised until 1976, so that chrome bumper cars still showed rear body lift on corners and the newer pre-1976 rubber bumper cars with raised ride height were even worse!

Hindsight is a wonderful thing because anybody can put matters right with the benefit of it. Hindsight highlights the fact that, had decent anti-roll bars like those now marketed by Ron Hopkinson been standard equipment from the start (see Chapter 5) or had the car been set up in the same manner as that of the MGB which Ron Gammons drove to 2nd place in the 1990 Pirelli Classic Marathon, then the MGB would probably never have been criticised for its handling. Such arguments fail to take account of the praise which was heaped on the handling qualities of the MGB in its early days! The manufacturers did not improve the car's handling because they did not at the time have to.

To sum up the MGB's handling, it is quite adequate for all save the fastest progress around bends. If the car is pushed to the point at which the rear end begins to slide then it is still relatively easily controlled. In comparison with many sports cars, the MGB is very easily pushed to the point at which things begin to happen but not so easily taken to the point at which the car is uncontrollable. Other sports cars are notable for behaving themselves superbly up to a point far beyond the MGB's change from understeer into oversteer, but when they do go there is very little the driver can do to salvage the situation.

To those who say that the MGB does not handle, the best response is to ask which sports car (of any make) has survived in such numbers as the MGB. Follow this by observing that any car which actually handled as badly as popular myth suggests that the MGB does could not possibly have survived in such quantities, because most examples would have by now been written-off on bends!

GENERAL CONSIDERATIONS

Life with an MGB can be very pleasant. The engine is an excellent starter, renowned for trouble-free, smooth and unstressed running. On most roads, gear changes can be reserved for pulling away from a standstill, because the engine will not complain unduly if you go through a 30mph limit zone legally in overdriven top and then slowly gather speed afterwards.

Driver and 'front' passenger comfort (there simply is no comfort for anyone in the back of the GT) depends on the year, with cars from 1969 having reclining seats which became increasingly comfortable as they were improved year by year. Leg room (in the front) is excellent, allowing the occupants to stretch out. The GT in good order is warm (though the performance of the heater leaves much to be desired on a bitter winter's day), dry and relatively noise free.

The controls cannot be unduly criticised in the context of their production dates, although the non-illuminated heater controls in early cars were almost impossible to see and operate in the dark, and the dashboard switches for lights, heater and wipers were just as bad.

Driver visibility in the GT is generally good, although the front screen pillar can present an uncomfortable right-hand cornering blind spot depending, of course, on the position of the driver's seat and the perspective this creates. Both the Roadster and the GT need wing or door-mounted rear view mirrors, because turning to look behind when pulling off can be at best a strain, and for safe overtaking they are essential.

In conclusion, the driver of a modern vehicle who drives an MGB for the first time will be acutely aware that he is sitting close to the road. In most other respects he will feel perfectly 'at home'.

He might also be aware that he is deriving far greater enjoyment from driving the MGB that from a modern vehicle!

2 • BUYING AN MGB

Unlike the intending buyer of most classic sports cars, whose choice of available cars can be very restricted by the low numbers of surviving examples, the prospective MGB purchaser appears to be spoilt for choice because the market place always seems to contain many more MGBs than it does any other classic sports car. This comparatively huge selection does not make the job of selecting the right car any easier, however, because a substantial proportion of those cars which are placed on the open market will require extensive repair. Some will be structurally unsound, and a few downright dangerous. Yet even the very worst examples will usually find unsuspecting buyers.

The reason why some people buy MGBs in poor or in dangerous condition is that instead of first finding out how to properly appraise an MGB, they will view a car with their heads filled with nothing more than a vision of themselves creaming along a country road on a summer's afternoon with the hood down and the wind in their hair. They look at the interior, they look at the chromework (a few even go so far as to kick the tyres) but they fail to notice even the most severe of structural faults.

In the United Kingdom, far too much importance is attached to the fact that a car possesses a current (often a newly acquired) Ministry of Transport (MOT) Test Certificate (most cars which come onto the market will possess an MOT certificate, because this makes them far easier to sell). The MOT test procedure does not permit the tester to remove glued-in carpets or interior panels, to scrape away underseal or remove bolted-on panels on order to be able to find the hidden rot most likely to afflict the MGB. The individual approved tester will not usually be an expert on MGBs; even if he were familiar with the car and knew where to look for hidden bodyrot he would not be permitted to do so, and the certificate should be viewed accordingly. The only bodyrot which is likely to be discovered by the MOT test at the time of writing is that which is visible from the inspection pit (castle rail, chassis member or perhaps a hole which passes right through the lower outer wing and sill sections) plus rot revealed if the main cross-member buckles as the car is raised by its jacking point, and rot revealed if a seat belt mounting pulls free when tugged!

To summarise, honest-to-goodness bodyrot can be revealed by the MOT test, but rot which is camouflaged might not be. Too often an MOT certificate is taken by prospective purchasers as proof that the car concerned is structurally sound and, so long as it looks reasonably smart, the deal is struck.

The worth of official test certificates will obviously vary according to the country in question and the stringency of test routines. In the future, we can expect all testing procedures in the UK and abroad to become ever-more stringent, and, at the time of writing, the UK MOT test is set to incorporate exhaust emission tests. There appears to be nothing in the pipe-line, however, which will give testers the power to seek out fundamental bodywork faults such as advanced rot and distortion. Other types of certificate, however, can be very useful. A motor engineer's report may be commissioned and go into great detail about not only the state of the mechanicals but also of the bodywork. Motoring organisations sometimes arrange these. With MGBs, the engineers often have quite a lot to write about!

The sad fact is that unless an MGB has been locked in an air-conditioned garage with controlled humidity, or unless it has recently been fully restored and thoroughly rustproofed then it will to a greater or lesser extent have some body rust. The simple rule which should always be stuck to when appraising an MGB is to expect the bodyshell to have some rust and to try to establish the extent and the rectification costs of that rust!

PRIVATE OR TRADE?

Before pursuing the question of which MGB to buy, a few thoughts on where to buy are appropriate.

There are five main alternative sources of the MGB:

1. Most classic cars which change hands are sold by one private individual to another.
2. MGBs are increasingly being traded by a growing number of dealerships specialising in classic and classic sports cars – some even dedicated to a particular marque or model.
3. A diminishing number of MGBs are finding their way into the hands of mainstream second-hand car dealers, but this does happen.
4. As MGBs become more collectable, more are being sold at classic motor auctions.
5. Very rarely, an MGB might appear at a general car auction.

The classic car auction is by far the safer of the two types from which to buy an MGB, and the fact that other intending and often very knowledgeable buyers are around can be a great help to the tyro. The general car auction is another matter altogether. There are few valid reasons why a sound example of a collector's car such as the MGB should ever find its way to such an event.

Each source has its pros and cons according to the aspirations of the buyer. You are unlikely to buy a real bargain, for instance, from a classic car specialist, but you will get little in the way of consumer protection if you opt for a private vendor.

Private – looking for a bargain?

The main drawback with buying from a private vendor is that once money has changed hands and the car has been driven or towed away then the vendor generally assumes that he has no further liability; if the car folds in half a week later because the sills are rotten then the poor buyer will often have to resort to legal action to recoup anything from the deal. The limited liability of the private vendor is in some people's eyes countered by the advantageous prices which can sometimes be negotiated, but buying privately is always something of a gamble.

But what are the chances of finding a bargain-priced MGB? The sad answer is that they are very low indeed and probably akin to winning a lottery. The 'B now possesses collectors' classic sports car status and few vendors will be unaware of this or slow to try to capitalise upon it. Worse, many non-enthusiasts assume ridiculously high collectors' values for their cars. Those who do not subscribe to the classic car press can only take their pricing information from the occasional woolly item which appears in the general press and which usually does no more to quantify the rises in value of collector's cars than to state that 'prices are rocketing'.

Some vendors get their pricing information from one of the price guides which are regularly published in classic car magazines. The great problem with such guides lies in their interpretation in as much as cars are usually graded 'A', 'B' or 'C' (or 1, 2, or 3) condition with appropriate prices for each, and most non-expert vendors 'up' their cars by at least one class and sometimes more because they are not qualified properly to assess the condition.

Thus, the 'Class A' car which you drive miles to see might well turn out to be a near-wreck not even rating a 'Class C' tag and worth perhaps a quarter of its asking price!

In truth, a vendor cannot put an absolute value on a car because it is worth exactly what you the purchaser are prepared to pay and not a penny more. Exactly how you ascribe a value to a car is up to you, but the following method might be of interest.

Begin with the current classic car or MGB magazine guide price for an example in the condition which you require. Subtract from this the costs of getting the car in question to that condition and the remainder can be thought of as its current value to you. If you take a current MGB specialists' spares catalogue with you, then you can easily arrive at a figure which will be necessary to get the car in question to the condition which you require.

Buying privately can bring a 'hidden' cost which will not be apparent until you have wasted considerable time and money travelling to view misrepresented cars! After reading the whole of this chapter you will probably be able to rule out the very worst cars more or less 'at a glance', irrespective of the glowing description given in the advertisement and the vendor's assurances that the car was in excellent condition when you telephoned to arrange a viewing. In some instances, closer inspection will be needed to find the rot when it has been expertly hidden (some people put as much time and effort into hiding bodyrot as would be needed to rectify it!). Anticipate many wasted journeys.

Many MGBs are advertised as 'recently restored' and if this is the case then the vendor has no excuse for not being able to provide a full photographic record of the restoration. Most professional restorers provide photographs of the job in progress as a matter of course. If photographs are not available then it is likely that the restoration was not too extensive or that photographs were supplied but reveal other bodywork problems which the vendor does not wish you to see! The advertisement for a 'recently restored' car raises the question of why the owner should go to all the trouble and expense of a restoration only to sell the car immediately. The most common reason for such a car being sold appears to be that a planned full body restoration was hastily turned into a 'cover-up' when the true extent of the bodyrot and the costs of rectification became apparent. Be very thorough when assessing such cars!

When buying privately, always make sure that you see the Vehicle Registration Document (form V5 in the UK or its equivalent overseas), which will show – amongst other things – how many owners the car has had in the last few years. Some MGBs (particularly those with severe bodyrot) change hands many times in a short space of time as each buyer discovers the car's problems and quickly sells it to the next! People can be so desperate to sell such a car that they advertise it whilst the registration document is still being processed by the authorities for the previous transaction.

The most serious problem with buying privately is the risk of unwittingly buying a stolen car. Seeing the UK registration document does not give you a guarantee that the vendor is the actual owner of the car; the person named can be merely the registered keeper and might not necessarily be in a position to sell the car. There is in fact no record on the UK Registration Document of who the owner of the vehicle is. If you buy a stolen car from a dealer then you have some legal redress as long as the dealer is solvent – if you buy it privately then you will probably loose both the car and your money. There can be no better argument for taking your business to a reputable dealer.

Many tricks are employed by the motor vehicle thief to make stolen cars appear legitimate. V5 Vehicle Registration Documents are forged or altered (always look very closely at these). Two cars are sometimes simultaneously sold in different parts of the country with the same registration plates and duplicate registration documents (check engine/ chassis numbers and look for alterations to the Registration Documents). Occasionally, cars will be stolen 'to order' to take the identity of a written-off example of the same model, year and colour.

Always ask to see the receipt given to the vendor by the previous owner. Some vendors will not wish you to see this if they are selling for a far higher price than they bought the car for; some vendors will not be able to show you the receipt because there is not one, in which case the car could well be stolen! If you can see the receipt then you have the option of contacting the previous owner, which will go some small way to assuring you that the car is legitimate.

Another reason for wishing to see the receipt from the previous vendor is to avoid buying a car which is the subject of an outstanding Hire Purchase (HP) debt. As the name suggests, in HP agreements the car remains the property of the lender (the HP company) until such time as the amount is paid in full. Only then does ownership pass from the HP company. If you are unfortunate enough to buy a car which has the slightest amount outstanding on an HP agreement, the HP company will repossess the car and be under no obligation whatever to offer you any compensation; neither do they have to assist you in any way in recovering your money. Always see the receipt!

Another check which can sometimes help to identify a stolen car is to contact the British Motor Industry Heritage Trust (Tel. 0572 85 4014). For a fee, the BMIHT will check their records and give you details of the original specification of any MGB when it left the factory, including the paint colour.

Even better, in the UK, HP Autodata (0722 422422) operate a computerised database listing stolen cars and any against which outstanding payments are owing. Your local Crime Prevention Officer can give you the current telephone number.

'Ringing' is a growing crime in which a car of a particular age and model is stolen to order to assume the identity of a similar but completely written-off example, or the identity of an existing example for which a duplicate registration document has been obtained. In the UK it is possible to obtain a duplicate registration document, so that a legitimate car's identity may be shared with a stolen vehicle. Two or more cars with the same registration number can theoretically exist! The car ends up appearing perfectly legitimate and all which has to be done to it is to fit new number plates, deface the old engine and chassis plates (or replace them as they are readily available to order) and spray the car in the correct colours. If the colour listed on the V5 differs from the original then carefully check the car, chassis and body number against those listed by the BMIHT.

FINDING AN MGB

Most people who wish to sell their MGB begin by placing an advertisement in a local publication, and this is as good a place as any to start looking. The beauty of using local publications is that you will not have to travel too far to see the car, whereas if you search the national press or magazines you will certainly find a lot of cars but probably very few close to home. Because many of your journeys will be wasted due to misrepresentation you can save time, money and temper by buying locally!

It is worth finding out in which editions of your local papers are featured the car advertisements, because you will often find many more cars advertised on particular days. Regional editions of national advertising publications will also have many local cars advertised within their pages.

If you embark on this course then you will have to move quickly whenever you find a suitable advertisement, because there is often a good deal of competition. Furthermore there are a lot of mugs out there who will pay a high price for any 'B (even one which is patently a pile of junk), so long as it has an MOT and four tyres, and they will be quite likely to be racing you to the telephone the moment they see the advertisement. This will not happen in every single instance but it does pay to be first off the mark anyway.

It is worth looking at every car even if the previous viewer handed over a cheque in full payment for the car, because many of the potential buyers that an MGB attracts will be likely to back out of the deal before the cheque is cleared. These are the dreaded 'dreamers', who write out cheques on empty accounts, who subsequently find that they cannot afford or get insurance for the car, or who simply change their minds. They are the people described in those adverts which begin 'Re-advertised due to time-waster'. So evaluate the car just as thoroughly as if it were still for sale and if it is a good buy then leave the vendor your telephone number just in case the deal falls through.

SPREADING THE WORD

Arguably the best way of acquiring an MGB is to find one which has not yet come to the market by letting it be known as far and as wide as possible that you are interested in buying one. A 'Wanted' advertisement in a local publication or even a shop window can sometimes work wonders, and it helps to mention to everyone you meet that you are looking for a 'B, because the person you speak to might just know someone who is thinking of selling one.

Word of mouth and other local advertising is an especially excellent way of finding 'restoration project' cars. There must be thousands of 'Bs languishing in garages and gardens, untaxed, well out of MOT and deteriorating for want of a planned restoration which will probably never actually happen. The owners of such cars might well be reluctant to put them on the market because they feel that to do so would be to admit defeat in some way. All it usually takes to persuade them to sell the car which, deep down, they know they will never restore, is the offer of money.

THE SECOND-HAND CAR DEALER

Largely gone are the days when mainstream used-car dealers lined MGBs up alongside family saloon cars on their sales forecourts. The MGB is – in the eyes of the dealer – an old-fashioned car which looks rather out of place alongside the rows of modern and characterless family cars. Occasionally a smart rubber bumper 'B might make it onto the forecourt, but normally an MGB which is taken in as a part-exchange will simply disappear into the motor trade and re-emerge at a more appropriate specialist outlet or at auction.

There is no harm in mentioning to a few dealers that you are looking for an MGB; they will be pleased to telephone you if they take a 'B in against another car because they know that they will get a better price selling to you than they could by passing the car on through the trade.

The limited opportunities to buy an MGB from non-specialist retailers unfortunately usually occur at the most dubious end of the trade. Whilst it is true to say that those who make up the 'cowboy' element of the motor trade as a breed are dying off in the UK, they are by no means extinct. You can still see them in action at motor auctions; kicking tyres, assessing upholstery and checking that the ash tray is empty – but never getting down on their hands and knees to take a proper look at the structural components of the body. Deal with them at your peril.

There is another type of second-hand car dealer also best avoided. This is the back-street trader who buys in rotten cars and who, with only a few pounds of body filler and a quick spray-over, turns them into smart-looking and saleable, but often unsound, cars. Such people often pose as private vendors when they advertise (which is illegal) and they give the game away very easily if you ask the right questions. When you telephone in response to the advertisement, do not reveal which car you mean nor where the advertisement was placed. The back street trader will be forced to ask you questions in order to discover which of his cars you are referring to, which will unmask him!

Specialist classic car dealers

Classic car magazines contain any number of advertisements by specialist classic car dealers. Many of them concentrate on a particular marque or even model, and there are more of the one-model businesses dealing solely in MGBs than there are in any other classic.

Buying from a specialist precludes any chance of getting a real bargain because the vendor will be only too aware of the true condition of the car and its current market value! Unlike the general dealer, the specialist will be thoroughly familiar with the MGB and will be able to carry out a comprehensive appraisal of each car that he is offered; he will reject the rubbish. The plus point of this expertise is that such dealers are most unlikely to misrepresent a car through ignorance. They are usually very proud of their reputation and loathe to jeopardise it by selling so much as a single unsound car.

Many people avoid the specialist dealer because they believe that his prices are always inflated. This simply is not true, because a dealer makes a living and pays his bills by dealing in rather than by hoarding cars which are appreciating assets! He has to sell cars in order to gain an income to pay his bills, and he knows that he cannot sell cars which are over-priced.

The much-maligned specialist has also widely been blamed for artificially raising the values and hence the prices of classics by asking too high a price (a notion which we have already discounted) and by taking classics out of general circulation and so creating a shortage. Again, this is not true; the only people who create a shortage are those who collect several classics and keep them off the road, often as pure investments.

The specialist classic dealer often possesses restoration facilities, and many of the cars on offer will have either been partly rebuilt to roadworthy condition or completely restored. Such cars will be among the safest of 'buys'.

However, here a caveat. There are a few individuals around who try to benefit from posing both as professional dealers and as private individuals according to the circumstances. If they seek to buy a car then they place an advertisement in the 'Cars Wanted' columns which will not reveal their status as a dealer, which is illegal. If you are selling another classic car in order to finance the purchase of an MGB then beware the undisclosed trade advertiser because he will almost certainly be practised in the art of acquiring cars at well under market value. When you reply to such an advertisement, say merely that you are telephoning about the car, omitting to state what type of car and whether you are buying or selling. If you are asked the question 'Which car?' then there is a strong possibility that you are dealing with an undisclosed trade advertisement. Mutter something about 'trading standards office' and replace the handset.

The person who deals in classics and either buys or sells them via undisclosed trader advertising is not a good source for your MGB. His premises will usually be a barn or shed, his facilities for repair nil.

Remember that a person who is prepared to run the gauntlet of The UK Business Advertisement Disclosure Order (1977) will probably also be in breach of planning laws and he will probably be less than honest with the Inland Revenue. If you bought from such a person then you could find that your guarantee is soon worthless because the vendor is under investigation or even in 'custody'!

The classic car auction

The classic – as opposed to the general – car auction can be an excellent place to buy an MGB. True, you generally do not have too much time to make up your mind whether to buy a particular car or not, but against this must be weighed the wealth of knowledge which can be easily tapped at such events by a little 'ear-wigging'. If a particular car takes your fancy then by simply staying in its vicinity you will overhear many comments from more knowledgeable buyers which will tell you a lot about the car. Listen to those people who tend to lift carpets, to shine torches into crevices and to get down on their hands and knees to examine and poke at the underside of the car. Ignore the comments of the tyre-kickers!

Of course, the great drawback to buying from a classic auction is that you are unable to test drive the car and so you could buy a car in need of mechanical attention. This is just a risk which you have to take, but bear in mind that mechanical faults are far cheaper to rectify than structural bodywork faults. Before you bid at auction, find out whether there is a 'cooling off' period in which you might change your mind about the car without incurring huge penalties.

GENERAL CAR AUCTIONS

A sound example of a classic sports car will very rarely be offered at a general motor auction because it will realise a very low price there. Quite simply, no-one goes to an auction expecting to see and buy an MGB, so no-one bothers to enter a decent example in a sale which so patently attracts the wrong people! Occasionally, a car which has for some reason been seized or confiscated by, perhaps, a liquidator might come to auction, but most MGBs at such events will be very poor examples which failed to sell through normal channels. It is best to steer clear of general auctions.

In conclusion, the safest place to buy an MGB is from a reputable specialist dealer in the marque. If, like the majority, you prefer to buy privately, make sure that the vendor is in a legal position to sell you the car.

WHICH MGB?

Before setting out on a dozen wild goose chases after an MGB it is well worth spending some time deciding exactly what you require of the car. If you seek one of the rarer examples (such as an MGC or a Costello V8) with investment uppermost in your mind, then the originality of the vehicle you choose is obviously an important consideration, which questions the desirability of any cars which have been fully restored. The quality of restoration work varies immensely, and only the very finest of restored cars will be worth the same sort of money as a really good unrestored example in original, if slightly tatty, condition. If you seek the same sort of car but intend to rely upon it to any great extent as regular transport, rather than to own it for the sake of owning it, then the medium-quality restored example might well be preferable.

Much the same goes for very early standard MGBs and GTs in so far as some components are no longer easily sourced (such as aluminium bonnets) and in the case of the mechanical components, unless you possess a unit to exchange then some businesses might be reluctant to supply you on an 'outright' purchase basis.

Most MGBs seem to be bought to be used as a primary or secondary means of transport rather than as investments, so a professionally restored or rebodied car will offer obvious attractions in longevity and reliability – at a price. A fully restored car of the highest standards should fetch as much as a new medium-quality family saloon car, as should a rebodied car.

Relatively few cars of this standard, however, come to the market place. Of those which do, some come from restoration businesses which find it either more profitable or less troublesome to buy in old MGBs, restore them and then sell them than to restore cars for other people, and this is probably the main source of newly restored cars. Few individuals will commission a full restoration and then immediately sell the car, as they would almost certainly lose money by doing so.

Sometimes, though, people are forced by financial circumstances to sell a car on which they have just lavished thousands of pounds in restoration costs. Unless they are in really dire financial straits the asking price will fully reflect the standard and extent of work carried out in the restoration.

Early MGBs were very basic; amongst the

optional extras were the heater, oil cooler, overdrive, anti-roll bar and wire wheels. Some of these later became standard equipment but the more factory options any car had from new (and still has) the higher its value. The British Motor Industry Heritage Trust service mentioned previously will supply all details of an MGB, which gives the buyer a chance to check which equipment was original when the car left Abingdon. The BMIHT will also give the original paint colour, so that you can check to see whether the car has been resprayed for some reason in the wrong colour.

But not everybody wants an original car. Although there are alternative sports cars which may be acquired for quite a lot less than a 'B, the MGB still remains popular amongst those with little interest in the marque or in the classic nature of the car, but who merely want a nice sports car. It is probably true to say that this group tend to buy most of the unsound cars; their lack of knowledge of the potential problems of the MGB coupled with a liking for glitzy stainless door steps and sill covers – the two items of hardware which appear to be most commonly used to mask severe rot – makes them easy prey.

Most people agree that chrome bumper cars are far more attractive than the later rubber bumper versions. In the past, the rubber bumper cars offered the attraction of being relatively recent and therefore reliable and rust-free enough to be the 'safer' buys. They hence commanded generally higher prices, but this advantage has been lost with the passage of time. A V-registration car is nowadays just as likely to require expensive renovation as a B-registration example which was manufactured seventeen years earlier. If the trend for the MGB to accumulate collector's value carries on, then the chrome bumper cars should acquire ever higher prices.

It is not unknown for owners of rubber bumper cars to 'convert' them to chrome bumpers for aesthetic reasons. This job entails far more than merely switching the bumpers, however, and is not recommended. Amongst other things, the two cars have different ride heights, different front wings (chrome bumper wings have profiled sections to accept the indicator/side light units which are missing on rubber bumper wings) and, of course, the entire interior of each is different. It would probably cost more to carry out a complete and convincing conversion than it would to sell the rubber bumper car and buy a chrome bumper model, and anything less than a 100 per cent conversion would almost certainly reduce the value.

The first decision an intending MGB buyer will have to make is that between the drophead Roadster and the GT. The open top of the Roadster, which can make summer driving so pleasurable, brings certain drawbacks. With the hood raised there will be all manner of draughts and it is difficult to waterproof the cockpit totally when the car is underway in the rain. Then there is the question of security. The boot offers a safe lockable area for valuables but the cockpit is very vulnerable to thieves. Furthermore, a rag top on a sports car is a favoured target of vandals, as anyone who has returned to their car to find the hood slashed will testify! Detachable hard tops are available for the Roadster and highly recommended both for the winter and for security reasons.

In the classic sports car world it is a general rule that drop-heads are worth more than their fixed-head equivalents, and in this the MGB is no exception.

The enclosed GT body lacks the 'wind-in-the-hair' appeal of the Roadster but makes up for it in draught-proofing, in keeping the occupants dry when it is raining and in security. Many people buy the GT to use as a 2+2 seater 'family' car, but the rear bench seat is practically useless for seating all but the smallest child. Not only is the headroom severely restricted but the seat back is perpendicular and very uncomfortable.

The GT is in reality best considered a two-seater with the ability to carry larger loads than are possible in an open car. It is not, however, an estate car, and many GTs are bought only to be sold shortly afterwards simply because the buyer has to face the fact that he cannot get the kids or even a large family dog in the back!

The same characteristics are equally true of the MGC and MGC GT. The 'C differs greatly from the 'B and both renovation and running costs are likely to be appreciably higher. Although the 'C has considerably more power than the 'B, its handling suffers from the even greater weight of the C series engine (the B series engine is quite heavy enough), which tends to increase the car's understeering characteristics. The MGC is the faster 'straight line' car but the MGB should (in theory) in most cases (depending on the state of the respective suspensions etc) have a slight advantage on the bends.

As an investment, however, the comparatively rare MGC appears to eclipse the ubiquitous MGB completely. For every MGC (including the GT) which left the factory there were no less than 475 assorted

Bs and BGTs. Unfortunately, some body and suspension components were unique to the MGC, and since the car has not been manufactured since late 1969 it is little wonder that sourcing some spares is extremely difficult (although the MG specialists are able to supply ever-more spares for the car). Unlike the MGB, this is not a car which offers the option of the breaker's yard as a source of cheap spares (saving those common to the B and C), because the car's rarity persuades people not to scrap it!

Due to the growing scarcity of some spares, the MGC might not be such a good answer to your problems if you anticipate doing a high mileage. It is essentially a collector's and enthusiast's car.

Relative to the production figures for MGBs and MGCs, a disproportionately high number of the latter appear in the 'cars for sale' pages of classic car and owner's club magazines. This should not be taken as a sign of owner dissatisfaction; it will be due in the main to the fact that the majority of MGB 'for sale' advertisements appear outside the classic car and owner's club press, whereas the 'C is so much an enthusiast's car that few will ever be advertised outside the specialist press. Nevertheless, some MGCs will be advertised outside the specialist press (which is read by a high proportion of knowledgeable enthusiasts) because the owner can foresee looming problems involving those spares which are the most difficult to source, and wishes to advertise to non-experts.

The MGB GT V8 has rather more power than the 'C but a lighter engine, and so should suffer less from understeer. The V8 engine is more difficult to maintain and repair than the B series engine (although, unlike the MGC, engine spares are widely and sometimes quite cheaply available) and both the MGC and V8 will generally be much more expensive than the MGB in terms of running costs.

Against all this, only 2,591 V8 cars left Abingdon, which makes it the rarest of the production variations (limited editions excepted) and which gives it a very high collector's value. The numbers of V8s which are advertised for sale is completely out of proportion with the number which the factory built, for MG was not the only company to fit the GT with the Rover 3.5-litre V8 engine. Apart from the already mentioned Ken Costello, many companies and even individuals have shoehorned the V8 into not just the GT but also the Roadster shell (the factory considered only the GT bodyshell up to handling the extra power). In the long term, genuine factory cars, Costello cars and those from the most reputable of third-party conversions specialists such as the V8 Conversion Company, Motor Fayre or Abingdon Classic Sports Cars will almost certainly command far higher prices than V8s converted by lesser-known businesses or private individuals.

Most people who buy a V8 will do so as an investment or simply because they love the car. Few will buy it purely as a performance sports car, since collector's values have pushed the price up so far that there is a plethora of alternative modern high performance cars which are easily capable of showing the V8 a clean pair of heels and which are available at far lower prices. Some former MGB V8 owners have expressed the opinion that the car has too much power in relation to its handling capabilities, something which is by no means unique to the MGB and true of other sports cars which have been fitted with this potentially very powerful unit.

It is possible to uprate the MGB V8s suspension so that it can handle vast amounts of power, as can be witnessed at various sporting events. Several people campaign the V8 in hill climbs, with the engine overbored to up to 4500cc and in states of tune which deliver in excess of 300bhp. The better professional conversions companies will build V8s which are capable of using the V8 engine's power to the full. In the case of the non-factory V8 converted car such modifications as are necessary to allow the car satisfactorily to use even the 137bhp of the 'Range Rover' V8 (which was in a lower state of tune than the same engine when fitted into Rover cars and Costello MGB V8s) are probably quite acceptable from the investment standpoint and should help increase the value over that of the amateur or poorer-quality professional conversion. Ever-more rare factory cars, however, need to be original in order to realise their maximum value, and modifications, however worthy, will probably be to the detriment of this.

In assessing an MGC or an MGB V8 the intending buyer should be especially thorough, and not only because of the higher amounts of money which will be involved. In the case of the MGC the originality of all components is vital. With the MGB 'factory' or Costello V8 and also the Downton and University Motors MGC specials it is essential that proof be obtained relating to the car's bona fides, especially as these variants will have far higher prices than counterfeit copies or cars which were originally converted in good faith but presented as one of the rarer specimens by a later owner.

3 • APPRAISING THE MGB

When looking for an MGB, bear one point in mind above all. There are many MGBs on the market to choose from; if the car you are viewing gives the slightest cause for concern then you have the luxury of being able to reject it, secure in the knowledge that there will be plenty of other opportunities to buy the car you want in the condition you want. If you buy in haste then you can usually expect to repent at leisure.

A mechanical fault, any mechanical fault, on an MGB is of relatively little consequence in comparison with most of the usual bodywork problems. This is partly due to the high costs of rectifying the latter but also to the ease with which reasonably priced mechanical spares can be acquired and the ease with which most may be fitted. The use of components by MG from the likes of SU and Lucas means that many new spares from the original manufacturer can still be bought. For components which are no longer made by the original manufacturer there are often pattern alternatives from a growing, almost 'cottage', industry dedicated to keeping MGBs on the road. Even items which are no longer made at all are often freely available as exchange reconditioned units.

The very worst mechanical problem that could occur on a 'B – say, a con rod snapping and going through the side of the block, or the loss of a gear – will, at worst, result in cost of the outright purchase of a reconditioned unit plus, perhaps, one day's labour, if you have the work done for you professionally. Bodywork repairs can be very expensive and can force the car off the road for days, weeks or even months. However, mechanical, transmission, suspension, electrical and other faults all cost money to rectify, and a combination of such faults could add up to cost as much as a partial bodywork restoration. Whilst bodywork remains the first and most important criterion for the selection of an MGB, mechanical assessments nevertheless deserve proper attention.

Assessment plan

Rather than merely giving a check-list of places to poke and of noises to listen for – not uncommon with buying guides – each aspect of the assessment will describe the components in detail, describe what they do and how they do it, how they fail and the consequences of that failure. It will also try to cover as many 'dodges' (employed by the unscrupulous to disguise or conceal problems) as possible, and describe in some detail how to expose such tricks.

At the end of the chapter is a thorough check-list which it is recommended you follow.

Remember that there is no fault so bad that it cannot be repaired, no car which cannot be restored. The person seeking a car to rebody will obviously be prepared to accept a car with a body so rotten that most people would reject it out of hand. The following is written from the viewpoint of the person who wishes to buy either a fully roadworthy MGB or a car which may be brought to roadworthy condition at minimal expense.

BODYWORK

Many very tidy-looking MGBs conceal major structural problems which can sometimes be due to uncorrected accident damage but which are more usually the result of years of corrosion. Unscrupulous vendors often go to great lengths to hide these problems and so a lot of first-time MGB buyers find

This Roadster with smart chromework and passable paintwork actually looked very presentable, and many people might have been tempted to buy it. Closer inspection revealed it to be totally unroadworthy and in need of either a complete body rebuild or, preferably, reshelling. The vendor did not know how bad the bodyrot was, and was originally asking five times the author's estimate of the car's true worth as an 'easy' restoration project. To the author's astonishment, he eventually received nearly his full asking price and the car was sold for reshelling.

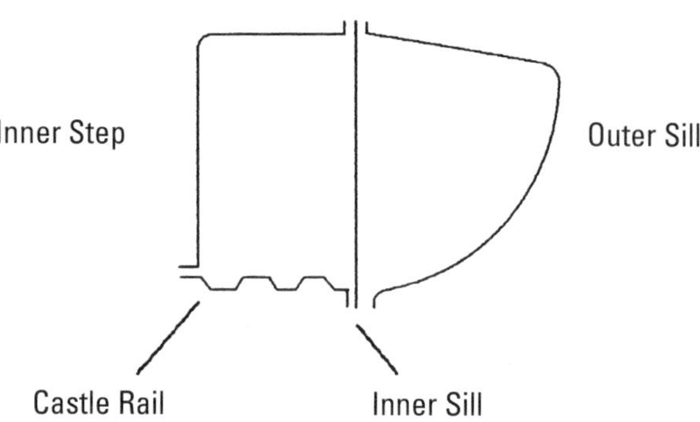

The four sill sections which combine to make two strong box sections. These were originally spot welded and, although it is possible to MIG or gas weld them, it is best to spot weld them for neatness and strength. The castle rail, inner sill and outer sill sections are not too difficult to replace; the inner step can be a very difficult section to replace without causing body distortion, and only experienced restorers should attempt it.

themselves saddled with a nice-looking car which, at best, requires immediate remedial attention to make it roadworthy and, at worst, is a death-trap.

Very often a 'B which is in terrible condition will be smartened-up in order to achieve a quick sale, and even the best-looking example can prove to be riddled with rust in the most important sections (which are naturally hidden from sight). It is a mistake to believe that later examples will be less likely to suffer extensive rusting, for all 'Bs are now old enough to have succumbed.

The very first indication of a possible camouflaging of serious bodywork problems is the presence of overspray. You can find this almost anywhere on the car from the petrol tank and suspension to the sides of the seats. Although overspray is by no means proof positive that certain work carried out on the car was of a fault-hiding nature, it does show that the person who has carried out work had a slipshod attitude which will probably be reflected in the quality of workmanship throughout the car.

The surest sign that overspray on the underside of the car or on a component of the suspension or drive is the result of the car being smartened-up for sale is when there is no dirt on it, because if that is the case then it must have very recently been put there!

If a small area of overspray is discovered in an otherwise beautifully restored car then it can suggest that the car has received accident or rust damage rectification of a lower standard than that of the earlier work. Such cars will probably carry a high asking price and hence deserve the most thorough of inspections.

An attractive-looking MGB can hide severe rust. Even a car which is regularly polished, garaged and rarely if ever used on the road, will suffer corrosion inside vital box sections of the body if the atmosphere in the garage contains moisture, because temperature variations will cause condensation to form – and so oxidisation begins. The original, unrestored MGB with a solid and rust-free body is very much the exception and such a car would undoubtedly command a very high price – probably more than the cost of a new small sports car in current production.

In order fully to appreciate why corrosion within body/chassis box sections is so damaging it is necessary to look at the overall structural design of the car. The MGB is of unitary construction, that is, the body incorporates strong chassis-like members

LEFT *These stainless sill covers were hiding rusted lower wing sections which in turn covered totally rotten sills. As the sill structures rot from the insides, there can be no benefit from whatever protection sill covers might claim or appear to offer. When appraising a car which is fitted with sill covers, ask the vendor to remove them in order for you to see the actual state of the underlying panels and, if the vendor refuses to do this, either budget for immediate sill replacement or reject the car. The sills of this particular vehicle could instantly be assessed by the state of the inner step, which simply did not reach the pedal box assembly at its front end!*

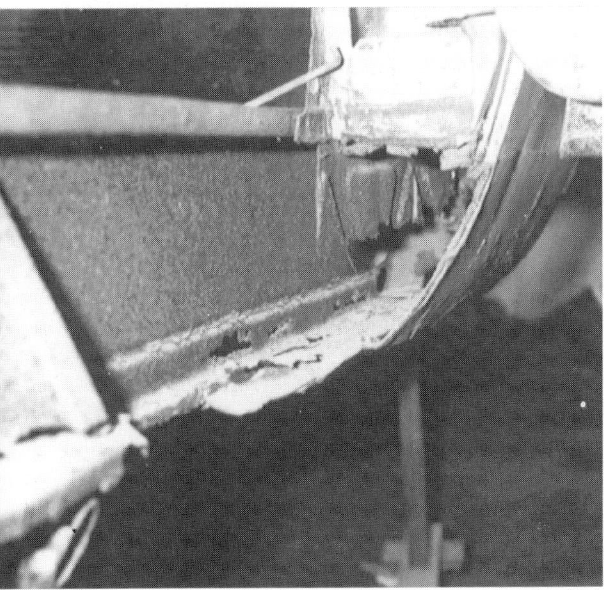

ABOVE *This is the sort of rust damage that stainless outer sill covers and 'centre sill repair sections' can hide. The castle rail is rotten, the inner sill upright is all but rotted away, the outer sill section is a distant memory and the inner step proved too weak for rescue. Bear in mind that if the lower wing is rusted then the sills will be at least equally as rotten – if not more so.*

RIGHT *Check that the gaps around the door are even, particularly on Roadsters which can sag in the middle when the sills have rotted. If the gaps at the top of the door sides are smaller than those at the bottom, then the car is probably sagging and should be rejected. If you attempted to straighten out such a shell at home and then to put new sills on it then the chances are that it would afterwards still have a distorted shell. Some professional workshops will undertake this type of work, but generally such cars are best considered ideal candidates for reshelling, particularly if mechanicals, trim and electrics are in good condition and salvageable. Uneven door gaps could be due to poorly corrected accident damage or evidence of earlier rust repair.*

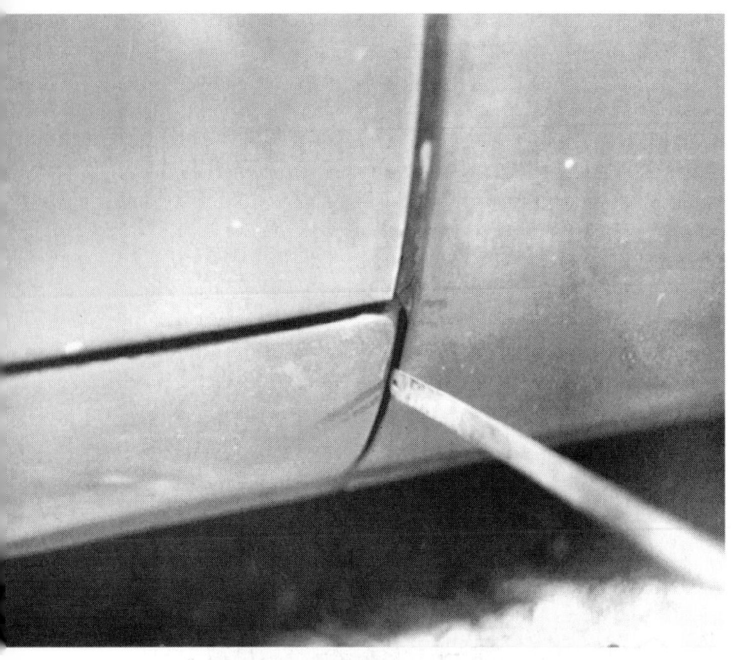

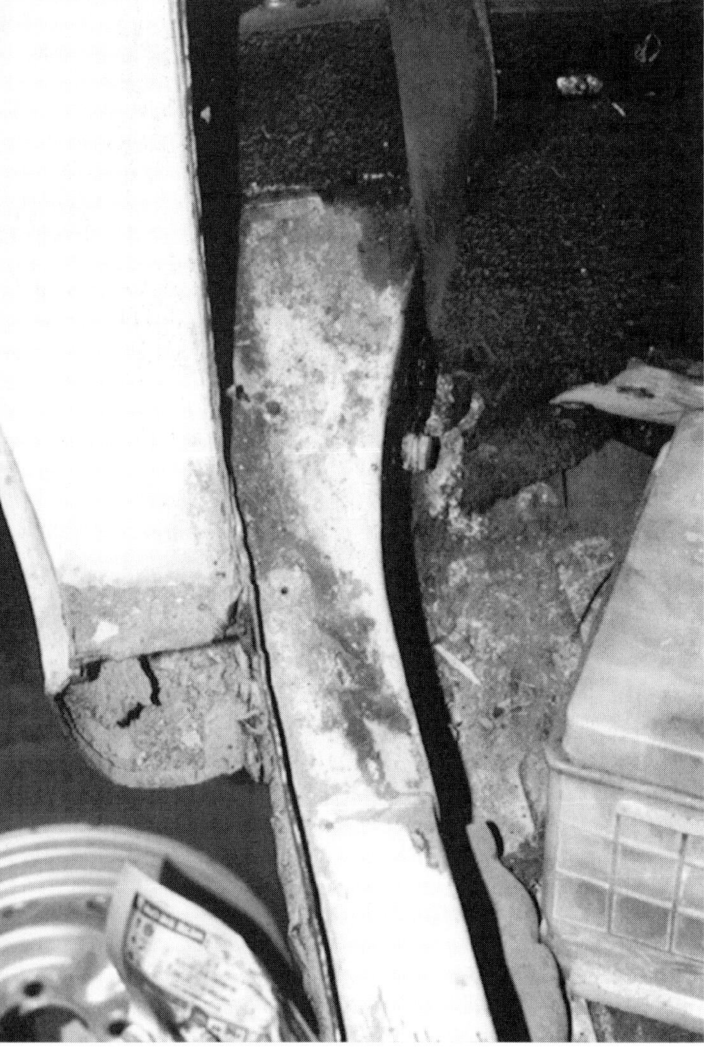

instead of having a separate chassis. In the case of cars which do have a separate chassis, the engine, transmission and suspension will all be mounted on and distribute their loads through the chassis, which is essentially a strong framework of steel box sections. In the case of the MGB, the loads are taken initially by the integral chassis-like sections and then distributed through virtually the entire body of the car. This means that many of the body panels which would not have great structural importance on a car with a chassis are vital to the integrity of the MGB.

At the front of the car, two sturdy longitudinal chassis rails support the engine and the front suspension; at the rear, two similar sections provide fixing points for the springs and hence the axle. Joining the chassis rails at the front half of the car to those at the back are the sills – the very backbones of the MGB. If the sills are allowed to rot completely then the car will first sag in the middle and eventually it could collapse!

To further emphasise the importance of sound sills on a car you are thinking of buying, bear in mind that to replace each side properly will take something like 20-40 professional man-hours, and far more if other adjacent metal also requires replacement, which is usually the case when the sills have rotted. If the sills are suspect, then subtract from the value of the car the cost of a minimum 40-80 hours of workshop time (assuming that other panels and chassis rails are sound) plus parts.

TOP LEFT *The outer sill sections run in a single length from the rear of the front wheel arch to the front of the rear wheel arch. Some people fit centre 'repair' sections to hide rotten sills. If a thin piece of steel such as this hacksaw blade or a piece of stiff plastic can be pushed at ninety degrees into the gap between the sill and either wing, then the car has been fitted with the dreaded sections and will require sill replacement. Some people are adept at camouflaging the gaps at either end of the centre sill cover section, so do not take the results of this individual test as proof positive of sound sills. Always carry out the other checks listed in this chapter.*

LEFT *The inner step is the most difficult of the sill sections to replace and consequently many people prefer to patch it when rotten. Rot usually strikes the front end and centre of the section, which are repairable. If the rear end is rotten, however, the job should be considered to have passed from the realms of DIY; opt for professional replacement.*

TOP *Lifting the door trim and counting the number of thicknesses of metal in this joint can reveal poorly-fitted sills. There should be three thicknesses – if there are more, then at some time in the past a rotten outer sill section may have been hammered-in and another welded on top. In such cases, the car must be considered unroadworthy. Look also for filler at the ends of the exposed door step where they join the bottom of the B-post panel. On the car in the photograph, the bottom edge of the B-post has rotted away, despite which, new sills were being welded into position. Presumably, the remaining gap would have been filled with bodyfiller, but the rot remaining in the B-post panel would soon have spread and lifted the filler, not to mention starting the rusting of the sills that much more quickly!*

ABOVE *If the car has been fitted with new sills, the standard of welding at the bottom of the A-post can tell you a lot about the probable standards of workmanship applied to the job!*

The jacking point is reinforced within the sill structure. If jacking the car produces creaks and other disquieting noises then assume that the sills are either rotten or have been badly repaired. It is not unknown for people to forget to weld new jacking point reinforcers in when replacing sills. Jacking the car in this way can also produce unhealthy noises if the fixed cross-member is rotten, so examine this carefully. Bear in mind that a car which does creak and groan when raised by the jacking point will quite possibly either have sagged or even buckled upwards when previously jacked up. If body distortion is thus suspected then the car is probably best considered a reshelling candidate.

The MGB's sills each consist of four long steel pressings which are welded together to form, in effect, two box sections. The *inner step* may be seen from inside the car by lifting the carpet (if fitted) and is the last of the four sections to rust through. The *outer sill* section is two-thirds covered by the front and rear wings but the centre section is visible under each door. The *castle rail section* runs along the underside of the car and, as the name suggests, is a profiled steel pressing which joins the sill to the floor section. The *inner sill* is the one section which is completely hidden and is a vertical pressing which runs from the rear of the front wheel arch to the front of the rear wheel arch. The inner sill is very prone to rust and vitally important to the integrity of the sills.

The sills rot in the main from the inside, although the outer sill can rot almost as quickly where it is covered by the front and rear lower wing sections. When this happens the wings themselves invariably rot from the inside and many people cover up both by fitting stainless steel outer sill covers and door steps. Rusting in the visible centre section of the outer sill is very often hidden by first knocking the rusted section inwards and then welding another mid-section on top, although even this seems too much trouble for some people and sills 'repaired' with GRP and filler are by no means unknown!

The castle sections come in for a hard time. Mud sprays on them from underneath, and on top they collect any condensation moisture from inside the sills! Subjected to such a two-pronged attack it is little wonder that castle sections usually have some corrosion. Some people cover their rotten castle sections with underseal prior to selling the car, others tack on a sheet of plain steel followed by underseal. Few replace just the castle rails because if they have rusted then it follows that the other sill sections and the two floor pans will also have rusted where they adjoin the castle rail and there will not be enough metal left to which to weld the edges of the replacement castle sections.

The inner step is the very last of the four sill sections to rust, and if extensive rust or signs of welded repair patches are apparent here then it is a racing certainty that the rest of the sill sections will have all but rusted away. In spite of this, many MGBs are bought in such a condition. Often, people weld a cover section over the inner step (particularly the front end) fabricated from sheet mild steel; sometimes holes are merely stopped with GRP and/or body filler, so look for both.

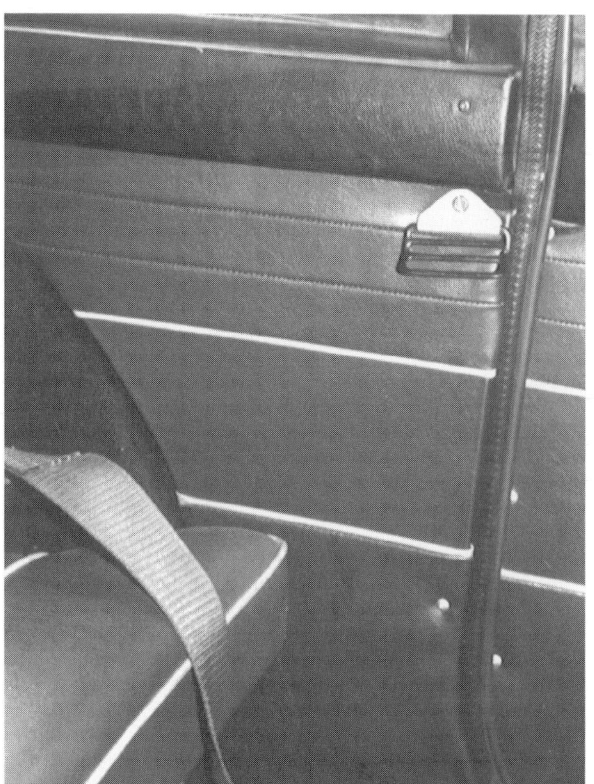

APPRAISING SILLS

LEFT *Removal of this interior trim panel takes a few minutes but can instantly reveal rotten sills, however expertly they have been camouflaged outwardly, because it allows access to the top rear edge of the outer sill section. Use a torch to illuminate and look at the sill, or feel carefully with a gloved hand.*

BELOW AND BELOW LEFT *If the vendor will permit it, remove the mud splash panel and, using a torch, inspect the outer sill front end and inner wing. Each panel should be held by three bolts – if it is found to be welded into position, suspect the worst! This view (front wing removed) shows the kind of horrors which can lurk behind the mud splash panel. Although the sills have been replaced (after a fashion), the A-post does not join the outer sill because it has rotted away!. The car shown in many of these photographs is presumably a DIY restoration project which halted because the true extent of the necessary work was not realised at the outset. Happily, this car found its way into the hands of Motor Fayre, and will be properly rebuilt or reshelled. Many cars in this sort of condition, however, are bodged and then offered for sale.*

Having covered some of the many and varied ways in which sill rot is concealed or disguised, it remains to find ways of exposing whatever tricks *may* have been used on the car you are thinking of buying. You will need a torch to see into nooks and crannies; a thin-bladed knife or a piece of hacksaw blade to poke into crevices; a half-inch spanner; an old screwdriver to poke into suspect metal; some means of lifting and supporting the car (preferably a small trolley jack and axle stands); a magnet to test for filler; and bags of patience – because a large proportion of the cars you examine will not be worthy of your hard-earned cash!

First, if a car is fitted with outer stainless sill covers then they have to come off and, if the vendor will not allow this, it may be best to reject the car because there is a good chance that the covers are hiding corrosion. With the covers off, look at the condition of the lower portions of the front wings which cover the ends of the sills and if they are rusted then the sills will probably be in a very poor condition since the sills usually rust before the lower wing sections and, more importantly, no-one in their right

mind replaces rusty front wings over sound replacement sills! See whether your magnet will stick to the lower wings. It should be strongly attracted unless body filler has been used.

If the lower rear wings have rusted (check for filler with the magnet if they look sound) then the sills will need replacing. This is because the rear wings, unlike the front wings which are bolted on, are welded into position and must be cut off (or at least the portion which covers the sill must be cut away) for a sill repair. The cutting process will render the cut off portion useless.

Next examine the gaps each side of the doors, because if they are smaller at the tops than at the bottoms this will show that the car is sagging in the middle. This might indicate rotten sills or, worse still, replacement sills which have been applied to an already sagging body! In either case the costs of rectification will be immense. To confuse the picture, uneven gaps around the doors can be an indication of poorly-positioned wings or sills, and might not necessarily mean that the car is weak. It is quite difficult to get the line of the sills exactly right when replacing them, and a perfectly sound sill replacement job could leave an uneven gap at the bottom of the door.

Look closely at the centre section of each outer sill, particularly at the front and rear edges where the section disappears underneath the wings. If no edge is apparent then filler has probably been flushed over, usually to cover up a 'bodged' repair, and in the absence of evidence to the contrary the sills should be taken to be rotten. If there is a gap which allows a thin piece of plastic (about credit card thickness) or perhaps a piece of hacksaw blade to be pushed straight into the sill body (at 90 degrees) then the sill has most probably been patched with a tacked-on outer centre section and the entire sill structure will almost certainly require replacing. Look along the sill centre section from an acute angle. If rivelling or other unevenness is apparent then you are probably looking at filler, something the magnet should verify.

Next remove the length of carpet or rubber mat which covers the inner step (it may be glued). If the vendor will not allow this then it may be prudent to adjust your offer to budget for full sill replacement. Using a torch, look closely at the front end of the step for signs of patching; even if the section has been painted some roughness should be apparent. On very bad MGBs the inner step might not even reach the front pedal box panel!

LEFT *Never be afraid to poke sturdy-looking sections vigorously. This cross-member appeared quite sound until a screwdriver revealed this hole. This section can be repaired without too much difficulty, but begs the question of what the rest of the car is really like, given the condition of this very heavy section. The car in question looked very smart and had been resprayed relatively recently. When its true condition was discovered, the poor owner had to pay for three weeks' workshop time to make the body sound again.*

BELOW LEFT *There will usually be some areas of rust which escape your attention, which is why it is so important to judge the entire car by its weakest point. This rot at the base of the C-post on the author's 1966 GT was not discovered for three years.*

Pay especial attention to the rear end of the inner step where the step/spring hanger/rear side chassis rail come together, for strength in this joint is crucial. If the vendor does not want the carpets in this area lifted (because the seat belt mountings will have to come off – another area which needs to be checked by tugging on the belt) then it may be wisest to account for substantial repairs in arriving at an offer figure. As stated previously, if the inner step is rotten then the rest of the sills plus sundry other panels are also certain to be useless.

It is worth lifting the trim covering the join along the top of the sill in the door aperture and counting the number of thicknesses of metal and also noting the welding method used to join them. There should be three thicknesses and they should be spot-welded; if there are four thicknesses then the extra one is quite possibly an outer sill centre section, indicating a cover-up. If the seam has three thicknesses and has been gas welded then the sills have probably received some attention, but this should not be taken as a guarantee of their soundness: first, the job could have been carried out some time ago and the sills could well have re-rusted and, secondly, this seam should ideally be spot welded for strength and neatness. If the job is to be done properly then there is little excuse for not hiring a spot welder for the odd day in order to gain the extra strength which it gives.

The next sill component to be checked is the castle rail section underneath the car. You will need to jack each side up in turn and (in the interests of safety) to rest the car on axle stands while you crawl underneath with a torch, or better still a lead lamp, for proper illumination. Some cars will not even stand being jacked up by the proper jacking points, because these are connected to the main cross member which transmits the jacking force to the sills! If you hear crunching noises as you begin to raise the car, lower it immediately and reject it or budget for new sills and possibly a new main cross-member. A car with sills this rotten could well be suffering body distortion.

Fresh underseal on the castle sections or on the floor underside is an obvious sign that either remedial work has recently been carried out or that problems have been covered up. Whether the underseal is fresh or not poke around with a screwdriver (floors as well as sills) and try to ensure that the metal is all sound.

The castle rail at the front comes right up into the bottom of the wheel arch, so an area of fresh underseal here can indicate a replacement. It can equally indicate a patch repair.

The one sill section which you cannot readily check is the all-important inner vertical membrane. This panel turns what would otherwise be a fairly flimsy box into two very strong sections. If serious rust is discovered anywhere in the sill then you can take it for granted that the inner membrane will have at least partly rusted away, in which case (and in the absence of direct checks) you should consider the car unroadworthy. If, however, you found a gap between the central outer sill section and either wing (ie a centre cover section) and you have a length of hacksaw blade, then poking the blade into the crevice and noting just how much of it is swallowed up will show you whether there is an inner membrane or none at all (which is by no means unusual!).

If the sills seem in good order and you are genuinely interested in buying the car then ask whether you can remove one of the rear interior side panels, which are held on with four screws. On GTs the leathercloth-covered wooden side trim rail will also have to be removed. This gives access to the top side of the outer sill section, normally hidden beneath the rear wing. If this is rusted then you can take it for granted that rest of the sill structure is rotten and expertly covered up!

There is one final check which can be made to the sills if the vendor will permit it (many will not). At the rear of the inner front wings are panels which keep the mud from the enclosed box formed by the front wing and the inner dash side panel. Removing each of the mud panels (they should be held on with bolts, if they are welded on this indicates very shoddy workmanship) will allow you to shine your torch beam onto the top edge of the outer sill. Very often

This is a good example of needless penny-pinching, or possibly of back-street 'cowboy' repairers' work. This flat strip of crudely gas-welded metal on a very smart 1967 GT had been fitted in place of the castle rail. It lacks the rigidity of the proper rail, and its replacement will probably reveal similar nasties in the other sill sections.

Rot around the spring hangers is bad enough, but when the rot extends to adjacent metal, causing the weight of the car against the spring hanger to buckle the entire assembly upwards, it is time to consider putting away the welder and ordering a Heritage bodyshell!

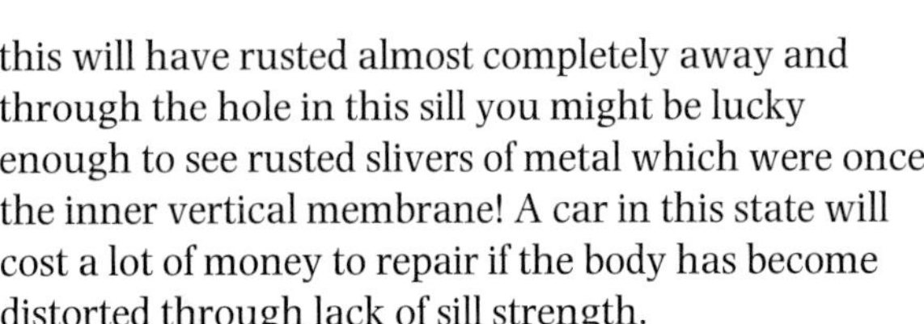

this will have rusted almost completely away and through the hole in this sill you might be lucky enough to see rusted slivers of metal which were once the inner vertical membrane! A car in this state will cost a lot of money to repair if the body has become distorted through lack of sill strength.

Many vendors will refuse to allow these essential checks on the sills to be carried out, sometimes because they (understandably) do not want carpets unglued from inner steps or interior panels removed, sometimes because they are secure in the knowledge that if you do not buy the car then they will gain an easy sale to one of the non-experts due to view the car. This can make the purchase of an MGB a very frustrating business, but the amounts of money at stake not only for the purchase of the car but also for any necessary bodywork should serve to encourage the reader to persist until the right car at the right price eventually appears. It is always a mistake to buy in haste in an appreciating market.

Quick check list for body rust points

1. Bases of roof pillars.
2. Triangular box sections within front wings/sill behind splash panel.
3. Front side chassis rails.
4. Sills where they meet wing edges.
5. Castle rail.
6. Inner step (from inside car) and rear sill top (from behind quarter trim panel).
7. Lower quarter wing.
8. Rear side chassis rails.
9. Top seam of rear wing.

OTHER STRUCTURAL PANELS

Because the structural chassis-like members of the MGB are built into the monocoque body they share the job of keeping the body rigid with various panels which many people erroneously believe not to be structurally important. When you consider that a few people believe that even the sills are not structurally too important it is easy to see why such confusion arises about lesser panels.

The basic framework of the front half of the car consists of the two longitudinal side chassis rails and the fixed centre cross-member (the 'U' section member running between the sills from one jacking point to the other), plus the radiator duct panel and its support pressing. If, as many people believe, this was the sum total of structural metal at the front of the car then the front framework would only join on to the sills by the two 90 degree welds to the central chassis member. It is fairly obvious to anyone who looks closely at this little frame as an entity that the centre cross-member does not support the front ends of the sills but merely provides a fulcrum for them. The side chassis rails are actually joined to the sills by a complex combination of panels. In fact, every panel in the vicinity plays a part not only in holding the whole together but also in spreading or dissipating the various forces which act upon the car when it is in motion.

A very important compound box structure is formed by the floors and transmission tunnel, the pedal box assembly panels, the side dash panels, the bulkhead and scuttle panel behind the dash, the A-post assemblies plus the front inner wings and their reinforcements. Even the unit which contains the radio speaker contributes to the strength of this area. Virtually every panel helps give strength to the car!

Because so many pressings contribute to the strength of the car, only the most severe rot in this vicinity will be sufficient to substantially weaken it. Severe rot is, however, by no means a rarity, and just as in the case of the sills, many unscrupulous people camouflage or conceal problems which should, by rights, result in the car's being taken off the road.

If in doubt regarding the structural importance of any panel then it is best to assume that any panels which are welded on are contributing to some extent to the strength of the body.

The front side chassis rails themselves are not especially trouble-prone because the undersides and the sides within the inner wing are often properly rust-proofed and any moisture on the inner and upper faces tends to evaporate because of heat generated by the engine. Some, however, will be found to have rotted badly, especially on cars which have been standing idle for a long period of time. The usual place is within the wheel arch when rust proofing and preventative maintenance were lacking, and rather than replace the entire member it is not uncommon to discover that previous owners have

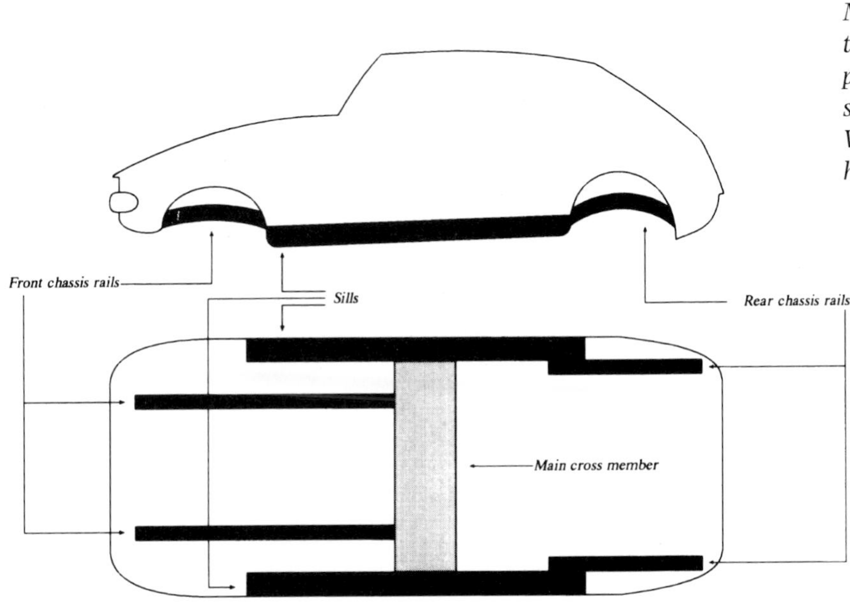

The main structural members of the MGB. This illustration demonstrates the structural importance of the panels which join the front end of the sill and the front side chassis rail. Virtually every panel in the vicinity helps towards the car's strength.

OPPOSITE ABOVE *The front side chassis rails support the engine and the front suspension. They must be sound if the car is to be considered roadworthy. Removal of the front wheel allows access for the rail to be probed with a screwdriver. Do not be deceived by fresh underseal, which is more likely to have been put there to hide rot than after it has been satisfactorily dealt with. The overspray which is just visible in this shot is actually the result of an innocent rust-treatment procedure; more usually, it indicates a hasty 'blow-over' when seen on a car which is being offered for sale.*

LEFT *This triangular box section (top right of photograph) rots mainly on its top face and, although this can be felt through the wheel arch, it is recommended that you wear leather gloves, because the jagged edges of a rotten example can cut! The engine bay side channels are also rotten. Replacement panels are now available for these sections.*

ABOVE LEFT *The horizontal panel in front of the pedal box assembly is one of the worst to have to deal with and is really a job for the professional, so be thorough when appraising its condition. Some surface rust is quite usual around the brake and clutch cylinders, caused following spillage of fluid. If unattended, this will lead to serious rot. If rusting is extensive then the car is likely to require either a total rebuild or reshelling.*

ABOVE *The rear side chassis rails can be probed using a screwdriver or similar sharp implement after removal of the rear wheel. Pay special attention to the areas around the spring hangers and where the damper fixing bolts pass through. Whilst repair sections are available and inexpensive, serious rot here indicates a strong likelihood of extensive bodyrot.*

welded on patches of 20g steel or even used body filler and then tried to conceal the 'repair' with underseal.

It can prove very difficult to reveal the existence of a patch steel repair when the whole is covered with underseal. The only two signs which might give the game away are the presence of an area of fresh underseal or the discovery of adjacent weakened metal which yields under pressure from a screwdriver blade. Do not be afraid to poke quite vigorously.

If patched rot is suspected or discovered in a side chassis rail then there is bound to be even more advanced rusting in the thinner adjacent panels, and these should be checked very thoroughly in such cases.

The centre section of the main fixed cross-member benefits in many instances from oil protection because oil lost from the engine or transmission is blown back when the car is under way, although at its ends by the jacking points, rot is common. Repair sections are available for these, although many people try to fabricate their own from thin sheet steel, which cannot give a satisfactorily strong support for the jacking points. A home-made repair section will be self-evident, but the presence of even professionally manufactured sections will be apparent if you look for the welded seam.

The join between the side chassis rail and the inner wing (front wheel arch panel) is prone to rusting and it is, of course, the thinner of the two sections (the inner wing) which rusts completely through first. Again, some people will patch the area with thin sheet steel or even GRP and filler rather than face the expense of proper repair. Check the join from inside the engine bay for signs of rot or repair and check from within the wheel arches with the magnet for filler/GRP.

Joining and strengthening the inner wheel arches and pedal box assemblies are two triangular box section strengtheners which protrude into the top of the inner wheel arch. The flat tops of these pressings tend to collect mud and moisture kicked up by the wheels, and unless they are thoroughly protected or regularly cleaned then rot is very likely. The sides and base also rot. Replacing these pressings is not the most difficult of jobs, but as wing removal on the MGB is anything but a simple task and is necessary for a proper repair, rot in these panels is sometimes dealt with by knocking in the offending surface to form a concave section and then building up and flushing over with body filler. It is wise to don a glove before reaching up into the inner wing to feel for rot in the strengtheners, because the edges of holes can be quite sharp enough to cut. To reveal filler 'repair' use the magnet.

The forward rear spring hanger section is not too difficult to replace. Unfortunately, if this sturdy section is rotten then the panels through which it distributes its considerable loadings will also be rotten, and these are anything but easy to replace. If the hangers have obviously been recently replaced then probe around them thoroughly to find adjacent rot.

The top of the dash side assembly (adjacent to the reinforcing pressings just covered) also rots and can only be checked (through two square holes in panels spot welded to the rear of the inner wing) from within the engine bay. Because it is difficult to 'bodge' a repair to these, expect to find the access holes already mentioned plugged with acoustic matting or other material. If either rust damage or a bodged repair is found in this panel then there is a good chance that the lower portion is also rusted and that the join between it and the sill is weakened. Expect the car to have thoroughly rotten sills!

The bulkhead assembly situated behind the dash which contains the air intake and bonnet hinges is likely to be rusted on earlier examples. Access here is almost impossible and so rust can only be hidden by literally spraying paint through the various holes. Look from the inside of the car for signs of rust coming right through and also for signs of repair. The horizontal flat scuttle panel immediately ahead of this bulkhead will often have rusted on the driver's side because of brake and clutch fluid spillages. The extent of the rot may be seen more readily from inside the car by poking the underside of the panel along the join with the steering column cut-away.

Moving back down the car, the floor sections are very prone to rusting. Water finds its way here for obvious reasons in the case of the drophead, but the leakier examples of GTs which are left out in the rain soon acquire mini lakes in both footwells. Although regarded by many as not in the least structurally important, the floor sections play a rôle in maintaining the strength of the 90 degree joins between the side chassis rails, cross-member and sills. Quite often the floor sections will be found to be plastered in paint and/or underseal, patched with GRP or 20g sheet steel. The floor sections will often have been replaced on a car before it is offered for sale. Far from giving the intending purchaser any reassurance, this should immediately raise the question of whether the sills (equally likely to be rusted) were replaced at the same time.

The transmission tunnel rarely gives any problems, although its various welded joins to the floor sections and rear heelboard can be less than satisfactory. The floor welds are quite easily checked but the joint with the rear heelboard might be covered with fresh paint or carpet and should be thoroughly probed for signs of rot.

At the rear of the car, the importance of pressed-steel panels such as the boot floor is more obvious than perhaps are the panels at the front, because the two side chassis rails, which support the leaf springs and hence the axle, do not have a sturdy rear cross-member joining them.

The rear side chassis rails do rot, and rot badly in the vital areas of the spring hangers. Repair sections are available for these and they can give a perfectly satisfactory result. However, if rot is apparent in the spring hanger sections then the chances are that it will also have infected much of the rest of the rail. The rails are often patched with sheet steel, which is fairly unsatisfactory, and sometimes body filler and GRP are used, which is obviously wholly unsatisfactory. It is a good idea to remove the rear

The rearmost spring hanger. Although rot in the side chassis rail here is not so serious as rot at the front hanger, it is still a job which is probably better tackled by a professional restorer. If there is rot here, look very closely at the entire rear end of the car, because nearby thinner panels are prone to rot through more quickly.

LEFT *Any areas of bodywork which are covered by chrome trim – such as the light clusters and the rear wings – are susceptible to rot. Look for signs of recent spray at the edges of the trim and check for filler repairs.*

RIGHT *The quarterlight and mirror areas of the door skin are especially susceptible to rusting. The area of door skin underneath the quarterlight lower pivot bolt rots and splits in some instances. Look for signs of recently applied spray, which could indicate a hasty filler 'repair'.*

wheels in order to check the rails. Fairly vigorous poking with a screwdriver will usually reveal both rot and non-ferrous repairs.

The boot tray rots through water having been allowed to lie undisturbed, and the top of the petrol tank which lies underneath also rots for exactly the same reason. There is no excuse for anyone having 'patched' anything more than very small holes in the boot floor with sheet steel – or any of the internal panels at the rear of the car for that matter, because to do so in any degree of safety entails the removal of the petrol tank, and if you go to the trouble of doing this then you might as well complete the job properly afterwards, by installing a new boot floorpan! With the opportunity for a quick 'bodge' with the gas or electric welder hence ruled out, you may find attempts at GRP or even filler repair.

The inner rear wings are not of paramount importance from the structural viewpoint (though they do play a reasonably important rôle in maintaining the shape of the car), but they can rot badly and the temptation to repair them with GRP is obvious. That is fine except for the fact that, if the inner rear wings have rotted, then other, more important, panels in the vicinity are also likely to have rotted to a similar extent. Notable amongst these will be the all-important sill to rear side chassis rail junction and indeed the chassis rail itself, especially around the spring hanger.

It will doubtless have been noted that signs of rot in many body panels point also to the existence of rot in the sills. Sill rot can be so expertly hidden that anything which suggests the possibility of sill rot should be treated as actual evidence of sill rot.

To carry out a thorough check of the rear underside of the car you have to jack the car up and

support it on axle stands. Armed with a torch to see with and an old screwdriver to test metal with, systematically work your way down each side. Pay especial attention to the condition of the metal around the spring hangers

Dark patches on the petrol tank indicate that it is leaking, probably through a hole in the rust-prone top surface. Following the test drive, when petrol can be lost through a hole in the top of the tank as it is thrown around, your nose will act as a good petrol leak detector.

External panels

Pay close attention to the boat-tail sections underneath the rear lights. These frequently rot, and when they have rotted it is inevitable that the triangular trunk outer sections and most probably some of the outer rear wing will also have succumbed. The two trunk outer sections can be checked easily from inside the GT or in the boot of the Roadster. The boat-tails may have been repaired satisfactorily with steel, but body filler 'repair' is quite usual, so test with the magnet.

Only one screw holds each light cluster in place, so you might care to remove one or both for a better look. As with all exterior panels, make full use of the magnet to reveal non-ferrous body filler 'repairs'.

Any exterior panel could contain filler used to finish a dent repair or flush an area suffering heat distortion following gas welding. The presence of filler cannot be condemned out of hand because it is a perfectly legitimate way of obtaining a satisfactory finish on shallow, concave dents. A thin layer of filler will still allow the steel underneath to be to some extent attractive to the magnet, but where a thick layer of filler has been used or a hole has been bridged with GRP the magnet will not be the slightest bit attracted. Such misuse of bodyfiller often arises because it is used over a rusted hole rather than a knocked-out dent.

Check the rear valance and the join between it and each rear wing, paying especial attention to the lower rear wing which suffers stone chip damage. The front lower quarter of the rear wing might have a visible seam running from the doorway to the wheel arch, and this panel might have been fitted over new sills, or it might simply be a slapped-on cover for a badly-rusted section (which would be covering an equally rusted sill end).

Lower half wing repair sections are widely used and the seam lies hidden under the chrome strip. This seam will quite often have partly sprung open, and the first sign will probably be a visible crack immediately above the chrome strip. The fillet at the top rear of the wing often rusts and many cars have evidence of filler around this area. Although this is not especially serious rust, it is far from being an easy repair.

Above this line the GT is usually sound! There will sometimes be a poorly finished horizontal seam line apparent on the rear roof pillar four inches or more below roof level. This can mark where either a new roof section was welded onto existing pillars or vice-versa. It could indicate something as noble as a full rear wing repair, or it could be the only visible remaining sign of a heavily rolled car! If a similar, poor condition, albeit much shorter, seam is apparent in the front pillars then the roof section has probably been replaced. Look for signs of crash damage. Do not confuse these seams with the originals, which are always very neat.

The doors rust out at the bottoms and the sides, as well as under the quarterlight window pillar (where they split) and anywhere, in fact, that a fitting passes through the steel. Doors are not particularly cheap and door skins/repair bottom panels do not cost too much but can be difficult for the amateur to fit. The door hinges do wear and drop. They are by no means cheap and fitting them entails removal of the front wing, which is something to be avoided whenever possible!

Check for good door fit. Doors which are of an obviously different profile to the rest of the shell can be the result of a poor attempt at reskinning; more commonly, however, they are the result of badly repaired side impact damage or poorly positioned sills. Check that the window winders, door handles and locks work.

The front wings are bolted into place and some of those bolt heads are buried deep and inaccessibly under the dashboard. This encourages people to cut off a rusted lower rear quarter and tack a repair panel over the top rather than spend a lot of money on a new wing which is tiresome to fit. A seam or unevenness can normally be felt if this has happened. It may indicate a slipshod rust repair or it may indicate a 'quickie' or cost-conscious sill repair. It is up to the buyer to establish which.

The areas around the front lights are very prone to rust; body filler usually being the response. As usual, cases of misuse of filler appear to outnumber cases of sensible use, so if filler is apparent to the magnet test then count on having to make good the repair or – if the damage is severe – to replace the front wing at considerable cost.

Earlier MGBs were fitted with lightweight aluminium bonnets, and the weight of the bonnet or the magnet test will immediately show whether the car has the original bonnet or a more recent steel replacement. Part of the largely aluminium bonnet assembly will rust at the front because a pressed steel framework there holds the bonnet latch plate.

Lastly, check the front valance, particularly at each end where rusting is very likely.

ENGINE AND ANCILLARIES

The MGB, C and V8 are very different from each other mechanically. As the mainstream model, the 1800cc MGB is dealt with first, with additional notes on the C and V8 to follow.

The B series engine is one of the most reliable, long-lived petrol car engines ever manufactured, and is capable of lasting for hundreds of thousands of miles. Serious problems normally only occur following neglect or abuse.

Visual. The state of the exterior of the engine can tell you a lot about its probable condition. A very dirty engine which is covered in a mixture of oil and general muck is unlikely to have been looked after very well, and furthermore, there is the question of where the oil came from. Look especially for grime covering any components which should receive regular attention, such as the distributor and oil filter. Obviously old and perished hoses, plug leads and so on also tell of neglect.

Look for oil leaks from the rocker box cover seal and from the head gasket; the former is not serious but does show neglect and the latter could indicate looming expense. Look at the dipstick, to check for correct oil level, and inside the rocker box cover, to see the state of the oil. Thick black oil shows neglect, droplets of water or a thick creamy substance indicate head/block/piston/gasket problems: tiny particles of metal indicate real problems!

Look for non-standard and missing fittings. If, for instance, chromed 'pancake' air filter holders are fitted, this might have some effect on the 'originality' value of the car. A total lack of air filters is another

ABOVE RIGHT *The MGB engine allows reasonable access for many maintenance jobs, although certain tasks, such as removal of the earlier inertia-type starter motor, can be extremely difficult. This is the bay of a car which has been reshelled by the Bromsgrove MG Centre, which explains why everything is unusually spick and span. The 1800cc 'B'series engine is tough, understressed and can give longer service than most other petrol engines. Look for signs of oil and water leaks from the head and block, plus the head gasket.*

RIGHT *The mighty V8 Rover unit should not be too stressed driving an MGB along the roads of Britain! When attention is needed, however, then the bulk of the unit makes access to it or its removal that much more difficult. Look especially for oil and water leaks.*

BJD 166H

matter and indicates abuse of the engine. Examine the state and tightness of various bolt heads, nuts and screw slots. Rounded hexagonal nuts and chewed screw slots point to the engine's having been worked on by someone who did not possess the correct tools and who was therefore probably unqualified to do the job. Any such damage on the outside of the engine will probably be mirrored on the inside.

Take a look at the ground under the car for signs of oil and either move the car to clean ground or slip a piece of cardboard or something similar underneath to reveal current oil/water leaks. Remember to do this before starting the engine.

Audible. Make sure that the engine is cold before starting it – or, at least check to see whether it is warm or cold – because vendors usually warm up 'difficult starters' before the viewer arrives. Start it up yourself rather than letting the vendor do so, but ask firstly how much choke it likes, to be fair to the vendor. Watch the oil gauge and listen to the sounds of the starter motor and the engine as it fires up. The oil pressure with a cold engine at fast idle should register 50-60psi. Unpleasant sounds from the starter could indicate problems with the motor, pinion or (more seriously) the ring gear, which means engine removal. Look in the interior mirror (or have an accomplice standing at the back of the car) to check for a puff of blue smoke on starting, which indicates worn valve guides. Oil which seeps past worn valve guides/stems into the cylinders burns and gives off blue smoke when the engine first fires up. A 'cloud' of steam, or more properly water vapour, on the other hand, signifies the possibility of a cracked cylinder head or blown gasket which allows coolant to enter the cylinders.

The engine should take a little time to warm up, so if it ticks over without choke straight away then it is probably running rich, no great problem in itself but an indication of poor maintenance. Extended running with too rich a mixture can wash oil from the cylinder walls and accelerate bore wear. The head could be badly carboned up from the mixture's being too rich and it could be in need of a decoke. This may be confirmed if the engine 'runs on' after the ignition switch has been turned off, although some running-on is not uncommon with the MGB and should not be a cause for great concern in itself.

Stop the engine after a minute or so and go to the

front of the car and touch the top hose. If this is already hot then the thermostat has been removed, probably to counter an unsolved overheating problem.

Remove the oil filler cap and look inside the rocker box (using a torch, if available) for signs of foaming or for black sludge, either of which indicates wear of the valve guides and/or of the piston rings/bores. Droplets of water denote cylinder head/gasket problems, although it is far from unknown for persons of low mechanical awareness to top-up the coolant through the oil filler cap! Droplets of water in the oil (or oil in the coolant) could indicate serious problems.

Ask the vendor to re-start the engine and listen to the engine noise. Some tappet noise (which emanates from the rocker box cover) could be apparent and may be ignored unless it is excessive or uneven. The timing chain, situated at the front of the engine, can be the cause of a 'tinkling' noise which indicates the need for reasonably troublesome attention which can – at a pinch – be given with the engine *in situ*, and untoward rumblings from the bottom end of the engine could mean an engine-out rebuild.

Individual suspect noises can be traced by holding a long screwdriver against various parts of the engine and using it like a stethoscope, noting at which point the noise is loudest. Unless you can recognise and differentiate between tappet, big end and small end noises, take along someone who can.

The engine should now be brought to normal running temperature, which varies according to the time of year, but which should fall within an indicated 160 to 190°C. If the temperature does not reach this, then the thermostat has probably been removed to hide an overheating problem.

Take a look under the engine to see whether oil or water is being lost.

As soon as the engine is at the correct temperature (the moment the thermostat begins to open and the top hose starts to become hot) switch off and check all hoses, the radiator and its cap, and the head gasket join for leaking coolant. The indicated temperature might now rise by as much as 30 °C because the thermostat opens very slowly and will not have allowed the initial water in the head to escape under the pressure from the water pump. Do not worry, it will push the water pressure up nicely

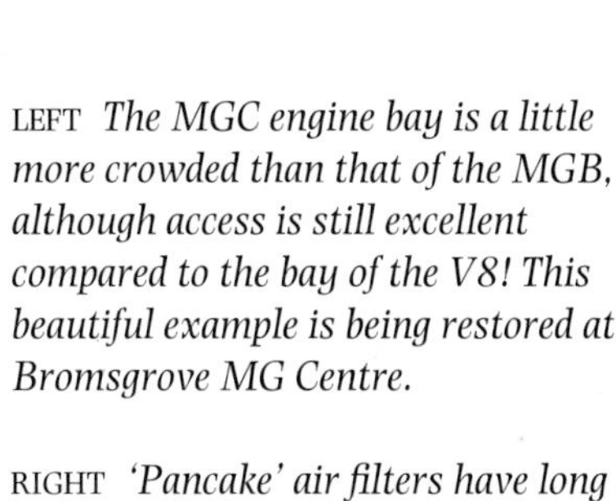

LEFT *The MGC engine bay is a little more crowded than that of the MGB, although access is still excellent compared to the bay of the V8! This beautiful example is being restored at Bromsgrove MG Centre.*

RIGHT *'Pancake' air filters have long been a popular way to achieve mild increases in performance, but with originality assuming ever-greater importance in the valuation of MGBs, the standard air filter covers are becoming more desirable. Any non-standard fittings can adversely affect the value of the car, especially very early examples and MGCs.*

LEFT *Never remove the radiator cap until coolant pressure has dropped. Feeling the top hose (which might be hot!) will reveal this.*

BELOW *Brown wires are permanently live, that is, they can be traced straight back to the main battery feed and have no fuse to protect them. If any other wires share a terminal with a brown wire, then they will not be fused and should be rewired into a fused circuit immediately. Non-standard colour wires, a predominance of sticky black insulation tape or uninsulated spade connectors point to shoddy electrical work having been carried out.*

and reveal any coolant leakage problems!

Wait for the pressure that can be felt within the top hose to drop. When the pressure has completely gone very carefully remove the radiator cap, using a thick layer of cloth to protect you from anything which does fly out. You should be able to see coolant, although sometimes there is insufficient to make the check worthwhile. Try squeezing the top hose to raise the level within the radiator, and if this fails you will either have to let the engine cool before topping up the level and then rewarming the engine, or top up with hot water.

Any sign of oil in the coolant indicates that there are problems with the head gasket or possibly (and more rarely) with the block or head itself. If the coolant is a russet red, it is because rust is present.

ELECTRICAL EQUIPMENT AND CONTROLS

At first sight electrical faults might not appear too important, but some can have the gravest consequences. An electrical fire can write off the car. An electrical failure can leave you stranded miles from home, and certain failures could be the direct cause of an accident. If you are buying an MGB which you intend to use straight away, rather than one for restoration, then do not underestimate the dangers of faulty electrical components.

The battery or batteries (two 6-volt units are standard on all but the most recent of MGBs, although many people fit a single 12-volt unit in their place) are situated behind the seats (Roadster) or under the rear seat (GT). Lifting the carpet or removing the seat reveals a plate held by slotted-head fasteners which can be removed with a large screwdriver. The condition of the batteries shows the level of care which they have received. Check the electrolyte level by unscrewing each cap in turn; you might have to use a torch for extra illumination in the case of the GT. Keep a damp cloth handy for wiping your hands afterwards, before you touch (and get battery acid on) anything else. Check that the terminals are properly connected, that the batteries are properly held and unable to move around (an MOT failure point) and check the condition of the insulation on the non-earthed lead. (Early cars had a positive earth, later cars a negative earth). It is well worth examining the insulation of the lead where it runs underneath the car.

The main battery feed lead runs straight to the starter solenoid, where it is joined to a number of brown wires. The brown colour signifies permanent live, which means that there is no fuse to blow fitted in the circuit. If a brown wire shorts to earth the wire will very quickly glow red hot, melt off its insulation, and a fire may result before the wire acts as its own 'fuse' and burns clean through. Because of this it is imperative that the insulation of all brown wires is in excellent condition, and this should be checked, especially where a brown wire passes through a bulkhead (a rubber grommet should be fitted) or where it might rub against a moving part (this should not happen, but it pays to check). No wire of any other colour should share that terminal, and if one is discovered then an explanation for its existence should be sought from the vendor.

Also keep an eye open for uninsulated spade connectors which can easily earth if they drop off a terminal or if anything drops onto them. If you find any connectors which do not have insulation then list their whereabouts and, if you buy the car, replace them at the first opportunity.

Look for loose wires which run alongside the loom (the tightly bound bunch of wires), because they will also be additions which could have been fitted following electrical problems such as a breakdown of insulation.

You should test every piece of electrical equipment (lights, horn, wipers, etc). While you are in the driver's seat take the opportunity to test the seat mountings/floor strength; push the seat backwards by pushing hard on the floor with your feet. Try adjusting the seat forwards and backwards; if this proves difficult then check the condition of the floor pans again, as this could indicate weakness. Also, grab the steering wheel and try to lift it and push it downwards, to move it to the left and to the right. If there is movement or a clunking noise is audible then the column bush could be worn or problems might lie in the universal joint.

Operate all three pedals and feel for roughness in the travel of the clutch and accelerator pedals, sponginess in the brake pedal (air in system). Apply continuous pressure to the foot brake. If the pedal slowly sinks under pressure then the system has a faulty master cylinder. Side-to-side pedal movement could signify worn bushes. Check the seat belt anchorage points by tugging sharply on the webbing and test inertia mechanisms if fitted in the same way (they should lock when tugged sharply).

Open the driver's window then look at the offside front wheel while you move the steering wheel one way then the other. If the perimeter of the steering wheel moves an inch or more before the front wheel moves then remember to find the source of the problem when you look at the front suspension and steering gear.

Check all instrumentation for originality, because replacements can be quite expensive. Using the torch for illumination, inspect what you can of the wiring behind the dashboard. Wires which go nowhere indicate amateur attempts at fitting non-standard accessories. Wires with charred or burnt insulation point to there having been an electrical fire at some time. A new loom is expensive and fitting it is not the easiest of jobs.

If overdrive is fitted, put the car into third or fourth gear, switch on the ignition (do not start the engine) and operate the overdrive switch, which on earlier cars is located at the right-hand end of the dash, and on later cars on top of the gear change lever. An audible click should be heard from under the car as the solenoid operates. Remember to switch the overdrive and ignition off. If no click can be heard and the overdrive proves inoperative during the test drive, then a faulty solenoid or faulty wiring will be either the sole reason or a contributory reason. However, a caveat here. An unscrupulous vendor wishing to sell a car with a mechanically inoperative overdrive can put an obvious electrical disconnection into the circuit in the hope that the buyer will find this and assume it to be the sole reason for the non-functioning of the overdrive. To fit a replacement overdrive will entail removal or partial removal of the engine/gearbox unit.

Finally, feel the carpets for dampness.

SUSPENSION AND STEERING

Rear suspension. With the car mounted on axle stands, check the leaf springs for cracks and breakages, and if their condition is generally poor (heavily pitted with rust) then replacement will probably soon become a necessity. Also look at the condition of the threaded ends of the 'U' bolts which join spring and axle. If they are bent or otherwise damaged then they will have to be cut off when the time comes to work on the springs or axle. Check the nuts on the 'U' bolts for tightness.

Check the axle for oil leakage, and if you have the correct square drive tool remove the plug and check the oil level. Low axle oil could signify future problems. Examine the brake backplates for signs of fluid leakage, and if you have the appropriate tool with you gently try to turn the adjusters, which will very often be found to be completely seized. Both low axle oil levels and poorly adjusted or seized brake adjusters show that the car was poorly maintained.

Put the handbrake on (car out of gear) and try to turn each rear wheel. If either does turn, check the cable for slack, although the problem could be poor adjustment, badly worn brake shoes or fluid leakage.

Ask the vendor to apply the foot brake and try turning each rear wheel. Slight movement which terminates in an audible 'clonk' (definition for this purpose: a thud with metallic overtones) is probably worn splines on the hub or wheel, although wire wheels with loose wires could also be suspect. If the tyre and rim move before the spinner starts then the wires will indeed be loose. Drag a pencil or ballpoint pen around the spokes of the wire wheels. Good spokes will give a ringing tone, and bad ones a dull tone. A new set of wire wheels will prove very expensive.

With the handbrake off and the car in first or reverse gear turn the wheel firstly one way, then the other. A clunk emanating from the middle of the underside of the car could well be due to a worn universal joint on the prop shaft. This can be established only if you can get far enough under the car to grasp one of the two yokes at each end of the shaft with each hand and hold one still whilst applying a turning force to the other. A noise best described as half-way between a click and a clunk could indicate that the bearings are on the way out. A grinding noise indicates that the roller bearings are chewed up and in immediate need of replacement.

While the rear wheels are off the ground, examine the tyres for wear, bulges etc. If the wear is very uneven, all on one side, then ask whether the tyres have been rotated (ie have been moved to different locations on the car). Rear tyres that show uneven wear might have worn in such a way when fitted to the front of the car, indicating a maladjustment of the tracking. Uneven wear acquired when the tyres were fitted to the rear indicate that the misalignment is in the rear axle or body – a much more serious condition and a problem of an entirely different nature.

Lower the car to the ground. Measure from the

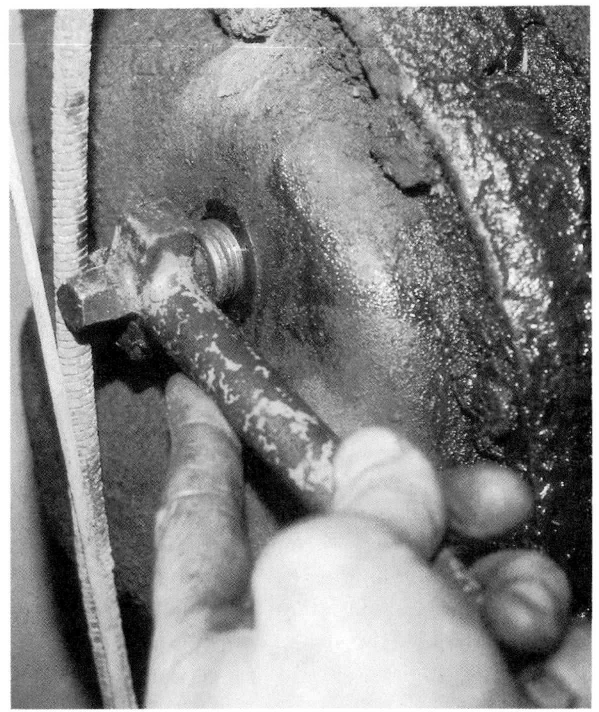

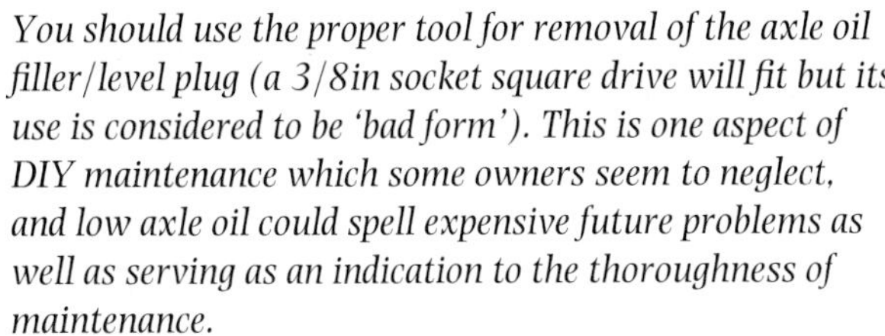

You should use the proper tool for removal of the axle oil filler/level plug (a 3/8in socket square drive will fit but its use is considered to be 'bad form'). This is one aspect of DIY maintenance which some owners seem to neglect, and low axle oil could spell expensive future problems as well as serving as an indication to the thoroughness of maintenance.

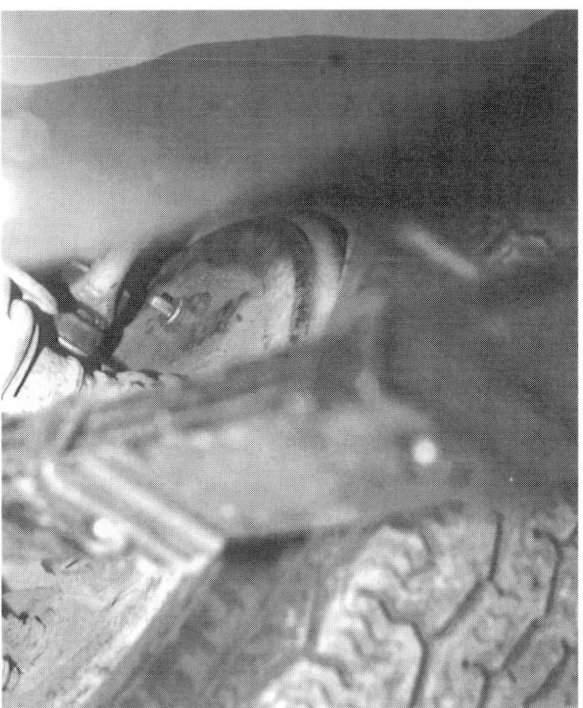

Use the correct tool when moving brake adjusters – although a spanner will fit, it cannot grip the adjuster stud properly and will distort it, so weakening it. If the adjusters will not turn easily, then the chances are that they have not been attended to for a considerable length of time. Although seized adjusters are not in themselves a serious problem, they indicate a poor level of maintenance. Use releasing fluid on the exposed threads and, if this fails to free an adjuster, there is no alternative to removing the adjuster assembly and either replacing it or applying sufficient heat to free it. See Chapter 5.

centre top of each wheel arch to the centre of the wheel. If the two measurements differ significantly this indicates a collapse on one side. Bounce each corner of the car downwards sharply. It should quickly come to rest and there should be no apparent resistance at any point in the travel. If the car bounces up, back down and up again or if you feel resistance during the travel then the shock absorbers probably require replacing.

Front suspension. Jack the front end off the ground and support it on axle stands. Examine the tyres for evenness of wear. If both are worn on the inside or the outside then the tracking is probably in need of adjustment.

Look for signs of leaking brake fluid and check the condition of the brake pipes. Using the torch, try to assess the condition of the wishbone bushes. If a bulge of perished rubber protrudes then the bushes need replacement.

Try turning the steering wheel from lock to lock and feeling for signs of roughness which can indicate steering rack wear, and then grasp one of the front wheels and do the same. If the steering is very heavy then the kingpins will probably require lubrication, possibly replacement. Spin each wheel in turn and listen for roughness which will indicate worn wheel bearings. Grasp each wheel in turn top and bottom and try to rock the wheel. Movement and a clunk indicate the likelihood of worn kingpins but could also be due to wheel bearings.

Lower the car to the ground and 'bounce' each corner to check the dampers. Measure from the centre of each wheel to the top of the wheel arch, if the two measurements differ significantly then the coil springs need replacing.

INTERIOR

Most items of interior trim are being manufactured once again and, as time passes and yet more such

Wishbone bushes perish and permit unwanted wishbone movement which affects steering and roadholding. Their replacement unfortunately entails a complete front suspension strip-down, which is not a job to be undertaken lightly!

items become available, the importance of the interior of a viewed car will diminish. Having the original steering wheel for the year and variant adds to the value of the car, because many were replaced by smaller 'sports' steering wheels.

Leather seat covers are widely available, as are vinyl alternatives; the former at considerable cost and the latter at the costs of authenticity and looks! In the eyes of many enthusiasts, however, a set of well-worn but basically sound seat covers is preferable to modern replacements, so if the existing covers are unusable or if, on the other hand, they are obviously too 'recent' then this could form a bargaining point.

The interior of the car is to many people the single most important facet of a vehicle. In the case of the MGB, it can be one of the least important considerations.

THE MGC AND MGC GT

Few people will buy the rare and valuable MGC or GT for use as an everyday car, therefore the criteria by which the car will be judged will differ from those applied to the ordinary MGB.

Paramount will be originality, as with any collector's car. The slightest departure from the specification of the car on the day it left Abingdon, such as a respray in the wrong colour, or even the wrong type of paint, will be viewed by the buyer as something which has to be 'put right'. If a component which is unique to the car, such as the original aluminium bonnet (steel replacements are available, if frowned upon) is missing, its replacement will either be expensive or the result of a lifetime scouring scrapyards.

The car is so highly sought after that even a rusting hulk which still has the registration document, the original registration number and the vital engine and chassis plates still fixed to what little remains of the body, will command a high price. If your standards are higher than your pocket is deep then the chances are that time and time again you will make what you consider to be a generous offer for a 'C only to be outbid by a collector who wants it at almost any price.

There is no reason why you should not carry out most of the checks outlined above for the MGB when assessing an MGC, paying particular attention to the state of the torsion bar-based front suspension (which is unique to the car). The six-cylinder 2912cc engine which was used in the MGC is also found in a unit of lower tune in the Austin 3-litre saloon, and some enthusiasts keep one of these cars as a spares supply for their MGC. Obtaining spares for both the suspension and the engine can prove a problem. The costs, however, of mechanical repair and increasingly of full restoration represent a diminishing percentage of the car's likely eventual worth and hence they are generally now considered to be of diminishing importance.

The MGB GT V8 manufactured by MG or Ken Costello will probably follow – if it is not already doing so – the lead of the 'C in becoming a collector's car first and a classic driver's sports car second. When inspecting either car, look closely for originality. Likewise, when looking at a V8 or purported MGC 'special', also look for proof of the car's provenance.

The V8 engine is heavy on engine mountings and on the transmission and final drive. It is worth paying special attention to these areas, especially the gearbox. Because the V8 is a far more expensive unit to service than the 1800cc 'B' engine, there is more chance that maintenance will have been skimped in the past. However, because this engine has seen, and will probably continue to see, use in a wide range of cars, spares are likely to remain available for many years. Furthermore, the Rover cars to which the engine has been fitted do not last anything like as long as the MGB, and so spares from the breaker's yard should be freely available for many years to come.

The original wheels are no longer available, so make doubly sure there is a spare! The extra power of the MGC and particularly the V8 over the standard 1800cc 'B make sound bodywork doubly important, so be extra vigilant when assessing these variants.

ROAD TEST

Make sure that both the car and yourself will be road legal. You should see the current tax disc in the lower left-hand corner of the windowscreen, the MOT certificate and, after thoroughly checking the car, be assured regarding the legality of tyres, brakes and controls. Make sure that your insurance policy allows you to drive this car. Very often a clause in your insurance policy will allow you to drive any other car with the owner's consent. If you cannot arrange insurance cover then the vendor will have to drive. Unless the vendor is a very experienced and capable driver, most of the really revealing tests are best avoided. The same will apply to you, of course. The purpose of the following tests is to determine as accurately as possible the condition of the car, and the way it actually performs. In order to do this the car must be put 'through its paces'. Only you can judge whether the car and the prevailing conditions are right for each one of the tests that are described, and only you can take the responsibility for carrying them out. The author and publishers accept no responsibility for the consequences of any of the following tests.

If the Vendor Drives

If the vendor has to drive, most of the above injunctions still apply. Ensure first that the car is in safe and road-legal condition. Throughout the test, note down (and describe) any untoward noises and their suspected sources.

Let the vendor drive for a couple of miles before making any special requests and during this period, watch for the following. If he keeps his hand on the gear lever then it could be to stop the car jumping out of gear. If he makes frequent, small corrective movements to the steering then it is probably to compensate for problems with the steering column universal joint, the steering rack or the kingpins. If he makes more occasional and apparently unnecessary corrections to the steering then perhaps the rear wheels are not pointing in exactly the same direction as those at the front (unjigged crash repair).

Try to judge (this is a subjective and very difficult judgement to make) whether he has to apply equal force to the steering wheel coming out of a bend as going into it. The steering should try to correct itself, but cannot if the kingpins are unlubricated or otherwise tight.

If the driver suddenly begins talking during any perceivable manoeuvre or action (such as pulling away from a standstill, whilst in a certain gear, etc) then it might be to mask a sound which he does not wish you to hear! Ask (politely!) for the manoeuvre to be repeated.

If he 'pumps' the brakes before braking then suspect a faulty master cylinder, air in the system or a fluid leakage. If he has to 'fight' the steering wheel on braking the car then the brakes are obviously pulling to one side, which could be due to fluid leakage, worn disc pads or a damaged disc. If the steering wheel wobbles at a certain speed then it could mean merely that the tyres need balancing, although it is best to go over the suspension again after the road test.

Ask the driver to pull up on a hill and apply the handbrake. If he will not take his foot off the footbrake then the conclusion is obvious! As he pulls off again listen for the tell-tale clonk of a seized prop shaft universal joint and also for pinking as he changes up into second and so puts a load on the engine.

Before the following tests, make sure that the road is empty ahead and that no traffic is following. Request that the car be accelerated hard in third gear from 30 mph. If it veers in the slightest then the rear axle may be loose, and equally severe deceleration will prove or disprove this if the car veers the other way. A clonk during acceleration or deceleration could be due to worn prop shaft universal joints or to the axle (expensive).

To test the gearbox the driver should be asked to accelerate hard in second and third gear and to decelerate from at least 3,000rpm (more revs if possible); a poorly adjusted or worn selector mechanism will cause the car to jump out of gear, as will a number of other gearbox maladies, all of which require that the engine and box be removed from the car. If gearbox noise is detected in a particular gear then the teeth are probably worn, and if the gearbox is generally noisy then the bearings could be worn. If the noise is only just audible, the oil level could be low. Still attending to the gearbox, observe whether the driver has any difficulty in getting the car into a gear (excepting 1st gear on three synchro boxes fitted to pre-October 1967 cars), because this could show up a worn or faulty selector mechanism, a clutch fault or simply worn synchro units.

If overdrive is fitted then it should be operative in third and fourth gears on pre-1977 cars and fourth only thereafter (and on V8s). In either gear it should engage and disengage cleanly and quickly, and when changing up from third/overdrive it should not disengage. On early cars the overdrive will disengage only when the accelerator pedal is depressed, there being a vacuum switch is in the electrical circuit.

Take the car off the road to carry out a clutch test, which you should do yourself. With the handbrake on (or the foot brake if you have already established that the handbrake or the shoes need attention), bring the revs up to around 1,000rpm in second gear and slowly let out the clutch, pressing it down again the moment the engine begins to labour appreciably, or if the pedal reaches anything like full travel. In the latter case the clutch is slipping.

After the test drive, feel the temperature of the rear brake drums: if a drum is very hot then the brake is binding. Also, repeat the tests for the coolant and oil levels.

If You Drive

If you have never driven an MGB before, it is a good idea to try to arrange a test drive in one which you know to be in good condition, so that you can become familiar with the handling characteristics, noises and general foibles of the car.

Begin by driving the car gently for the first two miles and try to familiarise yourself with the controls and the characteristics of the car while the engine warms to normal operating temperature. During this period you should satisfy yourself regarding the ability of the car to safely undergo the more vigorous tests which will follow.

Brake gently to see whether the car brakes in a straight line, if not, then suspect worn pads or shoes, rear brake maladjustment (adjuster could be seized/broken), a disc or drum contaminated with fluid, or a partial seizure of one or more brake caliper pistons. Do not carry out any higher speed testing with the brakes in this condition, because if you have to brake hard you could lose control of the car.

Gently apply the handbrake at slow speed, keeping your thumb on the release button. See whether the car pulls to one side, which could indicate contaminated shoes/drums, worn shoes or maladjustment.

If the car shows any signs of floating, if it pulls to either side on acceleration, deceleration or braking all other tests must only be carried out – if at all – very gently and at low speeds.

If the car floats then this probably indicates worn out dampers. If you have to constantly make small corrections to the steering then suspect play in the steering column universal joint, the steering rack or the kingpins. If the car shows any tendency to pull to one side on acceleration or when your foot is lifted from the accelerator pedal then the rear axle is probably loose (easily rectified), although the fault could also concern the rear leaf springs/spring hangers (could be very expensive). If the car exhibits a constant pull to one side then the fault could lie merely with the tyres or, more catastrophically, with wheel misalignment, ie irremediable chassis misalignment following crash damage.

It does no harm to seek out very small bumps or holes in the road and purposely steer over them, noting any effects this might have on the rear wheels. A car with body distortion problems behaves quite alarmingly when driven over a pothole. If you have never driven an MGB before, however, be warned that the car is naturally rather prone to bump-steer.

If the handling of the car proves particularly suspect at this early stage then it is probably safest to terminate the test drive there and then!

As the engine warms up, periodically check the oil pressure and the temperature gauges. Increase speed only when you are satisfied that there will be no danger to car, occupants or other road users by doing so.

When you exit a corner, the steering wheel should try to correct itself unless the kingpins are very stiff, and this indicates either a lack of lubrication (poor maintenance), partial seizure or sometimes a combination of these.

Stop the car, change into reverse, then reverse the car a short distance, listening for a clonk which indicates a seized prop shaft universal joint. When pulling away again, listen for the same noise. Go through the gears, taking the revs to around 3000 to 3500rpm in each and suddenly lifting off the accelerator pedal. If the car jumps out of gear then suspect either a worn or maladjusted selector mechanism.

In fourth gear, slow down to around 20 mph and then apply full throttle. Pinking indicates that the ignition is too advanced, which, in the long term, can cause considerable damage to the engine. If the engine misses or splutters then suspect a too-lean carburation setting which can cause valve damage in the long term.

Test the overdrive and clutch as previously described, and remember to feel the temperatures of the brake drums and calipers afterwards, to check for problems.

QUICK REFERENCE CHECK LIST

Super-quick check

The person who does not wish to buy a car which requires partial restoration can rule out many of the cars that he sees simply by checking the condition of the sills. On the other hand, however, sound sills do not by any means denote a wholly sound car, and if a car passes the 'sills test' then the more searching tests detailed below should follow. This test is designed to enable you to ascertain quickly whether a car is likely to require more than 40 hours of professional workshop time plus parts (ie sill replacement) in order to make the body roadworthy. It does not require you to so much as get your hands dirty.

Stainless sill and doorstep covers off! If the vendor will not remove them then the car should be deemed to have failed the sills test.

Check that sill seams exist at the front of the rear wings and the rear of the front wings – if not, suspect sill cover-up.

Check whether the portions of the wings which cover the sill ends are in the same or worse condition than the exposed centre sill section – if so, then suspect sill cover-up.

Check for rivelling in the exposed centre sill section by looking along it at an acute angle – if it exists, suspect filler 'repair'.

Check whether the centre sill section visibly tucks under the front and rear wings – if not, suspect cover-up.

Check whether door gaps are consistent top and bottom either side of doors – if not, car has 'sagged' and should be avoided irrespective of whether new sills are fitted or not!

Look along all major body panels with your eye within two or three inches of the panel, to check for rivelling or other unevenness.

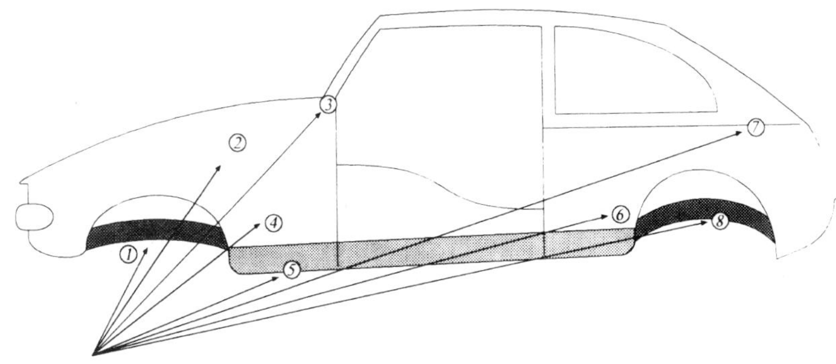

Main body rust check areas

1. Front side chassis rails
2. Triangular box sections
3. Base of roof pillars
4. Lower front wing
5. Sills and castle rail
6. Lower rear wing
7. Rear wing top sections
8. Rear side chassis rails

The main rust points of the MGB GT. Individual cars could have serious localised rot in areas not covered by this guide. This could be due to poorly treated accident damage, or to the effects of water having been allowed to lie undisturbed for a period of time. Check the entire car thoroughly even if these rust points all prove sound.

Main checklist

1. Bodywork.
Stainless sill and doorstep covers off!
Check visually:
- gaps around doors;
- all external panels for rivelling;
- overspray.

Check visually and with magnet:
- condition of lower front and rear wings covering sills;
- upper wing sections (especially around fillets);
- centre sill sections;
- centre sill sections to wing, probe with hacksaw blade;
- door bottoms/sides/skins.

Check visually, with magnet and probe with old screwdriver:
- inner front wings/chassis rails;
- inner front wing triangular box strengtheners;
- inner rear wings/chassis rails;
- sill inner step/seatbelt mounting;
- floors;
- transmission tunnel/rear heelboard;
- boot tray;
- boot floor outers;
- under-dash panel (esp. around steering column cut out).

Lift bonnet, check and probe:
- inner wing/chassis rail;
- dash side assembly (through hole top rear inner wing);
- around brake/clutch cylinders.

Jack up each side of car in turn, check and probe:
- castle rails;
- cross-member and jacking points;
- floors;
- spring hangers;
- rear wing boat-tail sections.

2. Engine
Check visually:
- state (clean, dirty, oily);
- general condition of hoses, electrics;
- state of coolant;
- oil level and condition;
- state of bolt heads, nuts and screw slots;
- cables;
- fan belt, fan blades;
- oil leaks;
- non-standard components.

Audible/visual checks:
- starter motor/ring gear noise;
- exhaust – blue smoke on starting;
- exhaust – steam on starting;
- top hose temperature rise;
- tappet noise;
- timing chain tinkle;
- bottom-end rumble;
- temperature;
- oil/coolant loss under car;

Electrics:
- batteries, levels, security, terminal insulation;
- main feed to solenoid;
- brown permanent live wires;
- under-dash wiring;
- all lights and equipment;
- fuses;
- uninsulated spade connectors;
- instrumentation originality.

Steering/suspension/brakes:
- steering column;
- kingpins tightness/play;
- state of wishbone bushes;
- steering universal joint play;
- steering rack wear/roughness;
- effectiveness of dampers;
- state of rear springs/fittings;
- state of tyres;
- handbrake effectiveness;
- front discs effectiveness.

3. On the road
Tendency to float or pull;
- Steering self-correcting after bend;
- Straight-line acceleration/hard deceleration;
- Wheel 'wobble';
- Oil pressure/temperature gauges;
- Gears, noise in, jumping out of, synchromesh;
- Overdrive;
- Transmission clonks, whine;
- Handbrake;
- Footbrake;
- Clutch;
- Engine, pinking, spluttering, knocking.

4 · MAINTENANCE

One of the greatest attractions of the MGB is that it is amongst the most economical of sports cars (not to mention classic sports cars) to keep on the road.

Most obsolete cars have higher day-to-day running costs than current vehicles. First, they will obviously require more regular attention and spares will need replacing on a more frequent basis than with a newer car. Secondly, the costs of the individual spare for most classics will almost always be higher than those for current cars. The MGB is another matter. The costs and availability of replacement components for an MGB (but not the MGC, alas!) in the UK can compare very favourably with those for most modern vehicles. On the question of availability, the MGB owner is spoilt for choice even when the car is compared with the best of the modern cars (with the sole exception of the Austin Rover Mini), because there are so many outlets and indeed types of outlet.

Many components used in the MGB over the years have also been fitted to other Austin Rover/ British Leyland/BMC cars, and so the modern Rover Group dealer network can provide MG owners in the UK with some spares. In addition, businesses specialising in carburation usually keep everything the MGB owner could possibly need for his SU or Zenith carb(s). Most large towns also possess a Lucas specialist to satisfy any electrical/ignition requirements.

MGB owners in the UK and in some of the major MGB export markets are fortunate in having access to many MG specialist businesses whose depth of stocking often surpasses that of the stores at the largest new car franchise. Furthermore, the range of spares available from such specialists is growing constantly as more and more once-obsolete spares come into production again.

At the other end of the scale, the breaker's yard can be an excellent source of low-cost spares, especially for the more knowledgeable MGB owner. He might, for instance, ask for an inertia-type starter motor drive spring (sold new by some companies only as part of a complete drive head assembly) for the Mk1 MGB, and add that it was also used on the Land-Rover and other BMC vehicles. A breaker will usually charge a fraction of the cost of a new drive assembly. If you are able to suggest alternative vehicles to which a component was fitted this greatly increases the chances of success.

Those who do not wish to carry out their own mechanical repairs will also find that the MGB can be repaired at the widest variety of garages at reasonable cost. The car mechanically is comparatively straightforward and most work is easily within the capability of even the apprentice mechanic. It can also be accomplished with a speed which should help to keep the labour charges down.

The simplicity of the mechanical components brings basic maintenance within the range of almost anyone with a minimum of facilities, with obvious savings over garage service charges plus considerable peace of mind in the knowledge that the job was thoroughly done!

The savings which can be made by DIY maintenance are considerable. In the short term, of course, there will be no charge for labour; in the longer term, the thoroughness which the doting MGB owner will apply to the job can prevent serious and expensive faults (and their often attendant even more serious and expensive consequences) from developing at a later date.

Most maintenance will be concerned with several separate areas. The reduction of component wear through proper lubrication is perhaps the most obvious and, indeed, many garage 'services' only go this far – even then they might not include checks on gearbox and axle oil, let alone attention to grease points! Second comes the correct setting-up of the carburation and especially of the ignition system for economy and to avoid unnecessary engine wear. The long-term consequences of skimping in these areas can prove more than mere increased fuel consumption, because badly set carburation or ignition can quite quickly wreck even a robust engine like the 'B' Series 1800cc.

Maintenance is also concerned with the safety of the car, with adjustments to and replacement of brake and suspension components. Lastly, and beyond the scope of normal garage servicing, comes the question of proper corrosion preventive maintenance. Remembering the huge costs of body rebuilding, proper attention to this often-overlooked aspect of car maintenance can bring the greatest long-term savings of all.

Safety

The price of ignoring the safety recommendations given in the text can be severe personal injury – even death in some cases. Nevertheless it is not possible to cover every conceivable aspect of safety here, and often accidents follow the unforeseen and unforeseeable circumstance, so you must act safely and judiciously and take responsibility for what you do.

Never work under the car while it is supported only by a jack, but ensure that it is firmly supported on axle stands or solid ramps which themselves are on a solid surface. Before raising any two wheels from the ground, place chocks fore and aft against the other two; if all the wheels are clear of the ground then ensure that the whole assembly cannot rotate off the axle stands. The low slung, heavyweight MGB can easily crush you to death if it falls whilst you are working underneath.

Always disconnect the battery or batteries before starting work on the fuel or electrical systems and before starting any major repair. An electrical fire caused by a short to earth is easily accidentally started and at best will wreck the wiring loom.

Remove the fuel tank and pump before carrying out any welding to the rear or the underside of the car. When welding, always keep a proper fire extinguisher very close to hand. Stop welding frequently to let the surrounding metal cool, because the relatively thin metal sheets used in car construction transmit heat very efficiently, and unseen soundproofing material, paint or underseal could come into contact with red-hot metal.

Beware of inhaling possibly toxic fumes which can be given off by fuel and by many of the products used in car repair. Bear in mind that many such fumes can also be explosive and, being heavier than air, will 'fall' into and fill an inspection pit. Never have a naked flame near the pit or in any circumstances when fumes might be present. Even in winter, allow the maximum workshop ventilation.

Whenever possible, make the fullest use of protective barrier creams and clothing such as goggles, respiratory masks and heavy leather gloves to avoid injury. Avoid any apparel, such as ties, etc, and metal items such as watches, that could become entangled with moving components.

Service intervals

With an old car like the MGB there can be no hard and fast recommended'service intervals', because there are too many variables involved. Not only does the MGB possess thousands of individual components, ranging from those which are as good as they were the day the car rolled off the production line, to others which are nearing the end of their useful life and which could fail at any time, but also so much depends on the way the individual car is driven. An old car which is driven hard or in adverse conditions will obviously require more attention more regularly than one which is gently driven only on dry, warm days.

Sticking to certain service routines, however, will help to ensure that the car remains roadworthy. The recommended weekly maintenance routines are all centred around safety considerations. Parts of the other recommended services listed below are also primarily safety orientated.

The recommended intervals relating to lubrication err on the side of caution for the average car operated in average conditions, but should be taken as minimum requirements for a car which is used in a very hot or dusty climate, or one which is driven hard.

To change engine oil, remove first the sump drain plug then the oil filler cap. Check the condition of the sealing ring and renew if necessary. An old plastic oil container with one side cut away is ideal for catching the old oil, which can be kept for rust-preventative maintenance. If you do need to dispose of the oil, think Green and do not pour it down the drain – take it to your local garage, who will have a more acceptable method of recycling it. When changing engine oil, always renew the oil filter at the same time.

An early oil filter can be fitted with this adaptor which makes life so much easier when the element has to be changed! The earliest oil filters, which do not have this adaptor, face downwards and must be removed from underneath the car, using a ratchet and extension bar. This can be very messy. Before refitting a downward-facing filter body with the new element, part-fill it with new engine oil.

MECHANICAL MAINTENANCE

Whenever you drive the car

Listen to the sounds of the engine and gearbox and take note of and investigate at the earliest opportunity any new noises. Constantly monitor the oil pressure and water temperature gauges. If oil pressure drops then stop the engine the moment it is safe to do so; if water temperature suddenly rises then stop as soon as possible, and in both cases thoroughly investigate: do not run the engine again until the cause of the problem has been found and dealt with.

Remember that no mechanical fault or electrical fault can 'cure' itself. If a loud noise suddenly stops then it is more ominous than a new one starting. If the lights suddenly go off and then come back on then the fault will recur, probably when you least expect it.

Weekly maintenance

The primary object of weekly maintenance procedures is to reveal potential problems – especially any which can affect the safety of the car – at the earliest opportunity. A minor fault, if left untreated, can quickly develop into or cause another much more serious and expensive secondary fault.

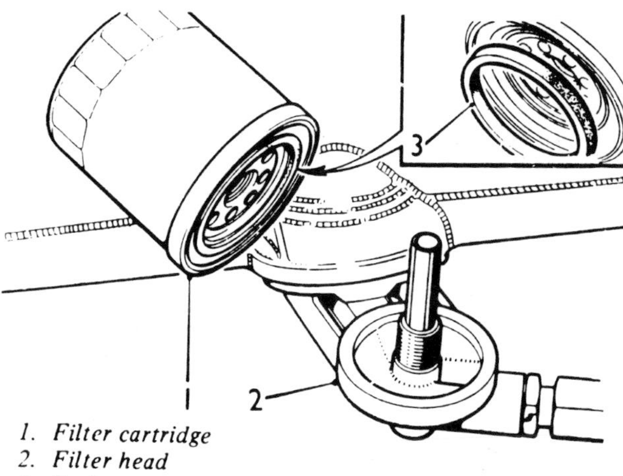

Disposable cartridge oil filter

LEFT *Cartridge filters are comparatively clean to work with, although sometimes they can prove reluctant to loosen. If a strap wrench is available, it will usually be sufficient, alternatively, an old screwdriver may be knocked into the cartridge and used as a lever. (courtesy Autodata)*

The only tools which will be necessary are a good jack to raise the car, axle stands to support it, a tyre pressure gauge and pump, and a coin or a screwdriver with which to unscrew the battery cover!

If you intend to carry out your own servicing then you should keep a stock of certain consumables. You will require distilled water for the battery(s), which can be purchased from most garages or motor factors, or alternatively, saved whenever you defrost a refrigerator or deep freeze; good quality motor oil; brake/clutch fluid; grease; and anti-freeze. This list will grow at each service interval, but the foregoing is sufficient for day to day maintenance.

Remove the rear seat (GT) or lift the carpet (Roadster) to reveal the battery cover, and remove it. Check the level of the battery electrolyte and the security of the terminal fittings. If the electrolyte is low then top up using distilled water. Remember to wash your hands afterwards and keep battery acid off your clothing! If a terminal fitting is loose then the opportunity to remove and clean the terminal and clean fitting should be taken before reassembling and covering the connections lightly with petroleum jelly or lanoline. Be sure to refit the insulation on the non-earthed terminal.

Jack up and support in turn the front and rear ends of the car, placing chocks on the unraised set of wheels to prevent the car from moving. Check the tyres for bulges, cuts and stones/nails. Check the tread depth and look for the first signs of uneven wear. Lower the car to the ground and check the tyre pressures and the tightness of the wheel spinners or nuts. Check the pressure of the spare wheel tyre.

BELOW *Lifting the strip of carpet (where fitted) from behind the speaker enclosure will reveal a rubber plug, beneath which is the gearbox/overdrive oil dipstick. If the level is low, refill using a pumping oilcan with a length of hose attached, or a funnel and hose. Stop frequently to ensure that you do not over-fill. Do not use any friction-reducing compounds in the gearbox/overdrive unit.*

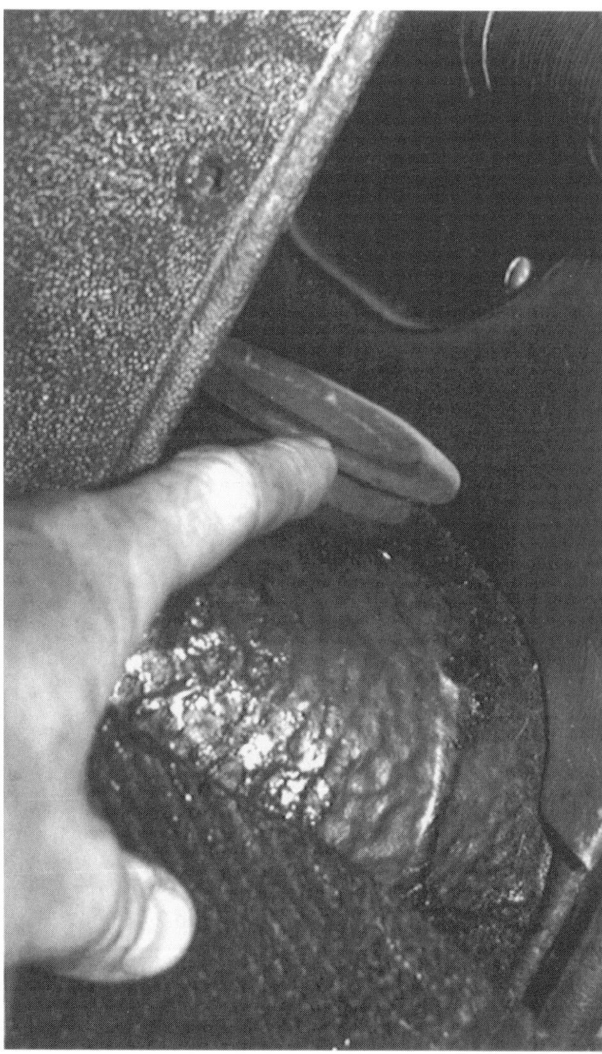

A grease nipple allows oil to be pumped into the splined area of the propeller shaft. Some cars have prop shaft spiders which have a grease nipple fitted, others do not. If there are grease points on the spiders then grease them whenever you grease the main prop shaft point.

Lift the bonnet. The engine may be warm but should not have run for some time. (When the engine has recently been running then oil will not have had sufficient time to drain down into the sump.) Check the oil level and top up if necessary. Carefully remove the caps from the brake and clutch reservoirs and check the levels of each. Top up if necessary, taking great care not to splash the fluid onto paintwork because it is a very effective paint stripper! If either level has dropped substantially since the last check then the reason for this should be investigated (see Chapter 5 dealing with the clutch and the braking system).

If the car has been run recently, ensure that the coolant system is not pressurised by feeling the top hose, then carefully remove the radiator cap. If the engine is cold this precaution will not be necessary. Check the coolant level. If this has dropped substantially then investigate the reason. Top up if necessary, remembering during cold weather to include anti-freeze in the appropriate proportion for likely climatic conditions. Check the level of the windscreen washer bottle, and examine the windscreen wiper blades for damage.

Test the lights, preferably by operating the switches and brake pedal while another person watches the lights coming on. Check the correct operation of all other electrical equipment.

Start the engine and listen closely for any noises which were not previously apparent.

EVERY TWO OR THREE MONTHS (OR AFTER 3–4000 MILES).

Tools and facilities

Although a normal tool kit and a warm, dry and well-lit place of work will suffice, many of the jobs will be made so much easier if a pit or a hydraulic lift is available. If you anticipate extensive work underneath the car then it is worth seeking out one of the modern 'DIY service centres' and paying the not unreasonable charges levied for the use of such facilities. Alternatively, enroling in a car maintenance course at the nearest college with similar facilities is an excellent idea for the novice. In addition to gaining the use of good tools, those who do enrol on such a course will benefit from the expert advice and assistance from the lecturer. Some colleges even run evening classes in car restoration – ask for a prospectus.

From the following recommended tool kit list, you will see that if you are starting from scratch and have to buy a full tool kit, the cost benefits of doing your own servicing will only become apparent in the longer term. Good tools are never cheap, and it is recommended that you buy the very best quality tools that you can afford, because in the long run they will save you time and trouble, expense and possible injury. A cheap spanner, for instance, can quickly become 'cow-mouthed' (the jaws open up). If you subsequently try to use it on a stubborn nut then you will find that it can 'round' the corners of the nut, so that more drastic measures may have to be taken to get the now useless nut off; you will also have to find a replacement for it. Even worse, a badly fitting spanner can suddenly break free whilst you are applying pressure with the result that your hand flies forwards, possibly to smash into something.

TOOL KIT:

1. Essential.

A selection of open-ended and ring spanners. The imperial sizes (earlier cars) 1/4in, 5/16in, 3/8in, 7/16in, 1/2in, 9/16in, 5/8in and 11/16in and/or metric (depending on year) sizes 7-21mm. All of these must be in excellent condition.

Imperial and metric socket set, preferably with 1/2in and 3/8in drive, with 5in and 10in extension bars and speed brace. (Special spark plug socket if not included.)

Selection of engineer's screwdrivers (parallel bladed – *not* carpenter's or electrician's screwdrivers, which have tapered blades), and cross-head screwdrivers.

Car jack, preferably trolley jack, with 2-ton capacity (for safety). Big bottle jack acceptable – scissor jack unacceptable. Sturdy axle stands.

brush. Emery cloth.
Grease gun and grease.
Pliers, long-nose pliers and side-cutters.
Brake adjusting and bleeding tools.
Feeler gauges, tyre pressure gauge and pump.
Oil and oilcan.
Copper/rawhide mallet (Wire wheels).
Light/medium-weight soft face hammer.
Small and large ballpeen hammers.

2. Equipment you will wish you had!

12-volt inspection light.
Hacksaw and junior hacksaw.
Mole wrench.
Allen keys.
'Strobe' timing light.
Thick leather gloves.
Overalls.
Goggles.
Impact driver.
Fire extinguisher.
Vice.

3. Non-specific Consumables.

Selection of self-tapping screws.
Selection of nuts, washers, bolts and set screws.
Selection of electrical terminals, fuses and wire.
Insulating tape.
Sticking plasters!
Set of appropriate lightbulbs for car.
Freeing agent (WD40 or similar).

Preliminary considerations

Before rendering your car immobile do your best to ensure that you possess all the parts necessary in order to get it back on the road! Before starting any mechanical work, examine every nut, bolt, stud, circlip and split pin which may have to be undone/removed, and if they show signs of corrosion or thread damage then order spares just in case you render the originals useless during removal. Most of the consumables required for even a major service will be widely available not only from MG centres but also from many motor factors. If you happen to live in an isolated small village with only a country garage for a local source of supply remember that (certainly within the UK) most can order spares on your behalf early in the morning for delivery the same afternoon.

Like many older cars, the MGB is likely to have many stubborn and totally seized nuts and bolts. Attacking these with too much gusto can not only risk damaging them but also the components they are fastening. A 'war of attrition' in which you soak the stubborn fitting in a freeing agent, then move it (however slightly), and leave it to soak in freeing agent again for a while before repeating the exercise is often the only solution. The use of heat where appropriate (and safe) can often help, but outright force is normally counter-productive.

Before starting the service, carry out the jobs and checks recommended in the previous service.

Test drive

Take the car for a short test drive, listening carefully for any 'new' noises. Park on a slope and check that the handbrake will hold the car. Making sure that the road ahead and behind is clear, gently apply the handbrake at about 30mph (keeping the release button depressed) and see whether the car pulls to either side. Brake normally (with the foot brake) bringing the car to a halt, again checking for any tendency for the car to pull to either side. (See Chapter 5, Brakes repair).

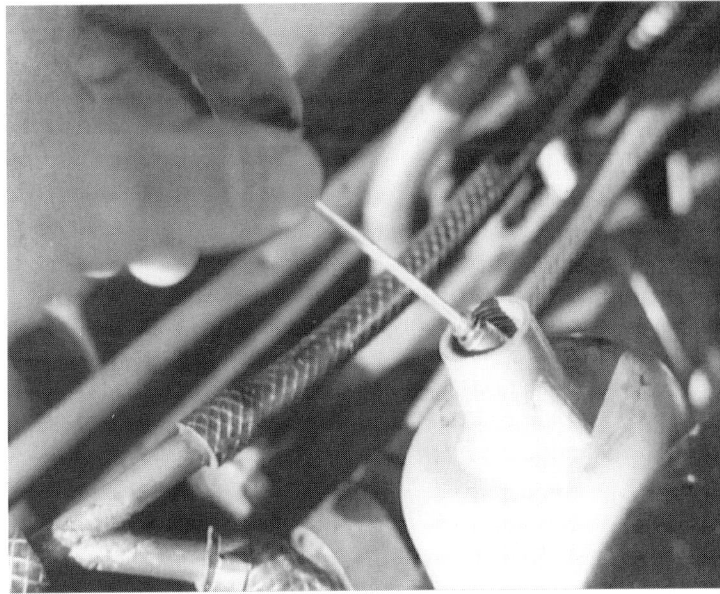

ABOVE *Fill the dashpot pistons to within 1/2in or so of the tops. If you over-fill, the excess will squirt out of the vent in the top.*

LEFT *Failure to grease the kingpins regularly will result in rapid wear, leading to an expensive and very unpleasant repair. Some early cars were fitted with kingpin assemblies which had only two grease nipples each, whereas later cars had three. Most early examples will by now have had an extra nipple fitted.*

Lubrication

The engine oil and filter (never change one without the other) may be changed if desired. This is advised if the car has been driven hard or in adverse conditions such as a dusty or very hot atmosphere. Firstly ensure that you have sufficient of the correct grade of oil and the correct filter (early cars used a replaceable element whilst later models use a cartridge-type filter). With the engine warmed, but not hot, or with a stone-cold engine (the oil has had sufficient time to drain fully into the sump) place a receptacle for the old oil (a 5 litre can with a side cut away is ideal, although special receptacles are also available at motor factors) under the sump drain plug and then remove the plug, allowing the oil to run out. While this is happening (it takes some time to drain completely), change the filter.

On early models the filter (if of the original type) will be contained in a case fitted with a central bolt to the filter head. On the earliest models this will face downwards and the bolt head can only be reached from underneath the car. This really necessitates jacking the front end of the car off the ground and supporting it with axle stands or using ramps, then removing the offside road wheel. Due to the especially great weight of the front of the MGB, both axle stands and ramps must be 'heavy duty' in the interests of safety. On later chrome bumper cars there is a fitting on the filter head which allows the filter case to point uphill, which makes matters much simpler, and there is also a drain plug situated under the filter head which allows you to drain and collect the waste oil from the filter prior to its removal. These earlier cars all use replaceable filter elements.

Discard the old filter element, wash the filter case with a little fuel and renew the filter and the 'O' ring seal in the filter head. Lubricate the 'O' ring with a little oil. Refit the centre bolt and, if the filter case is of the type which hangs below the filter head, fill the

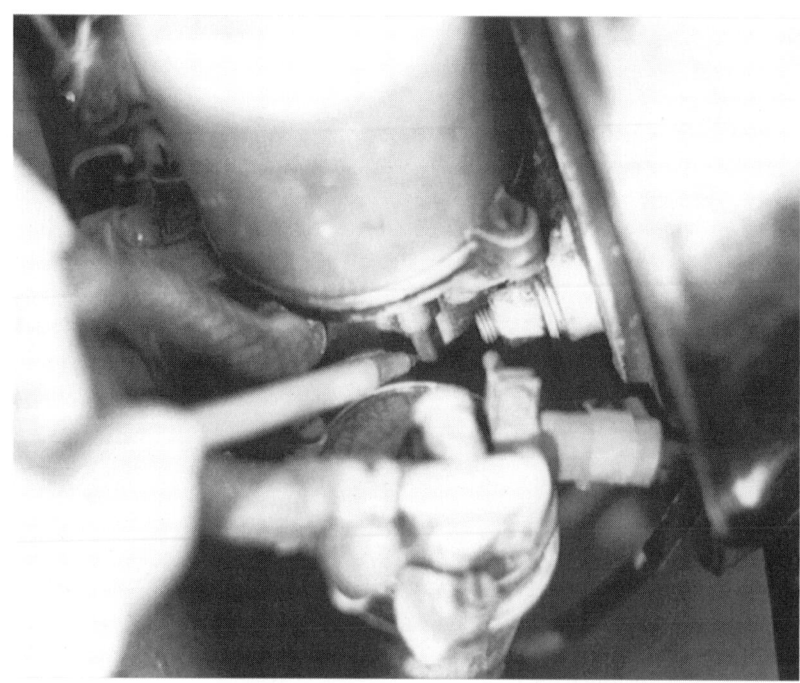

The piston lifting pins can raise the pistons just high enough to allow them to fall back onto the jet bridge and give an audible metallic click. This saves having to remove the air filters and manually lift the piston. Unfortunately, only those with fairly slim fingers will be able to reach the lifting pins!

case with new engine oil before bolting the assembly back onto the filter head. Oil filter elements usually come complete with sealing rings for the pump head. When reassembling the earlier 'downhill' type of casing, it pays to have an accomplice to help manoeuvre the components into position from on top, whilst you try to start the thread of the central bolt from underneath the car.

Later cars are fitted with 'cartridge' filters; special strap or chain wrenches are available to start these if they are reluctant to move, although you can simply drive the blade of an old screwdriver through the filter's outer casing and use this as a lever instead. Lubricate the in-built sealing ring in the cartridge with a little oil before refitting.

Refit the sump plug, ensuring that its sealing gasket is in place, and fill the engine with the correct amount of oil. Check the oil level using the dipstick, remembering that the oil will take time to drain from the rocker box down to the sump. Check for leaks (from the sump plug and the filter assembly) and if all appears to be in order start and run the engine for a minute or so and check again for leaks. Check the oil level again after a few miles of running.

Check the gearbox oil level. Because the overdrive is lubricated by the gearbox oil its well-being in this respect is taken care of automatically when the gearbox is checked. (If the overdrive refuses to operate always check the gearbox oil level at the earliest opportunity, because this can indicate a dangerously low oil level in the gearbox.) On earlier models a rubber cover is situated behind the radio speaker to the top off-side of the transmission tunnel. Removal of this gives access to the gearbox/overdrive dipstick. If the level is low then top up. The easiest method is to use a length of tubing attached to a funnel or a pumping oilcan. Avoid overfilling, because draining the excess will entail getting under the car to gain access to the gearbox or overdrive drain plug! On later models there is a filler level plug situated on the side of the gearbox which cannot be reached from inside the car but only from within the transmission tunnel. In this instance, the car will have to be raised and supported for checking and topping-up. Automatics have a dipstick situated in the rear offside of the engine compartment, and in this instance the level should be checked with the engine running (handbrake on and drive selector in 'P' position).

Check the axle oil level. If you can reach the axle oil level plug without raising the car then do so, ensuring that the car is roughly level. Otherwise, jack up the rear of the car as little as is necessary to see the axle and support it on axle stands. A plug with a square drive hole can be found on the back of the axle casing, and the oil level inside should come up to this plug with the car as level as is possible (this can be achieved by parking facing uphill on a very slight slope, chocking the front wheels and then raising the rear of the car).

Grease the prop shaft and the kingpins. Clean the grease nipples thoroughly before applying the grease gun to prevent forcing in grit. The prop shaft is best greased while the rear of the car is jacked up (out of gear, handbrake off); this allows the rear wheels to be turned by hand until the grease nipple(s) face downwards (some cars have grease points for the universal joints and the sliding collar, others just for the collar). Also, give the nipple on the handbrake cable outer (in the vicinity of the axle) a few pumps with the grease gun. The kingpins each have two or three grease nipples (early cars had just two, but the originals are by now likely to have been modified or replaced). Failure to grease these regularly will severely shorten the life of the kingpins. On some cars the steering rack is fitted with a grease nipple, and if so this should be greased.

Early cars were fitted with a grease nipple on the water pump and this should be given one or two strokes with the grease gun. Early cars were also fitted with a dynamo (alternators were fitted after late 1967). The rear bearing of this should be lubricated with light oil through the marked hole on the back of the unit. All hinges and door catches can be lubricated with a little thin oil, and the same lubricant can be worked into the choke cable to prevent its seizing in future.

Although not strictly speaking lubrication, the oil levels in the carburettor dashpots should be checked. At the top of each carburettor is a black screw cap, attached to which is a piston which is damped by oil. Low oil levels affect smooth running. An ordinary multigrade motor oil is not acceptable for this purpose; use SAE20 grade. The level should come to within 1/2in of the lower lip at the top of the unit.

It is well worth checking (especially if the engine tickover is lumpy or if the engine hesitates as you accelerate) that the carburettor needles are centralised. You can use the lifting pins if they are fitted. Alternatively, remove the air filters by undoing the two long bolts which hold each casing. Inside the throat of each carburettor you will be able to see the piston. Gently lift the piston about 1/4in (it should rise slowly and smoothly; if there is any roughness then do not force it) and let it drop down. If it hits the jet bridge with an audible metallic click then the jet is centralised. If not, centralise the jet following the instructions in Chapter 5, Fuel system.

Checks and adjustments

The fan belt tension should be checked. Along the longest run of the belt (from the crank pulley to the dynamo/alternator) it should not deflect more than 1/2in on early examples and half that on later models. If the belt is loose it can be tensioned simply by loosening the two nuts holding the main body to the brackets on the water pump housing and crankcase. Then slacken off the single bolt which clamps the tensioning bracket (under the dynamo/alternator) until the generator can be moved and the belt tensioned. Retighten the bolts firmly.

Check all brake, clutch and fuel pipes for leaking and signs of damage. Check the gaiters on the steering rack ends for cuts (an MOT failure point).

Check for play in the steering by turning the steering wheel and noting how far the periphery travels before movement is transferred to the wheels. If this is more than 1in then examine the steering column universal joint for play by pulling then pushing the steering wheel and listening for a clonk; if there is none then the fault could well lie with the dampers.

Check all light lenses for cracks (an MOT failure point), mirrors for damage and seat belt fixings for security.

EVERY 5–6000 MILES OR SIX MONTHS

Carry out all of the checks and adjustments listed previously, including all of those which were optional. Some of the more complicated jobs or those which require specialised equipment may be best entrusted to a professional. Most garages are pleased to carry out specific tasks rather than a full 'service'.

Extra tools

In addition to the previously suggested tool kit you will require the following (*Optional).

Strobe timing light.*
Feeler gauges.
Torque wrench.
Carburettor balancing equipment (twin carb models only).*
Wheel alignment device.*

Engine and ancillaries

If the engine oil and filter were not changed during the previous service then it is essential that they are changed as a part of this service. (See previous 3 month service.)

Check all cooling system hoses for condition and renew any which show signs of perishing, splitting or abrasion. Check the tightness of jubilee clips on the hoses.

Ignition

It is often cheaper in the long run to buy a complete 'ignition service kit' from an MG centre than it is to buy certain of the ignition components separately from local garages. Buying a complete kit means that you have all the likely spares to hand; any which are not needed in this service should be used as a matter of course during the annual service. When ordering these spares, quote the engine number in addition to the year to make absolutely sure that you obtain the correct components.

Check the plug leads. Remove the plugs, clean and reset them to the correct gap. If they show signs of old age then it is best to replace them. The state of the plugs can reveal problems with the ignition, the carburation or the engine itself. If they are badly carboned up (covered with a dry sooty layer) then the mixture has been too rich. This could be due to the carbs being set badly, or to worn jets, a sticking choke cable or clogged air filters (see Chapter 5, Fuel System). If the plugs are covered with an oily black layer then oil is getting into the cylinders past the valve guide/stem or the piston rings (see Chapter 5 Cylinder Head). Carboned or oiled plugs may be cleaned and reused.

If the electrodes are burning away, if the core nose is damaged or white (the electrodes will have a glazed appearance) then the plug is overheating for one of a range of reasons. Assuming that the correct plugs are fitted, the problem could lie with pre-ignition, too weak a fuel mixture or too low a grade of fuel. The fault in any instance should be traced and rectified before the engine is again run for any length of time, because serious damage could otherwise result. The plugs should in this instance be replaced.

To set the plug gap, first clean the plug thoroughly. Early cars fitted with the Lucas type 25D4 distributor should have plug gaps of 0.024in to

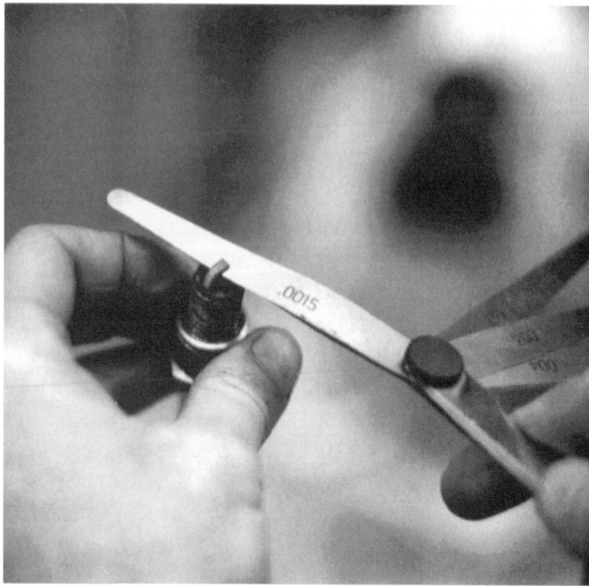

ABOVE *It is worth buying feeler gauges which come fitted with the correct tool for adjustment of the spark plug gaps. Always clean the plugs of carbon deposits before setting the gap, and pay attention to the condition of the plugs. If you ignore a warning sign, such as oily deposits, then the problem which caused it will only become worse and possibly necessitate more serious future repairs.*

BELOW *If the points are pitted they may be cleaned, although these are low-cost items and it is always advisable to change them. When setting the points gap, slacken the fixed plate screw then lever with a screwdriver in the arrowed notch. (courtesy Autodata)*

Distributor fixed plate securing screw and screwdriver notches

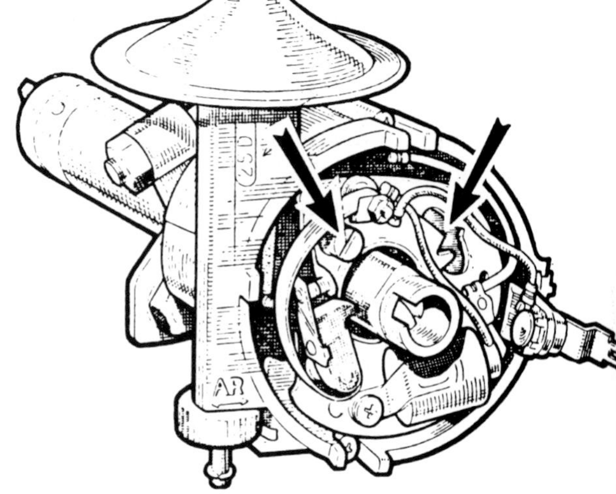

0.026in or 0.625mm to 0.660mm. Later cars, with the Lucas type 45D4 (or 45DE4) distributor, should have a plug gap of 0.035in or 0.90mm. Find the appropriate gauge (or use two or more which add up to the correct thickness) and gently push it into the electrode gap. Because electrodes slowly erode, the gap will normally be slack and should be adjusted using the correct tool (usually attached to the feeler gauge) until the gauge can be moved within the electrode gap and slight resistance felt.

Check that the screw barrel fittings on the ends of the plugs are tight. If they are loose then electrical losses will occur to the detriment of the spark efficiency.

Remove the distributor cap by pressing onto the centre of each fixing spring and lifting away the end. Examine the cap for cracks or burning, if any cracks are found then renew the cap, for any moisture here (such as condensation) will cause a short to earth and prevent the engine from starting! Examine the four metal contacts for signs of damage (six on the MGC and eight on the V8) and the plug leads for tightness.

Remove the rotor arm and examine the blade for fouling. Gently clean the contact area if necessary, or replace the arm if the blade is loose.

Examine the contact breaker points for wear and cleanness. The contacting surfaces should be free from pitting, level and clean. If a little light cleaning will not repair the surfaces then it is best to replace the points.

Lubricate the advance/retard mechanism, the cam and the contact breaker pivot. Either use a special grease, or the smallest quantity of light oil.

Refit the points. With the engine in gear, the handbrake off and the ignition switch 'off', push the car slowly backwards or forwards until the contact breaker arm is positioned on one of the cam lobes. Check the points gap using a feeler gauge, and if the gap is too large or too small then slacken off the screw which holds the plate and adjust the gap by levering the plate with a small screwdriver inserted into the notch adjacent to it.

If the points gap has to be altered then the ignition timing should be reset. This may be carried out either with the engine running (dynamic timing) or with the engine idle (static timing).

Static timing

The distributor cap must be removed. The number one cylinder (nearest the radiator) should be on its compression stroke. This may be found by removing the spark plugs and turning the engine over by hand until the cylinder shows compression, or by removing the rocker box cover and noting when number four cylinder's valves are open (rocker down) and number one cylinder's valves are closed (rocker at uppermost part of travel). Slacken the distributor clamp pinch bolt.

The crankshaft pulley has a notch and the engine should continue to be turned until this is aligned with the appropriate timing mark. The timing marks run from Top Dead Centre (TDC) anti-clockwise in 5 degree steps. The points at this stage should be starting to open. This can be checked by switching on the ignition and fitting a 12V test bulb across the low tension lead and earth, and the bulb will light as the

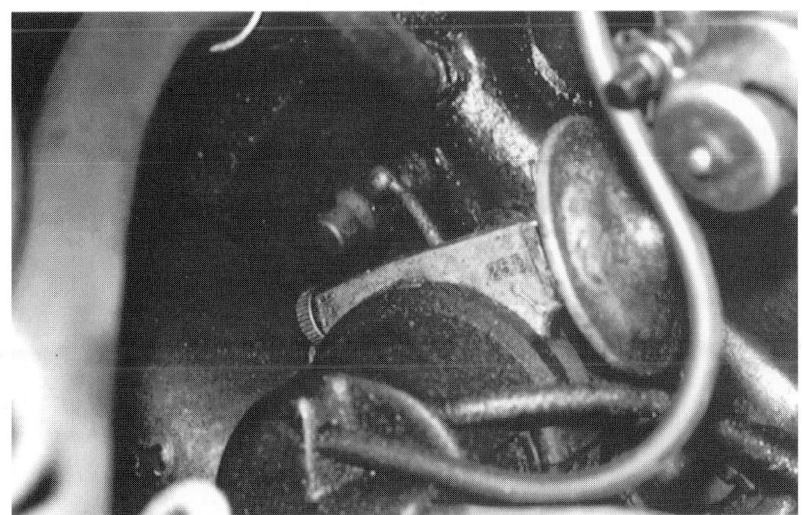

The vernier adjuster is clearly marked 'A' (advance) and 'R' (retard), and is used for making fine adjustments to the timing. After you have road tested the car, use the vernier adjuster to make any slight alterations to the timing rather than moving the distributor. Note the arrow next to the '25D', this shows the direction of rotation of the rotor arm.

points separate. Rotate the distributor until the bulb lights and then fix it in that position by tightening the clamp bolt. Low compression engines up to but not including 18V581F should be set at 8 degrees before TDC. High and low compression engines up to but not including 18V should be set at 10 degrees before TDC. 18V engines should be set at 5 degrees, 18V779F and 18V780F at 6 degrees, and more recent engines at 7 degrees.

Turn the crankshaft through a complete revolution and check that the bulb lights at the correct moment. If it lights too early then the ignition is advanced, too late and it is retarded. Small adjustments may be made using the vernier adjuster (where fitted).

Dynamic timing

This is preferable to static timing, and requires a stroboscopic timing light. A bottle of typist's white correction fluid is also very useful for marking the crankshaft pulley notch and relevant timing mark to aid visibility. Connect the stroboscopic timing light to the number one plug lead and plug and disconnect and plug or clamp the vacuum advance pipe.

Start the engine and shine the flashing timing light onto the rotating crankshaft pulley. The flashing of the light will apparently arrest the motion of the pulley, and the two marks should appear static. If the marks are out of alignment, turn the ignition off and adjust the distributor as in static timing. Retest and readjust until they align. Use the vernier adjuster for fine adjustments.

If the engine speed is increased, the timing mark should appear to drift to the left due to the mechanical (centrifugal) timing advance gear. If this does not occur then the mechanism is seized and should be freed. Reconnect the vacuum advance pipe, again increase engine revs. There should be a further, smaller advance. If this does not occur then either there is a leak in the pipe or the distributor requires attention.

A road test can be a useful final check on timing. Warm the engine, and accelerate from around 30mph in top. If the engine pinks then retard the ignition slightly using the vernier adjuster.

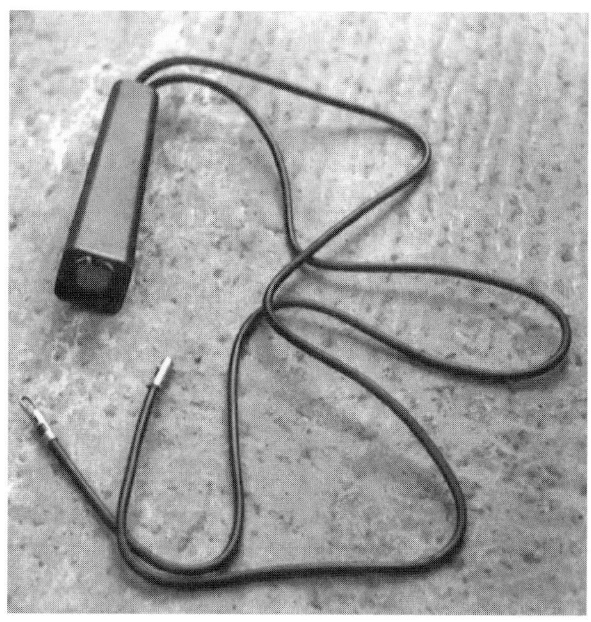

ABOVE *Stroboscopic lights such as this are inexpensive and allow the timing to be set more accurately than through static timing. The two leads are connected one to the spark plug and the other to the spark plug lead (both from number one cylinder). You will also need a bottle of typists' correction fluid to highlight the timing marks and pulley notch. Some stroboscopic lights are not terribly bright and you may have trouble seeing the marks on a bright day, in which case the work can be carried out in a garage, provided that the rear of the car is outside so that exhaust fumes do not build up within the building. Exhaust fumes include carbon monoxide, which is lethal. If you have a Mark 1 MGB and commission a mechanic to carry out this work for you, always point out first that the car has positive earth electrics – modern computerised garage electronic equipment will be instantly ruined if connected with a vehicle of opposite polarity!*

BELOW *The timing marks vary according to the year of manufacture. (courtesy Autodata)*

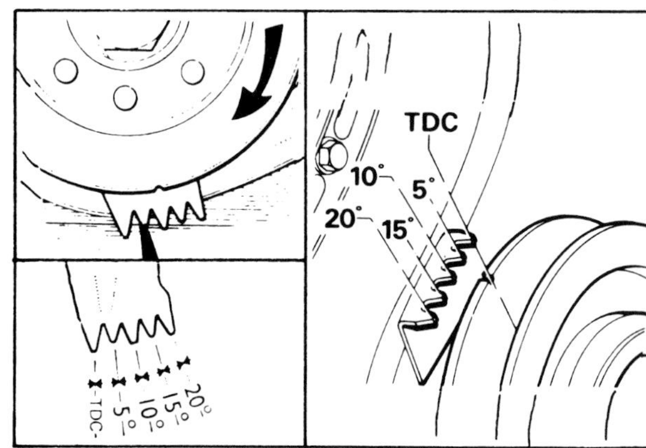

Carburation

Before attempting to adjust the carburettors, first set the ignition timing and ensure that all ignition components are in good order. Remove the bell housings from each carburettor, withdraw the pistons and examine the needles for ridges. Replace if necessary, along with the jets. Check that the jets are centred. If the engine runs 'lumpily', then begin by balancing the carburettors. (See Chapter 5, Fuel system).

Check the mixture. There are special kits available at reasonable cost which enable this to be carried out accurately, although the following can give fairly accurate settings.

First, examine the exhaust tail pipe. If the inside is blackened -- but not oily – then the car is probably running rich, if it is a light grey then the carburation may be too lean. This may be checked by lifting the carburettor pistons in turn (using the lifting pins) while the (warmed) engine is at tickover. Work first on the rear carburettor, then on the front, and then return to the rear one and so on until both respond correctly. If a carburettor is too rich then the revs will pick up when the piston is lifted, if it is too lean then the revs will immediately die away. If correctly set, the revs will pick up momentarily and settle back to the previous speed.

To richen the mixture, the jet adjusting nut should be turned clockwise (looking from the top) to pull the jet downwards, and vice versa. Only turn each jet adjusting nut by a single flat at a time, and work first on the rear carburettor, then the front, then the rear and so on until the correct effect is achieved when each piston is lifted.

Even the most avid DIY enthusiast would be well advised to have the twin carburettors professionally balanced and set up. This will bring long-term benefits in reduced fuel consumption and possibly also in engine wear.

For more details of setting carburation and balancing carburettors, see Chapter 5, Fuel System.

Valve clearances

Remove any fittings from the rocker box cover and the cover itself. As the engine will have to be turned over by hand, the car can be left in gear with the sparking plugs removed and the car 'rocked' backwards and forwards, or the sparking plugs can be removed, the car taken out of gear and the engine turned over by hand using the fan belt.

Turn the engine until valve number 8 is fully open, that is, the stem of the rearmost valve has been depressed to its maximum by the rocker gear. When valve 8 is fully open then the gap at valve 1 (nearest the radiator) should be set. Note that the sum of the valve numbers is 8+1 (9). The sum of the valve to be checked and that which is fully open always equals nine with the four-cylinder engine. Turn the engine until valve 6 is open, and check valve 3. The remaining sequence is (first number signifies open valve, second number is valve to be adjusted) 4+5, 7+2, 1+8, 3+6, 5+4, 2+7.

To adjust a valve if the clearance is not as recommended in the specifications, lock the ball end screw using a screwdriver and loosen the locknut with a ring spanner. With the feeler gauge in position, gently tighten the adjuster until the gauge can be moved and offers just a little resistance, and then tighten the locknut and recheck the gap.

Front wheel alignment

If the front wheels are out of alignment they will 'toe' in or out, that is, they will point either too far inwards or outwards, giving exceptionally high tyre wear on the outside or the inside of the tread respectively. This will also affect roadholding, and so it is very important that you have the alignment set correctly. Special kits are available which enable the DIY owner to carry out the measurement and set the alignment, although because this is only an occasional task and a fifteen minute job for a garage or tyre fitting business, the costs of having it done professionally are low.

Do not attempt to realign the front wheels 'by eye' because this is always a mistake. If very severe wear has taken place on one rim of the tyres do not be tempted to over-adjust the alignment to correct this, but have the alignment properly set and rotate (change the location of the tyres on the car) the tyres, provided, of course, that the front ones are still legal.

Lubrication

If the gearbox/overdrive and the rear axle oil were not changed as a part of the 3-month service routine, then do so now. The propeller shaft should be lubricated. Earlier cars had universal joint spiders

RIGHT *Each jet adjusting nut should only be turned by one flat at a time (one sixth of a revolution) when adjusting the mixture. If the balance seems completely lost between the two, then it might pay to start afresh. Turn each adjusting screw in turn anti-clockwise until both jets are level with the bridge. Then open the jets by two complete turns (twelve flats), and then proceed to set them individually, testing with the lifting pins as before.*

BELOW *Special tools are available for setting the valve clearances, and these are recommended for ease of use. Alternatively, a 1/2in ring spanner and straight-bladed (engineer's) screwdriver are perfectly acceptable. Do not use a tapered-blade (carpenter's or electrician's) screwdriver, because this will distort the slots and make future valve clearance setting more difficult.*

fitted with grease nipples (later cars did not) and they and later cars had a grease nipple on the sliding collar.

To grease the nipples, chock the front wheels, take the car out of gear and release the handbrake, then raise the rear of the car and support the axle on axle stands.

Turning one of the rear wheels by hand will bring the grease nipple(s) into such a position that the grease gun can reach them.

Brakes

While the car is jacked up, clean and lubricate the handbrake cables and compensating lever. Remove the rear wheels. Slacken off the handbrake adjuster and remove the brake drums. Check the condition of the shoes (replace them if worn; see illustration of rear brakes in Chapter 5, Brakes) and the drums (clean). The fine dust within the drums is dangerous asbestos, and so it is important to wear a face mask whilst the drums are cleaned out and to do so in the open air whenever possible. In this context, the brake-lining dust should be wiped out with a solvent-moistened rag, so keeping the amount of dust released to a minimum. If the shoes have been allowed to wear too far then the drums might be scored, in which case they should be replaced. Reassemble the brakes and adjust correctly using the proper tool. Screw in the adjuster until the shoes lock the brakes, and then turn the adjuster back by one notch. Apply the foot brake to centralise the shoes if they have been removed or replaced, then repeat the previous operation. Check for drag and turn the adjuster back one further notch if necessary. Refit the road wheels.

Check the condition of brake pipes, and renew any which show signs of corrosion.

Lower the car to the ground and transfer the wheel chocks to the rear wheels, apply the handbrake and place the car in gear. Loosen the front wheel nuts or spinners, and lift the front of the car and support it on axle stands. Remove the road wheels and check the condition of the brake discs and pads. See the illustration in Chapter 5, Brakes.

Check that the amount of friction material on each pad is within the recommended thickness range. If not, replace (See Chapter 5, Brakes). Examine the discs for pitting or scoring.

ANNUAL SERVICE

The annual service includes all jobs listed under weekly, 3 and 6 month services.

Lubrication

Drain the gearbox/overdrive oil, via the drain plugs in both units. (See illustration in Chapter 4). If overdrive is fitted, remove the filter cover which is situated to the nearside of the unit, and remove the filter and seals (See Chapter 5, Overdrive). Wash the filter out using neat petrol. Reassemble using a new filter cover gasket and refit the drain plugs before filling the gearbox with the (pre-measured) recommended quantity of SAE 20W/50 engine oil (three synchromesh gearbox/Laycock D-type overdrive, 4.5 pints gearbox only, 5.5 pints if overdrive fitted; four synchromesh gearbox/Laycock LH-type, 5.25 pints gearbox only, 6 pints if overdrive fitted). The overdrive is automatically filled with oil along with the gearbox because the overdrive draws oil from the gearbox.

Jack up the rear of the car and remove the axle oil drain plug then the level plug to drain the oil. Refit the drain plug and fill to the level plug using a proprietary oil to SAE 90EP Hypoid. Refit the oil level plug. The car should be as near level as possible to ensure accurate filling.

Miscellaneous tasks

If not previously done in an earlier service, it is as well to renew the distributor cap and spark plug leads. Ignition service kits consisting of points, spark plugs, distributor cap, rotor arm, leads and condenser can be obtained at prices less than the sum of the constituents.

Remove the rotor arm and apply a few drops of oil to the cam bearing. Apply a few drops of oil through the hole in the base plate to lubricate the automatic advance mechanism. Smear a little petroleum jelly on the distributor cam. Keep distributor lubrication to a minimum, as stray oil can cause ignition faults.

Drain the coolant from the radiator and the engine block. Flush the system using a proprietary product if desired, or plain water as an alternative. Refill the system using the recommended quantity of new anti-freeze (not alcohol based). For temperatures down to -13 °C use 25 per cent anti-freeze, for temperatures down to -19 °C use 33 per cent, and for temperatures down to -36 °C use a 50 per cent concentration.

Slacken the bolts which hold the dynamo or alternator and remove the fan belt. Fit a new replacement belt and tension it so that there is a maximum deflection in the centre of the longest run of 1/2in (dynamo fitted) or 1/4in (alternator).

Check all rubber hoses in the coolant system and renew if necessary, check hoses and seals in the hydraulic brake operating system and renew if necessary.

North American models only; renew the absorption canister and check the operation of the air pump.

BODYWORK MAINTENANCE

Having read this far, no-one should be in any doubt that the most lethal malady that can strike the MGB is bodyrot. Whilst it is true to say that no matter how badly rotted a car becomes it can still be rebuilt (albeit at considerable cost), there can be no doubting that prevention is always less expensive and less traumatic than cure. This section of the book looks at ways of extending the life of the bodywork in order to put off that time when extensive bodywork rebuilding will be required.

General care

In order for metal to rust it needs only to be exposed to water and oxygen, even in the very slightest amounts. Paint scratches and chips which expose bare metal will obviously permit this to happen, and so any such breaches of the paintwork should receive immediate attention, preferably before any moisture that does come into contact with the metal has sufficient time to let rust gain a foothold.

Very shallow scratches which do not go through to the metal may be gently cleaned out and hand-painted with a small brush. If bare metal has been exposed (to all intents and purposes corrosion begins the moment metal comes into contact with air which contains moisture) then it is usually best to take a small area of the surrounding paintwork down with 'wet or dry' abrasive paper (used wet) to reveal a little more metal than was originally exposed. The existing paint at the edges should be feathered, that is, there should not be a discernible shoulder around the area. This should be dried and thoroughly degreased before being treated with Finnegan's 'Number One' primer or Bondaglass Voss 'Bonda Prima'.

Either of these products should stop from spreading any tiny traces of rust which remain on the surface of the metal. If necessary, high-build primer can then be applied and flatted down before top coating.

All original MGB paint colours are readily available from any car paint shop with mixing facilities. Do not expect the shop to guarantee to supply the correct colour by name alone, but find the manufacturer's code and quote that as well. Cars manufactured during or after 1976 have their paint code usefully included with the chassis number.

Old paintwork will usually be faded, so that the new paint stands out from the surrounding area. If this is the case then cutting the old and new paint (allowing a suitable period for the new paint to harden first, which varies according to the type of paint used) with a proprietary mild cutting compound will remove accumulated road dirt and take a very thin layer off the old paint to lessen the difference, as well as improving the surface of the new paint. If you are unsure about the hardening period for the paint you have used, it is best to leave any new paint to harden for at least a fortnight before cutting it back.

Underneath the car, particularly within the wheel arches but also along the run of the sill castle-sections, the rear side chassis rails and the floor, mud accumulates and should be cleaned off at regular intervals. Mud not only holds moisture in contact with the car body for long periods but it holds the salt which is used on roads in the UK in winter. Little accelerates rusting faster than salt, as can be witnessed in cars which are regularly exposed to salt-laden coastal air.

Steam cleaning is the very best way in which to remove mud from the underside of the car, although most people make do with a powerful jet of water. Even a garden hose which has a 'choked' fitting to give a pressurised jet of water will remove most mud, although specialised high-pressure cleaners will do the job much faster and more thoroughly. If the paintwork of the car was applied badly, they can also remove paint, so take care! High pressure cleaners can also remove underseal which no longer adheres to the metal due to the spread of rust underneath. Far from being a problem, this is a great help because it gives you a fighting chance of dealing with the rust at the earliest opportunity. You can hire such washers by the hour or day from many DIY and equipment hire businesses. If you do use one then first make sure you have rust-arresting primer and some underseal to deal with the rusted areas which will be exposed!

Washing the car regularly not only keeps it looking good but also helps to show up any scratches or minor dents which could, if left untreated, lead to the onset of corrosion. It is a good idea to begin by washing the underside of the car and the wheels, since the use of a hose or high-pressure water device can splatter mud all over the place, including onto the paintwork you have just washed if you did things in the wrong order. The head of a stiff broom can be a help in removing mud from under the sill castle-sections, where it can be difficult to direct a jet of water. After cleaning the underside, switch your attentions to the roof and then work downwards.

Never use ordinary washing-up liquid to wash the car, because many liquids contain industrial salts. (Do not use it in the windscreen washer bottle, either, because some of this soapy water will find its way onto the paintwork). It is always safer to use a proper car shampoo. Begin by hosing the car down with fresh water to get as much dirt as possible into suspension and off the body. On very hot days work on just one section of the car at a time, because if you try to hose down the whole car at once then the roof will be dry and the dirt will have resettled before you can begin to use a leather or sponge. If you take the wash leather or even a sponge to bodywork covered in gritty dirt then the dirt will grind at the surface of the paint. Begin with the roof, work along the horizontal boot/bonnet surfaces, down each side to the chrome trim strip and lastly do the lower wings and valances.

After this initial hosing or washing down it is as well to use a chamois leather and repeat the exercise, gently helping all dirt from the surface with the leather. Then shampoo the car and hose or wash the lather away. When the bodywork is really clean then you can dry it off with a spotlessly clean chamois.

At this stage you should thoroughly inspect the paintwork for any signs of damage and attend to these before polishing. If the paintwork is very dull then you might consider cutting it back before you polish it, using one of the several products for the purpose which are widely available from motor factors. Finally, polish the paintwork. Car polish repels water, so that water which is kicked up from the road (and which contains dirt) will wash away before most of the dirt has an opportunity to come out of suspension and stick to the surface.

Rust

Whenever a replacement panel which is a part of a box section has to be welded into position, the opportunity should be taken to give as much protection first to the side which will end up inside the section. Obviously, the area of metal which is to be the actual join will have to be cleaned bright and degreased, but most of the panel can be treated to several layers of primer. Some of this paint protection will probably burn off during the welding process, but, as they say, every little helps!

The maximum protection against rusting will be gained by using one of the better 'rust arresting' primers rather than normal primer. The rust-arresting products previously mentioned also perform very well on clean metal; better, in fact, than normal primers.

The MGB, depending as it does on combinations of metal panels welded together for its strength, has a lot of box sections, most of which can (and usually do) rust from the inside. When a panel or panels from a box section is repaired the opportunity to give further protection to the metal should not be missed. As soon as the welding is finished and the metal has cooled, Waxoyl or a similar wax-based corrosion inhibiter should be applied. This will often entail drilling a 3/8in hole in order to gain access to the enclosed section, and the hole should afterwards be sealed with a rubber grommet.

The coating is applied either with one of the hand pumps supplied by the manufacturer or via a compressor-driven 'paraffin' or underseal spray gun. When cold, Waxoyl, and other materials of this type, are of too thick a consistency to spray properly, and so should be warmed until thin enough by standing the container in a bowl of hot water. A cheap alternative to a wax treatment is old sump oil, which will have to be thinned in order to get a fine spray. It does have the disadvantage that it runs off the panel surfaces to a much greater extent than do special-purpose coatings.

Areas which particularly benefit from such

ABOVE LEFT *Waxoyl can be applied using this small pistol pump, or with a larger and more satisfactory pump also available from the company. It should be thinned by standing the tin in hot water, both in order to make it easier to spray and to encourage the finest possible spray.*

ABOVE *In order to apply wax products to the insides of the sills, you have to drill access holes. Afterwards these can be sealed with rubber grommets. Do not forget that there are essentially two box sections to be protected in each sill.*

LEFT *It is just possible to squeeze the injection tube past the rubber edging of the mud splash panel under the front wing. It is better to remove the panel, clean the sill top and then apply the wax.*

preventative maintenance are the sills, the main chassis side rails, the box section behind the front wheel arch and the partially enclosed box section behind the heater.

Not only the bodywork but also items from the suspension benefit from protection against corrosion. Even the heavy cross-member which supports the front suspension on the MGB (not the MGC) can suffer from rust to such an extent that the car will fail an MOT. There are various ways in which the suspension may be protected.

If the underside of the car is steam cleaned, then components previously covered in a layer of mud will be revealed to possess a covering of rust underneath. It is not always practical to clean and repaint such components nor to partially clean and then use a proprietary rust arrester. Many people slow the corrosive process in such cases by spraying or painting on old engine oil.

When oil is applied to a ferrous surface, it spreads to form a thin protective layer which offers the considerable advantage of remaining 'self healing' for a period of time insofar as, if the layer is breached by a scratch then the oil will again spread to re-cover it as long as it remains thin enough to do so. In time, the oil not only thickens of its own accord but also because it is absorbed by dirt. Surprisingly the oil will also be washed away in time by the action of solvents in road water. To maintain a good level of protection the 'oiling' process should be repeated from time to time. If oil is used thus then be very careful not to let any come into contact with the front brake discs or the rear drums!

Proprietary wax products are used by many in place of oil (which can be very messy to apply), mainly in the protection of the underbody. Waxes remain reasonably fluid during the summer months and so can be self-healing, but in colder winter weather this will not happen.

Underseal is the usual product utilised for underbody protection. It is a very thick substance which can go some way to absorbing the impact of stones kicked up by the road wheels which would otherwise expose bare metal to the elements. Underseal forms a thick and hard 'skin' over the metal, and here lies its greatest drawback. Any rust which exists before the application of underseal or rust which forms afterwards can spread rapidly and virtually unopposed, unseen under the surface of the underseal.

Underseal works best on new panels which already have some form of rust protection, and is best considered a form of protection for the actual anti-rust protection.

Arresting rust

When rust is discovered on thin body metal, or even on sturdy chassis or suspension components, there are two options for dealing with it. Preferable is the complete removal of all traces of rust from the surface of the metal, followed by priming and top-coating. This can be a time-consuming process, however, and many people prefer to utilise rust arresting products. Sometimes the body panel metal can be so badly rusted and thin that completely removing the rust would result in a hole. In such circumstances a good rust arresting product can prolong the life of the metal, provided that it is not a structurally important panel.

The car accessory market offers a wide range of chemical treatments which are all 'guaranteed' to arrest existing rust and ensure that the metal never rusts again. In the experience of the author, and also according to various published reports of independent testing, not all these products work as advertised. Two which, from his own experience, the author can recommend are Finnegan's 'Number One' primer and Bondaglass Gloss 'Bonda Prima'.

Unlike many other products, Bonda Prima is not claimed chemically to alter the composition of rust. It is stated to work by infiltrating and encapsulating rust particles in a resin. Finnegan's Number One, on the other hand, is claimed to convert rust into 'black manganite' and to contain particles of glass which give the primer function a tough and smooth finish. Both certainly work.

In order to work properly, rust arresters should be applied only to flake-free, grease-free and dry surfaces, which should ideally have no more than a thin coating of corrosion. Finnegan's Number One is available either in a spray can or a tin. It is the spray type that is recommended for most car bodywork because it is much thinner than the paint contained in the tin (the manufacturers recommend that this is not thinned), which is itself best suited to use on heavier sections.

It is useless, incidentally, to use any rust arresting primer on metal that is to be filled. If you are straightening out a dent, for instance, then you have to remove all traces of rust before applying the filler. Filler will not normally adhere strongly enough to such paint and it will drop off rusted metal in next to no time.

To arrest rust, you should begin by thoroughly cleaning and degreasing the section in question. When it has dried then it first should be wire-brushed and then rubbed down with emery cloth or paper in order to remove any loose rust and to key the surface. Follow to the letter the instructions of any product you choose to use). In the case of Finnegan's Number One, this entails applying two separate coats with a two hour drying interval in between. The work should be carried out in a warm, dust-free and dry building if possible; otherwise on a hot and dry day outside. Bonda Prima also comes in a spray can or a tin for brushing or spraying with a compressor. After treatment, cellulose should be applied either within 6 to 24 hours or after seven days, other paints may be applied after four hours.

Areas which can really benefit from rust arresting maintenance are body panels on the underside of the car, such as the sill castle-rails and the floor pans. If underseal on such panels shows any signs of lifting then the following attention can greatly increase their lifespan (assuming that they have not rusted right through).

First, all traces of old underseal and paint have to be removed. The easiest way in which to achieve this is to use an electric drill (or an air drill powered by a compressor) fitted with one of a selection of wire brushes and 'flap wheels'. Protective clothing, especially goggles, must be worn to avoid injury from flying rust flakes. If the panel being treated is anywhere near the petrol tank then this should first be removed.

Next, as much rust as possible should be removed using emery cloth or paper (to work right into the corners) in addition to the drill and wire brushes and flap wheels. No more than a very thin coating of rust should remain. Apply the rust arrester, followed by a second coat and a topcoat at the recommended intervals. Underseal may then be reapplied if desired to finish the job.

Areas for special attention.

Inside the car at the front ends of each rear wheel arch, triangular trim panels can be removed for the application of a wax compound or old sump oil. This will protect the top faces of the rear ends of the sills, the fronts of each wheel arch and the front ends of the rear wings.

On the hottest, driest day of the summer it is a good idea to remove the seats, carpets and interior trim from the car, and to give as much of the newly exposed metal as possible anti-corrosion protection.

A thin coating of a moisture inhibiting wax may be applied under footwell rubber mats to protect the floor and inner sill sections. Even with this protection, if the carpets get wet then they should be removed immediately and dried out.

The heater air intake chamber situated under the grille is especially prone to rusting because it is open to the elements and the drain hole often blocks with autumn leaves, etc. It is very important to keep this drain open, and a stiff length of wire, pushed through the grille, can be used for this purpose. The grille may be removed for a more thorough job. If the drain hole is allowed to remain blocked, then the air box will corrode badly. This is probably the trickiest of all bodywork to deal with, so keep the drain clear!

Chromework presents special problems. The tiniest pin-hole will enable rust to become established under the surface of the chrome, and it spreads unseen until large areas begin to 'bubble', eventually to flake off. New chromework could be polished to provide some protection, but because the bumpers and other items with a chrome finish are vulnerable to stone chipping, there remains very little which can be done in the way of protection. The non-chromed side of such fittings does benefit from either wax or oil protection.

Where small chrome fittings meet painted bodywork, problems with rusting can arise. The chrome light surrounds and side chrome strip are all able to trap and hold water in contact with the bodywork, and furthermore, the bodywork paint is often breached as the pieces of trim are fitted into place. If a small piece of self-adhesive plastic tape is fitted under such chromework, then paint damage and consequent rust damage is far less likely to occur. Especial care should be taken when fitting the body side chrome strip and wing mirrors, because in both cases there are holes through the body metal underneath and some bare metal will almost certainly be exposed.

At the rear of the front wheel arches, mudguard panels should prevent moisture from being thrown back into the box which houses the front end of the sill and inner wing. These are sealed against the outer wing by rubber strips, which should be checked periodically for damage. On a hot, dry day the mudguards should be removed and the area behind inspected for rust before a wax or oil treatment is applied.

Still within the front wheel arches, the triangular box sections should be examined for rust. Light rusting on the sides or underside can be dealt with easily; rust on the top face entails the removal of the front wing and should be dealt with at the earliest opportunity.

Surface rusting

Some areas are especially prone to surface rusting which, if left unattended, will slowly but surely eat its way into the metal. Surface rust should be dealt with at the earliest opportunity, because the longer it is left, the more difficult the repair becomes.

Prime areas are the fillets at the tops of the wings and the areas around the light clusters. The first step in dealing with such rust is to remove the paint from

RIGHT *The fillets and adjacent metal at the tops of both front and rear wings are very prone to rust. The pitting in the wing next to the shoulder of the fillet was dealt with using a tiny amount of body filler after, of course, every trace of rust was removed. The problem with this type of work is that you can often keep finding more and more small patches which require attention, and end up performing a virtual body respray.*

BELOW *On this front wing, the areas around the light clusters and underneath the chrome strip were rusting. These are common rust spots, and if they are not dealt with at an early stage, then the spread of the rust will accelerate. Having taken the surface back to bare metal, the paint edges were feathered and the exposed metal given a coat of primer.*

BELOW RIGHT *The repairs primed. Ideally, had time permitted, the front bumper would have been removed and the chrome strip fittings' pop rivets drilled out. When spraying near a tyre, a plastic dustbin liner is ideal for masking off the wheel and tyre.*

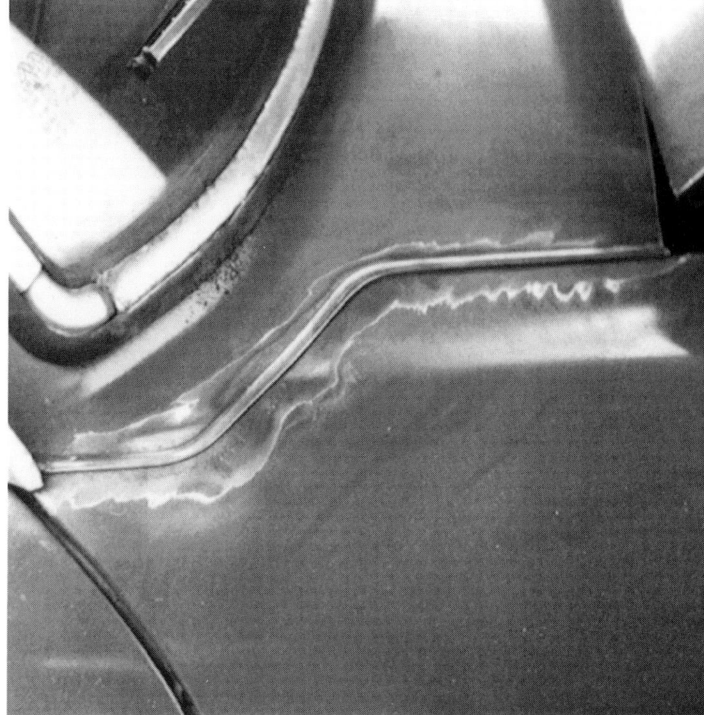

all suspect areas, then to remove every trace of rust using a wire brush. A cup brush mounted on an angle grinder makes light work of this. If the rust proves indeed to be light then the surface can be primed and any tiny undulations filled using body stopper.

If the surface turns out to be pitted, then when every trace of rust has been removed, body filler should be used to smooth over the surface before primer is applied.

Finally, the entire area should be flatted, cleaned, degreased and primed.

5 · REPAIR AND RESTORATION – MECHANICAL

INTRODUCTION

The full professional restoration of an MGB can be a hugely expensive exercise, costing hundreds of hours of skilled craftsman's time plus workshop overheads, and also requiring a considerable outlay for body panels, components and consumables. An MGB that is professionally restored to truly concours condition will, therefore, cost the owner at least as much as a brand new saloon car of good quality. It is little wonder that many owners of restoration-ripe MGBs chose to seek cheaper alternatives.

The DIY restoration is the cheapest route to ownership of a first-class MGB, provided that the person doing the work already possesses not only a full range of tools (and the skills to use them) but also a suitable premises and, not least, the commitment to see the job through.

Many people opt for a semi-DIY restoration, tackling the simple but tedious tasks themselves (which make up a major part of the labour costs of a complete restoration) and bringing in mobile skilled freelance craftsmen for the more demanding jobs such as welding or engine/gearbox removal. This will be a more expensive exercise than the true DIY restoration but it will still be an economical solution.

The next pricing level is to commission the MGB specialist to carry out (on his own premises) specific work, such as floor and sill replacement, side chassis rail and suspension hanger replacement, inner wings repair, and so on. The car can then be returned home for mechanical restoration and paint preparation.

Many professional restorers are happy to let (and some encourage) the owner of the car undertake quite a large proportion of the less skilled work themselves, such as stripping off all inner and outside trim and divesting the car of all mechanical and electrical components prior to body rebuilding. These components can be cleaned, replaced or swapped for reconditioned units whilst the body rebuild is carried out. Following the actual body rebuilding work, the amateur can also save a lot by stripping the old paintwork himself. Doing this can save the owner perhaps 40 per cent or more of the body restoration costs. This is probably the most popular method of DIY MGB restoration.

Merely to hand the car over to a professional restoration company and glibly request a full restoration can lead to a bill of unexpectedly large proportions. First, no-one (not even the most experienced restorer) can state with 100 per cent certainty exactly what work will need carrying out to the body until some of the welded panels have been stripped to reveal hidden metal (or a lack of it) underneath. Secondly, reputable restorers do not tend to employ low-paid, unskilled staff specifically to carry out tedious and time-consuming tasks, and so if the car has to be stripped to bare metal for a respray then the work will probably be undertaken by an over-qualified craftsman at quite a high hourly rate!

Of course, the availability from 1988 of brand new MGB Mk2 Roadster bodyshells has changed matters. Almost immediately following the introduction of these shells, the prices realised by rotted old Mk2 roadsters increased, and 1989 saw ridiculous prices being paid for cars just to get the engine-number plate, aluminium bonnet and windscreen surround! The new shells were priced at the equivalent of just over 100 hours of workshop time and were as good as the very finest restored body which could have cost many times the price. MGB GT bodyshells became available during 1990, and were able to accept Mk2 components but offered the option to fit a V8 – an alternative which many will find

A new British Motor Heritage MGB GT bodyshell under construction. Like the Heritage Roadster shell which preceded it, this is for the Mk2 version of the car (with reversing lights and four synchromesh gearbox). If you want to fit the components from your Mk1 GT into this shell then you will have to carry out the same modifications as those needed for the Roadster.

irresistible. This will doubtless lead to the creation of many new V8 GTs, so that those seeking a genuine V8 will have to be even more careful in guarding against buying a bogus car.

Early published reports of new MGB bodyshell car build projects showed that the cost of the new shell itself equated to just one quarter of the total DIY rebuild price if all components were also restored (reconditioned) or bought new. The Heritage bodyshell still offers the lowest-cost DIY way to obtain an 'as new' MGB roadster or GT. A top-quality one hundred per cent professional rebuild, whether based on a new bodyshell or on the existing shell, however, will cost as much as a new middle-range car.

So, there is no cheap solution to the restoration problems posed by a rotten MGB. The temptation to carry out a purely cosmetic 'restoration' should always be avoided; this approach is the source of so many nice-looking death-traps.

DIY RESTORATION

The cheapest way to restore an MGB is to do it yourself, provided that you already possess suitable premises and a full range of necessary tools and equipment. The outright purchase costs of a suitable garage, tools and equipment alone will represent a substantial percentage of professional restoration costs should you have to buy the lot to begin with.

As far as premises are concerned, it is essential only that they are dry and permit you sufficient light to see by and room to move around the car. There is, however, a great gulf between what is possible and what is practical. It is possible, for instance, to carry out a restoration on the roadside but it certainly cannot be considered a practical method of doing so. Similarly, it is possible to work in cold and cramped conditions, but to do so will have a terrible effect on morale and many people lose their motivation half-way through a restoration simply because they cannot face the prospect of returning to the work space again. It would be by no means impossible to work in a damp building, although any exposed

RIGHT *This SIP Airmate compressor has proved to be a very useful addition to the workshop, even when used only with a few basic accessories. For paint spraying, for powering heavier tools or for extended use with less air-consuming tools, a larger tank and more powerful motor would be needed. It is, however, possible – with patience – to carry out a full respray with a unit of this size.*

BELOW RIGHT *The MIG is versatile and (relatively) easy to learn to use. This SIP gasless Handymig has performed every task asked of it by the author and is quite sufficient for all DIY restoration work. Being gasless, the wire for the SIP is more expensive than plain wire, against which there is no gas either to have to pay for or to run out of! You can enrol in welding classes at most colleges, and it is worth learning how to weld properly since your life could depend on the strength of some of your efforts when the car is back on the road.*

metal would begin to rust overnight and tools would quickly become rusted and useless.

Ideally, the workshop should be wide enough to accommodate two cars (in order to restore one) and leave at least five feet clearance front and back. A garage 22 feet long by 16 feet wide would give a comfortable working area all around the car. Very large buildings like an old barn might seem ideal but will prove very costly to heat in the winter. Illumination should not be confined to the ceiling but should also cover the sides of the car, something best achieved by fitting strip lights (with protective covering) around the walls at a height of 3 ft or so.

The place of work should have some form of heating, not only for the sake of the person working on the car but also to assist in drying paints and in drying off any panels or components which have to be washed. Some heating systems are safer in a workshop than others, the best being electric stoves or self-contained solid- or oil-fuelled stoves of the type found in a house. Less suitable, but often used because of their ability to heat large spaces quickly, are diesel or paraffin space heaters, which have a hot exhaust. These could prove dangerous when flammable materials are being used, or even stored improperly.

The floor must be capable of supporting the weight of the car (upto 2,400lb) when concentrated into the four small footprints of axle stands. This calls for a concrete floor built on firm foundations. If a pit can be incorporated into the floor then so much the better, because its use can save hours.

Obviously, an electricity supply will be required, as will a main drainage system plus another separate system suitable for the disposal of toxic materials. A supply of running water is difficult to live without. It is often a good idea to incorporate a pumping system to empty the pit if the water table is high or if there is much surface draining around the building. It is by no means unknown for a pit continually to fill with water through its 'drain'. A drain must, in the UK, be built-in to a pit for the removal of fumes. Exhaust fumes which fall into the pit can quickly fill it and possibly kill the person working there. Petrol vapours will also fall into the pit and represent obvious dangers.

Security should not be overlooked. All classic cars are tempting targets for criminals as are classic car components and also good-quality tools. Furthermore, the possibility of attack by vandals also points to a need for proper security measures. The workshop should therefore possess locking doors and locking or barred windows. An alarm system is also a good insurance policy.

Unlike the normal domestic garage building which houses cars but not people, a garage/ workshop should have some measure of insulation in order to keep heat losses to a minimum. Garage workshops manufactured from precast concrete sections, steel or other sheet materials, offer very little in this respect, and some can let in draughts. Such buildings may be both draught-proofed and properly insulated, but do not forget to leave some ventilation, especially at ground level where heavier fumes, whether explosive or toxic, might otherwise lie undisturbed. Far more satisfactory is brick or breeze block construction, preferably with a proper pitched roof and joists strong enough to support an engine hoist.

The workshop should be designed and built so that it is easily kept clean. Fillets at the edges of the floor will make sweeping up much easier, lots of wall-hanging cupboard space and tool racks will keep the paraphernalia of restoration off the floor. The concrete floor should be sealed to prevent it from soaking up oil, and gulleys should be incorporated to assist in periodic floor washing. Vermin such as mice and insects should be discouraged by the avoidance of nooks and crannies for them to hide in during daylight hours. The typical workshop strewn with cardboard boxes and old rags makes a comfortable habitat for a mouse family and within a couple of months the third generation descended from the original invaders could be setting up home in the upholstery of your car.

The ideal building, then, could cost almost as much as a full professional restoration! In some cases, existing buildings may be adapted, in others, less than satisfactory buildings will have to suffice. The ideal building is not essential, but like the proper tool for any task, it does make the job far easier.

Gas welding is very versatile and the equipment can, of course, also be used for brazing. Here, John from Bromsgrove MG Centre uses gas to weld the steering column bracket onto the strengthening cross-member of an MGC which is being converted to right-hand drive. Use of the gas welding equipment does result in uncontrollable heat being applied to the metal, which can in some instances distort the panels being worked upon. It is recommended that anyone who decides to use gas for the first time should take a course on the subject, if for no other reason than fully to understand the safety precautions necessary when using that type of equipment. To be able quickly and accurately to heat reluctant nuts and bolts with a gas torch can be very useful.

BASIC FURNISHINGS

A workbench is an absolute essential. The workbench should be solidly constructed from rot-treated 4x4in timber and bolted to both a wall and the floor for rigidity. It should be between two and three feet deep and stand elbow high for comfortable working. On the wall behind the bench, shelving or cupboard storage should be built. A large board on which tools may be hung is a great aid, especially if the tools are traced round so that if one goes missing you can tell at a glance which tool it is.

Also very useful are small drawers to hold specific sizes of nuts and bolts, washers, set screws and self-tappers; to save hours of frustrating rummaging through mixed containers for these small items.

If strong joists are not used in the building then it pays to incorporate one central massive joist or preferably an RSJ on brick or block piers to hold an engine hoist. Portable hoists are quite expensive and take up a large amount of room, whereas an old garage hoist can often be acquired at a low price and may be easily stowed to one side out of the way when not in use. The fixed engine hoist should be situated at the far end of the building from the door, so that the engine can be lifted out and the car pushed backwards from underneath it.

Double doors are often preferable to a large 'up and over' single door because they allow a controllable amount of ventilation. Such doors with a vertical pillar can, however, make manoeuvring a car into the centre of the garage a problem. For the sake of safety, a small door at the opposite end of the building will permit escape should the front door be cut off by a fire; something which is terrible to think about but foolish to ignore. Also, a fire extinguisher at each end of the building could save your car and your life.

THE TOOLS AND EQUIPMENT OF RESTORATION

Good quality tools are very expensive, yet offer the cheaper alternative in the long run. Cheap spanners, screwdrivers and other tools actually last only a very short time if given the kind of heavy usage encountered during a full car restoration, and some will have to be replaced.

Today it is quite usual to find modern power-tools of the sort previously used only by professional garages in the workshops of restoration enthusiasts. All of these tools make life very much easier for the restorer and are very nice to have around if you can afford them. Remember, however, that there is nearly always an old-fashioned hand tool that can perform at lower cost the function of the modern powered equivalent, although the old-style tools will usually require a far higher degree of user skill and a considerable amount of stamina.

Probably the single most useful piece of equipment to the car restorer is the air compressor. This converts electrical energy into potential energy, stored in the form of compressed air which is contained within a cylinder. Unlike electrical power tools which each require a separate electric motor, air tools draw their power from the compressed air within the cylinder and are as a consequence not only cheaper than electric tools of equal quality but far more able to withstand heavy usage and less likely to break down. They are also less likely than electric tools to stall under very heavy loadings .

Air compressors are graded according to the horsepower of their electric motors, and the subsequent pressure and rate at which they generate compressed air, and the storage and pressure rating of their cylinders. Small compressors with low-power motors and low-capacity cylinders might be capable of operating a paint spray gun but will lack both the pressure and volume of air for a more power-hungry continuous-use tool like an air chisel or random orbital sander.

The restorer should as a minimum requirement look for a compressor with a 1.5hp motor and a 25-litre tank, although this will prove inadequate for anything more substantial than small 'blow-in' spray repairs or with most continuous-use tools. Better would be a compressor with a 100-litre or greater air tank and a motor of 2hp or more, which would allow most tools to be used for comparatively long periods. Even this might prove inadequate for some tools, which effectively means stopping work for a minute or two while the compressor again builds up tank pressure.

If the compressor has a small tank of 25 litres or less, even a paint spray gun can draw air too quickly at a typical setting of 45–50psi. This effectively means that the motor must run continuously in order to try and keep pace with demand. In doing so, the motor will quickly become very hot and preheat the air to the gun, which can cause dry spray (the paint dries in the air before reaching the surface). When spraying a large panel such as the GT roof or a wing, you cannot afford to stop half-way through the job in order to let the compressor cool, because this will give a 'dry edge' to the finish. The equipment of greater capacity is therefore recommended as the minimum requirement for respraying.

Many people think of compressors merely as power sources for paint spray guns. There is, however, a wide range of tools available, including air chisels, which make light work of cutting out rusted panels; sanders and grinders; which do not (unlike electric tools) become too hot to hold after extended use; wrenches; sand blasters; drills; sheet metal trimmers and workers; and so on. In addition to powering a paint spray gun, the compressor can usefully power a paraffin gun for cleaning off dirt and oil, and even the simple blow gun for putting out small welding fires or blowing away the rubbish you grind or sand off filler or metal.

If you intend to use a small compressor for spraying, then you will require at least one in-line oil/water trap and preferably two! A rubber air hose is far preferable to the plastic coiled hoses typically supplied with 'economy' spray kits.

The other important and expensive tool for the restorer is a welder. Four different types of welding equipment are in common use. These are arc, MIG, gas and spot welders.

Arc welding equipment is comparatively cheap to buy but has severe limitations regarding the thickness of metal it can be successfully used on. If the metal is less than, say, 1/8in thick (ie all body panels) the fierce arc welder will quickly burn right through the metal which it is supposed to be joining! Arc welders are best suited to use on heavy section metal and are useless for most car restoration work. An accessory called the 'Kel Arc Body Welder' is available, however, which is claimed to control the damaging high current from the arc welder and to produce a stitching motion which lifts the rod on and off the metal, allowing it to cool and preventing the rod from either sticking to or burning through the metal. The costs of the attachment and an arc welder will still be under the purchase price of a MIG welder.

The MIG welder surrounds its wire electrode in an inert gas, so excluding the corrosive and inflammatory presence of oxygen from the site of the weld. This lessens the chances of the weld burning through the metal and increases the purity of the weld. The MIG welder is ideally suited to joining panels of thin sheet steel so is perfect for use on car body panels. Two types are available. The more conventional MIG welder draws gas from either a small cylinder strapped to the unit or from a larger, remote cylinder. The newer type substitutes a substance contained in the wire for the gas. Because large gas cylinders are expensive and small gas cylinders have to be replaced frequently at high cost,

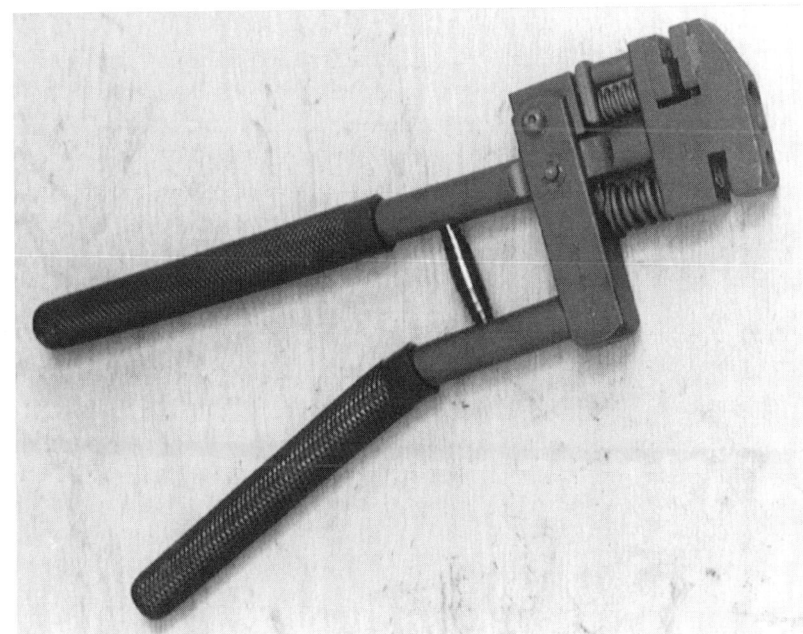

This tool is variously known as a joddler, jodder, jogger, joggler or, more properly, as an edge setter. It places a step in the edge of a panel so that it can overlap another, adjoining panel and, thus, give a flush surface. Other types of edge setter are available, but the advantage of this one is that you can reverse the head so that the second function comes into play and allows you to punch neat holes in the panel for plug welding.

this newer type of welder appears to offer advantages. The MIG welder is the best type for a newcomer to the art.

Gas welding is arguably the most versatile of all, and can produce excellent results in the hands of a skilled person. The greatest drawback is that by using a flame to heat the metal to be joined very high temperatures are generated which spread to more than just the local area; this tends to warp thin panels and so can easily give a new body panel a corrugated finish!

Spot welders are the easiest to use, although they are limited in range. This is because, in their simplest form, they can only join together two easily accessible metal 'lips'. For such joins they give an unbeatable combination of strength and neatness. A range of quite expensive special arms can extend the jobs that can be undertaken. Few DIY restorers would go to the expense of buying a spot welder because of their limited application, and most opt to hire them as and when necessary from a DIY store or tool hire business.

Most welding equipment can only produce neat and strong results if the operator possesses the appropriate skill. The quickest way to acquire such skills is to enrol on a short welding course, perhaps an evening class at a college. Whilst you can teach yourself to weld, it is not recommended that you do so (especially using your own car as a guinea pig).

USING THE MIG WELDER

Most DIY car restorers who take up welding will be using a MIG welder, and so some notes on its use have been included.

The fact that the MIG is the easiest of welding devices to use (save for the spot welder) does not mean that the novice will immediately be able to produce clean and strong welds on thin car body panels; operator skill and the right conditions are vital.

The chief problem is in preventing 'burning through', when the electric current raises the temperature of the metal so high that it burns through the pieces that are intended to be joined. This can occur if the wire feed is too slow, if the gun is moved too slowly across the metal, if the electric current is set too high, or if the shielding gas fails to protect the metal.

When metal which has become thin through corrosion has to be joined the chances of burning through are much higher. This is why the advice is always given to cut right back to clean and sound metal before attempting to weld.

Correct preparation of the metal is vital. Traces of rust, paint, oil, grease or almost any chemical deposit will result in not only poor adhesion but also in spitting, often producing a weld seam resembling bird droppings.

When welding a joint, both surfaces must be scrupulously clean and they must be firmly clamped together in some way to prevent either from buckling under the heat of the welding process.

Practice on scrap metal and do not attempt any welding on your car until you can produce a good bead of weld on typically thin body metal without burning through.

Safety

Never weld near a petrol tank or any other container used for the storage of combustible materials, even if the container is ostensibly empty; a tank or container empty of liquid will contain residual fumes which are even more susceptible to ignition than is a full tank.

Always use a proper welding mask. If you view the electric arc without proper protection then you will later suffer a painful and dangerous condition called arc eye, which will often require hospital treatment. Use protective clothing, especially gloves and a hat (to keep sparks out of your hair). The MIG gives off ultra-violet light which is dangerous.

Do not take risks by welding in damp conditions, because the electrical current drawn by a MIG welder can kill.

First steps

Begin by trying to produce an even run on a clean sheet of 20g steel rather than by trying to join two pieces. The gun should be held at 70 degrees to the surface of the metal, and can either be pushed or dragged across it. Cut the wire at the nozzle to a length of 10mm, then place the earth clamp onto the material to be welded. Put the leather welding gloves on, switch on the machine, place the gun into the starting position then pull the mask in front of your eyes and pull the trigger.

These small clamps, called Inter-grips, from Frost Auto Restoration Techniques (Crawford Street, Rochdale, OL16 5NU England, tel. 0706 58619) can be used to hold together two panels for butt welding. Sold in packs of five, the Inter-grips can clamp curved metal.

This is how the Inter-grips work. Such a simple idea, but very effective.

Once the panels are clamped, tack them into place, remove the Inter-grips and weld up normally. The tacks in the photograph are actually too close to the Inter-grips. they should be at least 10mm from the grips because as the weld cools it contracts, and if it is too close to the grips then the panels are pulled together, making it difficult to remove the grips.

The moment you squeeze the trigger, wire will spurt from the gun and probably catch you unawares before you have thought about moving the gun. Persevere until you can produce an even run of weld, and then move on to trying to butt and lap join two pieces of metal. You will find that altering the wire speed and lowering the power of the welder will enable you to weld thin metal without burning through. Experiment with different settings until you discover the best settings for varying thicknesses of steel and types of joint. Practice is the only answer.

The above instructions are really only a 'taster'; for further information, read *How to Restore with Metal Joining Techniques*, published by Osprey Automotive.

Exchange units

Much of the mechanical restoration of the MGB range may be carried out by the DIY mechanic at home. In many instances the work boils down to merely replacing old components with new or reconditioned ones.

Certain aspects of this work, however, will necessitate the highly skilled use of special engineering machinery, and there will be no alternative to taking the work to a professional company. This leaves the DIY restorer with a dilemma; whether to strip an assembly and take one or more of the components away for professional attention, or whether merely to exchange the entire assembly for one which has been professionally reconditioned.

In most of instances it will prove better to exchange the assembly as a unit. To recondition the engine, for instance, could entail the following work for the professional workshop: valve seats recut (perhaps inserts fitted); cylinder head skimmed; cylinder block skimmed; cylinders rebored; crankshaft reground; camshaft replaced. It would then be necessary to acquire a different head gasket, oversized pistons and rings, different sized big end and mains bearings, and so on.

While the above work is being carried out, there will always be a chance of some more serious fault, such as a hairline crack in the block or cylinder head, being discovered, not only causing a further delay while a replacement is acquired or a difficult repair is carried out but also entailing yet more expense. When your unit is taken in an exchange reconditioning deal, the company who supply the new unit have to stand the loss should there be some irremediable or expensive fault to rectify.

Exchange units are reconditioned in a cost-effective way on a purpose-built 'production' line. If you elected to commission each specific task and carry out the stripping and reassembly yourself, the chances are that the companies which carried out the work on your behalf would have to spend time (for which you would be charged) setting up their machinery to suit your unit. Obviously, this is going to add up and increase the final bill. A reputable company will not only guarantee the work that they have carried out on the unit, but will also guarantee those components which were merely inspected, passed as OK and refitted.

Many components will be readily available from the breaker's yard. It is not recommended that major components, such as an engine, gearbox, axle or overdrive are thus acquired, because faults in the units might only come to light after they have been fitted, necessitating another stripdown. Pay little attention to a breaker's 'guarantee' of a unit; this only guarantees a refund or replacement with yet another suspect unit should any problems come to light, which can be little compensation for all the work entailed in fitting then removing the unit.

What is acceptable, however, is to buy a unit from a breaker for subsequent exchange, where the breakers' price is less than the exchange surcharge.

It is especially recommended that the gearbox and overdrive are exchanged rather than reconditioned at home, because there is so much work involved in their removal and refitting; it would be heartbreaking to complete a restoration and discover after a few miles that either of these units had to come out again.

A very important matter for consideration is whether more than one job can be accomplished at one time. For instance, if the engine has to be removed and it is known that the clutch has only a few thousand miles left of useful life, then it would pay to fit a new clutch when the opportunity was presented, rather than later when the need arose, when the engine would have to be lifted out again. Similarly, the opportunity might be taken to paint the engine bay, to fit a new wiring loom, fit a starter motor, and so on.

Not only will combining jobs cut your overall man-hours, it can save money. Every time a major mechanical repair is undertaken there is a risk that some components might be damaged. Old, rusted-in bolts might shear, brackets, hoses and pipes might be crushed or split, paintwork can be scratched or panels dented.

Even more important than combining mechanical repairs, is that no opportunity should be missed to carry out bodywork repair that is made possible by the removal of mechanical components. A rear-end suspension strip should be combined with whatever work needs doing to the boot floor, wheel arches, battery containers etc.

The correct mental approach to mechanical repair work will save you time, money, temper and quite possibly injury as well! Always work at your own pace rather than pushing yourself unduly. When you try to work more quickly, things are more likely to go seriously wrong. Not only can injudicious haste make you forget important stages in a rebuild, dictating a restrip of the incomplete assembly that you have built up, but you are much more likely to strip threads, break studs and suffer similar frustrations.

The author is a frequent sufferer of achieving less speed through more haste, and offers this advice from bitter experience. A prime example came when he was refitting a cylinder head which had been removed merely in order to photograph the stripping sequence. In his haste, the author snapped an exhaust manifold stud (happily leaving enough proud of the block to permit its removal with mole grips). Obtaining a replacement entailed a thirty mile drive, and all for the sake of saving a few minutes.

The author spent a freezing winter's evening out of doors in the company of these two hardy brothers – Mark and Derek Blazier – to whom bitter cold and poor illumination are no barrier to MGB engine/gearbox removal! This is the donor car for a reshell.

ENGINE REMOVAL

Time: from 2hrs to 4hrs.

Special tools/equipment: engine hoist.

The 1800cc 'B' series engine is a relatively heavy unit which should only be removed with the aid of robust lifting gear. Portable engine lifting devices can be purchased or hired, or a proper garage chain ratchet winch (do not try to use any winch not specifically designed for the purpose) can be attached to a strong ceiling beam. If the latter is chosen then there should be sufficient room for the car to be pushed backwards from under the engine unit once lifted.

The engine can be removed on its own, or it can be removed complete with gearbox (and overdrive if fitted). The latter procedure is recommended, because the clutch is easily damaged during the former.

Engine only removal

Disconnect the batteries. Remove the bonnet (a two-person job), first scribing around the nut and bolt positions to aid accurate refitting. The coolant should now be drained. If the engine has been run recently and is not completely cold, first ensure that there is no pressure within the system by feeling the top hose; if it can be squashed readily then removal is safe. None the less, place a thick layer of cloth over the radiator cap before removing it. Remove the drain plug from the radiator (early models only) or disconnect the radiator bottom hose, the filler cap and finally the engine drain plug. On later models, first remove the cap from the expansion tank and the filler plug from the outlet pipe.

LEFT *Access to the rear oil cooler pipe block connection is not too easy. The other pipe connection is situated on the oil filter head. When removing the oil cooler pipes from the block, take the opportunity to examine them closely for wear and renew if necessary. The pipe and fittings are the same as used on some hydraulic equipment, and most agricultural equipment engineers can make up replacement pipes tested to thousands of psi; a point worth remembering if you ever have an oil pipe burst in the depths of the countryside! (A tip – if an oil pipe bursts, you can get home by 'shorting out' the oil cooler, in a manner of speaking, by using the good length of pipe to connect the two engine connectors.) If a worn pipe bursts, stop the engine immediately because the engine oil pressure will reduce to zero in seconds and the engine will be wrecked in short order.*

BELOW LEFT *The temperature gauge sender can sometimes prove difficult to remove. Removal of the thermostat housing and thermostat will enable you to apply freeing agent from both inside and outside. Take care not to damage the fragile sender pipe.*

ABOVE AND LEFT *The number of carburettor installation pipes will vary according to the year and degree of emission control equipment fitted. Disconnect them all; if you are worried about reconnecting the pipes in the correct places, label each with a tag made from masking tape.*
For a 'quickie' job, it is acceptable to leave some of the carburettor attachments in place and to rest the manifold and carburettors on some form of padding over the front nearside wing. The exhaust manifold can be tied out of the way, as shown in the photograph (ABOVE). *This saves having to undo the six nuts which hold the down-pipes onto the manifold, which can result in broken studs and so make extra and unnecessary work.*

RIGHT *Some mechanics hoist the engine by a bracket which they affix to a cylinder head stud. Alternatively, a rope or chain can be passed right around the engine. If this approach is adopted ensure that the engine cannot rotate or slip in its cradle irrespective of the undignified angles it achieves when being removed. It is important that the engine is held in such a way that it can be tilted when lifted. The lifting gear can consist of a simple chain hoist attached to a strong roof beam, or a mobile hydraulic engine crane.*

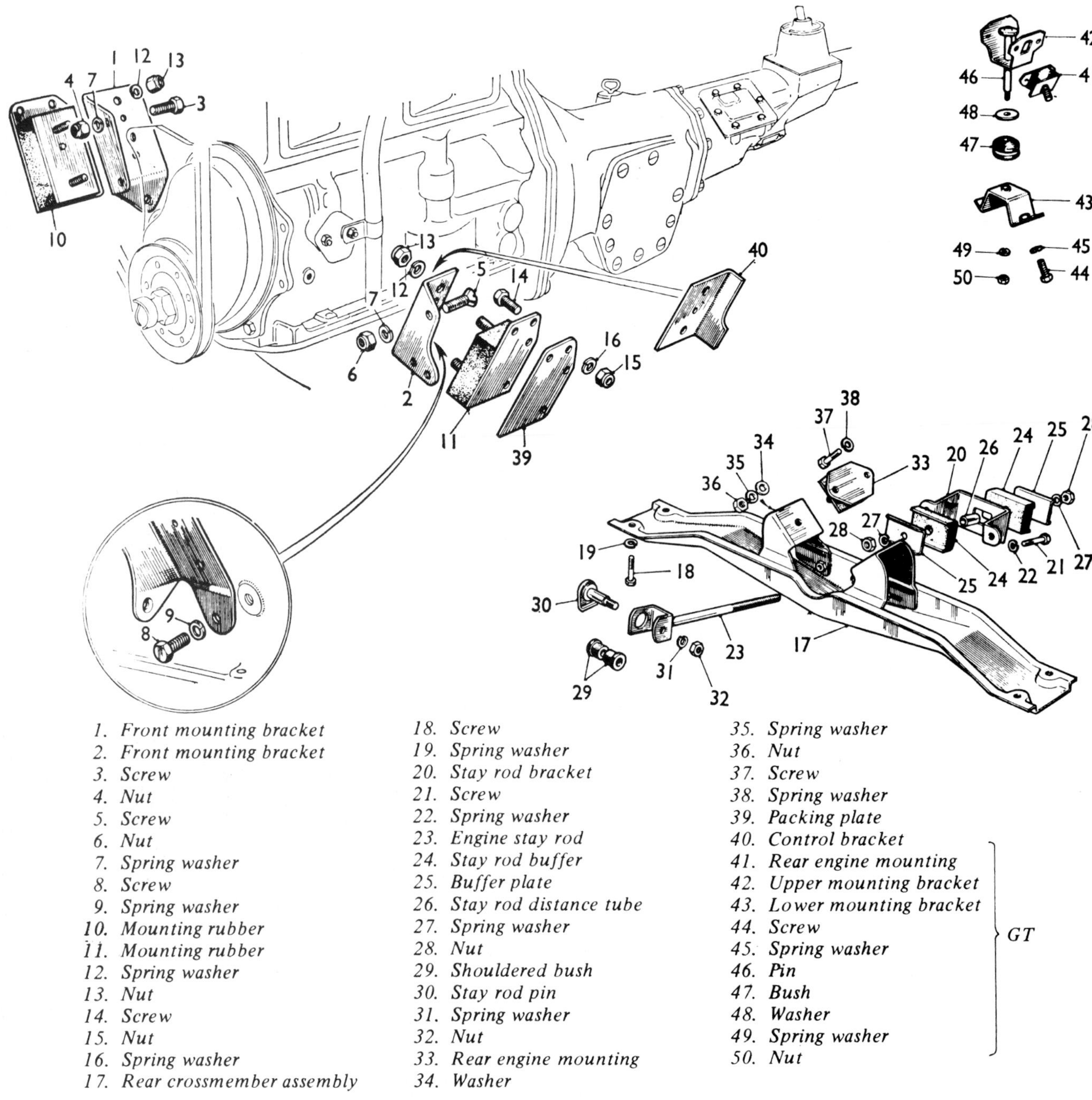

The engine mounting components

Drain the oil by removing the filler cap on the rocker box cover and the drain plug from the sump. Remove the oil cooler pipes from their connections at the oil filter and block. Remove the radiator top hose, the radiator surround and the stay set screws, and the oil cooler radiator set screws, and withdraw the whole assembly.

Remove the oil pressure sender pipe (situated next to the oil cooler pipe on the block), and the temperature gauge sender.

Remove the spark plug leads and the distributor cap, the low tension lead and the two, three or four (depending on year) wires to the dynamo or alternator. Disconnect the starter motor wire(s).

Remove the throttle and choke cables, and the return springs from the heat shield. Remove the air filters, petrol feed pipe, vacuum overdrive switch pipe, brake servo pipe (if fitted) and the auto advance/retard pipe from the distributor. Remove the crankcase breather pipe if fitted. Remove the heater

LEFT *The engine mountings. Note where and how the packing piece fits, and also remove any brackets which may have been fitted to the mountings, such as one to hold the coil. (Courtesy Autodata)*

RIGHT AND BELOW *It helps to move the engine forwards slightly in order to gain access to the starter motor bolts. The lower one is accessible from under the car and is relatively easy to get a spanner to, the top one is less accessible.*

hoses and valve. Remove the carburettors, inlet manifold and heat shield, then the exhaust manifold. The manifold may be left in position on the down pipe and tied back out of the way for engine removal if desired; this avoids risk of damaging the studs or brass nuts, easily done if the exhaust down pipe is disconnected from the manifold.

If the mechanical-type tachometer is fitted then the cable end should be removed.

The engine lifting gear should now be placed to take the weight of the engine. Either run chain or very strong rope around the engine and take up the slack in the lifting gear. Place a jack underneath the gearbox, preferably with a little wood packing.

Undo the nuts and bolts on the front engine mountings and place the shaped packing plate from the left-hand mounting to one side. Undo the bolts holding the starter motor, and remove the bolts which hold the engine to the bell housing. The engine and gearbox can simultaneously be raised until the

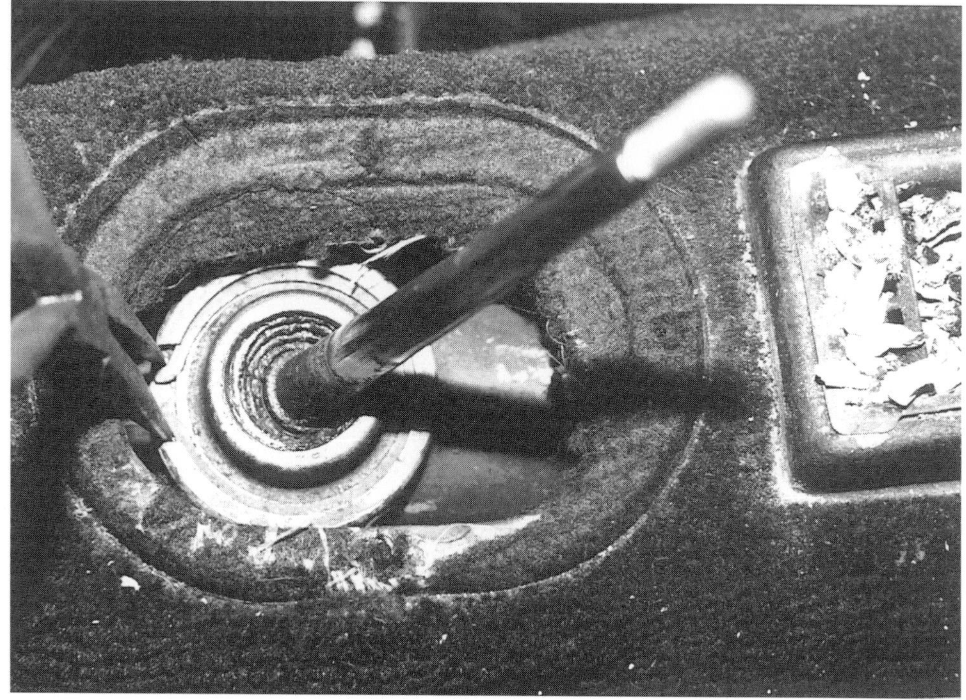

FAR LEFT *Access to the engine/ gearbox bell housing bolts is not easy. Some can only be reached from underneath the car; some from within the engine compartment.*

LEFT *After removing the prop shaft front end from the overdrive or gearbox flange, place a jack under the movable cross-member, remove the fixing bolts (there are two each end) then gently lower this in order to incline the whole engine/gearbox/ overdrive assembly.*

BELOW LEFT *Depending on the year, the gear lever is removed by first removing three fixing bolts or, on earlier models, a circlip, which is easy to remove but sometimes tricky to replace.*

ABOVE RIGHT *The clutch slave cylinder.*

RIGHT *Mark and Derek chose simply to wrap strong rope around the engine unit. That bonnet is about to prove a problem and get in the way of the engine crane arm; ideally it should have been removed first.*

When removing the engine and gearbox together, the unit has to be angled quite steeply to clear the engine bay.

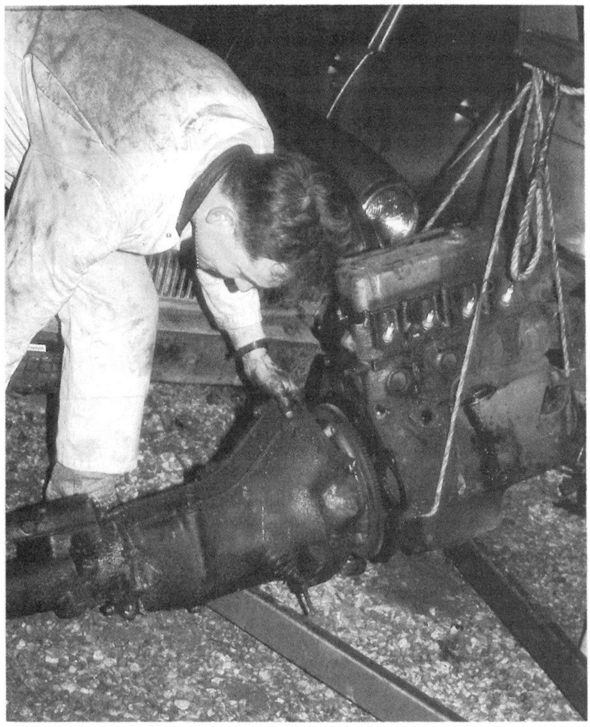

Separating the engine and gearbox straight away makes them easier to manhandle. The 'B' series engine is a very heavy unit to move around, the engine plus the gearbox is even heavier and far more awkward!

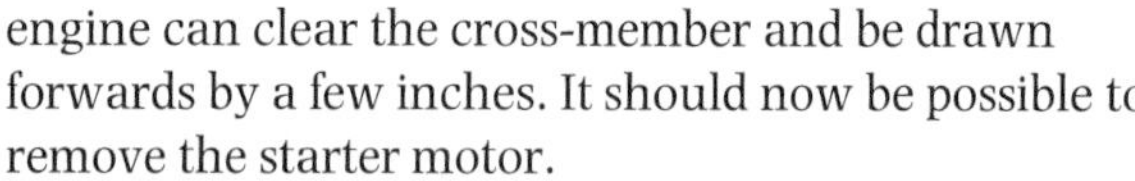

engine can clear the cross-member and be drawn forwards by a few inches. It should now be possible to remove the starter motor.

It is imperative that, as the motor is drawn away from the gearbox, no weight is allowed to hang on the input shaft, because this can result in clutch damage. This is why the jack is under the gearbox, so that its attitude can be altered to match that of the engine. When the engine is clear of the input shaft, it may be tilted and withdrawn from the engine compartment.

Engine/gearbox/overdrive removal

Proceed as before in respect of removal and disconnection of components related to the engine. Disconnect the exhaust steady clamp. On early cars, undo the four screws holding the gear lever surround to the transmission tunnel, lift the boot and remove the gear lever either by undoing bolts or by removing a circlip (whichever is applicable). On later cars, which have the overdrive selector switch fitted to the top of the gear lever, the centre console should be removed, the gear lever boot again lifted and the wires disconnected before removal of the gear lever.

Disconnect the four nuts and bolts connecting the propeller shaft at the gearbox end and 'telescope' it back out of the way. Place a jack underneath the gearbox and undo the four bolts that hold the movable cross-member. Gently lower the gearbox/overdrive assembly a little onto the fixed cross-member and disconnect the reversing light and overdrive switches.

Remove the set screws that hold the clutch slave cylinder in place, and set this to one side. Disconnect the speedometer drive cable. If fitted, disconnect the engine restraint rod from the gearbox, and remove the cross-member.

Begin to lift the engine and pull the engine and gearbox forwards over the front cross-member, angling the gearbox downwards as it clears the central cross-member. The whole assembly may now be withdrawn through the engine compartment.

THE CYLINDER HEAD

The cylinder head of the 1800cc B series engine performs many functions. It contains or holds the valves and rocker assembly, the inlet and exhaust ports, the main coolant return to the radiator and the thermostat, the heater return valve, the spark plugs, the temperature gauge sender unit, and the inlet and exhaust manifolds and associated equipment. It also contains oil galleries.

With so much happening at this crossroads of carburation, exhaust, coolant and lubrication, it is little wonder that the cylinder head is the part of the engine that most frequently requires attention. The DIY-inclined owner who wishes to carry out the maintenance and repair tasks associated with the head will need to be equipped with an accurate torque wrench, a valve lapper and grinding paste, and a valve spring compressor.

Cylinder head (and associated component) problems are often mere symptoms of faults concerned with badly-set or worn carburation or ignition components, which allow the engine to run too hot or too richly for a period of time.

The most common fault, the correction of which entails the removal of the cylinder head, is a blowing head gasket. Between the block and the cylinder head run a number of connecting water and oil galleries. The gasket helps to seal each of these and also the cylinders themselves. Damage to the gasket allows either water or oil into the cylinders when the engine is at rest (steam or blue smoke respectively will dominate the exhaust gases when the engine is restarted), or it can allow water and oil to mix, which is even more unpleasant for the engine and which should be rectified immediately. A damaged head gasket can also allow combustion fumes under very high pressure to escape into the oil galleries or the coolant galleries, or into other cylinders. None of these conditions is desirable.

Sometimes the cylinder block or the head can crack, giving the same results as a blown head gasket, albeit at far greater expense!

Many faults can occur to components associated with or covered by the cylinder head, the rectification of which entails the removal of the head. Exhaust valves and seats can burn allowing the loss of compression, valve guides can wear and allow oil to enter the cylinders (blue exhaust smoke on starting – also caused by worn piston rings and bore damage). The head can warp (same results as a blown gasket).

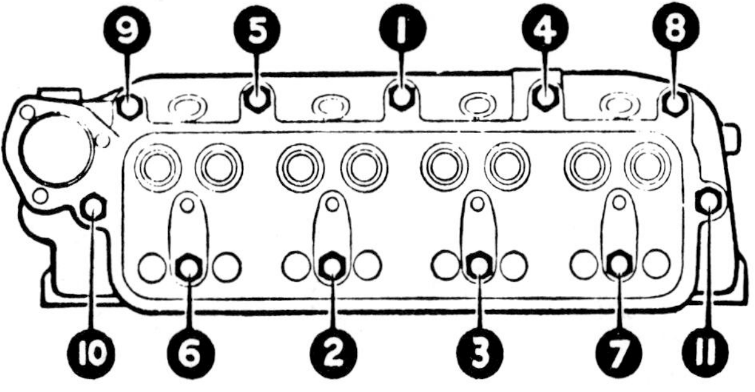

Cylinder head nut slackening and tightening sequence

Following the correct cylinder head nut removal sequence prevents the head from distorting as the immense pressure on it is released. (courtesy Autodata)

Even stripped spark plug hole threads require the removal of the head.

Removing the cylinder head

Time: 30 minutes.

Special tools/equipment: torque wrench.

You will need first to obtain a new gasket set, because the old gaskets should not be refitted once removed, even if they appear to be in good order.

First, disconnect the batteries. Drain the cooling system (See: Engine removal). Disconnect the top hose and the temperature gauge sender. If the earlier non-electric sender unit will not budge then remove the thermostat housing and thermostat, then douse the body of the sender and the external threaded joint with freeing agent and retry later.

Remove the air filters, the overflow pipe, fuel pipe hoses, return springs and vacuum pipe from the carburettors, then unbolt the two carburettors and their linkages as a unit. The carburettors can be placed on the nearside wing if it is well-cushioned, otherwise, disconnect all pipes and cables and remove the two as a unit from the engine bay. Take care not to allow dirt near the assembly or to invert the units (this could disturb sediment in the float chambers which will foul the needle assembly).

Slacken the inlet and exhaust manifold nuts at this stage, but decide whether to leave the manifolds in position to assist breaking the bond between the block and cylinder head (which entails undoing the exhaust downpipe clamps, a dirty, sometimes tricky and eminently 'avoidable' job), or whether to remove the manifolds and lose the advantage of the leverage they offer.

The rocker box cover is held by two capped nuts and should be removed along with its oil seal. Check that all hoses and other fittings have been removed

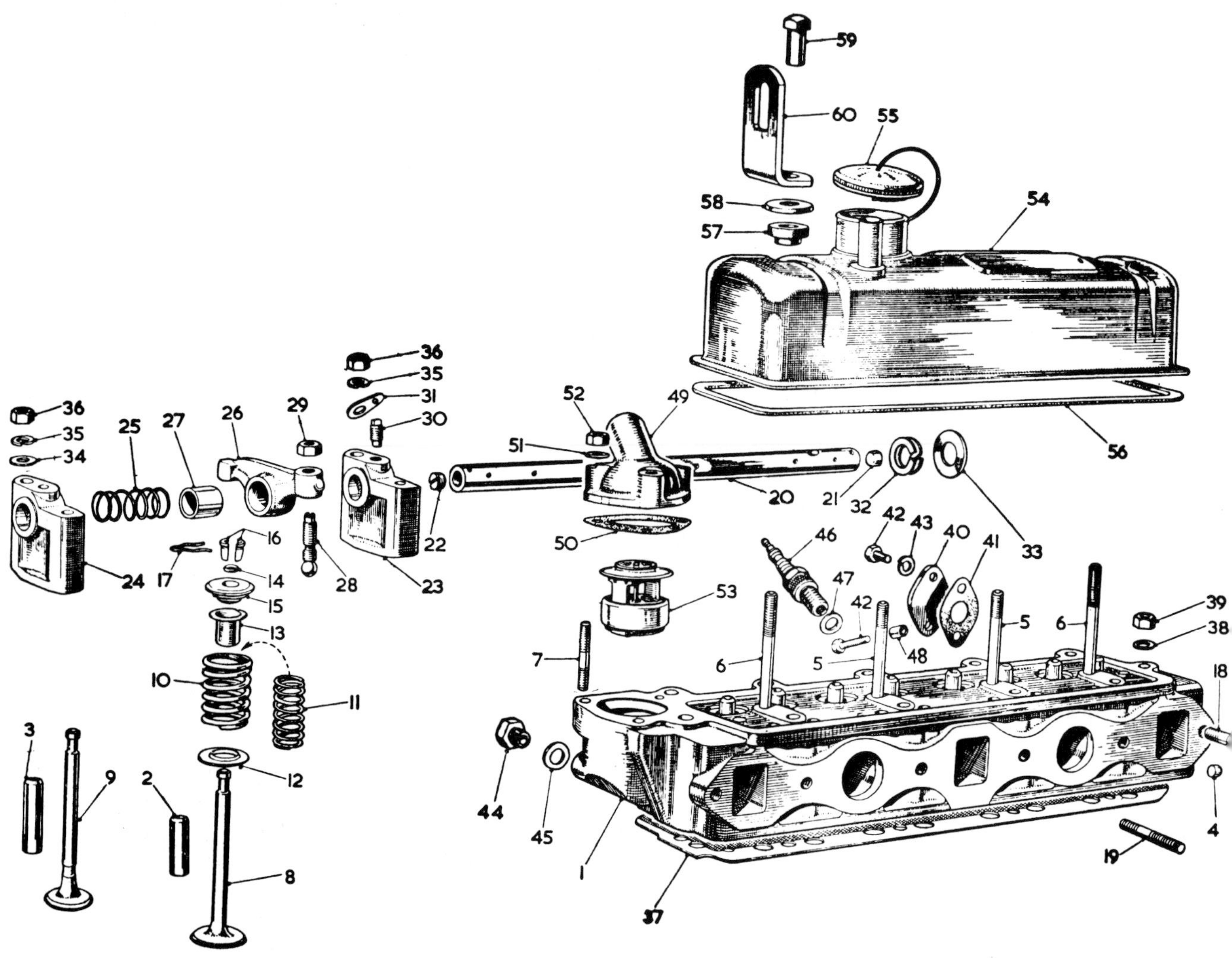

The cylinder head components

1. *Cylinder head*
2. *Inlet valve guide*
3. *Exhaust valve guide*
4. *Oil hole plug*
5. *Rocker bracket stud*
6. *Rocker bracket stud*
7. *Stud*
8. *Inlet valve*
9. *Exhaust valve*
10. *Outer valve spring*
11. *Inner valve spring*
12. *Spring collar*
13. *Valve guide shroud*
14. *Valve packing ring*
15. *Spring cup*
16. *Cotter*
17. *Cotter circlip*
18. *Stud*
19. *Stud*
20. *Rocker shaft*
21. *Rocker shaft plug*
22. *Rocker shaft plug*
23. *Rocker shaft bracket*
24. *Rocker shaft bracket*
25. *Rocker spacing spring*
26. *Rocker*
27. *Bush*
28. *Tappet adjusting screw*
29. *Nut*
30. *Screw*
31. *Lock plate*
32. *Washer*
33. *Washer*
34. *Washer*
35. *Spring washer*
36. *Nut*
37. *Joint washer*
38. *Washer*
39. *Nut*
40. *Blanking plate*
41. *Joint washer*
42. *Screw*
43. *Spring washer*
44. *Thermal transmitter boss plug*
45. *Washer*
46. *Sparking plug*
47. *Gasket*
48. *Distance piece*
49. *Water outlet*
50. *Joint washer*
51. *Washer*
52. *Nut*
53. *Thermostat*
54. *Rocker cover*
55. *Oil filler cap*
56. *Joint washer*
57. *Rubber bush*
58. *Cup washer*
59. *Nut*
60. *Engine sling bracket*

It is possible to disconnect the throttle and choke cables, then remove the carburettors and their linkages as a single unit. Take care not to invert either carburettor, as sediment in the fuel bowl can be disturbed and foul the main jet. Whilst the cylinder head is being attended to, it makes sense to strip the carburettors for cleaning and, if necessary, replacement of jets and needles.

To clean the outside of the carburettors, the author uses neat petrol and an old toothbrush. To obtain the petrol, the author reconnected the battery, held a glass jar under the end of the fuel delivery pipe, and asked an assistant to turn on the ignition for two seconds. If you do this, do not forget to disconnect the battery afterwards.

Remove the insulation blocks and the heat shield.

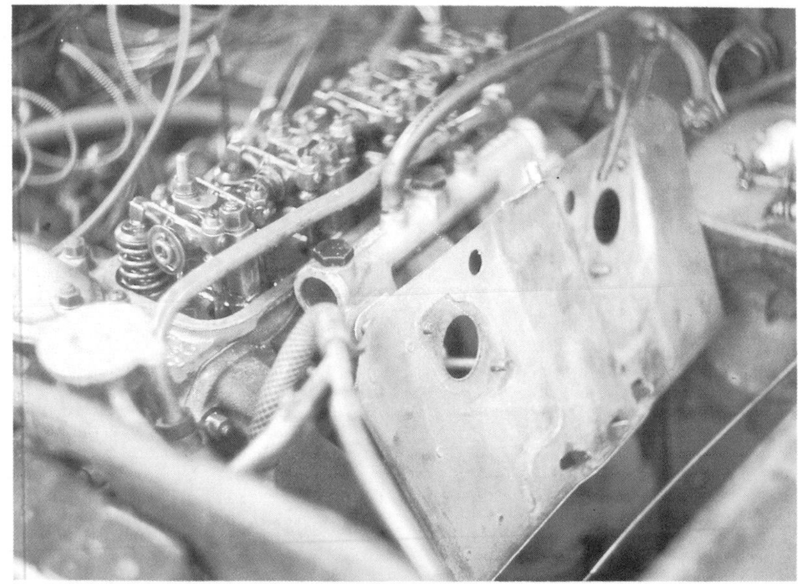

RIGHT AND BELOW LEFT *Remove the overdrive vacuum pipe and any other fitments from the inlet manifold, then undo the manifold nuts and lift away the inlet manifold. Then pull the exhaust manifold back from the head* (BELOW LEFT).

Do not place any kind of lever between the cylinder head and the block in order to free the head. If it is reluctant to move, tap it with a rawhide or other soft-faced mallet until it comes free.

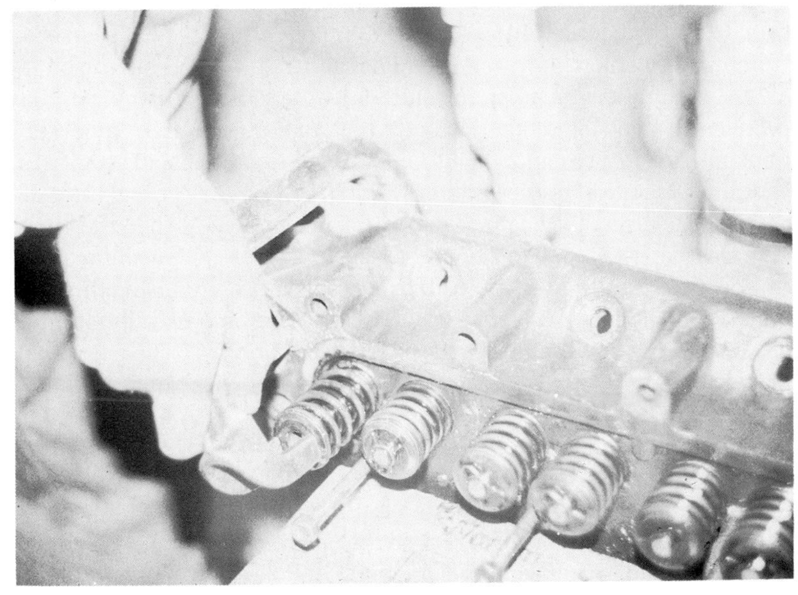

Before removing the valves, it pays to give each spring cup a light tap to free it from the collets. Remove the collet spring (where fitted), compress the spring as shown, then remove the collets and then take the pressure from the valve spring. The valve may now be removed. Some people place the valves in a numbered rack to show where each one lives, the alternative is to punch one, two, three or four small marks into each valve using a centre punch.

from the head. The number and type of these will vary according to the year and variant in question.

The eleven cylinder head nuts should now be removed in the order shown in the illustration. Move each nut a fraction of a turn in sequence, then by half-turns until all are able to be turned by the fingers alone. This is necessary to prevent distortion of the head; the same sequence must be followed when retightening the cylinder head.

The cylinder head can be reluctant to move. Usually, this is because it sticks on the threaded studs from the block. If gentle leverage of the manifolds, or then more vigorous rocking of the head, and finally, leverage under the ends of the head fail to move it, then tapping the head with a soft-faced hammer often breaks the seal. Do not place a large screwdriver or other lever into the join between the head and block, because this will lead to damage to the mating surfaces.

If the car is fitted with exhaust emission control equipment the same steps are followed, but there will be a number of extra hoses and pipes to be removed before the head may be lifted clear.

Cylinder head repairs

Tools: valve spring compressor; scrapers; valve grinding tool and paste.

An engine which has been running too rich, or has covered a high mileage, will be carboned up, that is, there will be a covering of carbon and other by-products of combustion on the piston crowns, the cylinder head and the valves. When the engine is running, the carbon glows red hot, and if it there is excessive quantities it can preheat fuel as it enters the cylinders, leading to pre-ignition and to detonation (pinking). It can also cause the fuel mixture to continue to ignite after the ignition switch has been turned off, causing the engine to run on. The removal of this carbon is referred to as a decoke.

To decoke an engine, you will require one large and one small scraper. Do not use old screwdrivers or chisels because these can score the piston heads and cylinder head. You will also require a valve spring compressor. Begin by stripping the cylinder head. Loosen the remaining four rocker bracket nuts, and remove the rocker assembly.

Using a valve spring compressor, remove all valves and place each one in a rack so that each component can be put back in its original location. The usual holder is simply a length of wood with holes drilled into it to hold the valve stems, with numbers written against each. To remove a valve, first compress the spring(s), then remove the two collets on each stem and slowly release the spring pressure. On early cars the collets were also fitted with spring clips, which should be removed before the valve springs are compressed.

Check the cylinder head mating surface with a straight edge for warping, or better still use a piece of plate glass and engineers' blue. If necessary, the head can be skimmed by a professional workshop to restore it to absolute flatness.

Clean all carbon from the head and closely examine it for cracks; if any are discovered then they should be repaired professionally. Some cracks might not be apparent until the valve seats are recut.

Examine the valves and their seats for pitting or burning. Test each valve in its guide for slackness or tightness, and renew the guides if necessary. If the valve seats are very badly pitted then inserts will have to be fitted; such work is best entrusted to professionals with proper facilities. Mild pitting can usually be dealt with by grinding in using paste or by having the seats recut. Although DIY equipment for recutting valve seats is available, the likely frequency of its use coupled with the need to obtain perfect results if the engine is to perform well afterwards, point towards having this job carried out professionally.

Check that each valve stem moves freely within its guide at all points of valve travel. A valve which sticks at a particular point in its travel may have a bent stem or the problem could be due to metal build-up on the stem. Renew the valve if necessary, along with the valve guides. It is possible to drift each new guide in to the correct depth, although it is more satisfactory to have them pressed into position.

If the valves and seats are not too badly marked then they may be ground back in. Using first a medium and then a fine paste, grind each valve/seat using the traditional dowel-and-sucker hand tool or a drill-mounted tool, frequently stopping to turn the valve until both the valve and the seat show an unbroken matt ring. If the valve and seat are cleaned of paste and the valve is lifted an inch or two from its seat and then allowed to drop on to the seat, it should bounce. If it does not then this indicates that the area of contact is not even.

If, on examination, the cylinder head appears to possess faults such as cracking or warping, then the

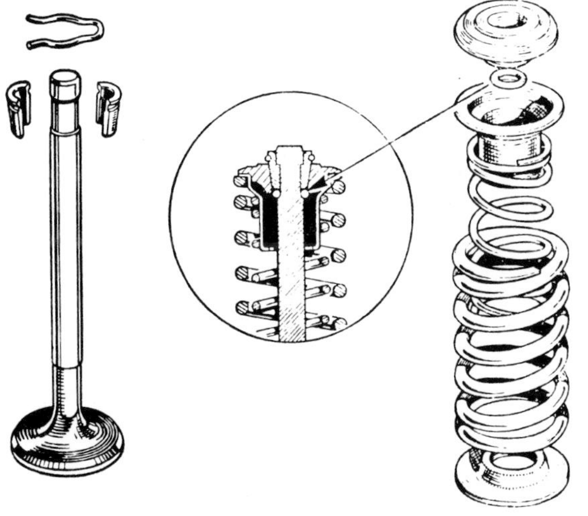

The valve assembly

When reassembling the valves and springs, do not forget to fit new oil seals. (courtesy Autodata)

best solution could be to exchange it for a reconditioned one. This gives the option of exchanging the head (at extra cost) for one which is compatible with unleaded petrol, or perhaps one which is modified to enhance performance.

Refitting the cylinder head

Make sure that the block and head mating surfaces are spotlessly clean. Use the correct scraping device rather than a chisel or screwdriver blade: the correct scraper is fashioned so that it will not score the surface, whereas it will easily be scored with makeshift tools. The piston crowns should be cleaned. Turn the engine over by hand until two pistons are at the tops of their travel, then stuff clean rags into the other two, in order to prevent carbon from falling into them (as it can lodge on the top piston ring and score the bore). Also, mask off all water and oilways for the same reason.

Lightly wipe a little engine oil around the bores of all cylinders and double check that none are scored.

Place the new head gasket onto the block. It should be marked 'Top'and 'Front' but even so, make sure that none of the oil or coolant galleries will be blocked when the gasket is fitted, just to ensure that you have the correct gasket and are fitting it right way up and right way round. Do not use any kind of sealant.

Lower the cylinder head into position. If tightness against the studs is encountered then they may be cleaned lightly. Replace the pushrods into the correct holes so that each locates correctly with its tappet.

Replace the rocker assembly, ensuring that the ball end of each screw adjuster locates correctly in the pushrod top.

Fit the eleven cylinder head and four extra rocker assembly nuts to finger tightness, then turn each of the cylinder head nuts half a turn in the correct sequence until they can be finally set at the correct torque using a torque wrench. Reset the valve clearances; this is described below.

Reconnect all hoses, cables, manifolds and associated gear and coolant/heater connections by reversing the stripping sequence, fitting new gaskets where appropriate. Fill the engine with the correct quantities of essential fluids. Run the engine until it reaches normal operating temperature, watching for signs of leaks from around the head gasket. Retorque all cylinder head nuts in sequence. It is as well to retorque the head after a hundred miles of use.

Setting valve clearances (see Chapter 4 for full details and photographs)

Tools: ring spanner; screwdriver; feeler gauge; proprietary valve adjusting tool optional.

With the battery disconnected and the cylinder head reassembled onto the block, remove the sparking plugs so that the engine can be turned over either by hand (via the fan belt) or by pushing the car with 4th gear engaged.

The valves should be checked in the following sequence (which saves the engine having to be laboriously turned over too much).

Valve fully open	Test/adjust valve no.
8	1
6	3
4	5
7	2
1	8
3	6
5	4
2	7

Note that the sum of the valve numbers is always nine.

Holding the ball-end adjusting screw with a screwdriver, slacken the locking nut using a 1/2in ring spanner. Insert the correct feeler gauge(s) and adjust the screw until the gauge is very lightly gripped but may still be moved. Holding the adjusting screw still, tighten the locking nut. Recheck.

Make doubly sure that you have the correct replacement head gasket and that you are fitting it the right way around by checking that its holes align correctly with the water and oilways in the block and cylinder head.

Do not over-tighten the manifold stud nuts, because they break quite easily, as the author has found to his cost in the past. Note in this photograph that the fuel line end has been blanked off with a nut of suitable size.

If the adjuster screw slots are badly distorted, then it pays to renew them, because this will allow more accurate resetting. The rocker gear has to be removed, which entails slackening each cylinder head nut in the correct sequence and then removing the four which hold the rocker posts and the four nuts on the head studs. Some adjusters have oilways which direct oil to the pushrod end and, if your car is fitted with these, then you may not be able to obtain the correct replacements. The author found himself in this position, and fitted plain adjusters without oilways. After the engine had covered a few miles, the rocker box cover was removed and the author was pleased to see that plenty of oil had splashed into the push rod tops, giving ample lubrication.

When the cylinder head has been replaced and the ancillaries reconnected, the engine might not run very evenly. As the ignition has not been disturbed, check the carburation. First check that the fuel bowl overflow pipe(s) are not blocked. If the engine requires copious amounts of choke to run, suspect an induction air leak. Check that the various connections to the inlet manifold and carburettors (overdrive and distributor vacuum switches, breather pipe, etc) are all in position.

There is always a danger that removing or refitting the carburettors disturbs sediment in the fuel bowl, allowing some to foul the main jet. Dismantle the carburettors and wash then blow out the system.

ENGINE STRIP

Time: 1 day +

Special tools/equipment: see text.

As with the gearbox, overdrive unit and cylinder head, the engine may be overhauled at home. Likewise, it is very likely that certain tasks will be necessary which can only be carried out by a skilled engineer. This not only costs money but also causes time delays while the work is undertaken and involves transportation of the units to and from the engineering premises.

Furthermore, in order properly to assess the condition of various engine components, you should possess and be familiar with the operation of both internal and external micrometers in order to check for wear and ovality.

The expense of commissioning each engineering task individually can be relatively high, because in each case the machinery will have to be specially set up for the engine in question. The difference in cost between this (plus the costs of replacement components) and merely buying an exchange reconditioned unit can be so little that the latter is in many cases the better option. In fact, looking through an MGB specialists' catalogue, the prices for the reconditioned and replacement components likely to be needed for a home rebuild come to more than the price for an exchange assembled half engine. Professional engine restorers will work on what amounts to a production line, and they will restore engines in batches and hence keep labour costs down.

The trade have a commonsense attitude to the subject of exchange units. Graham Sawyer of Bromsgrove MG Centre is quite happy to provide materials and components to those who wish to carry out their own engine rebuild, but points out that, in the case of an engine exchange, if the block or cylinder head of a customer's own engine turn out to be cracked then it is the business which stands the loss rather than the customer. If you choose to recondition your own engine then such a discovery would prove expensive.

One point to bear in mind when collecting a reconditioned engine for a late chrome bumper or early rubber bumper car is that the 18V engine was fitted in both, but with a different front plate. The engine mounting brackets are attached to the front plate, and if you obtain the wrong one then you will not be able to fit the engine without first obtaining and fitting the correct plate. It is better to check first with your supplier that you have the correct plate fitted.

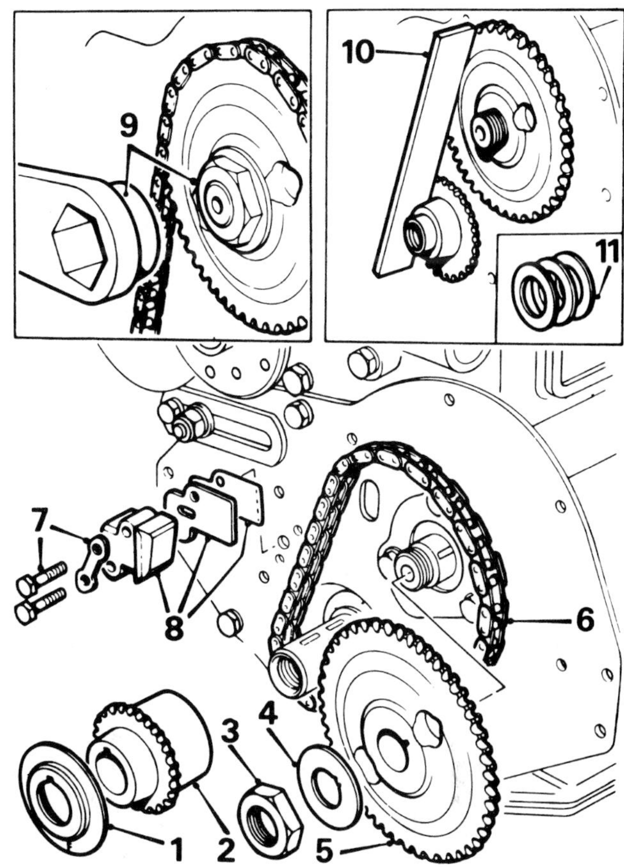

1. *Oil thrower*
2. *Crankshaft gear*
3. *Camshaft nut*
4. *Lock washer*
5. *Camshaft gear*
6. *Timing chain*
7. *Screws and lock washer*
8. *Chain tensioner assembly and gasket*
9. *Camshaft nut and tool 18G 98A*
10. *Check wheel alignment with a straight-edge*
11. *Packing washers*

The timing chain and gears

Take care not to mislay the crankshaft packing washers and, when reassembling, check for alignment using a straight edge. (courtesy Autodata)

The following describes the engine strip in sequence; if a specific area has to be attended to in isolation, refer to a workshop manual for a description of the precise stripping order for that specific task.

Preliminaries

To strip the engine, first remove the cylinder head as previously described and place the pushrods in a numbered rack. Remove the breather pipe and tappet covers, then lift out the tappets and place them in a numbered rack for identification purposes.

Remove the dynamo or alternator, fan belt, fan and pulley. Remove the distributor, the single screw which retains its housing, then the housing. Either screw a 5/16in UNF bolt down into the drive and pull it out whilst turning it to free the gears, or wait until the sump has been removed then push it out from the inside.

Timing chain, and gears

Fold back the tab on the crankshaft pulley retaining bolt, unscrew the bolt and withdraw the pulley. Unscrew the timing cover retaining bolts and remove the cover and gasket. The gasket should be renewed. Remove the bottom plug from the chain tensioner and, using a 1/8in Allen key, wind the tensioner back to the fully retracted position (double roller chain type). Remove the two securing screws then remove the tensioner and backing plate. A different type of tensioner is used on later engines. To remove this, first unlock and remove its securing nuts then gently prise it from the backplate, ensuring that the slipper head, which is under tension, is not lost.

Align the timing marks on the crankshaft and camshaft wheels, then bend back the lock washer tab on the camshaft wheel nut and remove the nut. The crankshaft and camshaft wheels may now be removed complete with the timing chain, although if either is reluctant to move then a special tool will prove necessary.

The crankshaft gear wheel has packing washers which must be refitted in the same order unless either the crankshaft or camshaft are replaced. In this case, refit both wheels without packing washers and use a straight edge across the camshaft gear teeth and measure the gap between the straight edge and the crankshaft gear teeth. Subtract 0.005in from this to

ABOVE *The engine front plate had to be changed on this 18V engine, because the same engine unit was used in both rubber and chrome bumper cars, but the plate and engine mountings were different. Do make sure when obtaining an exchange reconditioned engine that you have the correct front plate fitted.*

RIGHT *The crankshaft and camshaft keyways properly aligned prior to the fitting of the gears.*

find the thickness of packing washers required.

To refit, set the crankshaft keyway at the twelve o'clock position and the camshaft keyway at the one o'clock position. Assemble the gears into the chain with the timing dimples opposite each other. Fit first the crankshaft gear, turn the camshaft slightly to align its keyway then push both gears onto their shafts and refit the lock washer and nut onto the camshaft end.

Oil strainer and pump

Remove the bolts then remove the sump from the crankcase. The strainer is held by two bolts. After removal it can be cleaned using paraffin and a stiff brush. Early types can be dismantled for cleaning.

The oil pump cover is secured by two bolts and the pump by three threaded studs. Undo the three nuts then remove the pump, driveshaft and gasket. When replacing the pump, use a new gasket. If oil pressure has been low then replace the pump, lubricating it first with engine oil.

Big end bearings

Bend back the locking tabs (using a cold chisel) on the connecting rod (conrod) bearing cap bolts, then undo the bolts. Remove the caps and lower bearings, then push the conrod upwards so that the upper bearing can be removed. If the pistons/conrods are to be removed from the engine for a rebore, assemble each so that the components are not inadvertently mixed later.

When refitting, lubricate each bearing and journal thoroughly and torque the bearing cap bolts to 35-40 ft lb.

During this operation, check the condition of the crankshaft journals and, if worn, fit a replacement crankshaft which will be supplied with big end and main bearings.

Crankshaft

In order to remove the crankshaft it is necessary first to remove the flywheel. Remove the clutch assembly (see page 126), then remove the flywheel securing nuts. Remove the big end bearings as previously described above.

Remove the main bearing caps then lift the crankshaft from its bearings. When replacing, lubricate the new bearings with engine oil and torque the main bearing caps to 70 ft lb.

Pistons and Connecting rods

Following removal of the big end bearing caps, the piston/conrod assemblies may be withdrawn from the bores. The gudgeon pins will be retained with circlips (18GB engines), with press-fit gudgeon pins (which should be removed using a special tool held by Rover Agents) , or by a clamp bolt through the split little end (18G/GA engines).

The piston rings can be removed using a special tool or by lifting one end of the ring and inserting behind it a thin strip of metal (a 0.02in feeler gauge is ideal) then gently working the ring up onto the land above the groove. Clean out the grooves. Test the new rings in the cylinder bore by fitting each in turn and measuring the gap (ensuring that the ring is level within the bore) with a feeler gauge. It should be 0.008-0.013in. When refitting the rings, place their gaps at 90 degrees to each other and note that tapered rings must be fitted the correct way up, to which end they are marked with a 'T' (top). A piston ring compressor will be necessary for refitting the pistons, and the bores should first be lubricated with engine oil.

Camshaft

If a mechanical tachometer is fitted, remove the securing nuts and washers then withdraw the drive gear. The camshaft locating plate is secured to the cylinder block by three set screws and washers. After removal of these, the camshaft may be withdrawn. Examine the cam lobes for wear and renew if necessary. Assemble the retaining plate and chain wheel onto the camshaft and use feeler gauges to measure the gap (endfloat) between the camshaft journal and the retaining plate. If this is excessive (more than 0.007in), renew the retaining plate.

MGC

The advice given to obtain a reconditioned unit rather than attempting to strip and recondition an

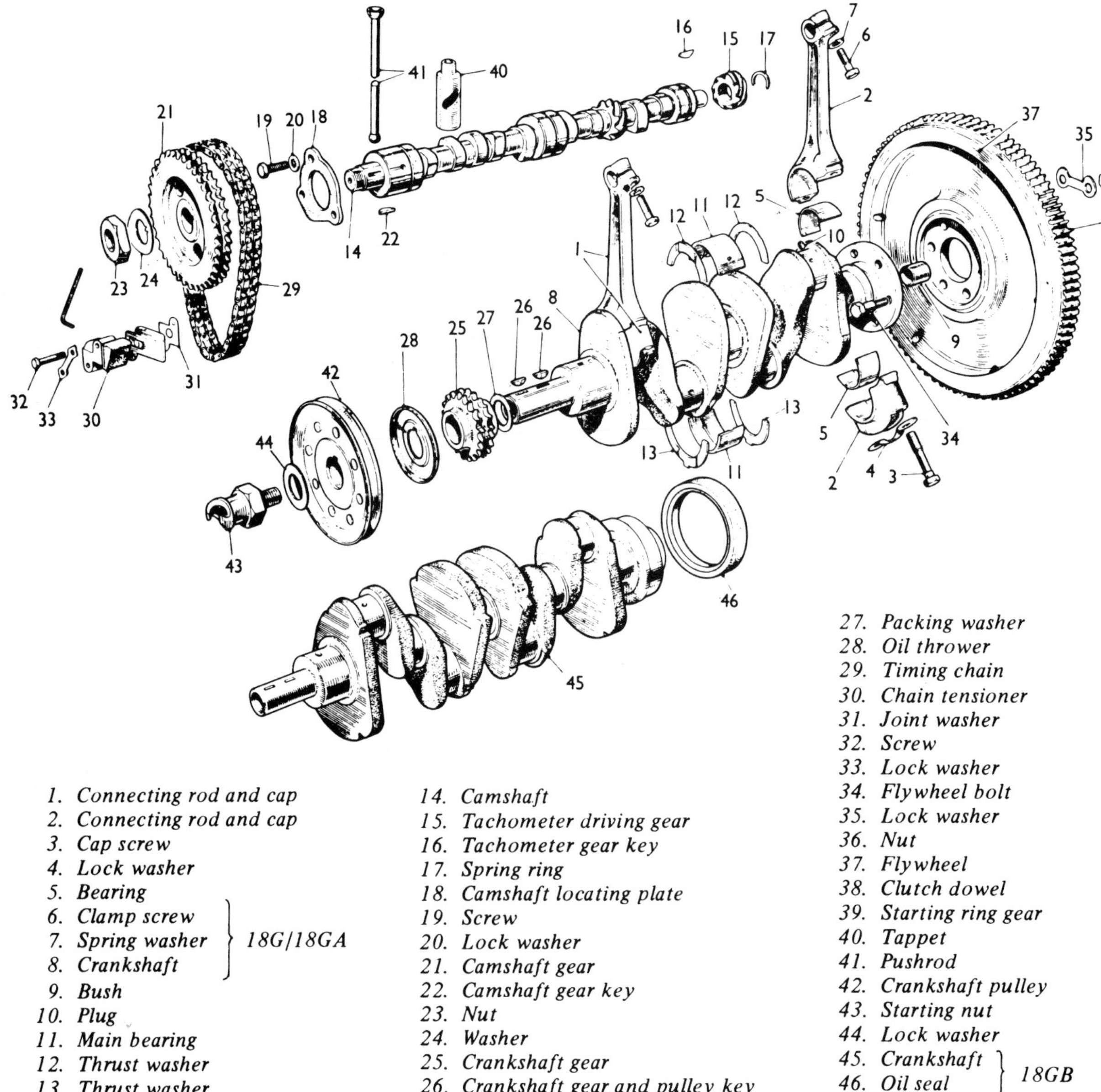

1. *Connecting rod and cap*
2. *Connecting rod and cap*
3. *Cap screw*
4. *Lock washer*
5. *Bearing*
6. *Clamp screw* } *18G/18GA*
7. *Spring washer* } *18G/18GA*
8. *Crankshaft* } *18G/18GA*
9. *Bush*
10. *Plug*
11. *Main bearing*
12. *Thrust washer*
13. *Thrust washer*
14. *Camshaft*
15. *Tachometer driving gear*
16. *Tachometer gear key*
17. *Spring ring*
18. *Camshaft locating plate*
19. *Screw*
20. *Lock washer*
21. *Camshaft gear*
22. *Camshaft gear key*
23. *Nut*
24. *Washer*
25. *Crankshaft gear*
26. *Crankshaft gear and pulley key*
27. *Packing washer*
28. *Oil thrower*
29. *Timing chain*
30. *Chain tensioner*
31. *Joint washer*
32. *Screw*
33. *Lock washer*
34. *Flywheel bolt*
35. *Lock washer*
36. *Nut*
37. *Flywheel*
38. *Clutch dowel*
39. *Starting ring gear*
40. *Tappet*
41. *Pushrod*
42. *Crankshaft pulley*
43. *Starting nut*
44. *Lock washer*
45. *Crankshaft* } *18GB*
46. *Oil seal* } *18GB*

The engine internal components

engine at home applies doubly in the case of the MGC. The individual components likely to be needed in a rebuild will be very expensive, and it may prove far more economical to opt for an exchange unit. The machining operations on the MGC will also prove costly if commissioned individually.

THE FUEL SYSTEM

Petrol is stored in a tank situated under the boot floor. The fuel is fed along metal pipes under the car to the carburettor(s) by an in-line electric fuel pump. Later cars have a filter in line to clean the fuel before it reaches the carburettors.

The carburettors allow a mixture of fine droplets of petrol and air to be drawn through the inlet manifold into the cylinders, where it is burnt to produce the energy to drive the engine.

Petrol tank

Three types of petrol tank were fitted to the MGB. Very early Roadsters had a tank which was fastened by two metal straps; these appear to be unavailable today, although you might be lucky and stumble across a piece of old stock somewhere. MGB GTs and roadsters from 1966 to 1977 were fitted with lipped tanks which were held by bolts which passed down through the boot tray. Roadsters and GTs from 1977 had a similar tank, but with one less hole, since the petrol gauge sender unit and the fuel outlet were combined.

There are two fairly common reasons for giving attention to the fuel tank. The more frequently arising of these is when someone accidentally fills up the tank with diesel (it happens!) or dirt- or water-contaminated fuel, in which case the entire fuel system will require flushing out. The tank should be removed so that a thorough job can be done. The other occasion is when a petrol leak is discovered, more often than not due to corrosion.

Petrol leaks give themselves away first by aroma but also if a dark patch is discovered on the side or bottom of the tank. Some leaks will be traceable to one of the inlet/outlet/sender joins, although most leaks are due to corrosion of the flat top of the tank on which water can collect. Owners of early Roadsters, for which original pattern tanks are unavailable, have the option of trying to effect a repair to the existing tank or (the recommended solution) fitting one of the later examples.

Petrol tank repair is not really a job for the amateur. GRP repair kits are available but can no more be expected to give a lasting repair than can GRP used on thin and rotted bodywork. Furthermore, a tank which is rotting and covered partially with GRP will start to wash tiny flakes of rust into the petrol, clogging the fuel pump filter. Small pin holes can, in theory, be treated using a type of sealant which is placed in the tank and splashed around, but non-rusted pin holes do not occur any too frequently; rust holes predominate.

A professional can repair a petrol tank, but the safety procedures for dealing with an empty petrol tank and the explosive consequences of ignoring them are so terrible that it is best not even to think about attempting the job yourself.

Converting an early Roadster to take the later bolt-on tank is not too difficult a job, consisting of accurately drilling the holes in the boot tray through which the bolts can pass. To remove the earlier tank, first disconnect the batteries, then chock the front wheels and raise the rear of the car and support it on axle stands placed as far each side of the tank as possible to give the easiest access.

A jumper lead is ideal for earthing two metal petrol containers to prevent static electric sparking between the two, prior to siphoning fuel. The dangers of explosion or fire is very real when siphoning fuel; do take the proper safety precautions, including making sure that no naked flames or other heat sources are present.

Place a receptacle under the fuel drain plug, remove the plug and then remove the filler cap in order to drain the tank. If the tank has no drain plug, then it will have to be siphoned. Always run an earth wire between the tank and the container into which petrol is being syphoned if the latter is made of metal,

LEFT *Rot in the top of the petrol tank is often localised but severe. Most of the surface can be perfectly clean and sound, yet a small area of rust can conceal many pinholes. This will allow minimal, but progressively worsening leakage, and will slowly release tiny rust flakes into the fuel, which will in time foul the fuel pump filter. This tank, removed from the author's own car, shows typical rust damage. Although 90 per cent sound, pin holes in the top face are apparent from the damp areas where petrol has leaked. This damage was not apparent until the tank was removed from the car, so even if the bottom and sides of your tank appear to be perfectly sound, it could be leaking fuel and contaminating your petrol with rust particles.*

BELOW LEFT *Before fitting the replacement fuel tank, take the opportunity to mask off the sender and filler pipe holes and give the top as much paint protection as possible, to help prevent future corrosion. Compare the new tank with the old to gauge the positions for fitting the rubber strips.*

ABOVE RIGHT *Removing the sender unit. Order a new gasket for this and possibly a new locking ring when you order the replacement tank. Also, check the condition of the tank-to-pump fuel line and replace it if is corroding. The one on the author's 1966 GT folded effortlessly in half when removed!*

RIGHT *The fuel pump points can corrode if the car is left standing for any length of time. This often happens following a restoration. When you try to start the engine again, listen for the familiar clicking noise of the pump to ascertain whether it is working. The points may be cleaned in situ, or the spring blade contacts may be removed for better access.*

to prevent static electricity from causing sparks to jump between the two. Never attempt to syphon petrol by sucking on the end of a tube; apart from the fact that petrol tastes unspeakable, the inhalation of petrol fumes at a high concentration, and, worse still, the ingestion of petrol into the lungs, is dangerous and can cause death. Use a syphon bulb of the sort available from many motor accessory traders. Take the petrol away and store it somewhere safe, although it is probably best to dispose of it, since it will invariably be dirty. Remove the sender wires and the rubber filler pipe from within the boot. Undo the fuel pipe union. The rear end of the tank should be supported while the two nuts which hold the strap fixings are undone. The tank can then be lowered.

Removal of the later types of tank is very much the same, except that the bolts holding the tank are removed from inside the boot of the car, and nuts are removed from threaded studs set into the boot floor from underneath. The safety procedures are identical and should be strictly followed.

An apparently empty petrol tank is more dangerous than one which is full of petrol, because it is petrol vapour which ignites so readily rather than liquid petrol. If the old tank is to be discarded then it is advisable to refit the drain plug immediately, place bungs in the sender and outlet holes and fill the tank with water to exclude petrol vapour. Ask your local garage to dispose of the tank for you. If the tank is to be cleaned and refitted then do this immediately by

flushing out with a little fuel two or three times, shaking and inverting the tank to clean out foreign matter. Clean the top of the tank thoroughly and examine closely for pin-holes. A tank which appears to be sound can be afflicted by localised rot. Refit and refill the tank at the earliest opportunity, in the interests of safety and to prevent rusting.

It is worth ordering the following items at the same time as your new petrol tank: cushioning strips, tank to boot floor seal, gauge unit cork gasket (models to 1977) or rubber seal (1977 on). Remove the sender unit by tapping off the threaded locking ring and salvage the captive nut clips from the old tank.

In order that the replacement tank should last longer than the previous one, you should use the rust preventative measures detailed in Chapter 3. The new tank will almost certainly already be painted but, at the very least, this should be keyed with emery paper or preferably taken right down and then treated with Finnegan's Number One Primer followed by a heavy-duty paint such as Hammerite from the same company. Before attacking the paintwork, be sure to plug all holes in the new tank to keep bits of old paint out!

The captive nut spring clips should be fitted to the replacement tank, along with the sender unit and its rubber or cork gasket. The cushioning strips are best glued into position. The petrol pipe union should also be connected before the tank is offered up into position and bolted into place. This entails either building an elaborate structure of wooden chocks to hold the tank while you bolt it up, or the help of an assistant. The latter is recommended.

Petrol pump

Two types of pump were fitted, both electric. The SU HP was used on earlier cars and the SU AUF 300 (or 305) on later cars. The pumps give little trouble. Occasionally, the filter can become blocked and restrict the flow of fuel into the unit and hence out to the carburettors. Sometimes, dirt will lodge under the non-return valve. Other faults can be tackled by simply exchanging the unit. The cost price is not too great, and if an old pump develops one fault then others will probably soon follow, questioning the desirability of having to remove the pump each time in order to carry out remedial action.

Cleaning the filter

First, disconnect the batteries. Disconnect the two wires attached to the pump, the inlet, outlet and vent pipes (having first placed a receptacle underneath to catch petrol), then the bolts which hold the pump bracket to the heelboard. On the SU HP fitted to earlier models, clean the outside of the unit then remove the base plug, its sealing washer and the filter. On the SU AUF 300 pump, remove the coil housing, the screws holding the clamp plate, the valve assembly and filter. The filter may be cleaned in paraffin.

If the car is off the road for a month or more

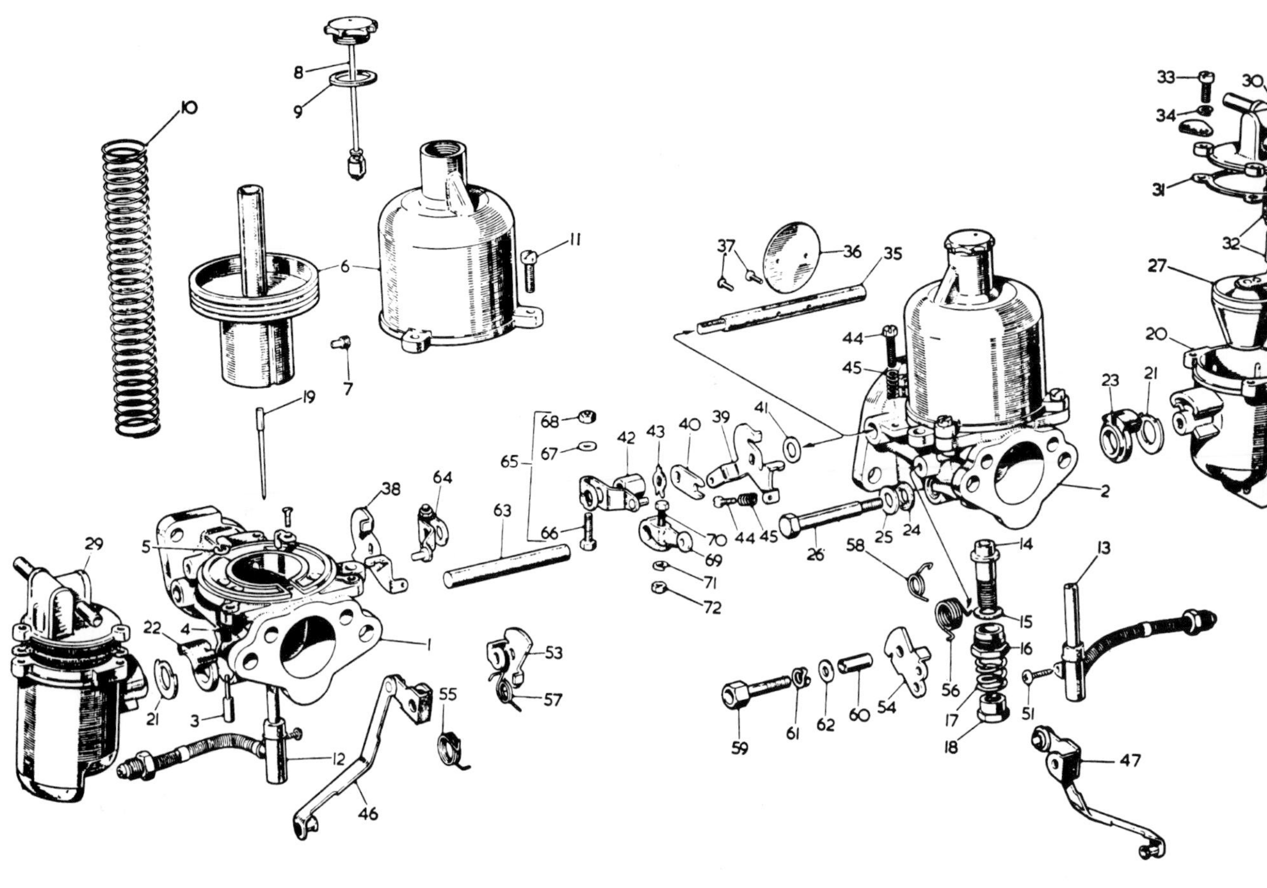

The carburettor components (SU HS4)

1. *Carburettor body*
2. *Carburettor body*
3. *Piston lifting pin*
4. *Spring*
5. *Circlip*
6. *Chamber and piston assembly*
7. *Needle locking screw*
8. *Cap and damper assembly*
9. *Fibre washer*
10. *Piston spring (red)*
11. *Screw*
12. *Jet assembly*
13. *Jet assembly*
14. *Jet bearing*
15. *Washer*
16. *Screw*
17. *Spring*
18. *Jet adjusting screw*
19. *Needle*
20. *Float chamber*
21. *Washer*
22. *Rubber grommet*
23. *Rubber grommet*
24. *Rubber washer*
25. *Washer*
26. *Bolt*
27. *Float assembly*
28. *Pin*
29. *Float chamber lid*
30. *Float chamber lid*
31. *Washer*
32. *Needle and seat assembly*
33. *Screw*
34. *Spring washer*
35. *Throttle spindle*
36. *Throttle disc*
37. *Screw*
38. *Throttle return lever*
39. *Throttle return lever*
40. *Lost motion lever*
41. *Spacing washer*
42. *Nut*
43. *Tab washer*
44. *Throttle stop screw*
45. *Spring*
46. *Pick up lever and link assembly*
47. *Pick up lever and link assembly*
51. *Screw*
53. *Cam lever*
54. *Cam lever*
55. *Pick up lever spring*
56. *Pick up lever spring*
57. *Cam lever spring*
58. *Cam lever spring*
59. *Bolt*
60. *Tube*
61. *Spring washer*
62. *Washer*
63. *Jet connecting rod*
64. *Lever and pin assembly*
65. *Lever and pin assembly*
66. *Bolt*
67. *Washer*
68. *Nut*
69. *Choke lever*
70. *Bolt*
71. *Spring washer*
72. *Nut*

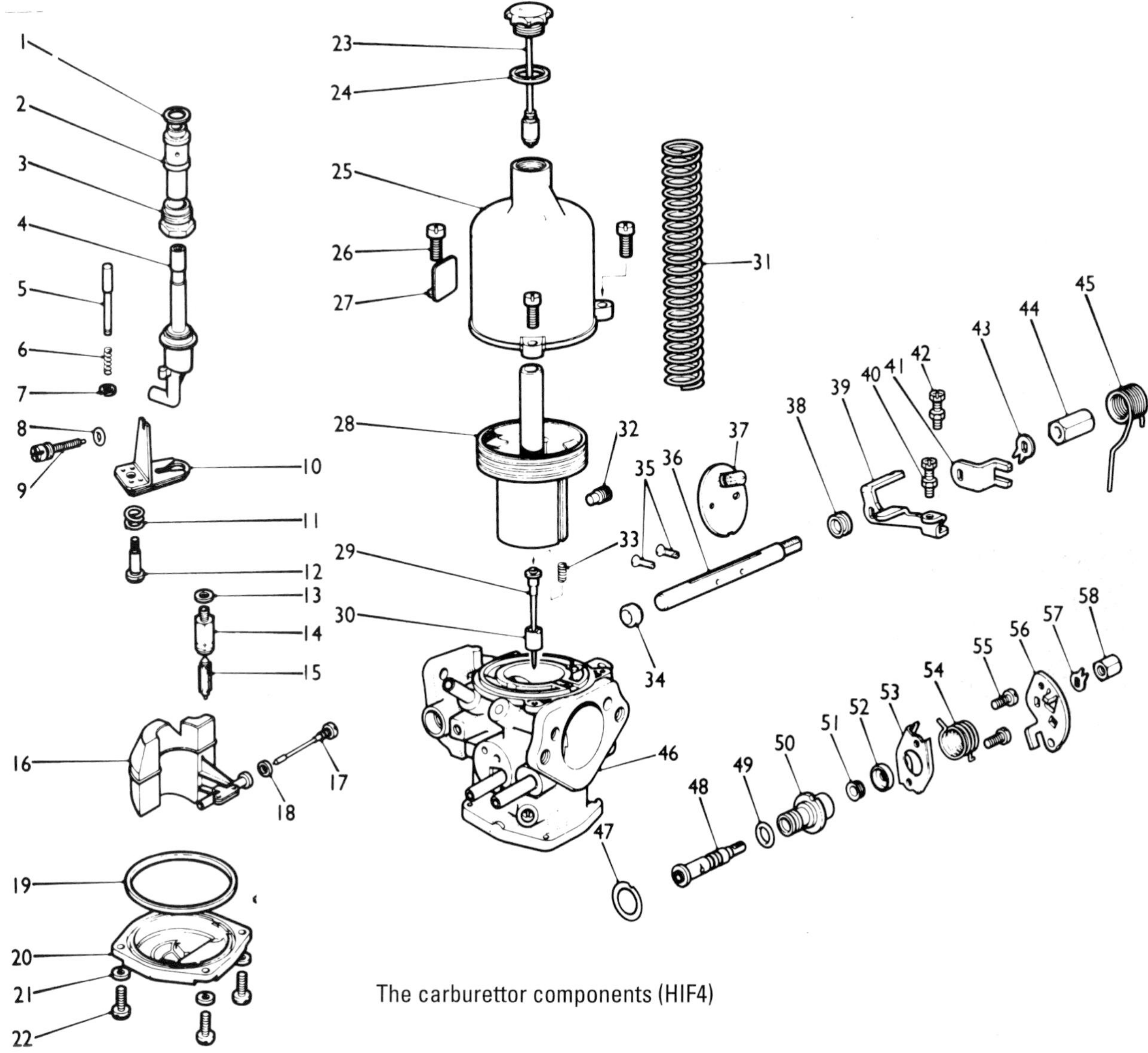

The carburettor components (HIF4)

1. *Jet bearing washer*
2. *Jet bearing*
3. *Jet bearing nut*
4. *Jet assembly*
5. *Lifting pin*
6. *Lifting pin spring*
7. *Circlip*
8. *Adjusting screw seal*
9. *Jet adjusting screw*
10. *Bi-metal jet lever*
11. *Jet spring*
12. *Jet retaining screw*
13. *Needle seat washer (if required)*
14. *Float needle seat*
15. *Float needle*
16. *Float*
17. *Float pivot*
18. *Pivot seal*
19. *Float-chamber cover seal*
20. *Float-chamber cover*
21. *Spring washer*
22. *Cover screw*
23. *Piston damper*
24. *Damper washer*
25. *Suction chamber*
26. *Chamber screw*
27. *Identity tag*
28. *Piston*
29. *Jet needle*
30. *Needle guide*
31. *Piston spring*
32. *Needle retaining screw*
33. *Needle spring*
34. *Throttle spindle seal*
35. *Throttle disc screws*
36. *Throttle spindle*
37. *Throttle disc*
38. *Throttle spindle seal*
39. *Throttle actuating lever*
40. *Fast idle screw and nut*
41. *Throttle lever*
42. *Throttle adjusting screw and nut*
43. *Tab washer*
44. *Retaining nut*
45. *Throttle spring*
46. *Body*
47. *Cold start seal*
48. *Cold start spindle*
49. *'O' ring*
50. *Cold start body*
51. *Spindle seal*
52. *End cover*
53. *Retaining plate*
54. *Cold start spring*
55. *Retaining screw*
56. *Fast idle cam*
57. *Tab washer*
58. *Retaining nut*

during rebuilding work, then the petrol pump contact points can become corroded. This will be apparent by the absence of pump noise (clicking) when the ignition is switched on.

To clean the points, first disconnect the battery(ies) and remove the battery (if fitted) from the offside compartment. The pump can be seen protruding into this compartment.

Remove the terminal nut, wire, and end cover nut, then pull the end cover away. The points may be cleaned in situ using light emery paper, although if corrosion is well established it will be better to remove them first.

Carburettors

Early cars are fitted with twin SU HS4 carburettors, later cars have the basically similar SU HIF4 carburettors, which differ mainly in having integral float chambers, a main jet held by a bi-metallic strip which automatically alters mixture richness according to temperature, a bypass passage, and a separate jet for cold starting. Both are very simple and trouble-free units. North American cars were fitted with a single Zenith 175 CD 5T carburettor. For certain markets, all three carburettor installations were fitted with exhaust emission control equipment. When such installations are tuned, the exhaust emission control equipment must be connected.

When you first buy a car, it is as well to check on the condition of the jets and needles and (in the case of the HS4 with the fixed needle in cars without emission control equipment) to ensure that the jets are centred before attempting to set the carburation. Refer to the accompanying illustration for the part numbers given to components.

First, remove the damper piston rod (8) from the bell housing, then undo the three screws holding the bell housing and remove both this and the spring (10). Carefully withdraw the piston, taking the greatest care not to damage the needle. Examine the needle for a ridge which indicates that it has not been centrally located in the jet (14). If a ridge can be seen then the needle should be renewed, along with the jet, which will also be damaged.

To remove the jet, first undo the petrol feed union (12) from the base of the float chamber. Undo the screw (51) holding the jet head to the link assembly, and withdraw the jet.

The needle is held in the piston by a screw; loosening this allows the old needle to be withdrawn and the new one refitted.

Remove the jet adjusting nut (18) and the spring situated on top of it and refit just the nut, screwing it up as far as possible. Slacken off the jet locking screw (16) until the jet bearing can be rotated. Refit the jet.

Gently push the piston back into the main body, ensuring that the needle properly enters the jet. Do not use force, but turn the jet bearing until the needle passes easily into the jet. Ensuring that the jet head is not at an angle, gently tighten the jet locking screw. Lift the piston and let it fall to the jet bridge, if it fails to land with a metallic click, undo the jet locking nut, readjust the bearing and try again.

When the jet is centred, reassemble the carburettor, taking care not to alter the position of the jet locking nut. Check that the piston still hits the bridge deck with a click before refitting the air filter covers.

Tuning

In the long term, arguably the cheapest method of dealing with carburation is to take the car along to an SU specialist who has a rolling road and exhaust gas analyzer, and ask him to check and set up the carburettors on your behalf. Having the carburation attended to professionally and with the best equipment, not only replacing worn components and setting the jets but also balancing the carburettors for the best economy, will pay dividends in both fuel consumption and reduced engine wear.

Whether you have the work carried out professionally or do it yourself, it is essential that before attempting any carburation tuning the ignition components should be in excellent condition and properly set, and that the advance/retard mechanism is working properly.

Balancing the carburettors

The most basic method of doing this (which you will see in many garages) is to remove the air filter casings and listen to the rush of air into the throat of each carburettor. This is done by holding one end of a rubber pipe just inside the throat of the carburettor and the other to the ear, with the engine on tickover and at normal operating temperature. This can be a reasonably accurate method for the amateur and a

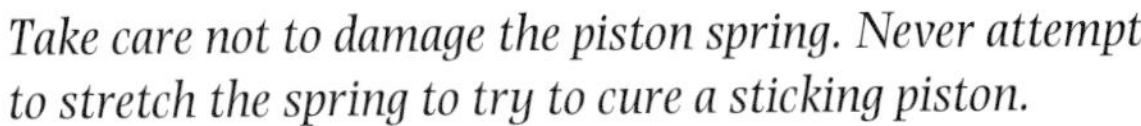

Take care not to damage the piston spring. Never attempt to stretch the spring to try to cure a sticking piston.

The needle is easily bent (and hence ruined), so be very careful when handling it. Examine it closely for ridges, and examine the jet for ovality, as the two problems usually occur simultaneously. Replace both the jet and the needle if any problems are found.

very accurate method for an experienced person, but it is recommended that the inexperienced use a special balancing kit which gives much more accurate results.

The engine should be at normal operating temperature for the following procedures. Remove the air filters. Remove the choke cable, slacken off the nuts on the pinch bolts to allow the carburettors to operate independently. If you have not already done so, check that the needles are centred. Lift each piston manually as far as it will go, and screw in the jet adjusting nut until the jet is flush with the bridge and then turn them back twelve flats each (two complete turns). Recheck that the needle is centred. Back off both throttle idle adjusting screws (44).

Start the engine and either listen for equalized 'hiss' in each throat or use the balancing kit while adjusting the throttle idle screws. When the carburettors are balanced, carefully retighten the connecting rod pinch bolts so that both carburettors operate simultaneously as the rod is turned.

Keeping the jet assemblies pressed in, adjust both by equal amounts until the highest consistent tickover speed is achieved. Then back off the idle adjusting screws by equal amounts until the desired tickover is obtained. Remember that the tickover speed affects fuel consumption on the overrun.

To adjust the mixture finely, lift each piston slightly in turn using the lifting pin or directly (lifting no more than is possible with the lifting pins) and listen to the effect this has on engine revolutions. If they rise then the mixture is too rich (screw jet upwards one flat and retry) if the revs die then the mixture is too lean (screw jet back down one flat).

LEFT *Slacken the nut on one of the pinch bolts in order to allow the carburettors to operate independently. It is important that the carburettors are properly balanced before mixture setting is attempted. The choke cable (foreground) should be disconnected first!*

BELOW LEFT *The time-honoured method of balancing carburettors: listening to the rush of air through each carburettor and making a judgement on whether they are equal, can give very accurate results for experienced persons. Trevor from the Bromsgrove MG Centre set up a triple carburettor MGC in this manner, and when subsequently tested on a rolling road, it was found that no further alterations could improve on the setting! The amateur might not always achieve the same results, and is recommended to take the car to a specialist who has a rolling road.*

RIGHT *The fuel overflow pipe can quite easily become clogged with dirt. Early cars have just one pipe on the front HS4 carburettor, whilst later cars have one per HIF carburettor. From time to time, check the ledge on the side of the engine block underneath the overflow pipe(s). This naturally tends to be covered in a layer of oil and dirt and, if the area immediately underneath the overflow pipe(s) is clean, then petrol is obviously leaking! Check the condition of the float chamber needle and jet, and the float itself.*

If the engine speed rises for a half second and then returns to normal, adjustment is correct. Work first on the rear carburettor and then the front one before returning to the rear, and so on until both give the desired effect when the piston is raised. Reconnect the choke cable and air filters.

Tuning problems

If the ignition system is in good order then setting the carburation as outlined above should give a smooth tickover and a clean pickup. There should be no 'lumpiness' nor flat spots throughout the rev range. Fuel consumption should average in the mid-twenties, according to the type of running.

If the engine still will not run properly, first remove the fuel overflow pipe and check that this is not blocked. A blocked overflow pipe prevents the fuel float from rising and cutting off the petrol feed, so making two cylinders run far too richly.

If the car uses too much fuel, check the brakes for binding, the fuel system for leakage, the choke for accidental operation and the air cleaners. If no obvious fault is discovered, then the problem may lie with a float chamber.

To dismantle a float chamber, first disconnect the inlet pipe then remove the three screws to allow the fuel chamber top to lift away. Lift out the float and check that it contains no fuel (if so, it will be holed and should be renewed). The float should be adjusted so that it closes the needle valve at the correct height. Invert the float chamber top so that the needle valve is fully closed. The float should be 1/8in above the chamber top, and this may be checked by inserting a 1/8in bar or rod under the float and on top of the chamber top rim. The float lever may be bent until the float is at the correct level.

SU HIF carburettors

This is a slightly more complex carburettor which incorporates the float chamber into the main body instead of having a separate chamber like the SU HS4. The jet is held by a bi-metallic strip (two strips of metal joined together which bend when heated), to vary the jet setting according to engine temperature. The jet is adjusted by means of the screw (9) which acts on the bi-metal jet lever (10). A separate jet is provided for cold starting and there is a bypass idle system. In most respects the instructions given for the SU HS4 will also cover the SU HIF. For further information on this and the Zenith 175 CD 5T, consult a workshop manual.

Exhaust emission control systems

The systems fitted will vary according to the year of the car and the country of export. Basically, the systems force cleaned air into the exhaust ports to assist in burning away any hydrocarbons. In addition, various crankcase ventilation and evaporative loss systems may be fitted. North American models were also fitted with catalytic converters to reduce the emission of nitrogen oxide in the exhaust gases. In such cases it is essential that any repair or tuning is carried out professionally by a company which has emissions test equipment, because any interference with the emission control apparatus can alter the emissions.

Ignition

If the engine will still not tick over smoothly, if it is hesitant or misses and yet no fault can be found with the fuel delivery and carburation systems, then check the ignition system thoroughly.

EXHAUST SYSTEM

The exhaust system performs two basic functions. First, the two silencer boxes cut the noise generated by the rapid expansion of gases which escape when the exhaust valve opens, which would otherwise be deafening. Secondly, the system should assist in drawing the gases away efficiently before the exhaust valve closes.

If a system is too restrictive because the bore is too small, the baffle plates too intrusive or the system simply partially blocked then the performance of the car will suffer, as the gases build up pressure in the exhaust and prevent from escaping properly the

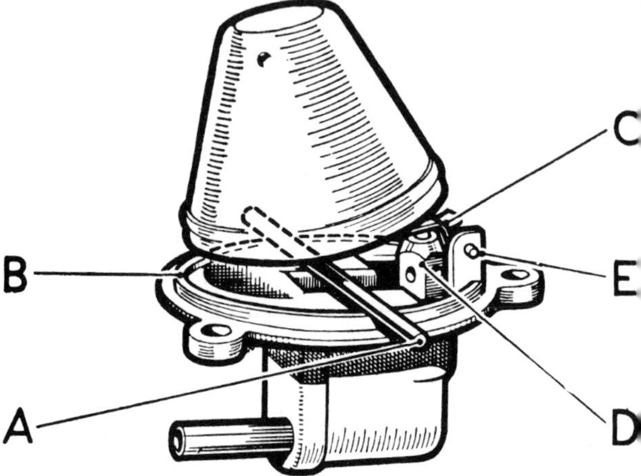

A. 0.125 to 0.187 in (3.18 to 4.76 mm) dia. bar
B. Machined lip
C. Float lever resetting point
D. Needle valve assembly
E. Hinge pin

Checking the nylon float level

The float level should be accurately set. Failure to do so could greatly increase fuel usage! In the SU HS4 carburettor, the original float consisted of a plastic float moulding with a separate metal link mounted on top, and this was adjustable. At the time of writing, the original part (AOD 9904) is not available from the Rover Group's own classic spares division, and alternatives appear to lack the facility for adjustment. (courtesy Autodata)

following gases from the next exhaust valve which opens . If, on the other hand, the exhaust system has too large a bore, the gas flow will still not be correct and the performance will still suffer. The system has to be exactly matched to the engine for optimum results.

The 'standard' exhaust system material used by most car manufacturers is mild steel which, like the steel used in car bodies, rusts. One of the substances emitted by an engine is water, and this water attacks the silencer from the inside. A second attack takes place from the outside, not only water from the road, but also from the highly corrosive salts that it contains. Not surprisingly, mild steel silencers can rust very quickly.

The first sign that an exhaust system is faulty will be 'blowing', that is, exhaust gas under pressure can be heard to be escaping through small holes in the exhaust body. It is illegal to run a car on the public roads if the exhaust is blowing, furthermore, not only will performance suffer but fuel consumption will also rise slightly as a result. When this happens there are a number of courses of remedial action. The hole can be patched using one of a number of special proprietary compounds that are widely available from garages and motor factors, or it can be patched with sheet steel which is welded or brazed into position (or simply stopped with a blob of weld). Alternatively, and almost always most satisfactorily, the whole system, or a part, can be renewed.

Exhaust repair compounds and bandages can be useful in extending the life of the exhaust as long as the rust is not too advanced. Very often a rusted exhaust will be found to have only paper-thin steel around the area of a hole, and this will be so weak that the hardened compound simply blows out after a short period of running. Much the same is true of sheet steel repairs: you cannot weld onto rusted or very thin metal and expect the repair to be long-lasting.

The exception is when exhaust damage has been caused by a blow of some kind such as a silencer box grounding. With good metal, welded repairs can last a long time and repair pastes and bandages can also be satisfactory.

Due to the temporary nature of most exhaust repairs and also to the fact that an engine's performance will be affected by an exhaust system which is blowing, the most satisfactory solution is to replace part or preferably all of the system.

Fitting an exhaust system

Time: 2 hours.

Tools/equipment: means of raising and holding the nearside of the car which keeps the rear suspension compressed. A pit or car lift will make this job a hundred times easier!

Protective clothing (overalls, hat, goggles).
Mole grips.
Half inch socket, ratchet handle, 5in and 10in (approx.) extension bars, speed brace useful.
Jointing compound (where a 3-piece system is to be fitted).
Freeing agent.

Fitting a new exhaust system can be a relatively straightforward job for the home mechanic if no problems are encountered along the way. It can just as easily turn into a nightmare. First, there is always the danger that the replacement exhaust will not fit, which can arise if you are sold an inappropriate system (rubber bumper and chrome bumper cars need different systems). Secondly, some of the fittings can be seized solid, of which the worst are the six nuts holding the down pipes to the bottom flanges of the exhaust manifold. If you are unlucky enough to 'round' one of these or, worse, to break off one of the manifold studs then you have to hacksaw off the old down pipes, remove the carburettors and their manifold and then lift out the exhaust manifold.

This job is also extremely dirty, and must be considered one of those tasks often best left to professionals with fully equipped workshops.

Preliminary inspection

Check the condition of the metal/rubber 'sandwich' rear and central mountings on early chrome bumper cars, the central mountings only on Mk3 chrome bumper and all rubber bumper cars. If the rubber blocks show signs of parting from the two steel brackets to which they are bonded, then it is best to order replacements. Do not be tempted to rip off the remaining rubber and then weld the two pieces of metal together, because this will not only allow vibrations from the exhaust to be directly transmitted into the bodywork (causing a constant 'drumming' noise), but it will place stresses on the system itself. The system must be flexibly mounted to account for engine movements.

Look at the exposed threads on the exhaust manifold studs; copious quantities of freeing agent applied to the threads and allowed to soak for as long as possible before commencing work, will make the job easier and reduce the risk of shearing a stud. The nuts fitted here should be brass and are easily damaged, so it is worth ordering six spares just in case. If steel nuts have been fitted and have seized then their forced removal could lead to broken studs, and if steel nuts have been used and appear badly rusted then spare studs should also be ordered as a precaution. Like the brass nuts which fit on them, studs cost very little and if they are not needed then they can be greased and put aside as valuable spares for future use.

When ordering a replacement system for a chrome bumper car be absolutely certain that you get one specifically designed for the car. Some manufacturers produce a 'one size fits all' design for all 1800cc MGBs; it will probably fit the rubber bumper car fairly easily, but could be almost impossible to fit satisfactorily to a chrome bumper model. If you are not 100 per cent certain whether a system will fit then compare the section of pipe situated immediately to the rear of the middle silencer box with that on the system to be replaced and easily visible underneath your car. The system for the chrome bumper car is much straighter than that on the rubber bumper model.

When a compromise system is built to fit all MGBs, it is made to be a better fit on more recent cars than on the less numerous earlier models. To the professional with a fully equipped workshop complete with pit, fitting such a mismatched system will often be possible with the aid of specially made-up brackets, albeit a time-consuming and unrewarding business. To the amateur working on his back under the car without special facilities it can be a completely fruitless exercise. If it will not fit then exchange it for one which does.

Stainless or mild steel?

Mild steel exhaust systems can last as long as three years but many cheaper examples may not live too long after their first birthday! If you intend keeping the car then it is well worth fitting a stainless steel system.

Even a stainless steel exhaust will not last forever, but a system of reasonable quality should serve you for ten years or more, in which time you could easily get through between three and five mild steel systems!

A stainless system will cost roughly two and a half times as much as the very cheapest mild steel alternative, so the financial arguments in favour of stainless steel are obvious.

The word 'stainless' is in itself no guarantee of quality, and you will find that some systems inexplicably weigh far more than others. The answer lies in the thickness of steel used; better systems make use of 16 gauge (ie 1/16in thick) steel whereas others will use thinner 20 gauge (1/20in thick steel). Examine any stainless exhausts you are offered; on most you can see the gauge of metal used stamped onto one of the silencer boxes. With both the mild steel and the stainless system, you generally get what you pay for, and there will few bargain-priced systems of good quality.

You sometimes have the choice between a three-, a two- or a one-piece system. The multi-piece sort do allow you to exchange any one of the sections if one becomes faulty or is damaged, but against this they can be more complicated to fit – particularly the three-piece – because the manufacturer intends them to fit any year of MGB 'at a pinch'.

With a multi-piece system always preassemble it before attaching it to the car to ensure that the female join areas have not been distorted. If you lay the assembled system on the ground alongside the car then you can compare its length and shape with that of the existing system; if it is longer then replace it with the correct system.

Removal

If you can beg access to a pit or to a car lift then do so, because either can easily cut 75 per cent off the time requirement for the job. Otherwise, proceed as follows. Raise the nearside of the car and support it with axle stands. The rear stand should be under the

A speed brace and an extension bar will be long enough to reach the exhaust manifold nuts. Use the absolute minimum of force to prevent damage to the nuts or studs. Undo each a fraction in turn, and repeat until all the nuts are loose before removing any. If you loosen one nut at a time, the clamp plate will move and place great strain on the remaining nuts, making them very difficult to loosen.

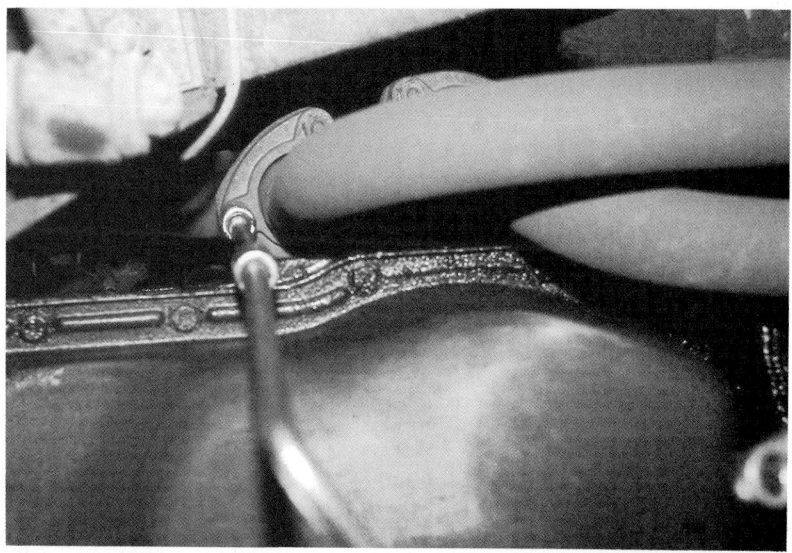

The exhaust steady can be removed using a half-inch open-ended spanner and a half-inch ring spanner or socket.

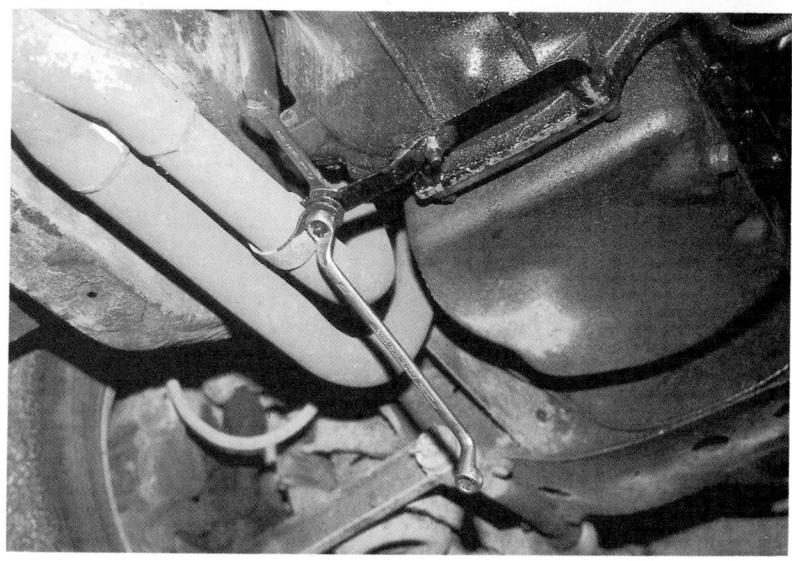

axle or rear suspension to keep it in the 'on-road' position. Open the bonnet to let more light onto the manifold area. Removing the roadwheel also helps.

Loosen each of the six manifold nuts. If any refuse to shift, try spraying freeing agent on the exposed thread and retry later. Do not use excessive force unless you have spare nuts and studs to hand and you like making extra work for yourself. If any of the soft brass nuts 'round' then you could try tapping on an old, fractionally-smaller, socket. If any of the studs break then you will have to remove the exhaust manifold in order to renew them. When all the nuts will turn then remove them.

Remove the steady bracket clip bolt (using two half-inch spanners), the centre hanger bolt, and lower the frontal end of the system onto some form of support. It may be necessary to use Mole grips, because the various nuts and bolt heads are often 'chewed' as a result of the previous owner's attempts at removal!

On early cars, the rear bracket may be opened slightly with the holding bolt removed and the system drawn away forwards. On later cars, simply undo the bolts holding the bracket. Withdraw the system.

You should now remove the steady bracket from the off-side pipe just ahead of the junction and fit it to the replacement system if it does not already have a new one.

Refitting: one-piece

Fit the rear bracket to the car first (early cars), as access to the bolts is very limited with the tail pipe in place. Lay the system on the ground underneath the car and locate the tail pipe in the rear mounting. Fit the two downpipe seals (asbestos facing upwards) before offering up the downpipes towards the manifold. Temporarily chock the system up so that the downpipes locate. Push the bolt through the centre bracket to support the system fully. Offer up each downpipe clamp in turn and start all nuts turning the socket extension bar in your hand or using a speed brace rather than with a ratchet to prevent cross-threading. Tighten the six nuts on the manifold. Be careful not to over-tighten these because the threads strip easily.

Fit the stay bracket, and then tighten all other fittings. Run the engine for a minute or so and listen for blowing, and then check all fittings for tightness.

Three-piece

It pays to 'trial fit' the system first to make quite sure that you have the correct one before smearing sealing compound around the jointed areas. Fit the downpipe as described above. Offer the mid-section to the downpipe section, and attach at the middle bracket. Fit the rear bracket and feed the tail pipe through this until you can move the section forwards onto the middle section. Keep all nuts loose at this stage.

If the system is well clear of all parts of the bodywork and all ancillaries such as the axle, damper arms and electrics, then you may go ahead and fit it. Otherwise, telephone the supplier and double check that the system is really suitable for your car.

Remove the rear section and centre bracket, then open the first joint and apply a jointing compound. Reassemble this and refit the centre bracket. Assemble the rear to centre sections with jointing compound and refit the rear bracket and the stay bracket, keeping all nuts loose. Recheck for adequate clearances. Fit clamps on the two joints and then tighten all nuts, starting with those on the manifold and moving backwards down the car.

Lower the car to the ground, start the engine and listen for any knocking sounds, especially when the engine first fires and when you turn it off. It is also a good idea to test drive the car, because minor bumps in the road can also help reveal whether the exhaust system needs further adjustment. It is always best to discover any such problems while all the tools needed to correct them are to hand.

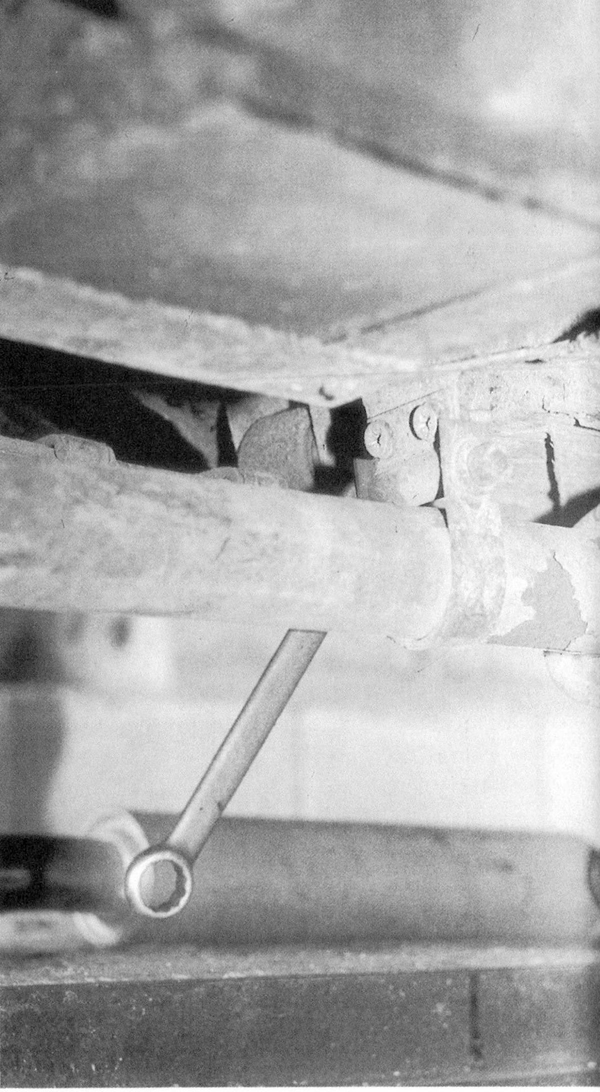

ABOVE *The centre bracket is held by a bolt and nut. If the nut is seized then it would pay simply to hacksaw it off rather than waste time trying to undo it.*

ABOVE RIGHT *The early rear bracket can be opened slightly using a large screwdriver to aid removal of the tailpipe. Both this and the centre bracket should be closely examined and, if the metal/rubber 'sandwich' shows signs of coming apart, replaced.*

RIGHT *The author made up this simple rear exhaust mounting bracket to replace the rotted one on his own car. A plate was welded onto the top, and the assembly then MIG-welded to the boot floor and spot-welded to the valance. The two nuts were also welded into position.*

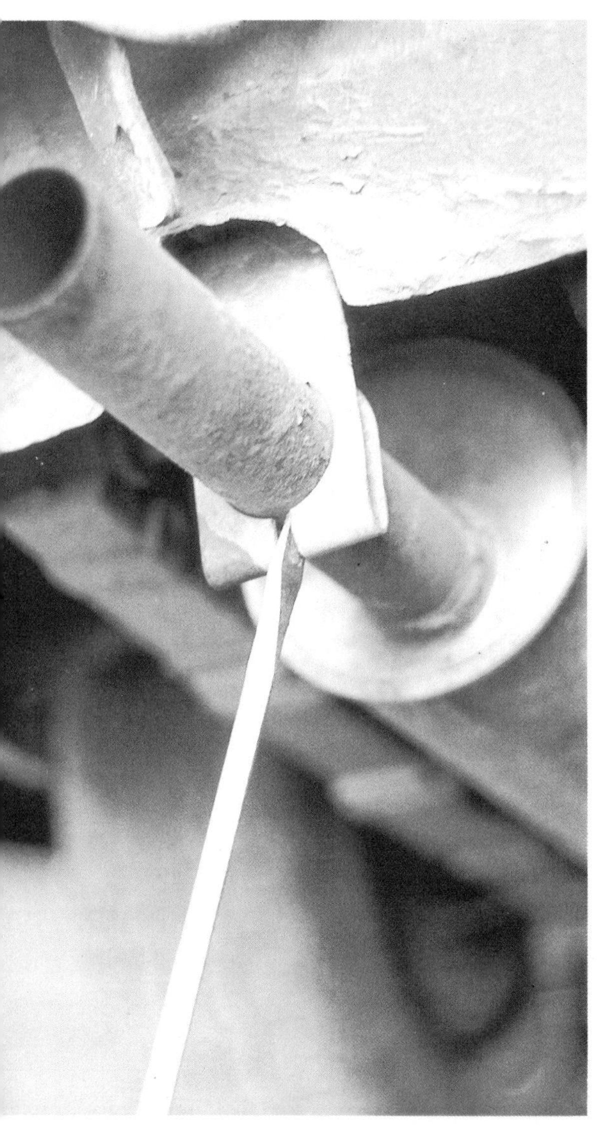

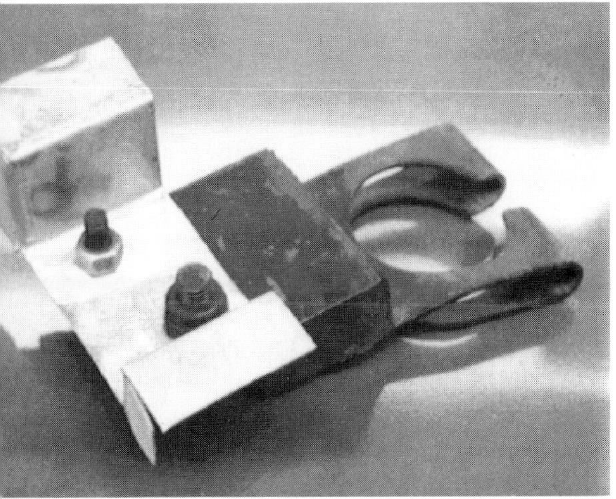

GEARBOX

A noisy gearbox can give many years of service (provided that you can tolerate the noise!) and the decision to remove and work on the gearbox just because there is a noise in one or more gears is not one to be taken lightly. The problem is that to correct noisy gears will sometimes demand that virtually the entire workings are reconditioned. Of course, when the engine and gearbox have been removed during a restoration then the opportunity to rectify any faults should not be lost.

It is perfectly feasible for the DIY enthusiast to recondition a gearbox at home, and kits are available for this purpose from a number of sources. It would be extremely galling, however, to recondition and refit a gearbox only to subsequently discover that you had made some mistake in reassembly or overlooked a fault. In such instances there would be no alternative to repeating the whole exercise.

Furthermore, it is quite possible to spend far more on new and reconditioned components than the price of an assembled exchange reconditioned gearbox.

For these reasons it is recommended that a reconditioned (and guaranteed) gearbox be fitted, to avoid the headache.

Engine/gearbox separation

Remove the starter motor and the screws which hold the gearbox bellhousing to the engine mounting plate. Withdraw the gearbox, keeping it square to the engine in order to prevent damage occurring to the clutch release plate drive straps.

Remove the nut and bolt from the clutch lever and the lever and its dust cover from the housing. Remove the engine stayrod (where applicable).

Automatic gearbox removal

Proceed as for the manual gearbox, but also remove the downshift assembly. Remove the six bolts which hold the gearbox to the torque converter housing, and withdraw the gearbox. Undo the bolts holding the torque converter housing to the engine and withdraw the housing. Four bolts hold the converter to the drive plate. On no account should the amateur attempt to work on an automatic gearbox.

THE CLUTCH

The clutch is operated hydraulically by a non-compressible fluid. The master cylinder piston is moved by pressure on the clutch pedal and forces fluid into the slave cylinder, where the pressure acts against the release bearing.

The high-friction driven plate is clamped between the pressure plate and the flywheel. When the clutch pedal is depressed, the pressure plate moves away from the driven plate, so releasing it from the sandwich between the pressure plate and the flywheel.

In order to renew the clutch components it is necessary to remove either the engine unit or the engine/gearbox complete. If only the clutch is to be worked on then it is easier to remove just the engine. Proceed as detailed in Chapter 5, Engine removal.

If the engine and gearbox have been moved simultaneously, first split the two units. Mark the flywheel and clutch cover to ensure that the two components can be refitted in correct relationship with one another. Undo the six bolts which secure the clutch assembly to the flywheel, turning each in sequence by a small amount to prevent distortion of the cover. The clutch assembly can now be withdrawn.

The driven plate and the release bearing should be renewed at the same time. The clutch cover and pressure plate should be examined for marks on the machined contact surfaces or damage to the diaphragm springs and exchanged if necessary. DIY repairs are not advised because these components should be balanced following repair, which is work beyond the scope of most amateurs. Obtain and fit an exchange unit.

When reassembling the clutch, ensure that the marks made on dismantling line up before fitting the cover bolts to finger tightness (so that the driven plate is gripped but can still be moved). The clutch driven plate must be centralised so that when the gearbox and engine are mated once again, the gearbox input shaft will enter the splined boss in the plate. Use an old gearbox input shaft or a proper clutch alignment tool to ensure correct alignment of the driven plate before tightening the cover bolts in a diagonal sequence and torquing them to 25 to 30 ft lb. Also, take care not to allow the weight of the engine on to the gearbox input shaft when refitting the unit in the car.

If air enters the hydraulic system then it must be bled in the same way as brakes are bled. The bleed screw is on the slave cylinder and fitted with a cover which must be removed before bleeding.

To bleed the system, push a length of pipe over the bleed screw and immerse the other end of this in brake/clutch fluid contained within a glass jar. Ensure that the master cylinder is topped up, then ask an assistant to push the clutch pedal fully down to the floor whilst you open the bleed screw. When the pedal is fully down, close the bleed screw and ask the assistant to release the pressure and pump again. Repeat until no air bubbles can be seen within the fluid pumped out of the pipe, then close the bleed screw, refit the cap and top up the master cylinder.

Master cylinder

The master cylinder must be emptied of fluid before removal. Go through the motions of bleeding the system but omit to top up the master cylinder.

Remove the clutch/brake master cylinder cover. It may help in loosening the screws, first to place a screwdriver blade into the heads of each fixing screw and give it a sharp tap both to clean out the screw head and to shock the threads loose.

Remove the split pin, clevis pin and washer from the pushrod and disengage the pedal lever. Clean the pipe connection at the rear of the cylinder, disconnect the pipe and plug it to prevent the ingress of dirt. The fixing bolts can now be undone and the cylinder removed.

Repair kits are widely available for the master cylinder. To strip the master cylinder, remove the rubber boot then press on the piston to take the pressure from the circlip, and remove the circlip and pushrod assembly. Pull the piston and associated components from the unit.

Clean all metal components in clutch fluid and renew all the rubber components. Cover all components in clutch fluid before reassembly, which can be accomplished by reversing the removal procedure.

Slave cylinder

To remove the slave cylinder first disconnect the hydraulic pipe and catch whatever fluid escapes. Undo the screws which fasten the cylinder to the clutch housing, then remove the cylinder, leaving the pushrod attached to the release fork.

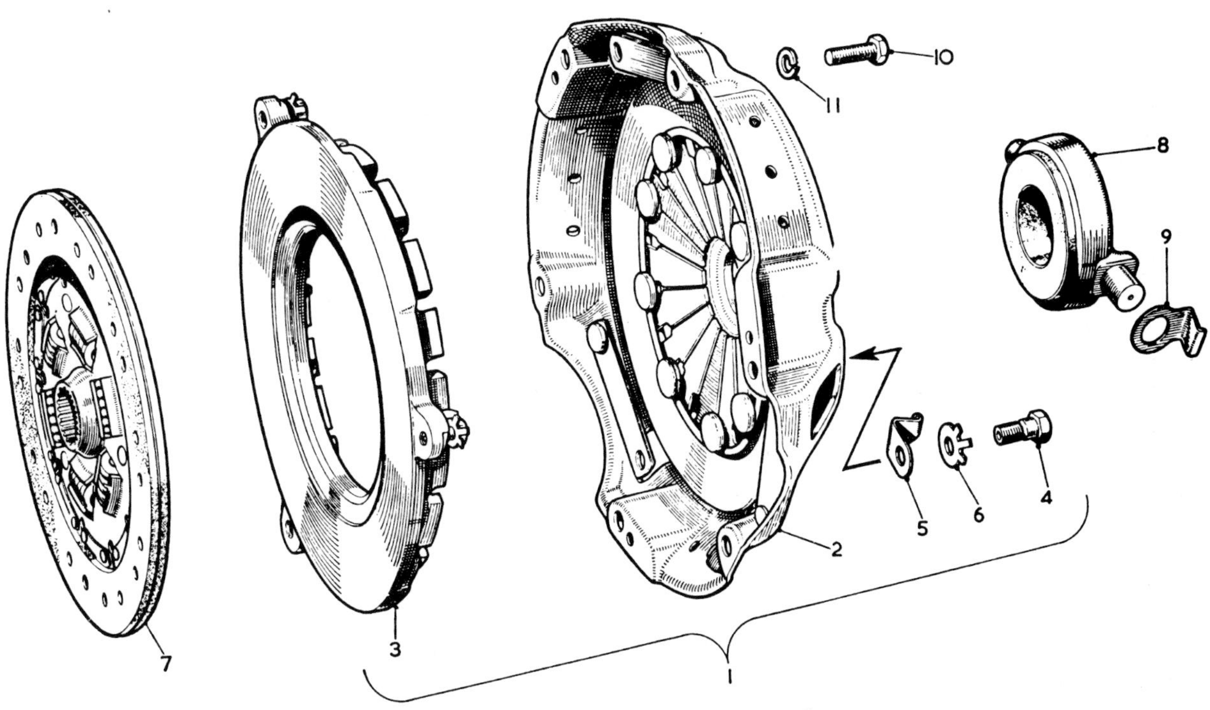

1. *Cover assembly*
2. *Cover with straps, diaphragm spring and release plate*
3. *Pressure plate*
4. *Strap bolt*
5. *Pressure plate clip*
6. *Tab washer*
7. *Driven plate assembly*
8. *Release bearing assembly*
9. *Bearing retainer*
10. *Clutch to flywheel screw*
11. *Spring washer*

The clutch components

ABOVE *Normally, clutch repair entails renewing the driven plate and the release bearing; never renew one without the other. It is possible to repair the cover assembly, but because the unit has to be balanced afterwards, it is usual and recommended to obtain an exchange unit. (courtesy Autodata)*

BELOW *Bleeding the clutch is just like bleeding the braking system, except that access to the slave bleed nipple is more difficult. A very heavy clutch action can be caused by collapse of the slave cylinder feed pipe, so take the opportunity to inspect this. (courtesy Autodata)*

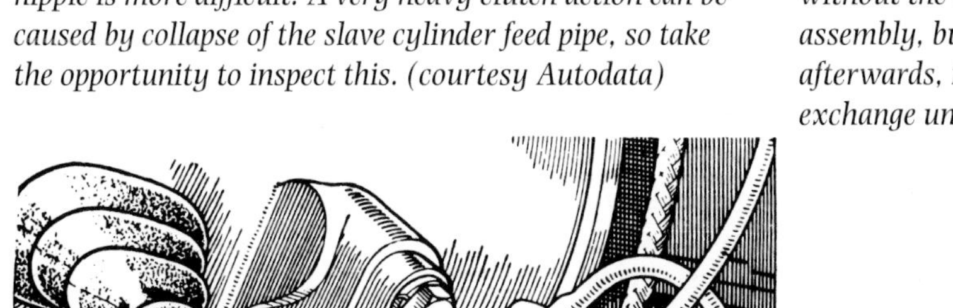

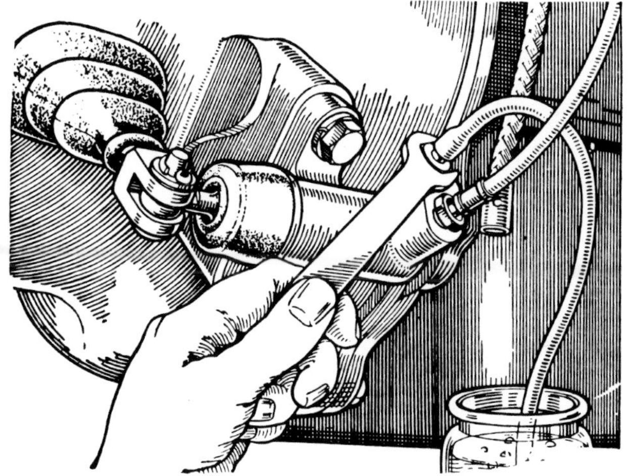

Bleeding the clutch hydraulic system at the slave cylinder

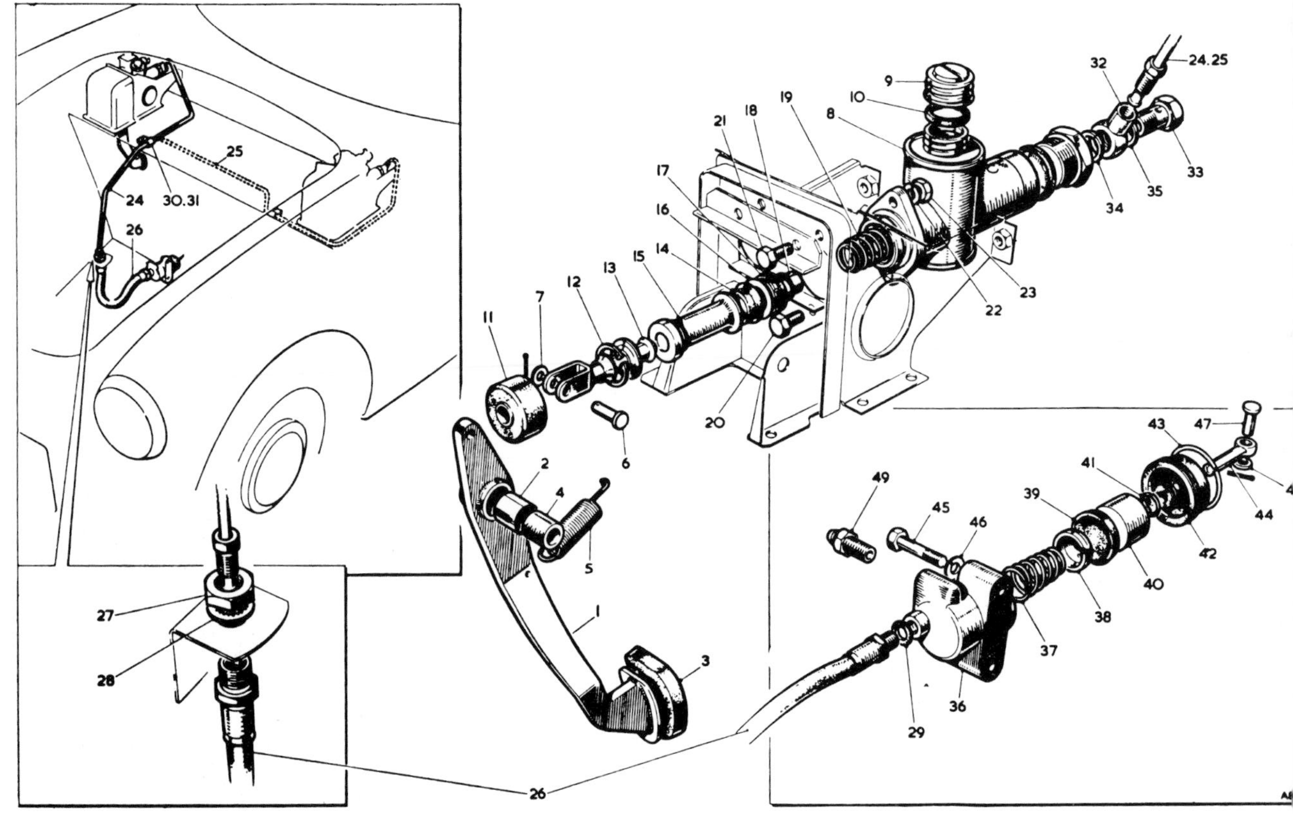

The clutch operating components

1. *Clutch pedal*
2. *Bush*
3. *Pedal rubber*
4. *Clutch pedal distance tube*
5. *Pedal pull-off spring*
6. *Clevis pin*
7. *Clevis pin washer*
8. *Barrel and tank*
9. *Filler cap*
10. *Cap seal*
11. *Boot*
12. *Circlip*
13. *Pushrod*
14. *Secondary cup*
15. *Piston*
16. *Piston washer*
17. *Main cup*
18. *Spring retainer*
19. *Spring*
20. *Cylinder to box screw*
21. *Cylinder and stiffener to box screw*
22. *Spring washer*
23. *Nut*
24. *Master cylinder to hose pipe*
25. *Master cylinder to hose pipe*
26. *Clutch hose*
27. *Hose locknut*
28. *Shakeproof washer*
29. *Hose to body gasket*
30. *Clutch pipe to bulkhead clip*
31. *Clutch pipe to bulkhead clip*
32. *Banjo connection*
33. *Banjo connection bolt*
34. *Gasket*
35. *Gasket*
36. *Body*
37. *Cup filler spring*
38. *Piston cup filler*
39. *Piston cup*
40. *Piston*
41. *Boot clip*
42. *Boot*
43. *Boot clip*
44. *Pushrod*
45. *Cylinder to gearbox bolt*
46. *Spring washer*
47. *Clevis pin*
48. *Clevis pin washer*
49. *Bleed screw*

THE OVERDRIVE

Two overdrive units were fitted to the MGB. Earlier cars to late 1967 (three synchromesh gearboxes) were fitted with the Laycock D-type overdrive as an optional extra; four synchromesh gearbox cars were fitted with the Laycock LH-type overdrive, again as an extra. The overdrive final ratio was slightly lowered in 1974 before the overdrive became a standard fitting a year later.

An overdrive is in essence like a second gearbox which is fitted behind the first, but it has just two 'gears'; straight through drive and overdrive. Unlike the gearbox, it is not operated directly by a lever but by an electrical circuit which is actuated by a switch situated either on the extreme driver's side of the dashboard or, on later models, on top of the gear lever.

The electronic actuation of the overdrive allowed the designer to incorporate additional switches into the circuit which only allow the overdrive to operate under certain conditions. A switch situated on the gear lever linkages prevents the overdrive from switching in if the car is in any gear other than third or fourth (fourth only on the V8 due to the higher stresses placed on the overdrive by the more powerful engine). Another, vacuum-operated, switch on earlier cars only allowed the overdrive to come in

The Laycock D-type overdrive was fitted to the early MGB and to many classic cars of its period. It is still quite easily sourced.

LEFT *The Laycock LH-type unit fitted to later cars is very similar in operation to the earlier D-type. Like the D-type, it is recommended that a non-functioning unit is replaced by a reconditioned one rather than being repaired at home.*

BELOW *The vacuum switch and relay. The vacuum switch allows the overdrive to operate only when there is a vacuum in the inlet manifold.*

when the throttle pedal was depressed (the vacuum is transmitted via a pipe from the inlet manifold).

The overdrive is a simple and extremely robust unit which rarely itself gives any trouble. A one-way clutch in the unit will be ruined, however, if the car is reversed whilst overdrive is engaged. This can only happen if you come to a halt with the overdrive still engaged (in third or top) and then reverse the car. It is an unusual circumstance, that might happen only, perhaps, following an emergency stop in which just brakes and not gears are used to assist in stopping the car.

When the car is in third or top gear and the overdrive switch is actuated, a circuit passes electricity to a solenoid. The solenoid consists of an electro-magnet, within which an armature is fitted. When current is applied to the coil of the magnet, linear movement is imparted to the armature. When the current is switched off the armature moves back to its 'at rest' position by spring pressure. In this instance, the armature operates a lever which simply opens a valve.

At the front of the overdrive unit is an oil pump which pumps oil from the gearbox continuously. When the overdrive is switched on and the lever described in the previous paragraph moves to open a valve, the oil is allowed into two cylinders which hold pistons, and under the pressure of the oil the pistons move forward and pull a conical clutch with them. This movement is the physical force which switches from direct drive to overdrive.

The output shaft from the gearbox drives a planet carrier; that is, an assembly which holds three 'planet' gears, so-called because they surround another gear called the 'sun' gear. In straight top drive, the conical clutch which holds the sun gear is in contact and rotates with the annulus, or output. When the overdrive is switched in then the conical clutch moves away from the annulus and into contact with a braking ring which stops both it and the sun wheel from rotating.

The planet gear carrier now rotates around the stationary sun wheel, so that the planet gears drive against it at approximately 1.25 times the speed of the gearbox output shaft rotation. They also drive against an internal gear cut into the annulus, so turning the annulus at a higher rotational speed for given gearbox output shaft revolutions and hence engine revolutions. A one-way clutch allows the output to freewheel as drive changes from straight to overdrive.

Most of non-working overdrive units will be found to have a fault with either the electrics or the pumped oil systems.

Fault finding

Time: could be hours!

Special tools/equipment: electrical test meter useful.

The most common overdrive fault is, happily, the easiest to identify and cure, and concerns the electrical circuit which feeds power to the solenoid. To test this circuit, switch the ignition on (do not start the engine) put the car into fourth gear and operate the overdrive switch, listening for a clearly audible click from under the car (the noise made by the solenoid as it operates). If a click cannot be heard then a problem exists with part of the circuit. Do not confuse this click with one simultaneously made by the in-line relay unit which is situated just under the bonnet of the car above the vacuum switch. If you are unsure whether the solenoid is working then stoop by the side of the car while a helper operates the switch.

A test meter is very useful when tracing electrical faults such as a mid-circuit disconnection. A 12V test lamp serves as an alternative which can show whether power is reaching terminals.

Check (in this order) the A3 fuse through which the overdrive is powered; the connections at the dashboard or gear lever switch; and the vacuum switch and the relay unit (both on the bulkhead to the right on the heater unit). Check the vacuum switch pipe for holes and for correct connection to the manifold. Repeat the ignition on/top gear engaged/ manual switch operation test but this time ask someone to listen to the under-bonnet relay unit for a click which indicates that it is operating. If none can be heard then recheck the relay's black earth connection and try again. If no click can be heard, replace the relay unit. Test to see whether the overdrive now works.

Check the single wire which runs to the overdrive solenoid unit for a short to earth caused by worn or damaged insulation, or for a break. If this seems in order then the solenoid could be faulty and presents the next easiest check. Simply cut the yellow/purple wire leading into it (it can be rejoined later using a proper connector) and touch the solenoid end momentarily against a wire attached to a live terminal. The solenoid should operate instantly; if not it is faulty and should be renewed. If the solenoid does work by direct connection, then the only remaining switch is that operated by the gear lever linkage. In order to check the connections the transmission tunnel plate surrounding the gear lever must be removed. The switch in question is on the offside of the unit and, unfortunately, quite difficult to reach.

If all connections are sound and switches and the relay unit appear sound, then there is a mid-wire disconnection which must be traced with a test meter or small circuit and bulb, and new wiring will have to be run.

If the solenoid is working

Because the overdrive takes oil from the gearbox, a low gearbox oil level will prevent the overdrive from working, and so this should be checked (see Chapter 3). Three other minor (non-mechanical) faults can be the cause of the problem. First, the overdrive oil filter could be blocked (to check this entails draining both overdrive and gearbox oil). This is an uncommon fault, and if the filter is blocked then that will be merely a symptom of further problems elsewhere. Secondly, the solenoid could be out of adjustment (to check both this and the blocked filter entails lowering the gearbox/overdrive unit after removal of the cross-member). Thirdly, the valve operating cam could be out of adjustment or have suffered a mechanical failure. The most easily checked of the three is the valve operating cam.

Remove the transmission tunnel plate and remove the hexagonal plug situated on the offside top of the unit, under which is a ball bearing valve. Operating the solenoid should raise this through 1/32in. If no movement is apparent then it is likely that the arm acting against by the solenoid will require adjustment. Occasionally, when a reconditioned overdrive unit is rebuilt, the tiny Mills pin which secures the cam is overlooked.

The very last check which can be carried out without removal of the overdrive, engine and gearbox is as follows.

Jack the rear of the car as high as possible and support it with axle stands. Place a jack under the gearbox cross-member and remove the four bolts which hold the movable cross-member under the overdrive unit. Slowly lower the cross-member a little, taking care not to damage any underbody fittings such as the exhaust or wiring. A plate held by three set screws immediately in front of the solenoid will be visible on the off-side of the unit, under which lies the solenoid operating lever. Remove the plate and operate the solenoid. If a 3/16in rod (the blunt end of a twist bit will do) can pass through the hole in the lever and into the 3/16in hole in the body casting then adjustment is in order. If not, then screw the solenoid arm nut in or out as appropriate.

While the unit is lowered the oil filter can be checked. It is situated under a small panel on the nearside of the unit. First, drain the overdrive oil via the drain plug. Remove the set screws and plate and withdraw the filter. The filter has a large surface area and if it is blocked with swarf then this could indicate severe problems elsewhere within the unit, and the overdrive should be removed from the car. If the filter is not blocked, take the opportunity to clean out the chamber behind it before reassembling.

OVERDRIVE REMOVAL

Time: 4-8 hours.

Special tools/equipment: engine hoist.

If no fault has been discovered then the overdrive will have to be removed from the car. There is no reason why an overdrive should not be stripped, repaired and reassembled by the enthusiast 'at home'. There is, however, a strong possibility that either replacement components will be required or that the overdrive fault will not be repairable by the amateur, in which case the home mechanic will be left with his car off the road until replacement components or a replacement overdrive can be obtained. For this reason, it is usually best to obtain a replacement overdrive *before* removal of the faulty one. These are widely available from MG specialists on an exchange basis, although if you opt for outright purchase then later you will be able to repair or have repaired the original unit to keep as a spare.

If you have access to a pit and engine hoist or a portable engine hoist, the overdrive unit can be changed without having to remove the engine and gearbox (contrary to popular belief). It is better that they are removed, but it is far from essential if they are instead manoeuvred into the correct position. This gives less opportunity for damage to occur, than whilst the heavy and awkward bulk of the three units is lifted out through the engine bay.

First, drain the gearbox/overdrive oil. Follow all of the steps recommended for engine/gearbox removal. Disconnect and telescope the prop shaft out of the way and remove the gearbox cross-member completely. Instead of lifting the three units from the car, lift the engine, tilt the overdrive downwards and push the car backwards (or pull the portable engine hoist forwards) until the engine occupies a position just above the panel which normally holds the oil cooler (chrome bumper cars). This should, of course, be heavily padded. The gearbox/overdrive unit can now be angled downwards until all appropriate fastenings (not forgetting the speedometer drive end) can be reached, the old unit removed and the replacement fitted.

To gain reasonable access to the overdrive fittings, remove the gear selector remote control assembly. The eight nuts which hold the overdrive to the gearbox can now be removed, and the unit carefully withdrawn.

Stripping the overdrive

With just a normal tool kit (plus a 1 1/8in deep socket for removal of the output drive flange castle nut) the home mechanic can perform an 80 per cent strip and rebuild of the overdrive unit. Some of the faults likely to be found can be repaired by the amateur by simple replacement of faulty components. There are some faults, such as damaged bearings, which are best left to professionals with appropriate equipment. Not all transmission specialists will work with overdrive units, but if this proves the case then they should be able to recommend someone who will.

To avoid damaging the (expensive to replace) solenoid, it pays to remove this first. The solenoid rod can be left in position if desired, although it is easy to manoeuvre it past the operating arm once the operating valve has been removed. To do this, carefully remove the plug at the top of the overdrive unit. This is unfortunately largely hollow and easily damaged during removal. Remove the spring, ball bearing and rod. Next remove the oil filter cover and filter, drain plug, non-return valve and plug. Allow the unit to completely drain of oil.

Operate the pump head manually to ensure that it is not sticking. If it does stick or is stuck at the bottom of its travel then this is the reason why the

(Cont. p. 137)

The nut (LEFT) *is hollow and easily damaged. The valve* (RIGHT) *is opened when the solenoid pulls its operating lever. In between is a Mills pin which is sometimes forgotten when overdrives are rebuilt. The valve pin lifts through 1/32in when the solenoid operates.*

OPPOSITE ABOVE *If the oil filter is clogged, then the overdrive should be stripped to discover why.*

OPPOSITE BELOW *The bifurcation on the pump can easily be spread if the unit is fitted to the gearbox with the latter's lobe pointing downwards. This causes the pump to stick at the bottom of its travel, which can prevent the unit from working.*

ABOVE *Remove the pump base plug, then the spring and ball bearing.*

LEFT *The pump body can then be pressed or gently drifted down out of the casing. Although the photograph shows a socket in position, the pump does not unscrew from the casing. It is a friction fit and is located by the small grub screw.*

RIGHT *The pump body, bearing and spring.*

BELOW *After folding back the tab washers, the nuts on the piston bars may be undone, the bars removed, and the pistons withdrawn.*

BOTTOM *Examine the piston bores and the pistons for marks, and replace the 'O' ring as a matter of course.*

OPPOSITE ABOVE *The unit separated. It is wise to remove the solenoid to prevent damage before progressing this far, because these are quite expensive items to buy.*

OPPOSITE BELOW *Remove the retaining circlip, then the sun gear can be separated from the cone clutch body.*

RIGHT *The output shaft can be drifted from the casing if required. Invert the nut and replace it onto the shaft to give the threads protection.*

BELOW *The marks on the planet gears and carrier are difficult to locate, but it is essential that they align before the sun gear is replaced.*

RIGHT *A thin spanner can make removal of the speedometer drive much easier.*

overdrive did not work. Remove the plug situated under the oil pump, the small spring and ball bearing within, and the small set screw situated on the front face of the unit (which locates the pump body). The pump body can now be withdrawn, but will usually require the assistance of a soft brass drift and a small hammer. Examine the pump head for damage. If the bifurcated arms are splayed then they should be gently straightened in a vice. This damage will have occurred when the overdrive was previously forced onto the gearbox output shaft, with the cam lobe of that shaft pointing downwards so that it pushed against the pump head roller – do not make the same mistake when refitting the unit!

Fold back the tabs on the four locking washers which hold the nuts on the piston bar rods, then remove the nuts and bars. The pistons can now be withdrawn; if either is seized then this could be the main or a contributory reason for the non-functioning of the unit. Examine the pistons and cylinders for wear or roughness, and replace the piston 'O' rings as a matter of course.

The two main body castings are held each side of a braking ring by eight studs and nuts. Turn the first nut by two flats, then the nut opposite, and so on, until the pressure from the four springs is released. Very often, the three main units will be seized together, in which case the nuts should be loosened by equal amounts and the body castings lightly tapped with a hide mallet until they part from the braking ring. Pull the units apart.

Lift away the cone clutch and captive sun wheel, then the planet gear carrier. Examine the clutch linings for wear and replace if necessary, although this may be a job best left to a transmission specialist, because the linings are riveted in place. Examine the planet and sun gears, plus the internal gearing of the annulus for damage.

The sun gear is held in the cone clutch body by a circlip; this should be removed and the sun gear withdrawn and inspected for damage.

The speedometer drive is located by a bolt. After removal of this, the unit can be pulled from the main casing. A thin-walled spanner might be of assistance in breaking the unit free if seized. To remove the annulus and output shaft, first remove the split pin and then the castellated nut from the output flange. Use a socket for this, ensuring that it is deep enough to reach the bottom of the nut, to prevent damaging the castellations. The nut may be reversed and replaced on the threaded end of the shaft to prevent damage whilst the whole is drifted out of the rear casing. If necessary, the rear bearing can be removed from the rear of the unit. The oil seal should be replaced.

The one-way roller clutch should not be removed unless obviously damaged. Examine all bearing surfaces for undue wear. It is recommended that any attention to the roller clutch or bearings be left to a transmission specialist.

Reassembly

Carefully refit the annulus/output shaft into the rear body casting, refit the drive flange and washer and torque the castellated nut to 110 ft lb before refitting the split pin.

Each planet gear will carry a mark which should be lined up with a scribed line on the planet carrier. In practice, these marks may be difficult to see. When all three are correctly lined up, refit the sun gear into the planet gears, then the cone clutch body and circlip. Offer this assembly as a whole to the annulus then refit the braking ring.

Place the plate and four springs over the thrust bearing legs and offer up the front body casting. Replace the eight nuts and tighten by equal amounts, working on opposite nuts to keep the three sections true. Further reassembly is the opposite of stripping.

PROPELLER SHAFT

The gearbox (or overdrive) is connected to the rear axle by the propeller shaft, universally referred to as the prop shaft. This is a drive shaft that has universal joints at both ends which allow for movements which alter the relative positions and attitudes of the axle and gearbox/overdrive while the car is on the move.

The prop shaft also has a sliding collar joint (with splines to transmit the drive) connecting its shorter front and longer back sections. It can thus be 'telescoped' for easier fitting and removal. Several different lengths of prop shaft were used on various MGBs, and when ordering a replacement it is important that the correct length shaft is obtained.

Three faults can develop or be present in the prop shaft assembly. Because it revolves at high speed in use, the shaft must be very finely balanced to prevent its setting up vibrations which would otherwise place

The sealed type of universal joint does not have a grease nipple. (courtesy Autodata)

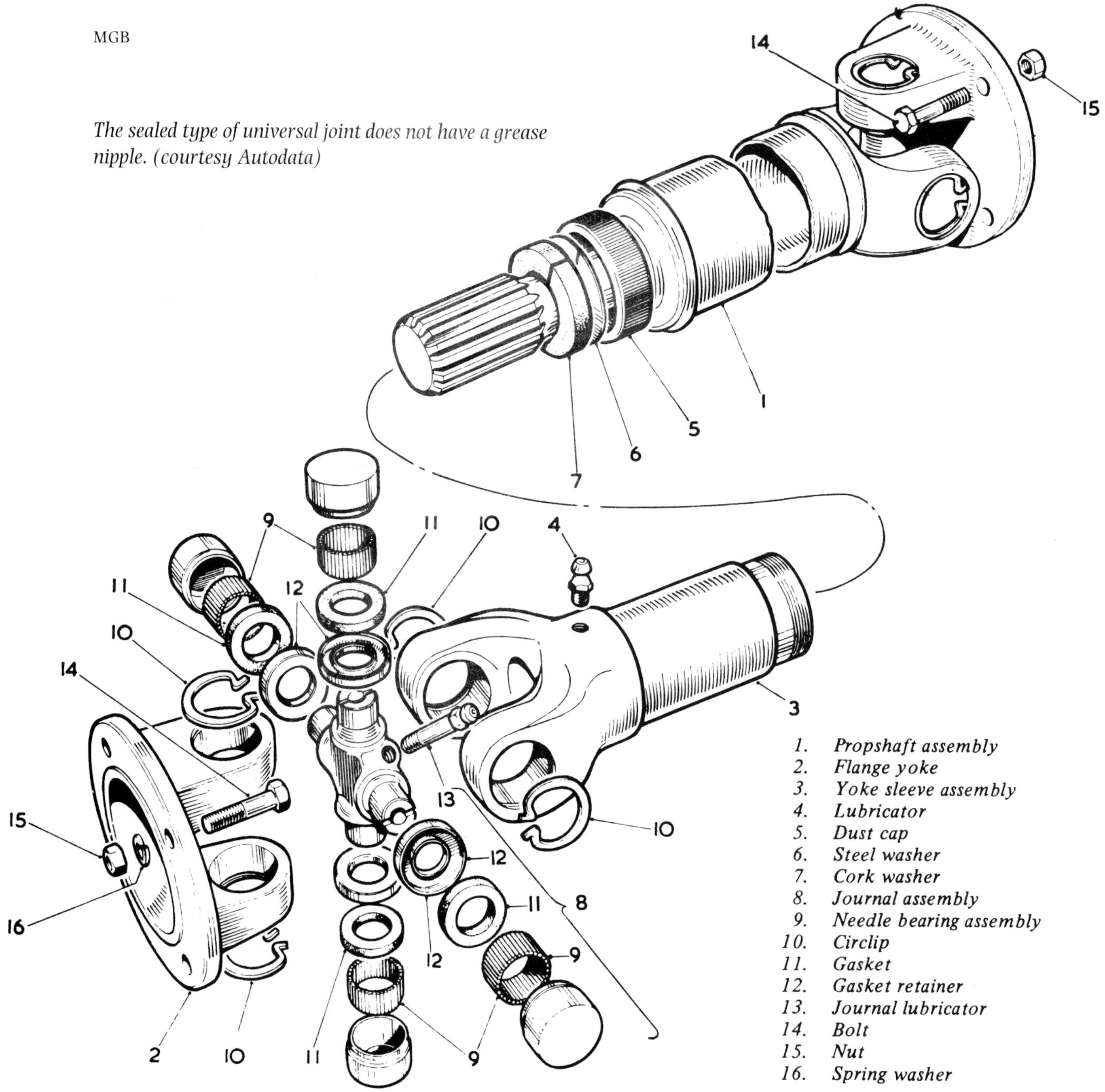

1. *Propshaft assembly*
2. *Flange yoke*
3. *Yoke sleeve assembly*
4. *Lubricator*
5. *Dust cap*
6. *Steel washer*
7. *Cork washer*
8. *Journal assembly*
9. *Needle bearing assembly*
10. *Circlip*
11. *Gasket*
12. *Gasket retainer*
13. *Journal lubricator*
14. *Bolt*
15. *Nut*
16. *Spring washer*

The propshaft components

great strains on the gearbox/overdrive and axle and be apparent from inside the car as a 'drumming' noise. It is extremely unlikely that a prop shaft would become unbalanced in normal use, but there is always the chance that a previous owner of the car removed it and refitted it incorrectly, for it must be replaced exactly the way it came off.

The second fault is a sticking and unlubricated universal joint. This will cause transmission clonks when the car is driven over bumps and pot holes, and when going from forwards to reverse (see Chapter 3, Appraising the MGB).

The worst fault that can occur is when the drive splines are damaged. In this case, a new prop shaft will have to be found. Bear in mind that several lengths of shaft are available, each of which is appropriate to a different variant of the MGB. It pays therefore to measure the shaft before removal to ensure that the correct replacement is obtained.

UNIVERSAL JOINT REPLACEMENT

TIME: 2–4 hours.

Special tools/equipment: normal tool kit.

To remove the prop shaft, chock the front wheels, take the car out of gear and release the handbrake. Jack up the rear of the car as high as is consistent with safety and support the rear axle on proper stands. The rear wheels must be off the ground.

Scribe a clear line over the two sets of mating flanges to aid accurate refitting, and then remove the
[illegible] rop shaft
[illegible] ou will
[illegible] uts. Rest
[illegible] cross-
[illegible] prop shaft
[illegible] er break
[illegible] olts which
[illegible] withdraw

[illegible] to be
[illegible] of the
[illegible] eassembled
[illegible] haft should

[illegible] yoke/
[illegible] e cleanliness
[illegible] nt roller

[illegible] t,
[illegible] se of grease
[illegible] nove the four
[illegible] Usually, the
spider and bearing cups can [illegible] be removed from the yokes, although sometimes slight assistance from a thin drift and hammer will be required. Occasionally, the roller bearings within the cups will have broken up and be jammed solid, so preventing the removal of the cups and spiders. If this is the case, then dispense with the thin drift and, holding the yoke in a strong and securely mounted vice, forcibly drift the spider out using whatever weight of drift and hammer prove necessary, brought to bear on the spider itself.

Renew the spider assembly. In the case of the sealed type (no grease nipples), first remove the bearing cups from the spider legs, taking care not to dislodge the roller bearings, which are retained by grease. Fill the spider grease holes with grease, making sure that there are no bubbles. Hold the spider in position and carefully press on each cup in turn through the yoke bearing hole. Ensure that none of the roller bearings become dislodged at this stage. It may prove necessary to use a vice and a suitably-sized socket to press the cups fully home. Refit the circlips.

With the non-sealed type, first press the gasket seals into position on the spider legs, using a suitably-sized hollow drift. Then fit the gaskets. Assemble the needle rollers in the bearing cups using grease to hold them in position. When offering the spider into the yokes, ensure that the grease nipple faces the prop shaft to give access for future maintenance lubrication. Fit the cups and circlips as before.

SUSPENSION AND STEERING

Dampers

Dampers are usually referred to in the UK as 'shock absorbers', although this term is actually a misleading misnomer. In the typical suspension system, the components which absorb shocks from bumps in the road are not the 'shock absorbers' but the springs.

After any suspension spring has been compressed by the absorption of a shock it will re-extend past its at rest length due to the energy which was imparted into it during its compression. After fully extending, it will begin to compress again, then re-extend and so on until the original energy has been dissipated. The rate of compression and extension is called the resonance of the spring, and the resonance of the spring will differ from that of the car body, which will of course rise and fall as the spring acts upon it.

The dampers are provided to damp the resonance in the road springs. If a car was driven without any dampers, then the slightest bump in the road surface, also the very process of accelerating hard or braking, would set up dangerous spring and, thus, body resonance. The effects of this are that the car is very difficult to control and dangerous to drive, because the weight falling onto each road wheel is constantly shifting from ultra-light to very heavy as the car pitches and rolls, with a consequent variation in individual tyre grip from virtually nothing to maximum.

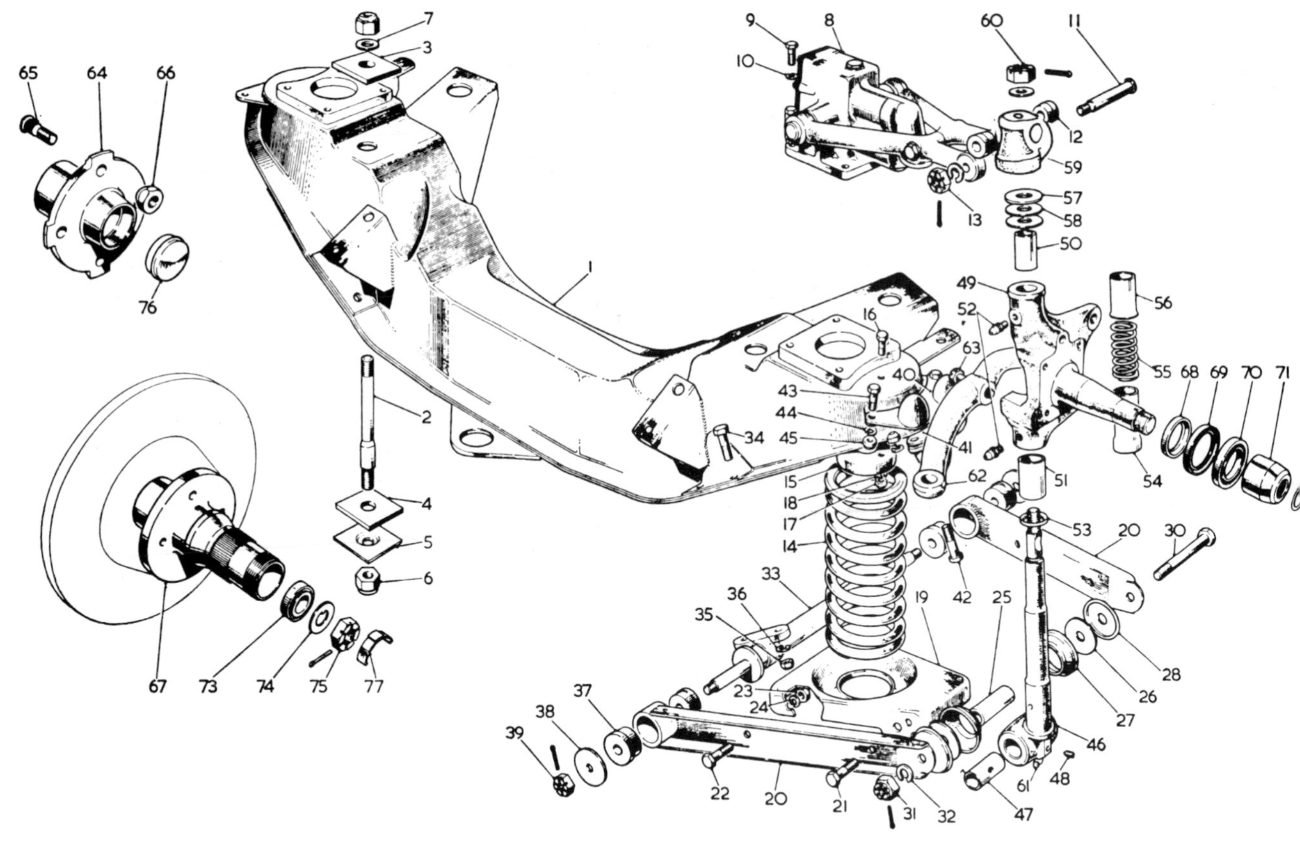

The front suspension components

1. *Crossmember*
2. *Mounting bolt*
3. *Mounting pad*
4. *Lower mounting pad (rubber)*
5. *Clamp plate*
6. *Nut*
7. *Washer*
8. *Shock absorber*
9. *Screw*
10. *Spring washer*
11. *Fulcrum pin*
12. *Link bearing*
13. *Nut*
14. *Coil spring*
15. *Spring spigot*
16. *Screw*
17. *Nut*
18. *Spring washer*
19. *Spring pan assembly*
20. *Bottom wishbone assembly*
21. *Screw*
22. *Screw*
23. *Nut*
24. *Spring washer*
25. *Link distance tube*
26. *Thrust washer*
27. *Seal*
28. *Seal support*
29. *Nut*
30. *Bolt*
31. *Nut*
32. *Spring washer*
33. *Wishbone pivot*
34. *Bolt*
35. *Nut*
36. *Spring washer*
37. *Bush*
38. *Washer*
39. *Nut*
40. *Rebound buffer*
41. *Distance piece*
42. *Bolt*
43. *Screw*
44. *Spring washer*
45. *Nut*
46. *Swivel pin*
47. *Bush*
48. *Grub screw*
49. *Swivel axle assembly*
50. *Bush*
51. *Bush*
52. *Lubricator*
53. *Cork ring*
54. *Dust excluder tube*
55. *Spring*
56. *Dust excluder tube*
57. *Thrust washer*
58. *Floating thrust washer - 0.052 to 0.057 in (1.32 to 1.44 mm)*
59. *Trunnion*
60. *Nut*
61. *Lubricator*
62. *Steering lever*
63. *Bolt*
64. *Hub assembly*
65. *Wheel stud*
66. *Stud nut*
67. *Hub assembly*
68. *Oil seal collar*
69. *Oil seal*
70. *Inner hub bearing*
71. *Bearing spacer*
72. *Shim - 0.003 in (0.76 mm)*
73. *Outer hub bearing*
74. *Washer*
75. *Nut*
76. *Grease retaining cup*
77. *Grease retaining cup*

Pictures pages 141–144: front suspension stripping. (See page 144)

With wire wheel cars, the hub nut split pin must be withdrawn through this small hole using long-nose pliers. Always replace the split pin with a new one, because it will prove far easier to remove again when the time comes. It is advisable to cover the workshop floor with newspaper or a cloth when removing the hub assembly, just in case the wheel bearing drops out. A tiny piece of grit can do more damage to the bearings than many years of normal driving, so place the hub and bearing assembly somewhere safe, such as in a sealed plastic bag.

There are several types of ball joint splitter, of which this scissors type is probably the most common and useful. It is sometimes possible to remove the track rod ends without the special tool, although it is common for the use of the tool to be absolutely necessary. When the joint breaks, there will be an almighty 'crack', which can be quite startling!

Either tie the caliper out of the way or find a stable support for it, such as the paint tin shown here.

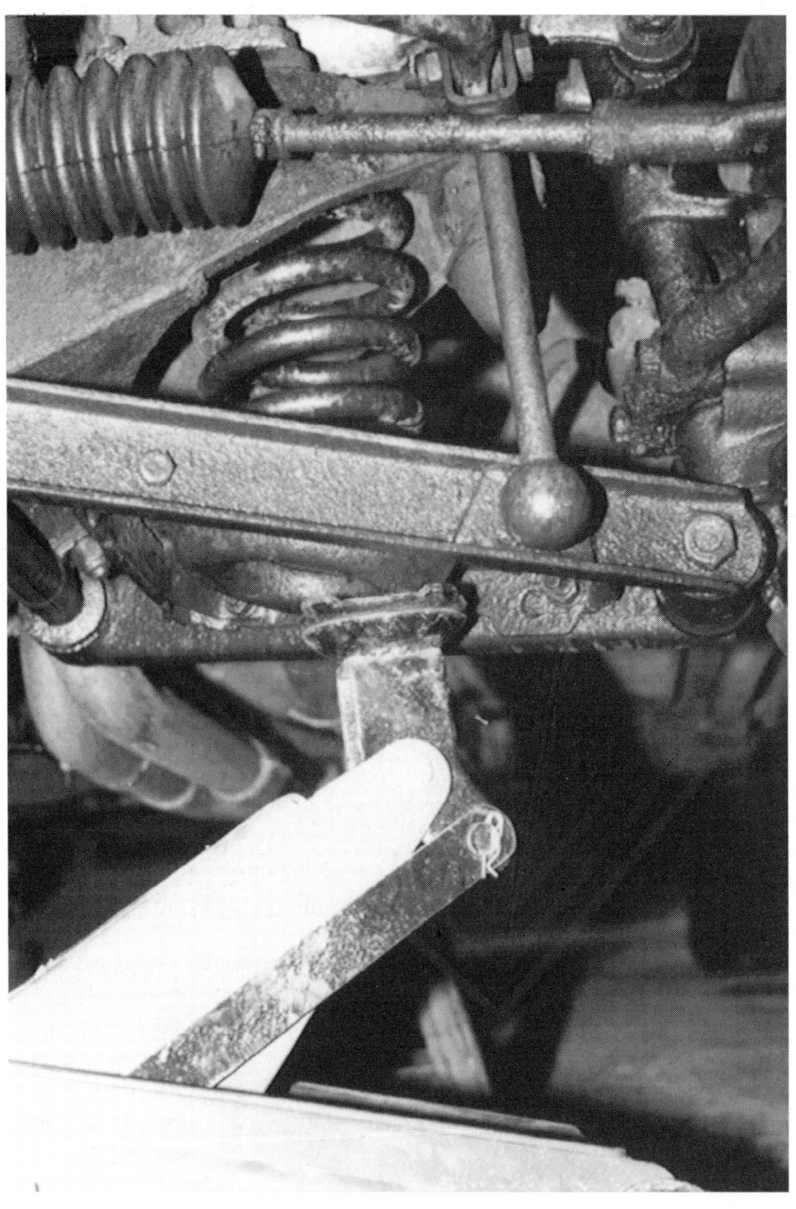

LEFT *Spot the deliberate mistake! The author, concerned with photography rather than accomplishing the suspension strip, forgot to undo the anti-roll bar drop link. This must be done before the suspension is compressed, otherwise, there will be so much pressure from the anti-roll bar that the bolt will not budge. By presenting the trolley jack from underneath the car, the author will be able to release the suspension from a position of safety away from the 'firing line' should the trolley jack slip and the suspension spring suddenly fly out.*

RIGHT *Undo the top arm fulcrum nut. The suspension is still 'safe' at this stage, as the trunnion bolt is still holding the assembly to the damper arms.*

BELOW RIGHT *When removing the trunnion bolt, try to stand to one side of the assembly, just in case anything does go wrong. If the trolley jack is at the correct height, then the bolt should drift out easily; if it sticks then slightly altering the height of the trolley jack might ease it. Kingpin fitting kits contain replacements for these and for the lower pivot bolt and its distance tube.*

It is very difficult to assess the condition of dampers properly. The unscientific and wholly unreliable method often adopted is to 'bounce' each corner of the car in turn and to note how many times the body rises and falls; movement which good dampers should suppress. In fact having good dampers is so fundamental to roadholding that if one is suspected of having even slightly reduced efficiency then it should be changed.

If dampers are deteriorating then the usual first signs are for the handling to become rather vague and for the car to seem to 'float' at speed. The full effects are not so obvious but include much reduced roadholding on bends and an increasing reduction in braking efficiency. This latter consequence of worn dampers is insidious and might not be noticed under normal braking but will become apparent in an emergency stop, increasing stopping distance greatly.

Road spring renewal should always include damper renewal, because newer and more resilient springs will require full damping power. (See Chapter 7, Modifications – handling).

Springs

The function of the springs is to absorb shocks imparted by uneven surfaces. To some extent, that is what pneumatic tyres do, because the compressed air within each tyre is in effect a small 'air spring' able to soak up some of the energy involved. In isolating the bodywork from the shocks imparted by road bumps

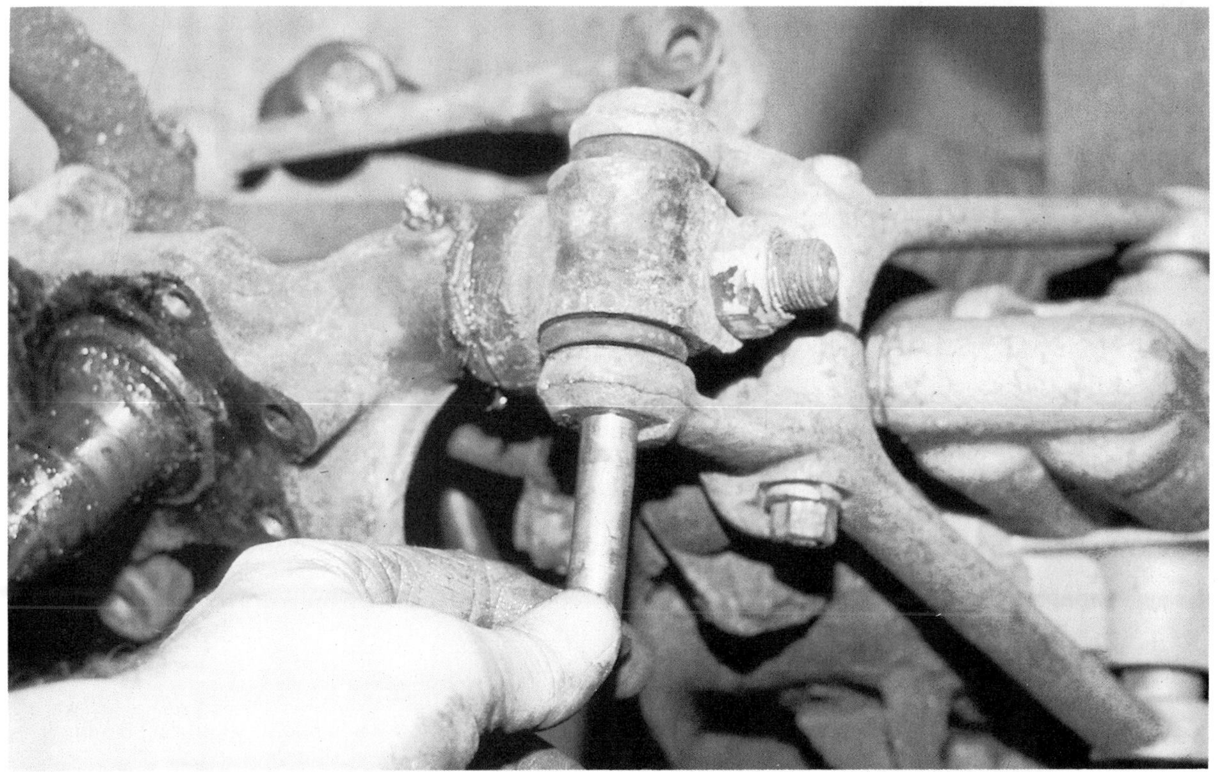

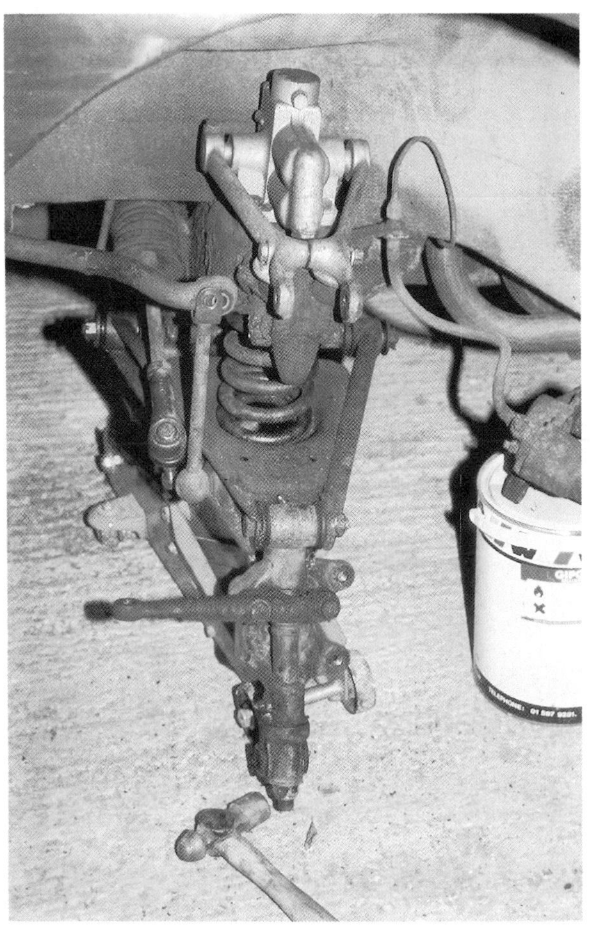

LEFT *Do not lower the trolley jack with the kingpin angled downwards, because this would force the top thread into the ground and distort it. You could remove the lower kingpin pivot bolt and then the kingpin assembly, although this can require a degree of force and could prove unsafe if the trolley jack were to slip whilst you were hammering away at the pivot bolt!*

FAR RIGHT *If, like the author, you have to work solo, then placing a block of wood as shown will guide the kingpin assembly as the spring pan is lowered. This allows you to keep out of danger's way whilst the immense pressure of the front coil spring is released. If you do not guide the kingpin at this stage, it can simply be forced into the ground. Release the spring pressure as slowly as possible, and be ready to stop immediately if anything goes wrong, such as discovering that the anti-roll bar drop link is still fastened!*

RIGHT *Ensure that all of the spring pressure has gone before trying to remove the spring. At this stage, you could remove the wishbones and spring pan to replace the bushes or to weld up the wishbone to spring pan bolt holes if they are distorted. You could replace the damper, or the kingpin assembly itself. It is not recommended that you try to repair the kingpin/swivel axle yourself; these are readily available on an exchange basis.*

and holes, powerful road springs improve ride comfort and prevent damage to the vehicle.

The front springs of the MGB are 'coil springs' which act upon the lower wishbone arm, which is able to rise and fall (the top arm is actually the damper arm). Even with the car at rest, the front springs are supporting the weight of the front end of the car including the heavy engine and therefore they contain much energy. This energy would, if permitted, cause the spring to extend violently and with great force. It is vital, therefore, that when stripping the front suspension, the energy stored within the front springs be allowed to dissipate in a controlled and safe way.

Front springs can break, in which case the failure will be immediately apparent. More usually, over an extended period of time, the springs will take a permanent set, that is, their at-rest length will be reduced because the springs have weakened. In this case, the front end of the car will be low to the ground and the tyre top to wheel arch distance will be less than normal. If the springs are allowed to become very inefficient then there is a danger that they will be unable individually to overcome the force of the anti-roll bar. If one spring is compressed by a bump in the road then the anti-roll bar will place a reduced force on the other spring; if this is inefficient the effect is to take the load off the opposite tyre, in extreme cases momentarily lifting the tyre from the surface of the road.

Front end rebuild

The front end of the car must be raised and supported on axle stands situated under the side chassis rails, and the road wheels removed. The brake calipers should be unbolted and tied out of the way so that no weight falls onto the lengths of flexible brake pipe.

Remove the track rod ends. The joints can prove difficult to part; use a ball joint splitter if possible, although hitting both sides of the steering lever end

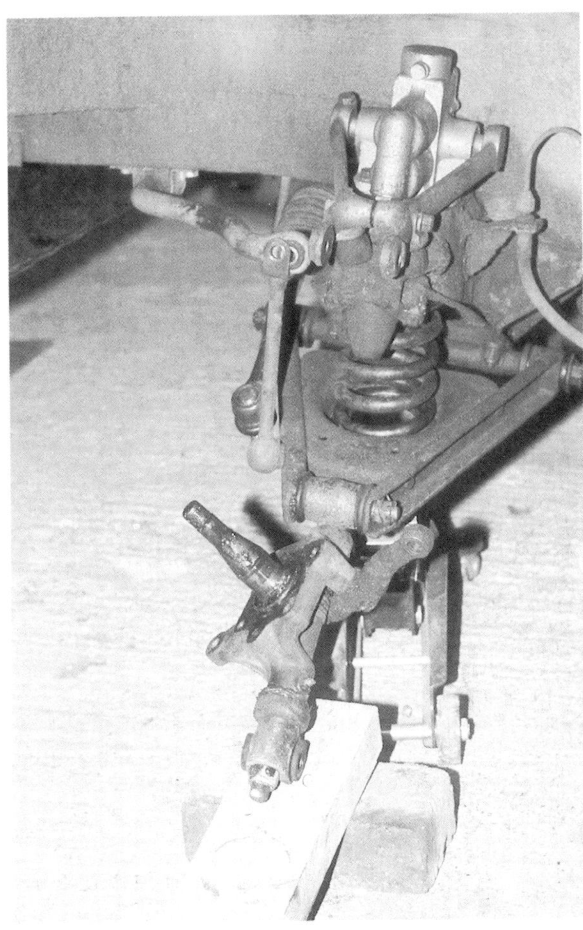

simultaneously with two hammers can sometimes distort the hole sufficiently to release the tapered shaft. Remove the nuts and bolts which secure the front anti-roll bar to the drop links.

The hub nuts can now be removed. These are large castellated nuts, secured with a split pin. On wire-wheel cars where the hub has a splined extension, the split pin is barely accessible through a small hole in the splined portion of the hub. When removing the hub assembly take care not to let the roller bearing fall onto the dirty floor! The disc dust cover and steering lever arm can now be removed.

The next stage is removal of the kingpins. During this job, the pressure of the large suspension springs must be gently released; as already stated, a special tool is available for the task, although most opt to use instead a large trolley jack. The pressure exerted by the springs is immense and, should the jack slip, is capable of releasing the spring at great speed and at great risk to people and vehicle.

The trolley jack should be placed under the spring pan, with wood between the two, and moved into position from underneath the car, so that the operator is out of the danger area should anything go wrong.

Partially compress the suspension spring but not to the extent that the car is raised in the slightest from its axle stand support. Ensure that everything is sound before proceeding further.

Slacken the nut and bolt which pull the two damper lever arms together, so that the trunnion can come out more easily. The split pin and nut should be removed from the top damper arm fulcrum bolt, and the bolt drifted out as gently as possible. The trunnion can now be removed. The whole kingpin assembly can be pivoted downwards and preferably rested against a wooden block in a horizontal attitude.

Clear all spectators out of the way and, from a position of safety, release the trolley jack as slowly as possible, allowing it to push the spring pan assembly downwards. If the kingpin assembly shows any signs of becoming jammed then raise the spring pan slightly, adjust the position of the kingpin and begin releasing the pressure again. Remove the road springs, check their length and renew if necessary.

The lower kingpin pivot bolt can now be removed, the damper unbolted and lifted out. The lower kingpin pivot bolt passes through a distance tube into which it will often be found to have seized.

It is as well to recondition or replace all of the wearing suspension components at once, if only to save having to do a complete strip-down at a later date if another component fails. The swivel hub can be overhauled by the insertion of new bushes followed by line-reaming to size to fit the new kingpins. The rather easier option is to use a reconditioned and rebuilt assembly, along with new bushes and fixings all round; these are available as a complete kit.

The spring pan assembly should be removed from the cross-member in order to replace wishbone bushes. The wishbone arms can be unbolted from the spring pan and the bushes removed: many people replace the standard items with the sturdier and longer-lived versions fitted to the V8 version of the car. If the wishbone arms have distorted holes at their ends or if the spring pan is weakened through corrosion then it is best to replace both.

Reassembly is very much the opposite of stripping, with an equal accent on safety whilst the springs are being compressed. Some of the rubber components are very difficult to fit, but a little lubrication with ordinary domestic soap eases matters greatly. It is also as well to slacken off the bolt which pinches the bifurcated damper arms before attempting to fit the kingpin trunnion, and sometimes the damper arms have to be physically prized open. Tighten all nuts to the recommended torque, and check these again after the car has been driven for a few miles.

Rear suspension

The rear springs are 'leaf springs'; that is, they are composed of flat-section leaves, held together by steel straps. It is important when replacing rear springs that a spring be used that has the correct number of leaves for the year and type of MGB be used. This varies essentially according to the different weights to be supported and the different engine power levels involved.

The rear leaf springs combine several functions. They support the rear bodywork, they absorb shocks from the road, they locate the axle transversely (and keep it square to the car) and they – to a degree – help to damp the tendency for the axle to twist and tramp under power.

Wear in or damage to the rear springs is usually made apparent by a reduction in the tyre top to wheel arch distance. Other problems associated with the rear springs include poor axle grip by the U-bolts (car veers to one side on acceleration and to the other on deceleration) and various 'clonks' from worn mounting bushes.

Rear spring removal is best approached one side at a time, and spring renewal should be combined with damper renewal so that both start at maximum efficiency. When the spring and damper are removed, the opportunity should be taken to probe thoroughly the chassis rails and especially the spring mounting points for rust. If any weakness is apparent or suspected, the best action is to strip down the rear end completely (especially the fuel tank, pipe and pump) and to rebuild it.

Rear suspension overhaul

Chock the front wheels, loosen the road wheel nuts, raise the car and support it on axle stands located under the forward extensions of the front leaf spring fixing brackets. Remove the road wheels and, with the trolley jack under the differential housing, raise the axle to the 'on-road' position. If the axle is to be removed, disconnect the handbrake cable assembly and the brake pipes at the 'T' connector (blocking off the main feed pipe); undo the nuts and bolts through the prop shaft/differential flanges; remove the dampers and the rebound straps (these can be cut

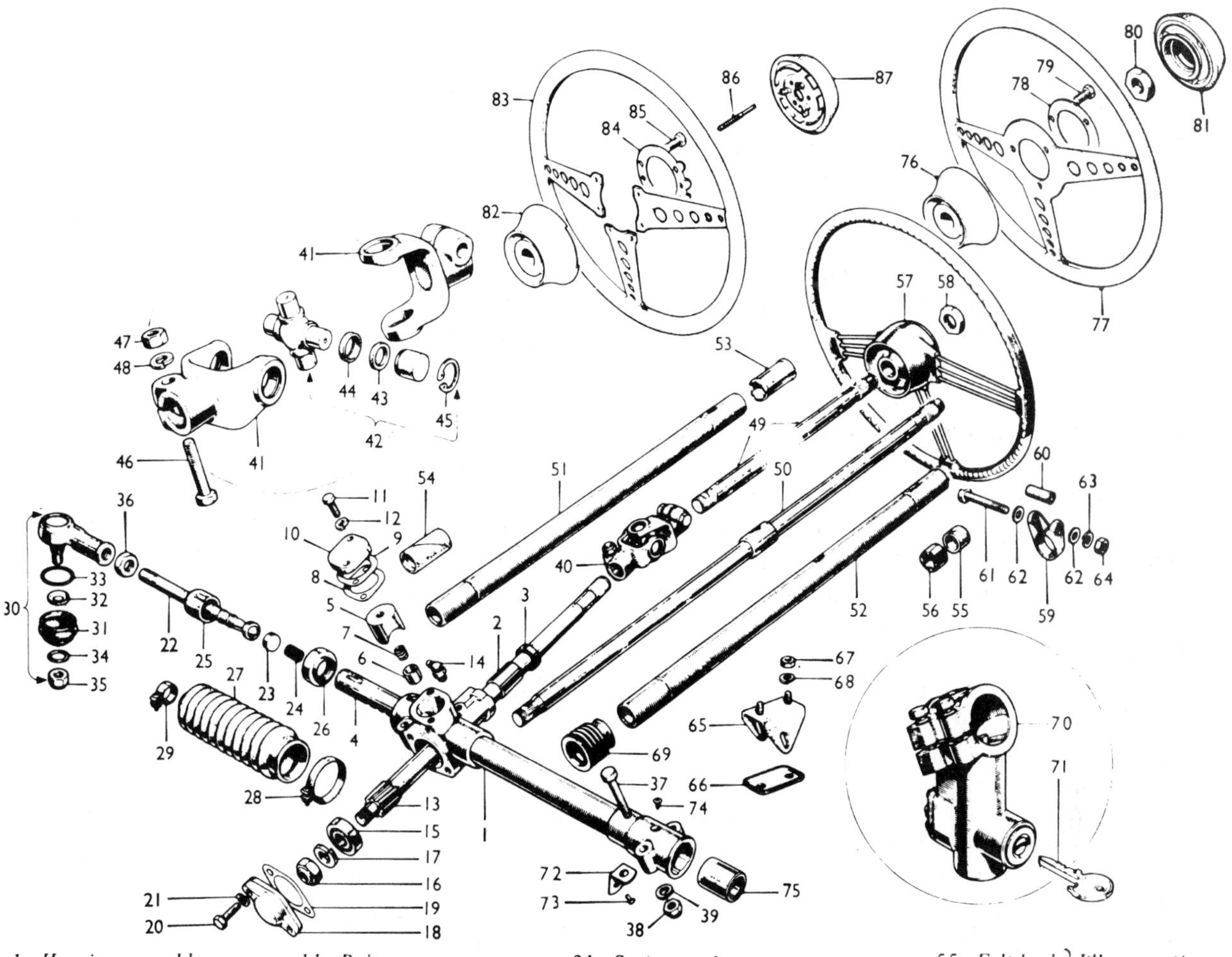

1. *Housing assembly*
2. *Pinion bush*
3. *Oil seal*
4. *Rack*
5. *Rack support yoke*
6. *Damper pad*
7. *Damper pad spring*
8. *Cover plate shim*
9. *Cover plate joint*
10. *Yoke cover plate*
11. *Bolt*
12. *Spring washer*
13. *Pinion*
14. *Lubricator*
15. *Pinion bearing*
16. *Nut*
17. *Spring washer*
18. *End cover*
19. *End cover joint*
20. *Bolt*
21. *Spring washer*
22. *Tie rod*
23. *Ball seat*
24. *Spring*
25. *Ball housing*
26. *Locknut*
27. *Rubber gaiter*
28. *Gaiter clip*
29. *Gaiter clip*
30. *Ball joint assembly*
31. *Rubber boot*
32. *Boot retainer*
33. *Spring*
34. *Washer*
35. *Nut*
36. *Locknut*
37. *Bolt*
38. *Nut*
39. *Spring washer*
40. *Universal joint*
41. *Yoke*
42. *Journal assembly*
43. *Journal joint*
44. *Retainer*
45. *Circlip*
46. *Bolt*
47. *Nut*
48. *Spring washer*
49. *Inner column assembly*
50. *Inner column assembly (RHD)*
51. *Outer tube*
52. *Outer tube (RHD)*
53. *Bearing*
54. *Bearing*
55. *Felt bush* } *When steering lock fitted*
56. *Clip* }
57. *Steering wheel*
58. *Nut*
59. *Column clamp*
60. *Distance piece*
61. *Bolt*
62. *Spring washer*
64. *Nut*
65. *Column bracket*
66. *Plate*
67. *Nut*
68. *Spring washer*
69. *Draught excluder*
70. *Lock assembly*
71. *Key*
72. *Shim*
73. *Rivet*
74. *Screw*
75. *Bush (GHN5/GHD5 cars only)*
76. *Wheel hub*
77. *Steering wheel*
78. *Lock ring*
79. *Screw*
80. *Nut*
81. *Motif and housing*
82. *Wheel hub*
83. *Steering wheel*
84. *Lock ring*
85. *Bolt*
86. *Horn push contact*
87. *Horn push*
88. *Steering column* } *From car No. 258001*
89. *Sealing tube* }

Steering rack components

LEFT *When raising the rear of the car to work on the suspension, position axle stands underneath the forward end of the front spring hanger, preferably with wood chocking in place to prevent distorting the two runners. Always fully chock the front wheels (front, rear and sides) to prevent the car from moving and toppling the axle stands.*

ABOVE LEFT *The MGC's torsion bars act directly on the lower suspension member at the front.*

LEFT *At the other end, the torsion bar is held by this bracket. The forces acting against this are so great that the MGC had to be fitted with a massive cross-member and large members to take the place of the side chassis rails. The floor is stepped to allow room for the cross-member, and hence standard MGB floor pans will not fit the MGC, although they are used in the MGC after being heavily tailored and added to. The suspension is adjustable, and also offers the benefit of telescopic dampers at the front.*

ABOVE *This photograph highlights just how great the differences are between the MGB and the MGC. The special cross-member is physically joined to the side chassis rails and the large engine mountings are welded onto it. The assembly also houses the mounting for the top (telescopic) damper fitting.*

through if they are to be replaced); detach the two rear spring fixing shackle plates; and lower the axle to the ground – pivoting it on the front spring bolts – by lowering the jack.

The front spring fixing bolts can now be removed and the entire assembly withdrawn.

To remove the springs and dampers only, support the axle in the 'on-road' position. Disconnect the damper arms from their drop links, remove the four self-locking nuts from each bottom spring plate. Remove the rear shackle plates in turn and lower the springs to the ground. The two front eyebolts can now be removed and the springs withdrawn.

The two nuts and bolts passing through each damper unit can now be removed and the dampers withdrawn. The lever arm dampers, both standard and uprated, are available on an exchange basis, although telescopic dampers can be fitted using special kits and are preferred by many; also offering the option of adjustable damping levels for differing conditions (see Chapter 6 Modifications).

Reassembly is the opposite of stripping. It is worth pointing out that stripping the rear suspension and especially the suspension and axle gives an ideal opportunity to go that little bit further, by removing the fuel tank, pipe and pump and cleaning, painting and re-undersealing the entire rear underbody area.

Steering

Although repairs are possible, faults with the rack and pinion steering of the MGB are usually rectified by replacement of the unit with a reconditioned one.

To remove the steering rack, first chock the rear wheels and jack and support the front of the car at a comfortable working height. Remove the road wheels then the track rod ends as detailed previously.

Turn the steering wheel to full lock (left on RHD cars and right on LHD cars). Undo the lower end of the steering column universal joint, then the four bolts which hold the rack to the cross-member. Take care not to lose any shims, and remember where any shims are fitted, because they will have to be refitted into the same positions to maintain correct alignment of the rack.

MGC front suspension

The 2912cc six-cylinder 'C' series engine fitted in the MGC is a very deep unit, and in order to shoehorn it into the available engine bay depth the designers did away with the main cross-member which, on the MGB, holds the front suspension. An alternative suspension, based on torsion bars, was fitted.

A torsion bar is quite simply a length of spring steel rod, which absorbs shocks through a twisting action. It is adjustable from the rear of the main cross-member.

THE COOLING SYSTEM

Petrol engines waste a large proportion of the energy that is produced when the petrol mixture is burnt. Some energy is lost to friction within the engine and drive train, which manifests itself as heat, but the single greatest energy loss is through heat wasted directly in the combustion process.

The heat lost in the combustion process is so great that unless some means of dissipating it is used, the engine would overheat in a matter of moments and be destroyed.

Removing the thermostat housing. Always replace the gasket when refitting.

Some engines are cooled only by a flow of air past them, the heat being dissipated by cylinder fins, as commonly seen on motorcycle cylinders, often assisted by a fan and ducting. Most car engines are cooled to a very small extent by a flow of air past the block but mainly by a liquid coolant (water and anti-freeze) which circulates through galleries within the engine and then through a radiator. The flow of air through the radiator cools, in turn, the coolant.

A fan, which is mechanically driven on earlier MGBs but electrically driven on later models, assists in drawing air through the radiator.

Although too great an operating heat level can destroy an engine, too low a temperature will not permit the engine to operate efficiently. When an engine starts up from cold the coolant is prevented from passing into the radiator by a thermostat (until its temperature has reached a predetermined level), which is a simple temperature-sensitive valve. As soon as the coolant reaches the required temperature (around 160°F) then the thermostat opens and allows the coolant into the radiator. The coolant is forced around this system by a pump which is driven, together with the dynamo/alternator, by the fan belt.

The coolant also provides the heat for the car internal heater, which consists of a small radiator

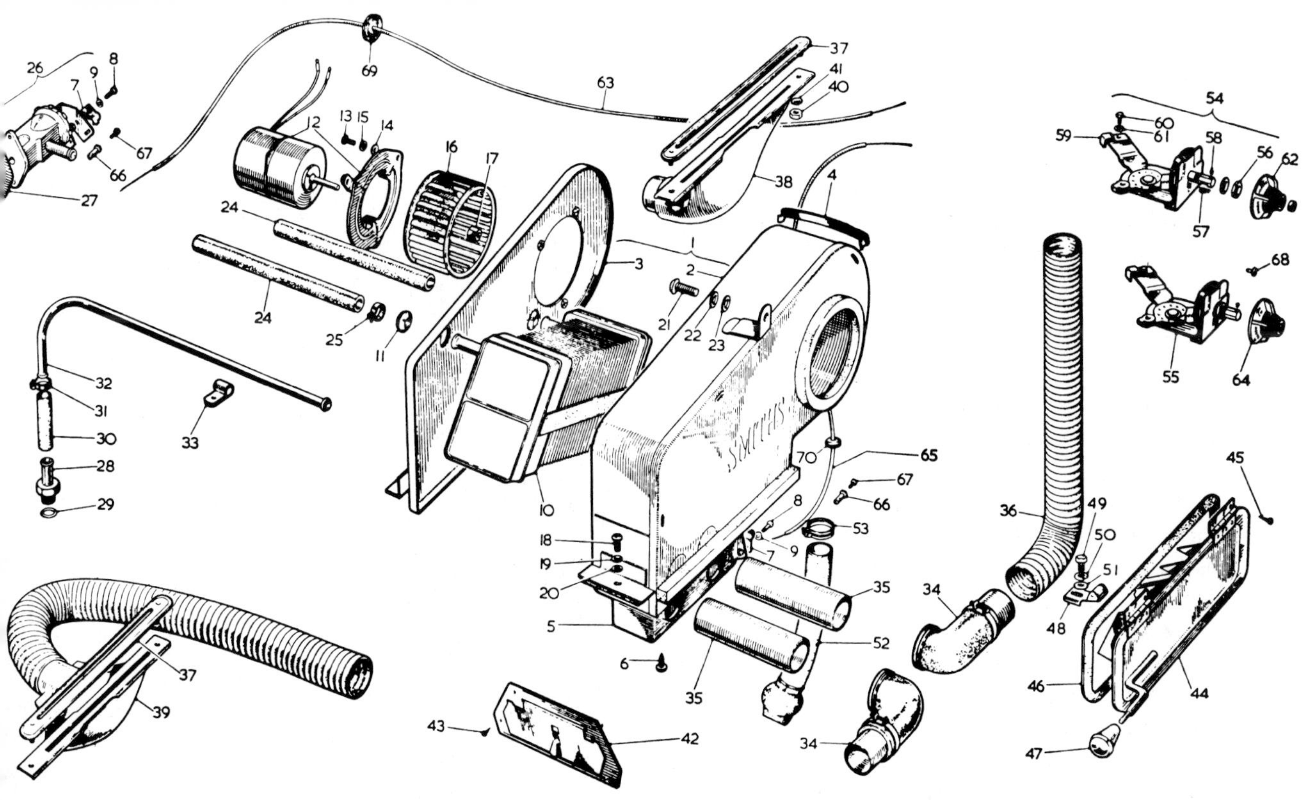

The heater components (early cars)

1. *Heater assembly*
2. *Cover*
3. *Cover*
4. *Cover clip*
5. *Outlet duct*
6. *Screw*
7. *Cable clamp*
8. *Screw*
9. *Shakeproof washer*
10. *Radiator*
11. *Washer*
12. *Motor and mounting plate*
13. *Screw*
14. *Washer*
15. *Spring washer*
16. *Runner*
17. *Collet*
18. *Screw*
19. *Washer*
20. *Spring washer*
21. *Screw*
22. *Washer*
23. *Spring washer*
24. *Hose*
25. *Hose clip*
26. *Water valve*
27. *Gasket*
28. *Water union*
29. *Washer*
30. *Hose*
31. *Hose clip*
32. *Return pipe*
33. *Inlet manifold clip*
34. *Demister elbow*
35. *Connector tube*
36. *Demister hose*
37. *Demister escutcheon*
38. *Demister nozzle*
39. *Demister nozzle*
40. *Nut*
41. *Spring washer*
42. *Heater outlet flap*
43. *Screw*
44. *Fresh air vent*
45. *Screw*
46. *Seal*
47. *Knob*
48. *Vent spring*
49. *Screw*
50. *Spring washer*
51. *Washer*
52. *Drain tube*
53. *Tube clip*
54. *Heat control*
55. *Air control*
56. *Locking nut*
57. *Knob clip*
58. *Knob pin*
59. *Cable clamp*
60. *Screw*
61. *Spring washer*
62. *Heat knob*
63. *Heat control cable*
64. *Air knob*
65. *Air control cable*
66. *Trunnion*
67. *Screw*
68. *Rivet*
69. *Grommet*
70. *Grommet*

which dissipates the heat from the coolant into the car. Use of the heater thus increases the overall cooling effect on the engine coolant, and switching on the heater can sometimes offer a useful 'get-you-home' ploy in cases of mild engine overheating.

In winter, water can freeze solid and, in doing so, expand. If pure water were to be used as a car engine coolant then such expansion would (and does) crack the metal of the cylinder head and block. Because of this, an anti-freeze is added to the water in a sufficiently strong concentration to prevent freezing at likely winter temperatures.

Restoration

From the restoration viewpoint, the cooling system comprises components which are simply replaced when necessary by new or reconditioned ones.

As a matter of course, rubber hoses would normally be replaced during a restoration, as would the thermostat. This is housed at the front of the cylinder head, and access is through a casting secured by three nuts. To change the thermostat (do not do this if the coolant is still hot), drain the cooling system then slacken each of the three nuts by equal amounts. Lift the thermostat housing clear and

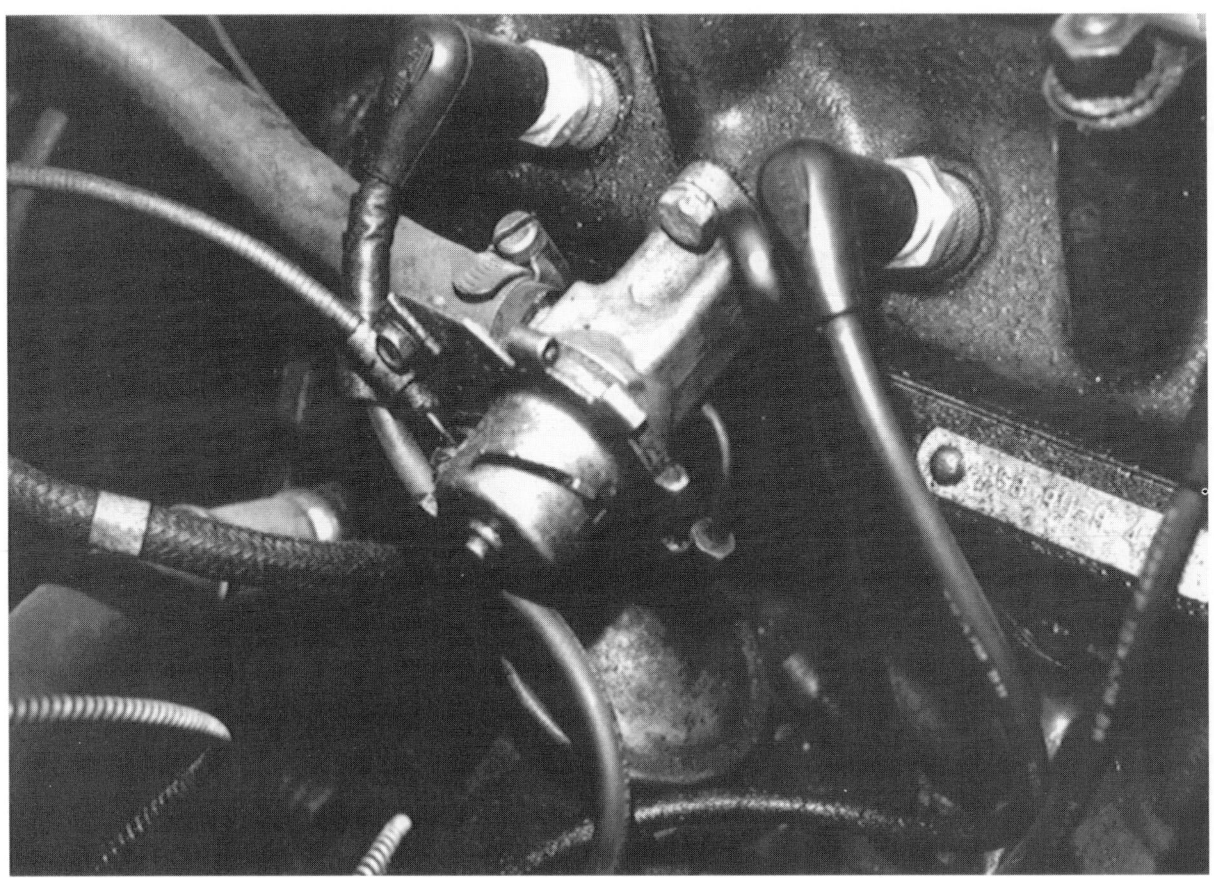

The heater valve assembly is inexpensive, so if any faults develop with it then simply replace it. Poor heater performance can be due to a previous owner fitting the unit using sealant, some types of which can melt at high temperatures and partially block the unit. Use a new gasket when refitting. The valve can become too stiff to operate through old age, although such problems are more usually due to the operating cable.

remove the thermostat. This can be checked for correct functioning by lowering it into heated water and noting whether it opens; in practice, the units cost very little and are best replaced periodically. When refitting the thermostat, always use a new gasket.

The ratings of the thermostat (temperature) and radiator cap (pressure) must be balanced and in accordance with the engine type and operating environment. If a too-highly rated thermostat allows the water to become too hot, it will generate too high a pressure within the cooling system and so permit some of the pressurised coolant to escape through the radiator cap.

The heater unit contains a small radiator (the matrix) which can in time become partially blocked, which reduces the efficiency of the unit. In this instance, replacement with a new element is the best cure. Disconnect the batteries and drain the coolant system. Remove the heater motor wires, loosen the jubilee clips and remove the heater hoses. Remove the overdrive vacuum switch (early cars). Remove the screws which hold the unit to the bulkhead then, from inside the car, move the centre console (or speaker panel) to gain better access and unscrew the demister tube clip screws then the demister tubes. Remove the temperature control cable and slacken the air control cable clip then remove the cable. The heater unit can be withdrawn.

The heater unit is held together by three clips. When the unit is opened, the matrix can be withdrawn.

The heater valve allows water from the cylinder head to be fed into the heater unit. These valves and their operating cables both deteriorate with age, becoming too stiff to operate. The valve itself can also become blocked, and it can be the cause of coolant loss. All are dealt with by replacement of the unit. Do not use sealant when fitting a valve, because the hot coolant can melt this, so that it clogs up the system.

RADIATOR

The main radiator can become partially blocked. This can sometimes be established by noting cooler areas on its front surface. Proprietary fluids are available to flush the system; alternatively, the radiator can be desoldered, cleaned and reassembled, although this is usually a job for professionals.

Radiator leaks can be dealt with temporarily by a range of products, although it is recommended that a permanent repair is effected during restoration by replacing the unit with a reconditioned one.

ELECTRICAL SYSTEM

There is a fundamental difference between mechanical and electrical components: before a mechanical component fails, it will very often give warning signs of impending failure such as an unfamiliar noise, a drop in oil pressure or a rise in temperature; when an electrical component fails it is usually without any warning.

The consequences of sudden failure of an electrical component can be severe, jeopardising the vehicle and its occupants. A lighting or ignition system breakdown on a crowded motorway at night presents immediate and obvious dangers. An insulation breakdown in the permanent-live circuits can cause a fire, perhaps in an inaccessible area such as behind the dashboard, which can fill the car with choking fumes in seconds, or ignite upholstery, sound-proofing materials or petrol.

It is essential, therefore, that the electrical circuits and components are checked quite regularly for adequate standards of insulation. Wires should be checked for insulation damage including cuts, crushing or abrasions; terminals and in-line connections should be regularly checked to ensure that they are not vibrating apart or being pulled apart. A set of spare light bulbs and fuses should always be carried.

The following notes on safety are written for those with little or no understanding of electrics. When a wire shorts to earth (a short-circuit is a direct connection which has no resistive load and hence allows maximum current flow), the battery discharges at its maximum amperage (current) rate through the wire. The resultant wattage (energy) passing through the wire is far higher than it is able to tolerate . If a fuse is in place, the fuse will melt, interrupting the circuit, thus rendering it safe until a repair can be made. Where a fuse is not fitted, the wire will quickly become hot, the temperature rising until, at a particular hot-spot in the wire's length, the wire will burn through. In the meantime the insulation will have melted, possibly catching fire, which can spread.

An electrical fire can start just about anywhere on the car. If it starts near a fuel line or the petrol tank then the results can be explosive. If an electrical fire begins behind the dashboard then the car can be full of choking fumes within a very short while.

No matter how strong the desire to make a car absolutely original, there is a strong case for fitting a battery isolation switch, which can be reached from the driver's seat and which can be operated immediately to disconnect the battery should there be any sign of an electrical fire. Such switches are widely available. A switch of this type cannot be operated accidentally because it must be lifted and twisted simultaneously in order to disconnect the battery. A battery isolation switch will usually come complete with suitable wiring and fitting instructions; if not, it is as well to buy from a company which can carry out the fitting or at the very least make up suitable lengths of wiring and advise on the fitting.

Electrical power is generated either by a dynamo (cars to 1967) or an alternator (cars 1967 onwards), and stored in the battery for use in starting the car and in making up any shortfall when demand outstrips supply (if almost all devices are simultaneously switched on). The dynamo wires run to the control box (voltage regulator) and then to the starter solenoid; the alternator wires run directly to the starter solenoid. A solenoid is an electro-mechanical switch that uses a small current from the ignition switch to bring together the points of a heavy-duty switch. In this case they complete a circuit with a much more powerful current which is sufficient to turn the starter motor.

Component repair and replacement

The Lucas components used across the entire MGB range – which include the dynamo/alternator, switches and relays and the ignition system -- can still be obtained either brand-new or, in the case of larger items such as the starter motor and generator, on an exchange basis as fully reconditioned and

ABOVE *The dynamo fitted to earlier cars does not generate so much electricity as the later alternator, and if you are in the habit of driving the car with all electrical accessories switched on simultaneously, the dynamo might not be able to keep pace with demand.*

RIGHT *The alternator was fitted to all negative earthed cars and should easily supply sufficient charge to handle normal electrical accessories without draining the battery.*

guaranteed units. There cannot, therefore, be any legitimate reason for attempting DIY repairs to any of these components, bearing in mind that a poor DIY repair to an electrical component can fail and at best leave car and driver stranded and at worst cause an electrical fire which could be terminal for both car and driver.

Many of the car's electrical circuits are fused. A fuse is a thin strand of wire which has no insulation and which is of a specific thickness and material specification. It will melt at a precise temperature if the electrical energy that passes through it exceeds a predetermined level. Fuses are rated according to the current that they can carry, and their job is to protect wiring and electrical components from damage due to too-high electrical energy. If a fuse 'blows' then there will be a reason, and on no account should the blown fuse be renewed until the fault has been found and rectified. A blown fuse should *never* be replaced with one of higher rating, or with such things as bits of metal foil, old nails, etc.

Battery

The battery must be firmly clamped into position within its compartment. Any potential for movement is an MOT failure point. Also, spilled battery acid will quickly destroy paintwork and corrode metal.

The battery installation (which consists of either a single 12-volt or two 6-volt lead/acid batteries) is situated under the rear seat (GT) or behind the seats (Roadster). A battery should require little in the way of maintenance, but checks should be carried out regularly at the recommended frequency. The level of the electrolyte (fluid) should be periodically checked and maintained (using only distilled water) at a height of 1/4in above the lead plates. Every three to six months the battery can be removed, disconnecting first the earthed then the live side, and the specific gravity (SG) of the electrolyte checked using a hydrometer. This should range between 1.210 and 1.290 for a fully charged battery and 1.050 and 1.130 for a fully discharged one. In temperatures over 27°C the readings should be at the lower end of these ranges and at temperatures under 27°C they should be towards the upper end.

If variations in the SG are noted between the cells then either a plate will have buckled and the battery will soon fail, or the electrolyte in the low reading cells contains too high a concentration of distilled water. In this case, some can be siphoned off and replaced with fresh electrolyte, which is readily obtainable from garages.

If the car is used only for short trips or in conditions of high current drain then the battery can need recharging from time to time. It is recommended that the battery be charged at the lowest possible rate of amperage (current) and that 'boost' chargers are not used, because frequent use of too rapid a charge rate can cause damage to the battery.

When the battery is removed from the car, clean the terminals and cover them with a thin layer of petroleum jelly or lanoline; also, inspect the battery for cracks or leakage and the battery compartment for corrosion.

One terminal of the battery is earthed (connected to the car's bodyshell) and the other is connected by a thick wire to the starter solenoid. Early cars had a positive earth, which can complicate the fitting of certain electrical accessories.

The loom

The wires which carry electrical energy via fuses and switches to most of electrical components are contained tightly-bound within the loom. The wires are colour-coded so that they can be traced easily and compared with colour-coded wiring diagrams. Also some colours are used widely to denote certain functions. Brown, for instance, signifies that a wire is permanently live and can well be independent of any fuse. All black wires run to earth, and red wires are usually found in circuits which operate independently of the ignition switch, such as parking light circuits.

In many examples of the MGB it will be discovered that previous owners have run wires of inappropriate colour, sometimes to bypass a length of damaged wire and sometimes when fitting an electrical accessory. Such wires should be replaced with others of the correct colour, so that future problems can be traced more easily.

If a car has too many lengths of inappropriate wire or if the loom itself shows signs of damage, then it will be worth replacing the loom. These are widely available for all years and models of the MGB. The early braid looms are still available, although some MGB spares stockists can only supply PVC varieties.

Dealing with electrical faults

Electrical faults never 'cure' themselves, and intermittent faults which can appear to correct themselves are bound to re-emerge, possibly at such a time that they present a danger. eg lights going off at night. Even more importantly, an apparently inconsequential intermittent fault can, in fact, be a symptom of a far more serious fault, such as a loose spade connector on a permanent-live and non-fused brown wire which, if allowed to fall away and come into contact with the bodywork (earth) could cause a fire within seconds.

ALWAYS trace and rectify electrical faults as soon as they become apparent. If for any reason you are unable immediately to tend to an apparent fault then at the very least you should note down the exact nature of the fault and the circumstances in which it occurred (ie which devices were in use at the time, whether it was raining, etc).

THINK SAFETY. Always begin by disconnecting the battery. Check the relevant fuse to see whether it is either blown or heat-discoloured, in which case too high a current has passed through it. Remember at this stage that a blown fuse is not a fault but a symptom of one; do not merely replace a blown fuse without locating the real fault.

You will require a circuit testing device, which could range from a multi-meter down to a small battery, bulb and crocodile clip tester.

The first step is to identify the components associated with the fault, which in addition to the component in which the fault is apparent (ie, wiper motor, light bulb etc) might include a switch or switches, fuse, relay and wires, and which can be traced via the circuit diagram. Locate each component in turn and ensure that it is the correct one for your particular car; a previous owner might well have substituted an almost identical alternative which can have different connectors.

On the wiring diagram, back-trace the wires which lead from the faulty unit through any switches or relays to the power source. It is often helpful at this stage to make a small simplified sketch of the circuit, clearly marked with relevant details, such as wire colours, terminal numbers and so on. This will be far easier to work with than a full wiring diagram. Check that the wires of the correct colour are actually fitted to the power source, switch, earth, etc.

Remember that one side of the battery is earthed, that is, it is connected to the bodyshell of the car. One side of any electrical unit can also be earthed, so that the bodyshell acts in effect as a length of wire between the two. This reduces the amount of cabling in comparison with that needed in GRP-bodied cars, but it also increases the chances of a short-to-earth fault occurring, because any live wire or connector which comes into contact with any part of the bodywork will cause a short-circuit which allows the battery to discharge at its maximum rate (until the wire actually melts). In order to stress the dangers of accidentally shorting a live wire to earth it only needs to be stated that maximum battery discharge involves more than sufficient power to turn the starter motor with the car in gear; in other words, enough power to move the car.

Think logically. If a unit fails to operate and a fuse is not blown somewhere within its operating circuit, then either there is an open-circuit (poor or total disconnection) in the power feed, or the earth connection is suspect. Check the earth first, and if this proves sound then use the circuit tester to check continuity between the various elements in the circuit back to the main power feed. Check also that the relevant switch is operating properly, using the circuit tester. If no faults in the circuit are apparent then the unit is faulty.

If a unit fails to operate and an in-line fuse is found to have blown, then there will be a short to earth somewhere in the wiring or the unit itself. Isolate each section of wiring and each electrical component in turn and use the circuit tester, with one terminal earthed, to check for a short circuit. If none is found then the fault could lie with the component itself, or there could be an intermittent earth problem somewhere within the circuit.

If in doubt, always consult an auto-electrician.

Fitting a loom

This can be a tricky and sometimes frustrating job with the potential – should you get your wires crossed, in a manner of speaking – for disaster, resulting in damage to your new loom or a fire.

Before touching the existing loom, lay the new loom out along the floor or on a table surface next to the car, so that the front lights, rear lights and dashboard wires are all adjacent to their corresponding areas.

Using a wiring diagram and making comparisons with the wire colours of the existing loom, note and label each terminal on the new loom; a ballpoint or fine felt pen and masking tape are ideal for this purpose. Do not proceed further until every single connector on the new loom is thus labelled and double-checked; if you have been given an incorrect loom by mistake, then it is better to discover so before it is half fitted!

If your car is fitted with an overdrive then you will also need the smaller separate overdrive loom.

Disconnect the battery(ies). Cut the old loom out, leaving a short length of wire on every terminal to

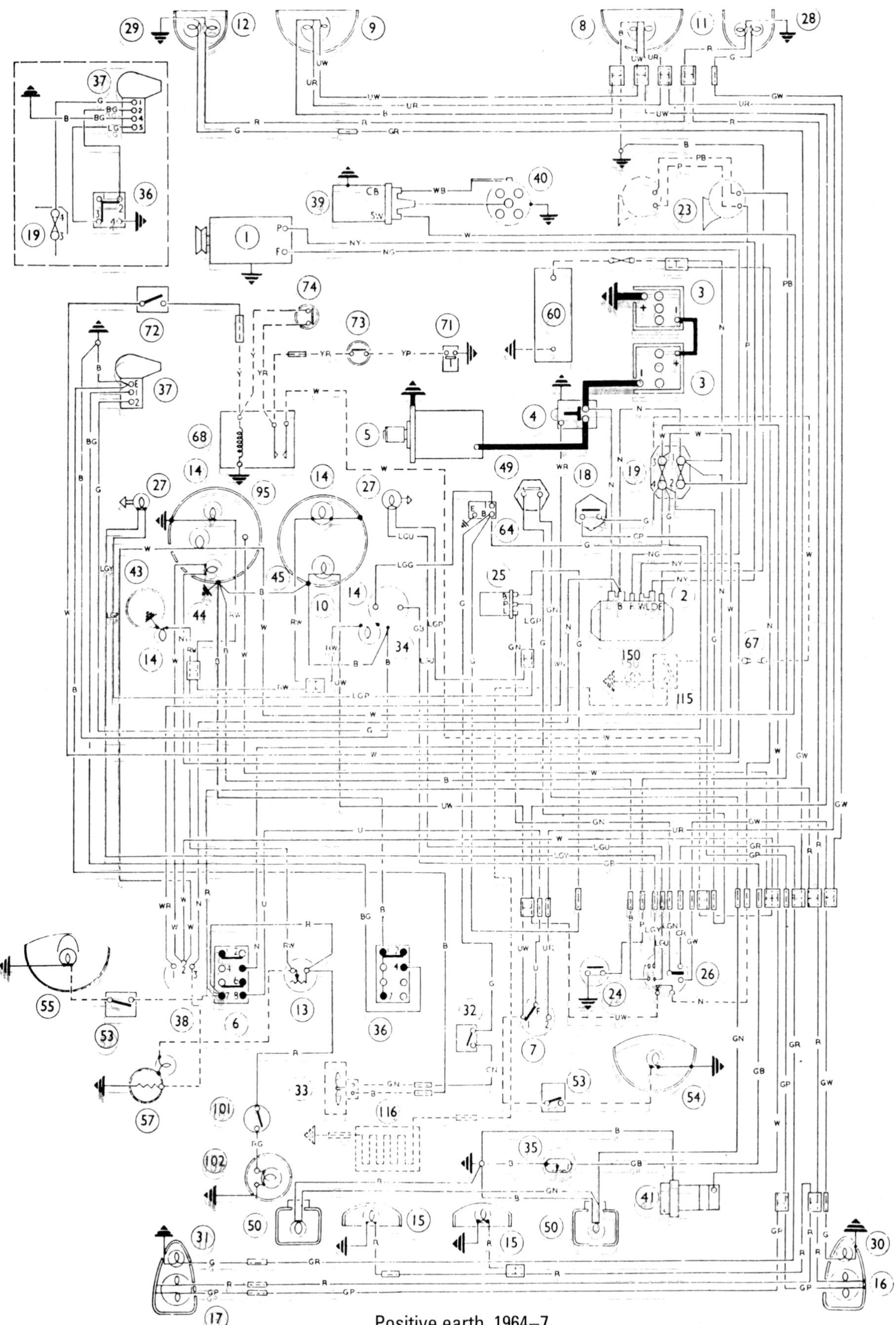

Positive earth, 1964–7

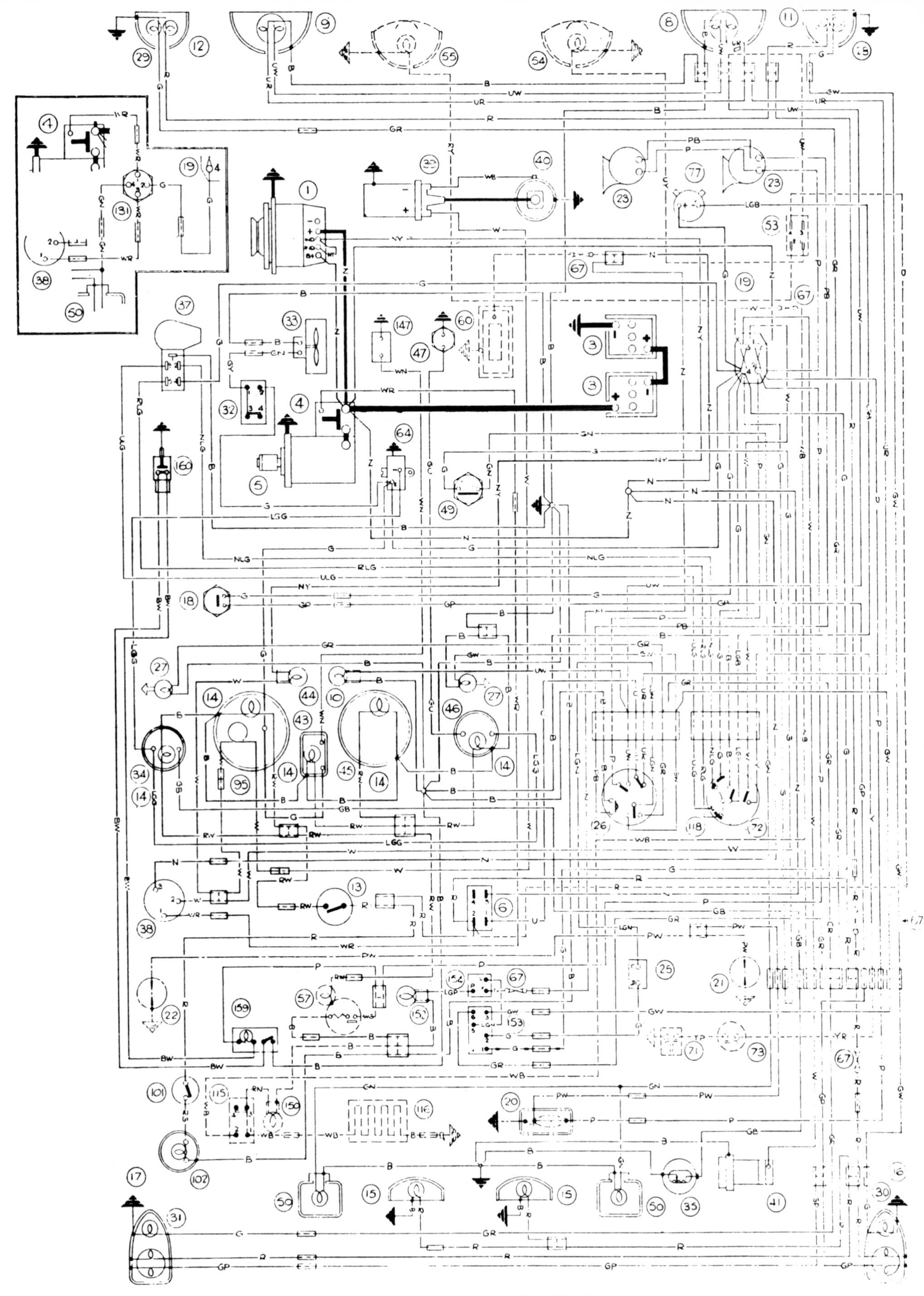

Negative earth (US), 1968–9

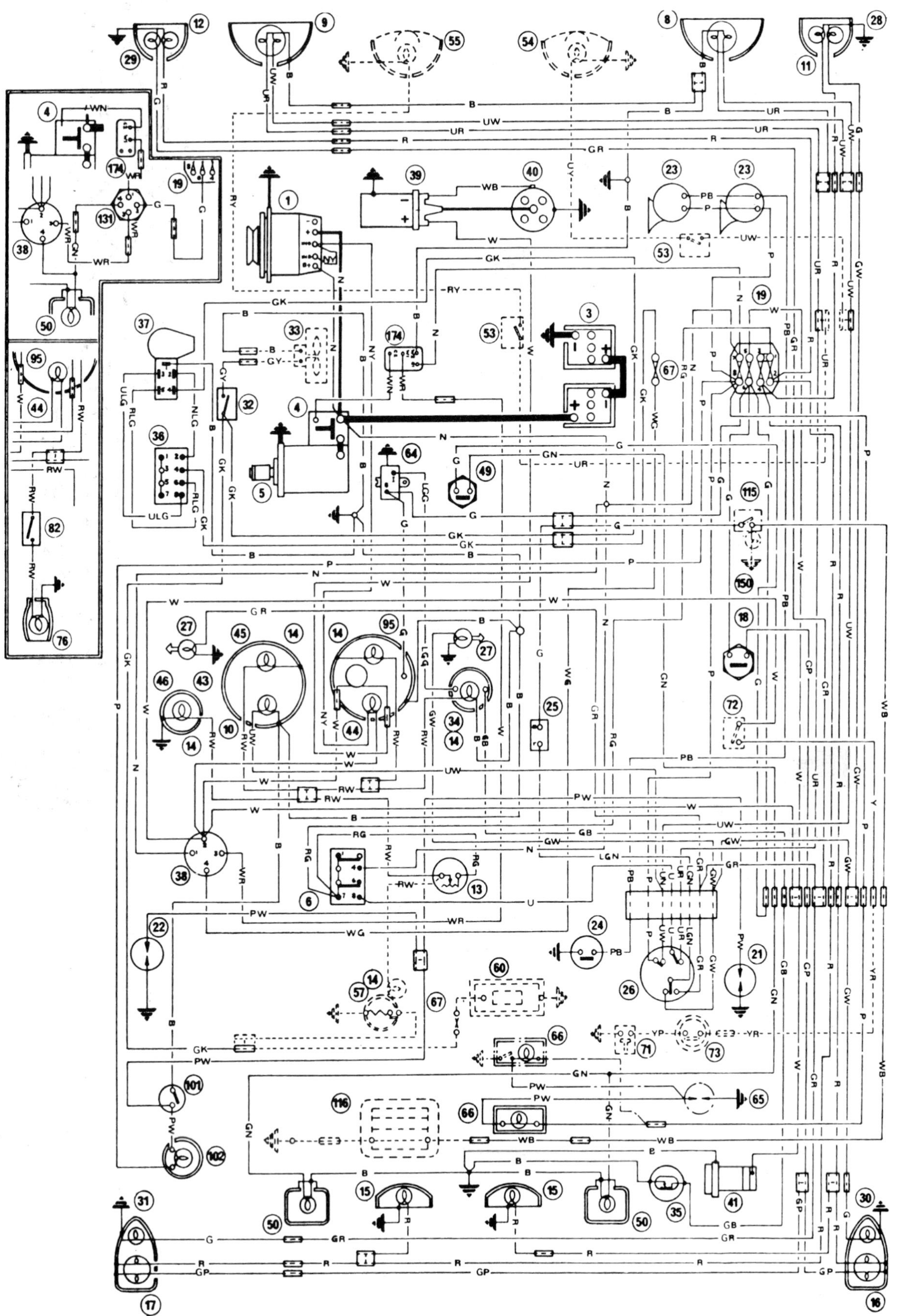

Negative earth, 1970–1

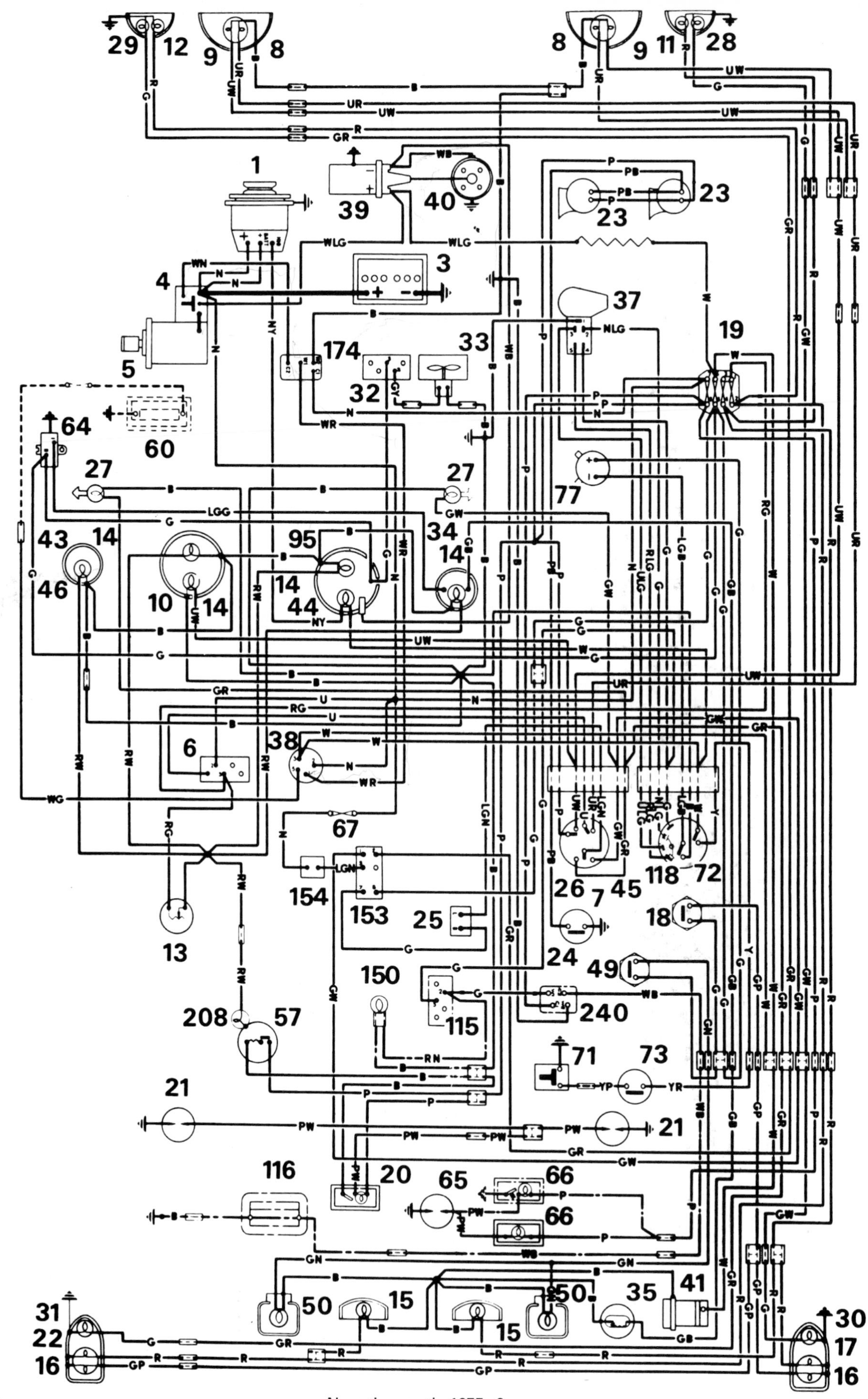

Negative earth, 1975–6

Key to wiring diagrams

Alternator or dynamo
Control box
Batteries (6-volt), battery (12 volt)
Starter solenoid
Starter motor
Lighting switch
Headlamp dip switch
R.H. headlamp
or
Headlamp dip beam
L.H. headlamp
or
Headlamp main beam
Main beam warning lamp
R.H. parking lamp
L.H. parking lamp
Panel lamp switch or rheostat switch
Panel lamps
Number plate lamp
R.H. stop and tail lamp
or
Stop lamp
L.H. stop and tail lamp
or
R.H. tail lamp
Stop lamp switch
Fuse unit
Interior courtesy lamp or map light
Interior lamp door switch
Interior lamp door switch
or
L.H. tail lamp
Horns
Horn push
Flasher unit
Direction indicator switch
or
Direction indicator/headlamp flasher
or
Combined direction indicator/headlamp flasher/headlamp high-low beam/horn push switch
or
Combined direction indicator/headlamp flasher/headlamp high-low beam switch
Direction indicator warning lamps
R.H. front flasher lamp
L.H. front flasher lamp
R.H. rear flasher lamp

31. *L.H. rear flasher lamp*
32. *Heater booster motor switch*
33. *Heater booster motor or fresh air motor*
34. *Fuel gauge*
35. *Fuel gauge tank unit*
36. *Windscreen wiper switch*
37. *Windscreen wiper motor*
38. *Ignition/starter switch*
39. *Ignition coil*
40. *Distributor*
41. *Fuel pump*
43. *Oil pressure gauge*
44. *Ignition warning lamp*
45. *Speedometer*
    or
45. *Headlamp flasher switch*
46. *Coolant temperature gauge*
47. *Coolant temperature transmitter*
49. *Reverse lamp switch*
50. *Reverse lamp*
53. *Fog lamp switch*
    or
53. *Combined fog/driving lamp switch*
54. *Fog or driving lamp*
55. *Fog or driving lamp*
57. *Illuminated cigar lighter*
58. *Driving lamp switch*
59. *Map light switch (early cars)*
60. *Radio*
64. *Instrument voltage stabiliser*
65. *Luggage compartment lamp switch*
66. *Luggage compartment lamp*
67. *Line fuse*
68. *Overdrive relay unit*
71. *Overdrive solenoid*
72. *Overdrive manual control switch*
73. *Overdrive gear switch*
74. *Overdrive throttle switch*
76. *Automatic gearbox gear selector illumination lamp*
77. *Windscreen washer pump*
82. *Switch illumination lamp*
95. *Tachometer*
101. *Courtesy or map light switch*
102. *Courtesy or map light*
115. *Heated back light switch*
116. *Heated back light*
118. *Combined windscreen washer and wiper switch*
131. *Combined reverse light switch and automatic transmission safety switch*
147. *Oil pressure transmitter*
150. *Heated back light warning lamp (GT only)*
152. *Hazard warning lamp*
153. *Hazard warning switch*
154. *Hazard warning flasher unit*
159. *Brake pressure warning lamp and lamp test push*
160. *Brake pressure failure switch*
168. *Ignition key audible warning buzzer*
169. *Ignition key audible warning door switch*
170. *R.H. front side marker lamp*
171. *L.H. front side marker lamp*
172. *R.H. rear side marker lamp*
173. *L.H. rear side marker lamp*
174. *Starter solenoid relay*
196. *Running on control valve*
197. *Running on control valve oil pressure switch*
198. *Driver's seat belt buckle switch*
199. *Passenger's seat belt buckle switch*
200. *Passenger's seat switch*
201. *Seat belt warning gearbox switch*
202. *Warning light - 'fasten belts'*
203. *Line diode*
208. *Cigar lighter illumination*
211. *Heater control illumination lamp*
240. *Heated back light relay*
244. *Driver's seat switch*
245. *Sequential seat belt control unit*

Wiring Colour Code

N.	*Brown*
U.	*Blue*
R.	*Red*
P.	*Purple*
G.	*Green*
LG.	*Light Green*
W.	*White*
Y.	*Yellow*
B.	*Black*
K.	*Pink*
O.	*Orange*
S.	*Slate*

When a cable has two colour code letters, the first denotes the main colour and the second denotes the tracer colour.

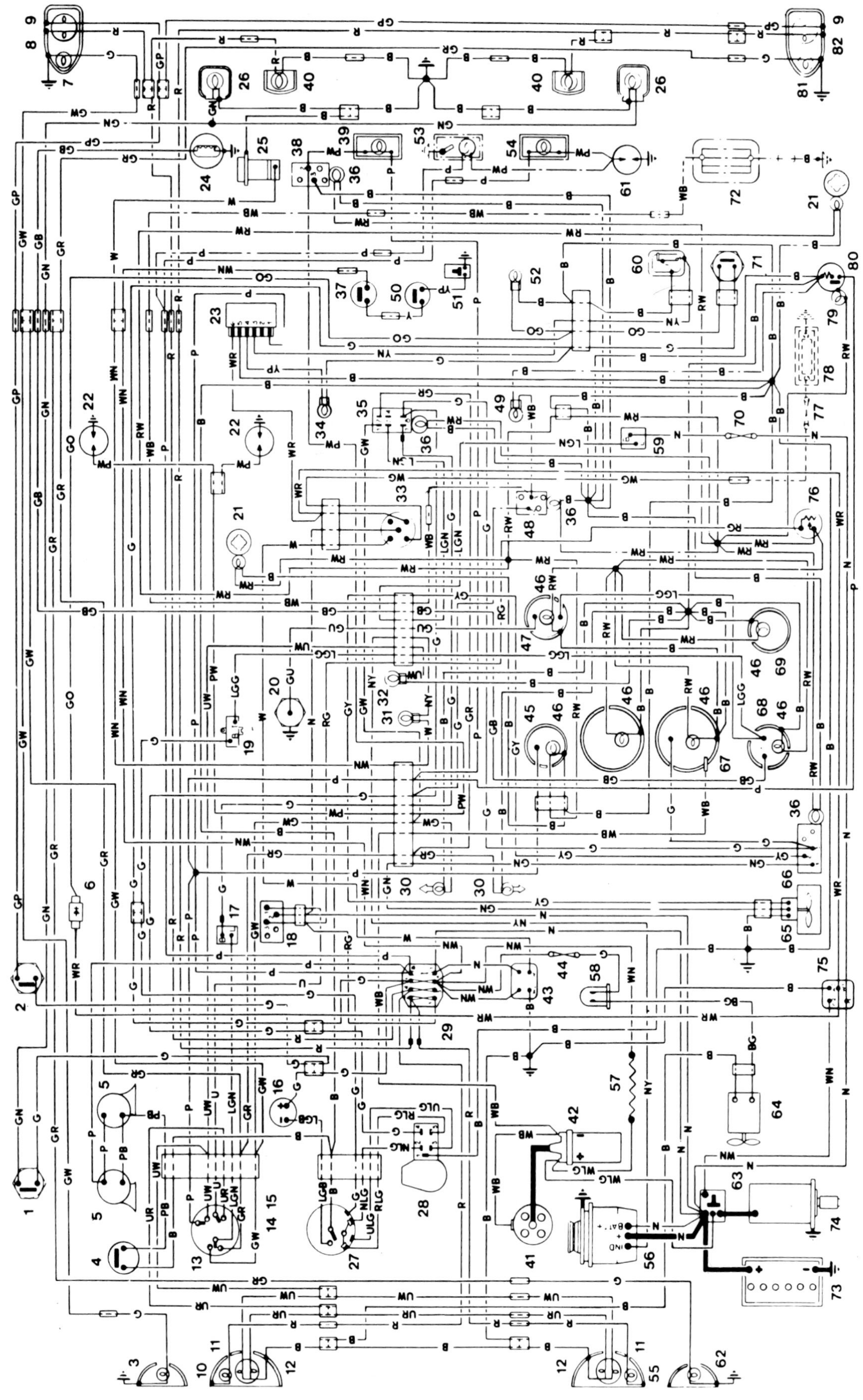

1977 onwards

Key to writing diagram, 1977–on

Several of the components listed in this key may not be included in the specification of all models

1. *Reverse lamp switch*
2. *Stop lamp switch*
3. *R.H. front direction lamp*
4. *Horn-push*
5. *Horn*
6. *Diode for brake warning*
7. *R.H. rear direction indicator lamp*
8. *R.H. tail lamp*
9. *Stop lamp*
10. *R.H. parking lamp*
11. *Headlamp main beam*
12. *Headlamp low beam*
13. *Direction indicator switch*
14. *Headlamp dip switch*
15. *Headlamp flasher switch*
16. *Windscreen washer pump*
17. *Flasher unit*
18. *Lighting switch*
19. *Instrument voltage stabilizer*
20. *Coolant temperature gauge*
21. *Heater control illumination*
22. *Interior courtesy lamp door switch*
23. *Time delay unit*
24. *Fuel gauge tank unit*
25. *Fuel pump*
26. *Reverse lamp*
27. *Combined windscreen washer and wiper switch*
28. *Windscreen wiper motor*
29. *Fuse unit*
30. *Direction indicator warning lamp*
31. *Ignition warning lamp*
32. *Headlamp main beam warning lamp*
33. *Ignition starter switch*
34. *Seat belt warning lamp*
35. *Hazard warning switch*
36. *Switch illumination lamp*
37. *Overdrive manual control switch (if fitted)*
38. *Interior courtesy light switch*
39. *Interior courtesy light*
40. *Number-plate illumination lamp*
41. *Distributor*
42. *Ignition coil*
43. *Ignition switch relay*
44. *Line fuse for radiator cooling fan thermostat*
45. *Clock*
46. *Panel illumination lamp*
47. *Coolant temperature gauge*
48. *Heated rear window switch (GT)*
49. *Heated rear window warning light (GT)*
50. *Overdrive gear switch (if fitted)*
51. *Overdrive gear solenoid (if fitted)*
52. *Hand brake warning lamp*
53. *Luggage compartment lamp (GT)*
54. *Luggage compartment lamp (Tourer)*
55. *L.H. parking lamp*
56. *Alternator*
57. *Resistive cable*
58. *Radiator cooling fan thermostat*
59. *Hazard warning flasher unit*
60. *Driver's seat belt buckle switch*
61. *Luggage compartment lamp switch*
62. *L.H. front direction indicator lamp*
63. *Starter solenoid*
64. *Radiator cooling fan motor*
65. *Heater motor*
66. *Heater motor switch*
67. *Tachometer*
68. *Fuel gauge*
69. *Oil pressure gauge*
70. *Line fuse for hazard warning*
71. *Hand brake switch*
72. *Heated rear window (GT)*
73. *Battery*
74. *Starter motor*
75. *Starter solenoid relay*
76. *Panel lamp switch*
77. *Line fuse for radio**
78. *Radio**
79. *Cigar lighter illumination*
80. *Cigar lighter*
81. *L.H. rear flasher lamp*
82. *L.H. tail lamp*

** Optional fitment circuits shown dotted*

CABLE COLOUR CODE

N	Brown	W	White
U	Blue	Y	Yellow
R	Red	B	Black
P	Purple	K	Pink
G	Green	O	Orange
LG	Light Green	S	Slate

When a cable has two colour code letters the first denotes the main colour and the second denotes the tracer colour

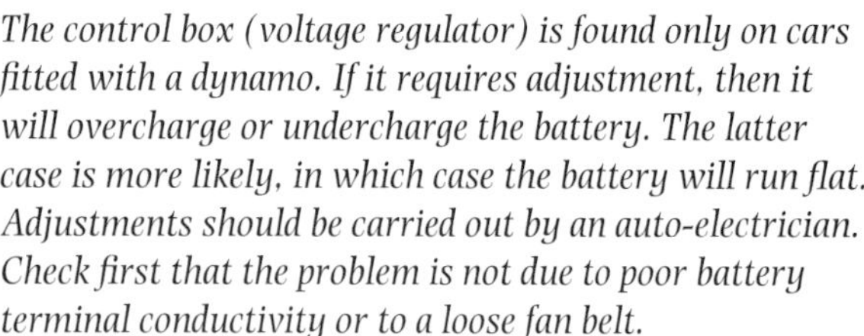
The control box (voltage regulator) is found only on cars fitted with a dynamo. If it requires adjustment, then it will overcharge or undercharge the battery. The latter case is more likely, in which case the battery will run flat. Adjustments should be carried out by an auto-electrician. Check first that the problem is not due to poor battery terminal conductivity or to a loose fan belt.

When fitting electrical accessories, always try to run a wire of the appropriate colour and always use wire which can easily handle the amperage needed by the accessory. If you find old, discarded, spade connectors as in the picture, you should ensure that they are not live, then cut and properly insulate them. Even better, you should trace them to source and remove them altogether.

assist in identification. Take care when removing the bulkhead grommet not to damage it, because these are not available at the time of writing. Begin fitting the new loom through the bulkhead grommet to the dashboard area, then run the sections under the bonnet and under the car. Further fitting is a matter of disconnecting old spade and other terminals, and replacing them with the appropriate wire from the new loom. If this sounds an oversimplification – it is! Quiet and patience are required in abundance.

If you decide to fit electrical accessories, then it is wise to take advice from an auto-electrician or even to undertake the physical fitting of the accessory and leave the wiring to a professional. Never fit extra units to a fused circuit without ensuring that the fuse rating is sufficient to meet all eventualities, and do not be tempted to uprate the fuse because it is matched to the existing units' safety levels. Each circuit, in addition to requiring wiring of the correct colour, also needs wiring of the correct rating for the anticipated current loads. Drawing too much current through too thin a wire (therefore of too high a resistance) will cause the wire to overheat.

Notes on engine electrical components

When fitting a replacement dynamo on early cars, always polarise the unit before connecting it up and starting the engine. This entails bolting the unit into place then momentarily touching a live wire to the smaller, field terminal of the dynamo. Reconditioned dynamos from reputable sources will always come complete with fitting instructions. If you turn on the ignition and discover that the ignition light is behaving in an unusual manner, such as remaining on after the ignition has been turned off, immediately disconnect the unit and repolarise it.

Starter motor removal

To remove an inertia type starter motor when the engine is in the car, disconnect the batteries and disconnect the heavy cable from the starter motor terminal. Remove the oil filter housing, the distributor and the coil with its mount. Undo the two screws securing the starter motor (one can only be reached from underneath), then withdraw the unit from within the engine bay. In practice, this is far from easy and a great source of skinned knuckles! Levering the engine against its mountings can provide a little extra clearance and make the task easier.

When removing the pre-engaged type of starter the procedure is similar, although the smaller physical size of the unit makes manoeuvring it out easier. It will not prove necessary to remove the coil, although when removing the type 2M 100 starter motor it is necessary first to remove the clutch slave cylinder.

Distributor removal

Type 25D4. Disconnect the batteries. Remove the distributor cap then turn the crankshaft until the rotor arm is pointing at the number one cylinder terminal. Remove the low tension lead and the vacuum advance pipe. Undo the split housing plate screws and withdraw the distributor.

Type 45D4. Disconnect the batteries and remove the distributor cap. Turn the crankshaft until the timing groove in the crankshaft pulley aligns with the static timing mark, and the rotor arm is pointing at the number one cylinder terminal. Remove the low tension lead and the vacuum advance pipe. Undo the clamp plate screws and withdraw the unit.

THE BRAKING SYSTEM

The MGB has a hydraulic braking system, with disc brakes at the front and drum brakes at the rear.

When the brake pedal is depressed, a piston

Front disc brake components

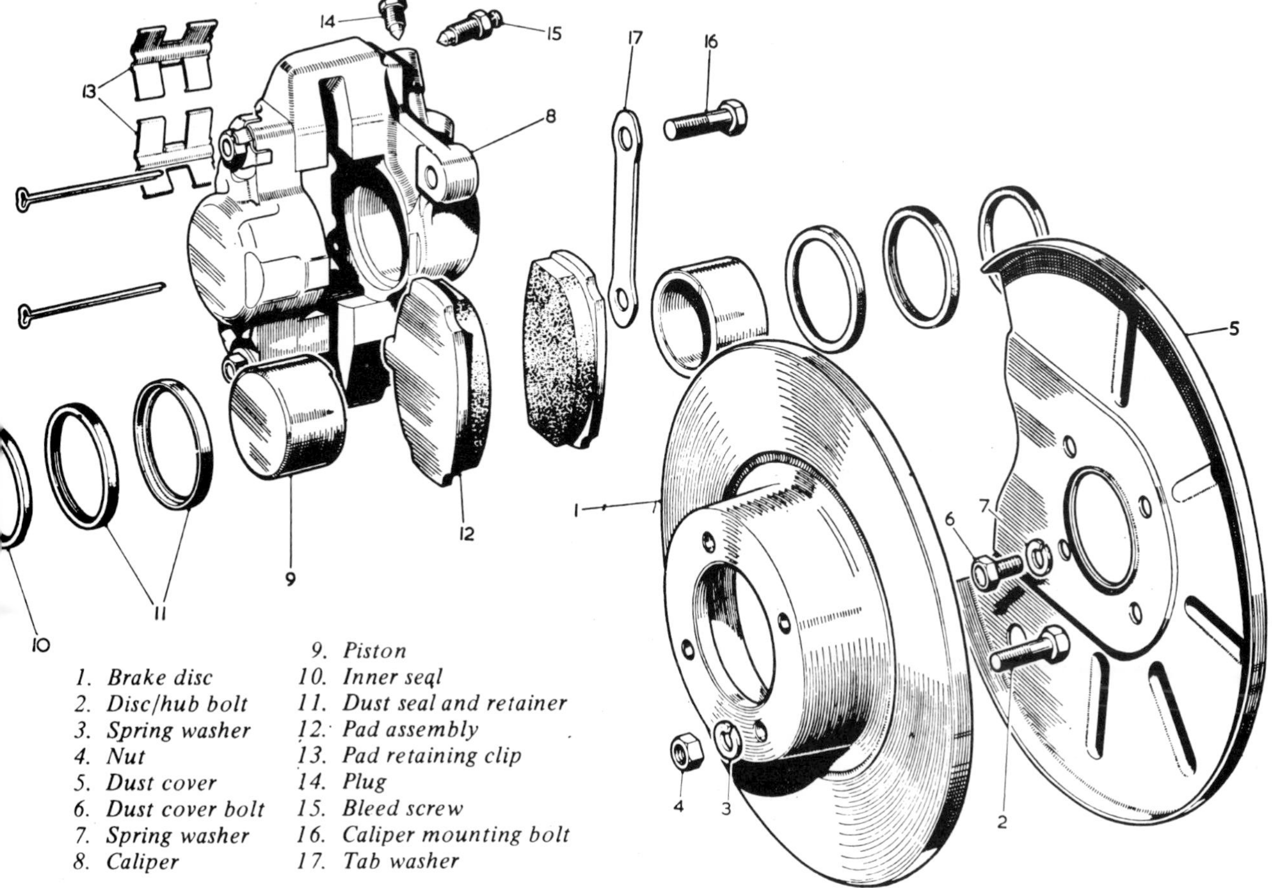

1. Brake disc
2. Disc/hub bolt
3. Spring washer
4. Nut
5. Dust cover
6. Dust cover bolt
7. Spring washer
8. Caliper
9. Piston
10. Inner seal
11. Dust seal and retainer
12. Pad assembly
13. Pad retaining clip
14. Plug
15. Bleed screw
16. Caliper mounting bolt
17. Tab washer

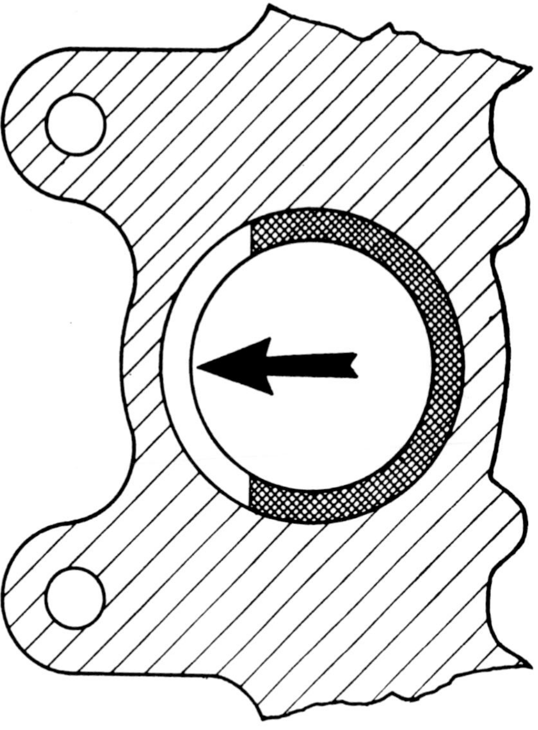

Piston cut-out position relative to the caliper

within the master cylinder is moved to force a non-compressible brake fluid through the brake piping. The fluid moves two pistons that are contained in each caliper assembly at the front wheels to push brake pads onto the discs, and two pistons contained in each of the rear wheel brake cylinders to push brake shoes onto the inside of the brake drum. Friction between the pads and discs and the shoes and drums causes the car to be retarded. Some years and models of MGB are also fitted with a brake servo unit, which provides power assistance to the pedal and decreases the amount of pedal pressure necessary for any given braking circumstance.

The handbrake operates independently of the hydraulic system via a cable attached to the handbrake lever. When operated, this mechanically causes the rear brake shoes to expand and make contact with the drums.

Restoration

Unless they are obviously in good condition, the brake pipes should be renewed. Corrosion can seriously weaken the pipes, and, in the case of copper alloy piping, vibration can cause work-hardening, which is usually followed by cracking.

Brake pipes are available for all models of the MGB, preshaped and with the correct end fittings in place. Alternatively, many garages will make up pipes, using your own as patterns. Take great care when fitting new pipes, because if they are accidentally pinched or kinked then the length concerned should be scrapped and again replaced. Flexible brake hoses should also be renewed, and these are widely available .

Disc brakes

The brake pads are contained in calipers, which are bolted onto the kingpin/stub axle assemblies. The pistons can be removed from the caliper by clamping one in place, then gently pressing the brake pedal to push the other until it can be removed by hand. Alternatively, the caliper can be removed from the flexible hose and the pistons removed using low-pressure compressed air. (Use a foot pump in preference to an air compressor, unless the latter can be set to give just a few psi of pressure. If you feed high pressure into the caliper, a piston will be forced out at high velocity). To remove a caliper, follow the instructions in Chapter 5, Suspension and steering, then clamp the length of flexible brake hose to minimise brake fluid loss, using a proprietary clamp or a self-gripping wrench with the jaws suitably padded.

To part the hose and caliper, do not twist the hose but, after 'starting' it, hold it stationary and turn the caliper, ensuring that the small amount of brake fluid which can escape falls into a suitable container.

The bores and pistons should be examined for marks, then cleaned. If the pistons are scored or corroded then they should be renewed together with the seals, and with the dust seals if necessary. Pistons should be lubricated and replaced so that the cutaway faces towards the hub.

Drum brakes

The most common problem affecting rear drum brakes is a seized adjuster. Do not try to move a reluctant adjuster using force alone, because the square driving stud is easily broken. Always use the correct tool for the job rather than an ordinary spanner. The adjusters can often be moved using heat

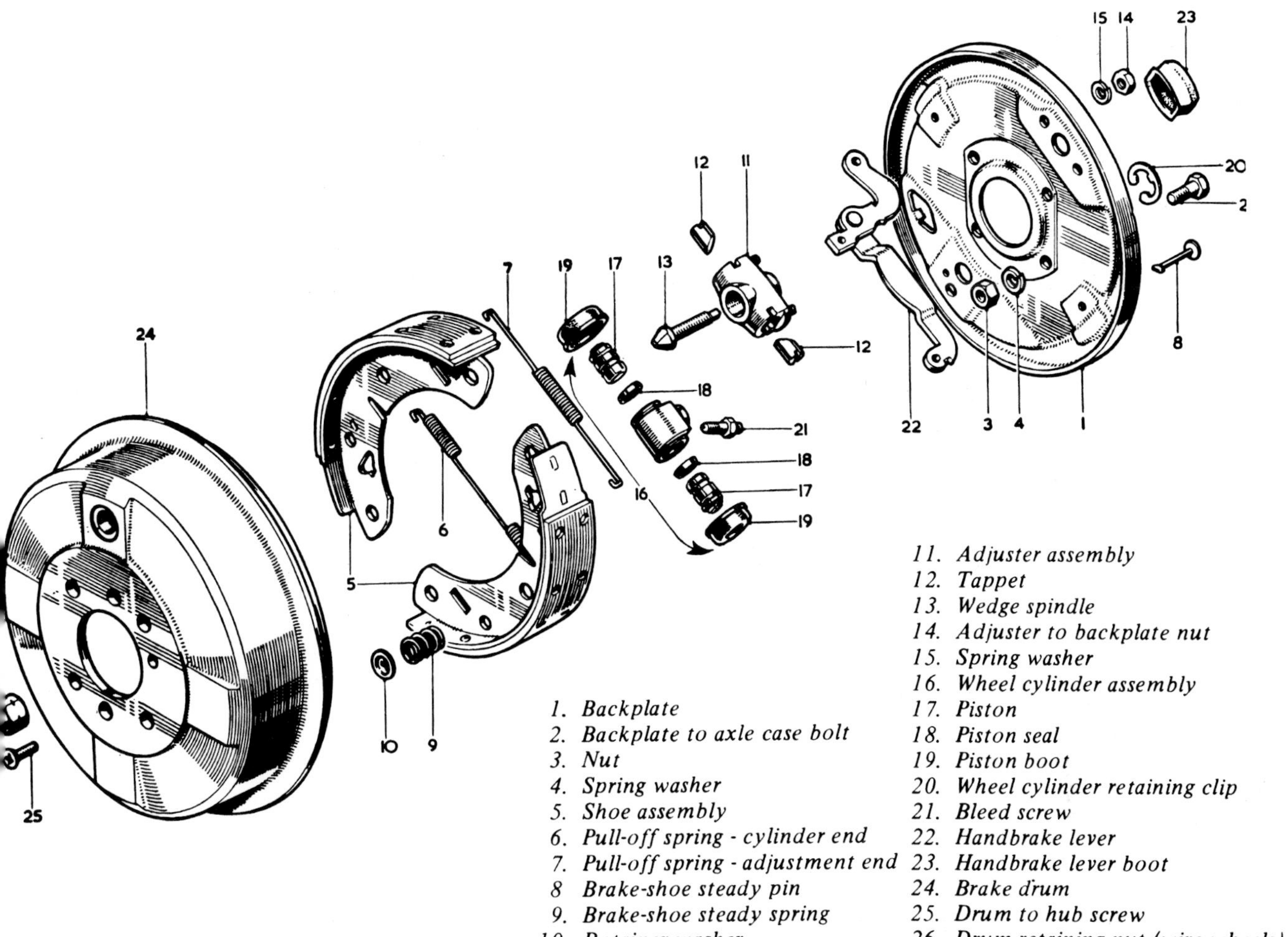

The rear brake components

1. *Backplate*
2. *Backplate to axle case bolt*
3. *Nut*
4. *Spring washer*
5. *Shoe assembly*
6. *Pull-off spring - cylinder end*
7. *Pull-off spring - adjustment end*
8. *Brake-shoe steady pin*
9. *Brake-shoe steady spring*
10. *Retainer washer*
11. *Adjuster assembly*
12. *Tappet*
13. *Wedge spindle*
14. *Adjuster to backplate nut*
15. *Spring washer*
16. *Wheel cylinder assembly*
17. *Piston*
18. *Piston seal*
19. *Piston boot*
20. *Wheel cylinder retaining clip*
21. *Bleed screw*
22. *Handbrake lever*
23. *Handbrake lever boot*
24. *Brake drum*
25. *Drum to hub screw*
26. *Drum retaining nut (wire wheels)*

and/or lengthy soakings in freeing agents. If the adjusters still prove reluctant to move, then remove the adjuster assemblies from the car and apply as much heat as is needed. If this fails, replacement assemblies and wedges are widely available. These should be fitted as a matter of course if the unit is hopelessly seized or if the square section adjusting stud is broken or twisted.

The piston boots will often prove to be perished and should be replaced if necessary. The pistons and their bores frequently become scored and if this proves the case then replacement is advisable. To examine the pistons, remove one drum and shoes at a time, ask an assistant to press the footbrake pedal gently. Have a receptacle handy to catch the small amount of fluid which will be lost. Fit new seals before reassembly. Finally, bleed the system and adjust the brakes.

Bleeding brakes

This will prove necessary if air is allowed to enter the system or following some types of work on a caliper or drum.

Both the disc calipers and drum assemblies are fitted with bleed screws. Clean the screw in question and push over its end a length of tight-fitting bleed pipe. Immerse the other end of the pipe in brake fluid contained within a jar to prevent air from re-entering the system. An assistant should now press the brake pedal to the floor whilst you open the bleed screw to allow fluid (and any air) to be pumped out into the pipe. When the pedal reaches the floor, immediately retighten the bleed screw. Repeat until no air bubbles can be seen in the fluid in the pipe. This action should be repeated at all four brakes.

If you have allowed air to enter the master cylinder, perhaps because the entire system has been stripped from the car or because you failed to top up the master cylinder while bleeding a brake, then air can become trapped in the master cylinder (not the

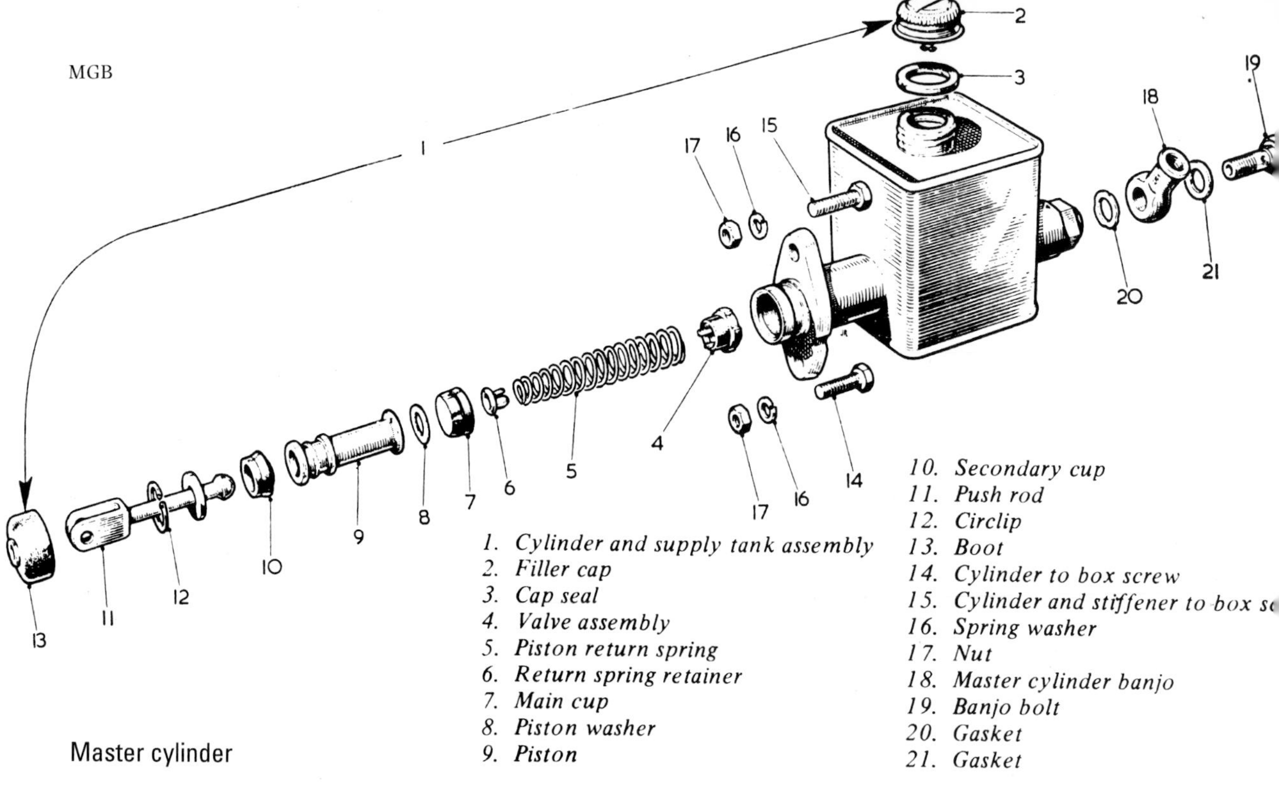

1. *Cylinder and supply tank assembly*
2. *Filler cap*
3. *Cap seal*
4. *Valve assembly*
5. *Piston return spring*
6. *Return spring retainer*
7. *Main cup*
8. *Piston washer*
9. *Piston*
10. *Secondary cup*
11. *Push rod*
12. *Circlip*
13. *Boot*
14. *Cylinder to box screw*
15. *Cylinder and stiffener to box s*
16. *Spring washer*
17. *Nut*
18. *Master cylinder banjo*
19. *Banjo bolt*
20. *Gasket*
21. *Gasket*

Master cylinder

tandem type). In such instances, you can bleed the brakes in the normal manner several times yet still find that the brakes are spongy because of this air which cannot be moved through the system in the normal way. A different method of bleeding the brakes will have to be adopted.

Set up a pipe on the bleed nipple and immerse the end in clean fluid as before. When the valve is opened, the brake pedal should be pushed strongly down to the floor, then worked through three quick and short strokes over the bottom third of pedal travel. The pedal should be held down whilst the bleed nipple is tightened, and then the person operating the pedal should let his foot slide off the pedal so that it returns sharply. This usually dislodges the air in the master cylinder and allows it to bubble up through the reservoir. If it doesn't work the first time, try again.

Master cylinder

The MGB was fitted with a single master cylinder (early cars), or a tandem cylinder/servo (later models). Repair kits for both are widely available, as are replacement units.

The brake and clutch master cylinders are underneath a cover which is held by four self-tapping screws.

To remove a cylinder, first bleed a single brake to drain all fluid from the master cylinder, then disconnect the pedal clevis pin and the pipe union. The cylinder can now be removed.

Brake servo

The brake servo is 'powered' by the vacuum present in the inlet manifold, which is transmitted by a pipe attached to a union on the manifold and one on the servo unit. The vacuum acts upon a diaphragm contained within the servo unit which applies an assisting force to the brake pedal when the pedal is operated. This reduces the amount of pressure that needs to be applied to the brake pedal by the driver's foot to achieve a certain braking performance. A brake servo cannot improve braking efficiency, so it cannot make up for a poorly maintained or set up brake system.

Repair kits are available for brake servos, although the repair of the units requires the use of special tools, and it is recommended that any repairs are carried out professionally. After refitting a repaired unit, bleed the brakes.

Brake light switch

The brake lights are operated via a pressure switch, of different design and location depending on the year of

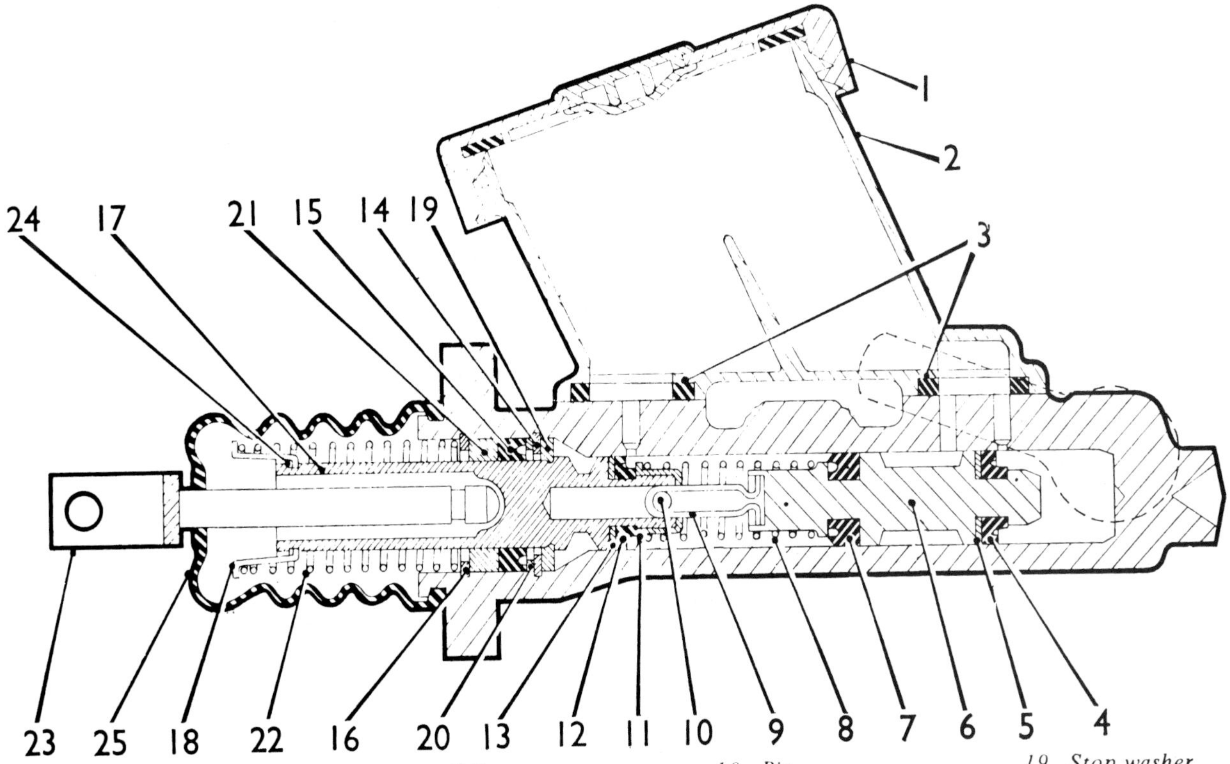

Cross-section of tandem master cylinder

1. Filler cap
2. Plastic reservoir
3. Reservoir seals
4. Main cup
5. Piston washer
6. Piston
7. Main cup
8. Spring
9. Piston link
10. Pin
11. Pin retainer
12. Main cup
13. Piston washer
14. Circlip
15. Cup
16. Circlip
17. Piston
18. Spring retainer
19. Stop washer
20. Washer
21. Bearing
22. Spring
23. Pushrod
24. Spirolux ring
25. Rubber boot

car. If the lights fail to operate, check the electrical circuit first, and if no fault can be found, the problem lies with the switch. After fitting a new pressure switch, always bleed the system, because trapped air will reduce braking power.

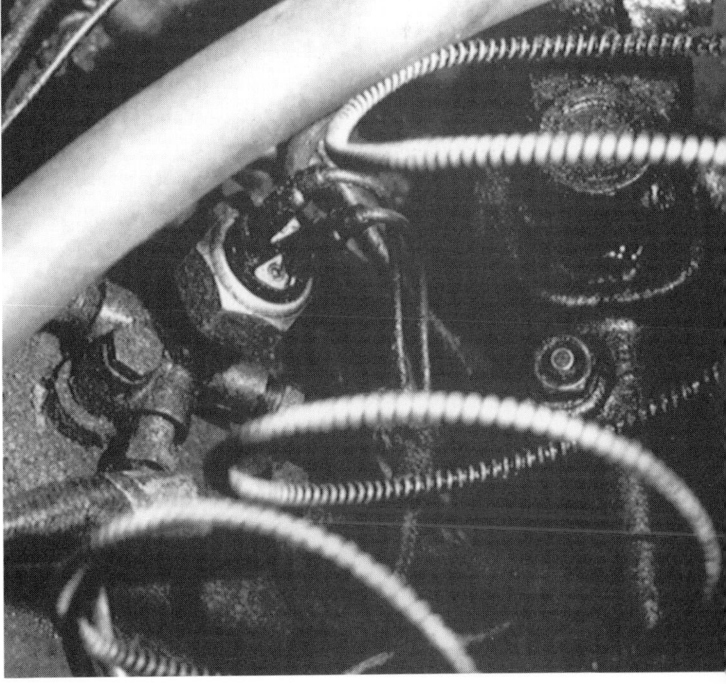

The pressure switch fitted to early models. If the brake lights fail to operate, always check the electrical circuits first, paying especial attention to the earthing of the light units, which is usually the culprit. Then check the switch terminals and connectors. If all else fails, renew the switch and then bleed the system.

6 · REPAIR AND RESTORATION – BODYWORK

Before embarking on bodywork restoration it is essential that you first ascertain the extent of bodyrot and assess honestly whether your capabilities and your workshop's facilities will allow you to see the job through, before you commit large sums of money on replacement panels.

The author has seen examples of MGBs which have been partly 'restored' by their owners but offered for sale before finished when they realised that the work was really beyond their capabilities and facilities. In some instances, the individual tasks had been carried out in the wrong sequence (or very badly done) and in order to make these cars sound and roadworthy it would have been necessary to begin by removing every panel which the owner had welded on. Removal of welded panels usually renders them useless, and so all the expense to which the unfortunate owner has gone is totally wasted.

If you have any doubts regarding your ability, commitment, or the facilities at your disposal, then seriously consider having this section of the restoration carried out professionally. This entails stripping the car to a shell (or a rolling shell) and then trailering it away to a bodyshop. Whilst the bodywork is being attended to, you can usefully spend your time cleaning and reconditioning other components ready for reassembly.

Preliminaries

Certain preparatory tasks usually precede serious bodywork restoration. First, the batteries are disconnected and removed (to prevent spillage of corrosive battery acid and accidental electrical fires). If welding at the rear of the car is envisaged then the petrol tank and preferably the pump and fuel line should be removed.

All body repair and restoration work follows a certain pattern. First, the full extent of the rot must be determined. It is sometimes necessary to remove some panels in order to be able to see others clearly, such as removing the front wing in order more clearly to determine the extent of rot in the sills and inner front wing. Because the front wing bolts on and is strictly non-structural, there is no need to support the body in any way before removing it. In the case of most other body panels, it is advisable to provide sufficient support in order to prevent the weakened body from distorting before the panel is cut away.

When the full extent of the rot is apparent, the decision to patch or replace the rotten panel must be made, and will be based on several factors. If a non-structural panel has only a small area of rust, then a patch can easily be cut and welded into position. If most of a non-structural panel is rotten then sometimes a replacement can be fabricated, although all MGB body panels are available at such reasonable prices that it is usual to obtain a replacement.

There are degrees of structural importance. The sills are of the greatest importance and should never be patched. The entire affected panel must be replaced. On the other hand, whilst the floor panels strictly speaking are of structural importance, their contribution to the overall strength of the car is not so great as that of the sills and side chassis rails and, if the affected area does not adjoin a structurally important panel (a welded seam), a small hole can be patched.

When the extent and severity of rusting has been established, it is as well to order all replacement panels before cutting any existing metal. Ensure that each replacement exactly matches the one that you will be replacing, because different marks of MGB have slight differences in many panels. Furthermore, some 'pattern' replacement panels can be inaccurate in form. A new panel that is only very slightly out can be a major headache to fit; this can be exacerbated when two rather 'approximate' panels are adjoining.

The new panels are needed so that they can be offered into position and their edges scribed around to save you from inadvertently cutting away too much of the existing panel. This is not, however, always possible with replacement panels such as the floor and the full GT rear wing with pillar. In such circumstances you will have to rely upon careful measurement.

One final matter to be taken into consideration before rotten metal is cut out is the way in which the body is to be supported. The shell, either in its entirety or in regard to the section being attended to, must be supported in such a way that it is safe to work on and will not collapse as parts are cut away and renewed. In practice this means supporting solid parts of the body on sturdy hardwood or box-section metal runners. Never support the body on axle stands alone because they give so small an area of support that they can act as pivots rather than supports. Also of importance is to ensure that the body is supported in alignment so that when new panels are fitted and welded up the completed assembly is not distorted.

Checking alignment is by no means always an easy task, and professionals (if they do not possess a jig) usually resort to taking a series of measurements from the car before any other work commences or, if the shell is thought or suspected to be distorted, by taking measurements from another example of the car which is known to be 'straight' (if you know the whereabouts of a Heritage shell then this is obviously the most accurate source of measurements).

Measure from the heelboard outer lower corners to points on the opposite A-post and from the top of the B-post to the bottom of the opposite A-post. Measure the door apertures and diagonals, and so on, until every important 'datum point' can be accurately located by the measurements or by triangulation.

The author also checks for body twisting before and during the restoration by placing straight edges across the width of the body at various points and resting a spirit level on top of these. This ensures that the front and rear wings (the tops of the flitch panels if the wings are removed), the door tops, front chassis rails, etc. are all at the same attitude regardless of whether the car is level or has one side raised. By fixing small blocks to the ends of a straight edge, it is possible to do the same test for the bottom edge of the sills and for the rear spring fixing points. Most of the measurements and placements for the spirit level straight edge will vary according to whether a Roadster or GT is involved.

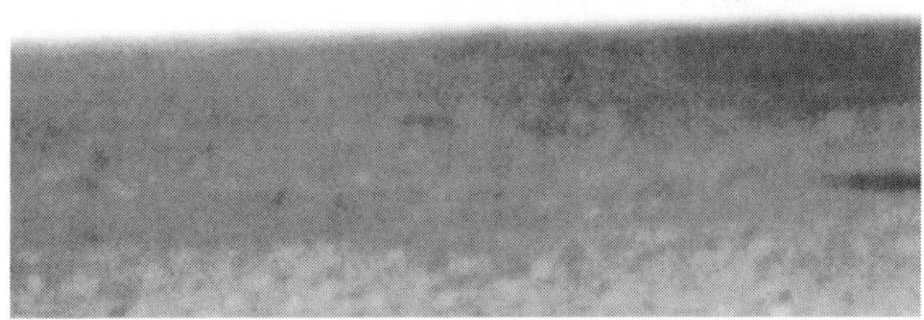

Three self-tapping screws hold the lower edge of each front wing. They are normally rusted solid and have to be ground, or preferably drilled, out. (See page 173).

It is by no means unusual to find, part-way through the body restoration, that you need extra measurements (perhaps to help in the accurate placement of a panel) which you did not previously take. The best option is to find a Heritage shell and take your measurements from this, if the owner will allow. Your friendly local Heritage-approved dealer may well have a shell awaiting delivery and permit you to use this.

When you have raised the car onto the supports ready for work to begin, check your measurements again, and adjust the height of the supports if necessary to bring the shell back into alignment.

Of the forces which can act upon the bodywork, none is so great as that of the weight of the MGB's engine. If the weight of the car were to be taken by supports aft of the engine then they would become pivot points against which the weight of the engine, which falls mainly upon the mountings, could act.

When the replacement panel has been offered up and its edges scribed around, scribe an inner, cutting, line which allows sufficient overlap for the join.

There are numerous methods of cutting out old panels, including hand shears, chisels and hammers, metal 'nibblers' and angle grinders. The tool and method chosen will depend on the panel and the ease of access relating to a particular job, and often a combination of tools will give the easiest and best result. Always be wary of cut metal edges; they are always razor sharp until finished.

If a welded seam or flat join has to be dealt with, it is often permissible merely to cut out the old panel at the edge of its welded seam and then weld the replacement on top of this seam to give a multi-layered join. It is, however, neater to part the old welded seam so that the resultant join has the correct number of thicknesses, and also helps moderate future corrosion. This also gives a stronger join.

Parting spot-welded seams when one of the layers is to be retained has to be done with great care to avoid damaging the retained layer. The spot weld remover tool, which fits into a hand drill, is highly recommended for this work. Other methods, such as grinding down the area of the weld and then parting the sheets with an air chisel or sharpened bolster chisel, will inevitably cause some distortion of the layer which is to be retained. If this is unavoidable, always straighten the panel using a planishing hammer and dolly before proceeding further.

Remember that a spot-welded flange is inherently stronger than one which is MIG or gas welded along the top edge, because the spot weld holds the two sections flat against each other. If you cannot obtain or hire a spot welder for such a seam, then it is highly recommended that you use the 'plug spot welding' method, in which holes are drilled into the uppermost of the two sections. The weld is then made through these holes to the underlying panel with a MIG welder.

Before starting to weld up the new panel, ensure that *all* traces of rust, oil and other contaminants have been removed from the two areas that will form the join. Also, ensure that they are tightly clamped (or temporarily pop-riveted together) and that their 'lines' are correct, taking measurements where necessary. It is by no means unusual to discover MGBs whose outer sills are out of alignment with the doors because not enough attention was given to their lines before they were welded into position.

The engine bay side channel bolts are the easiest of the front wing fixings to remove, so leave these until last. Two of the bolts are longer than the rest and hold the radiator steady brackets.

Finally, remember that all welding generates great heat which can easily distort thin body panels. When welding a large panel, first 'stitch' weld every few inches before joining these up with continuous runs of weld.

Obtaining replacement panels

Virtually every component of the MGB Mks 1, 2 & 3 is now available, including most body panels. In the UK there are many companies which sell such panels, and in many overseas countries there will be one or more sources. The MGC is not so well catered for, and both UK and export versions of this fine car have components (including a number of body panels) which are unique to them and which are not currently being manufactured. The situation is improving progressively, however, as some specialist

British spares suppliers increase the number of components that they are having made.

In cases of difficulty, contact the spares suppliers listed at the back of this book. They have all gained inclusion on the list because of their helpful attitude and, if they are unable to supply the requested part directly, most will be able to suggest the most likely source or suggest alternative components which might be tailored to fit.

Acid dip

Although this book is mainly concerned with the repair and replacement of individual body panels, there is a strong argument for adopting a completely different approach to the bodywork restoration. Rather than carrying out the restoration piecemeal, the bodyshell can be stripped completely and restored before any components are refitted. This has the advantage of making the bodywork restoration rather easier to carry out since the bare shell can be easily manhandled (if enough friends can be persuaded to lend a hand) and it reduces the chances of a fire occurring during welding operations. Perhaps even more importantly, it removes the main distorting force (the engine) from the car, so greatly reducing the chances of bodywork distortion. In fact, it would be fair to state that distortion of a bare shell would be unlikely unless it was totally riddled with rot or very roughly handled.

Many DIY restorers begin the task by stripping the car to a shell and then having it acid dipped. This removes all traces of rust and of rotted metal, and provides a clean shell with which to work, saving countless hours of painstaking paint removal later on. It also reveals the true extent of rot. It is essential, however, that all traces of soundproofing material are removed from the shell prior to dipping. These materials cannot be effectively dealt with by the acid, and will protect areas of rust from the action of the acid. For the same reason every bit of underseal that can be removed should be removed.

In the case of a car needing major bodywork repairs, this approach is highly recommended. However, because most restorations will be of the piecemeal variety, each task is covered from this angle.

Front wing removal

In order to gauge the extent of bodyrot in the all-important sill area it is necessary to remove the front wings. These are the only large body panels that are bolted rather than welded on, and which, thus, can be removed without damage, although their removal is rarely a straightforward business.

It is possible merely to cut away the lower quarter of the wing to reveal the sill forward section; repair panels which make this possible are available. The mutilation of a good front wing in the cause of saving half an hour's work can hardly be recommended. This is especially so taking into account the fact that welding on the new lower quarter and obtaining a reasonable finish using lead loading or epoxy filler will take up more time than would have removing the whole wing in the first place.

In the case of the Roadster, the windscreen must be removed first. This can be accomplished by first removing the dashboard to improve access to the set screws, although it is possible to do the job by merely removing the glove compartment. Remove the two set screws situated in each dash side panel which hold the screen surround legs in place (a shortened 1/2in ring spanner is the best tool for the job). Remove the two bolts from the screen tie rod, then the windscreen and surround can be lifted away.

The light, side light and indicator light wires should be traced back to bullet connectors situated under the bonnet lock panel and disconnected. If you are unsure of your ability to replace the various wires correctly, simply tag each one with a strip of folded masking tape and write the wires' location on to this. Feed the wires back through the holes in the inner wings. Remove the lights from the wing.

The lower rear end of each wing is fastened by three self-tapping screws which will usually be found to have rusted-in solid, and the heads of which often have to be drilled or ground away. If you are very unfortunate then you may find that a previous 'restorer' has welded these seams! Rather less troublesome are the two larger set screws situated at the front of each inner wing under the bonnet lock platform.

Three bolts situated behind the dashboard hold the wing top. These are very awkward to get at unless the dashboard has been removed and, again, a ground-off 1/2in ring spanner is the best tool. A further three bolts under the footwell side trim panel are easily removed (although they can be difficult to restart when the wing is refitted).

The wings are joined to the front valance by nuts and bolts which usually rust solid and consequently have to be ground away. The final run of set screws is along the engine bay side channels. These run into captive nuts, although two also have secondary nuts fitted underneath which fasten the radiator steady panels. Prop the doors open before removing the last of these set screws to prevent damage when the wing is lifted away, and try to get someone to take the weight of the wings as a further precaution.

With the front wings removed, the front ends of the sills can be examined properly. Often these will have rusted almost completely away, sometimes the rust will be limited to the top face of the outer panel. In either case, the sills should be renewed.

When refitting a Roadster front wing, always loosely bolt the wing into position first, then fit the screen. You can then properly position the wing so that the screen posts match the lines of the quarterlights. The wing can then be bolted into position (the screen can be removed if the car is to be sprayed). Failure to fit the wing in this manner can cause many problems if the car is to be subsequently resprayed. I have seen a new and recently sprayed bodyshell (with front wings fitted by a third party) on which the screen did not lie correctly against the quarterlight. In such instances, moving the front wing subsequently to remedy the misfitting will ruin the paintwork along the wing top fillet and, of course, in the engine bay side channel (when the fixing bolts are removed).

FLOOR AND SILL REPLACEMENT

Before becoming financially committed to repair and replacement work on the sills and floor sections, it is recommended that the side chassis rails are closely examined, both front and rear, to ensure that any necessary repair work to them will be within the scope of the amateur and that the costs of the work are not so high that a new bodyshell offers a more practical alternative. See the notes at the beginning of Chapter 6, Rear bodywork repairs, for more details.

Floor section replacement

The floor sections join together and help to maintain in a rigid rectangular formation the transmission tunnel, side chassis rails, sills, heel board, pedal box assemblies and main cross-member. They are therefore a good starting point for body restoration and should be replaced whilst other sections are left in situ in order to capitalise on whatever strength even rusted adjoining panels can offer.

If the car has been stripped to a shell it can be turned on to its side (with suitable padding) and rested against a wall. This makes the cutting and welding much easier. Otherwise, raise the car to a comfortable working height and support it by the axle and engine cross-member. The higher you can raise the car the better, because you will have to carry out some of the work on the car from underneath.

Disconnect and remove the batteries, petrol tank, pump and fuel line. Remove all wiring and the brake pipes from under the floor pan sections. Inside the car, remove the seats, all carpets, mats, trim and wires.

Begin by removing sound-deadening material then clean up around the edges of the floor so that the existing spot welds are exposed. An angle grinder with a cup brush makes light work of this. Both floor pan sections can be brought to this point together, although further work should concern one side at a time, so that the fixed side helps retain the positioning of the transmission tunnel.

There are two methods of removing the old floor

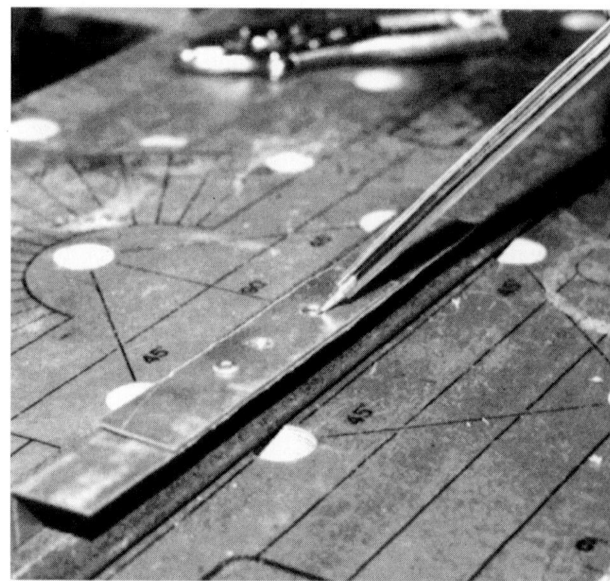

Plug welding

LEFT *Clean the surface of the lower panel thoroughly where the welds will be. Drill 3/8in holes in the uppermost of the panels. Draw together the two panels to be joined using pop rivets, clamps or self-tapping screws, ensuring that the metal visible through the holes is tight against that of the top panel.*

TOP RIGHT *Fill the hole with weld, and build up to slightly proud of the surface.*

CENTRE RIGHT *In this photograph the two holes have been plugged with weld, and the first has been ground flush with an angle grinder.*

RIGHT *Drill out the pop rivets, fill their holes with weld and grind flush.*

This car, the author's 1966 GT, had been described by the vendor as 'rot free'. Removal of the front wing showed differently. The outer sill section and the inner have rotted badly, with the lower half having rotted completely away. Some unmentionable individual had welded centre sill sections into place, and made a good job of camouflaging their presence. It was probably the same person who also welded on new castle rail sections to complete the illusion that the car possessed solid sills.

Cut out all rotten panels and then thoroughly clean traces of surface rust from the inner step, unless this, too, is to be replaced.

Worcester MG Centre (otherwise known as Sansome Walk Service Station) believe in replacing the inner step rather than patching or covering it. In this instance, only the front half was really bad, and the rear section behind the jacking point reinforcer was very sound. The step was cut through, then carefully parted from the floor and side dash panel. Note the run of holes in the old step and in the side dash panel, where the old spot welds were drilled out. Provide plenty of support for the floor and castle rail (if fitted) in order that the new section will sit naturally in the correct position before fixing and welding.

pan sections. The first is to drill out (preferably using a proprietary spot weld remover) the spot welds between the floor panel and the transmission tunnel, heel board, sill inner step and pedal box, then the welds joining the floor to the fixed cross-member. Take great care not to distort the flanges on the transmission tunnel, pedal box assembly and heel board. If any distortion occurs, carefully dress the flanges until they are true.

Alternatively, you could cut into the old floor sections at the edges of their overlaps with adjoining metal, working from underneath the car so that you can clearly see the flanges and avoid cutting into them. Taking this course of action will result in each seam having one extra thickness, but all will be out of sight. The seams must be thoroughly cleaned and trued prior to welding.

The best method of attaching the new floor panels is MIG 'spot welding', in which 3/8in holes are drilled into the top of the two surfaces (the floor), to be plug filled using a MIG welder. The two panels must be held tightly together and this is most easily accomplished using pop rivets, which can be drilled off afterwards and their holes plugged with weld. Alternatively, the new panels can be stitch welded and the excess weld ground away afterwards. MIG 'spot' welding is the better and stronger alternative. Before any welding takes place, of course, the old adjoining metal must be polished until bright.

The edges of the new floor sections should be sealed from the inside. Then you can fit seat runner nuts and transfer the various pipe and cable brackets from the old floor sections before undersealing and painting.

MGC floor panels differ from those of the MGB but are not available at the time of writing (although this situation might alter in the future as specialist companies manufacture ever-more spares for the MGC). At the time of writing it is necessary to obtain ordinary MGB panels and alter these to fit.

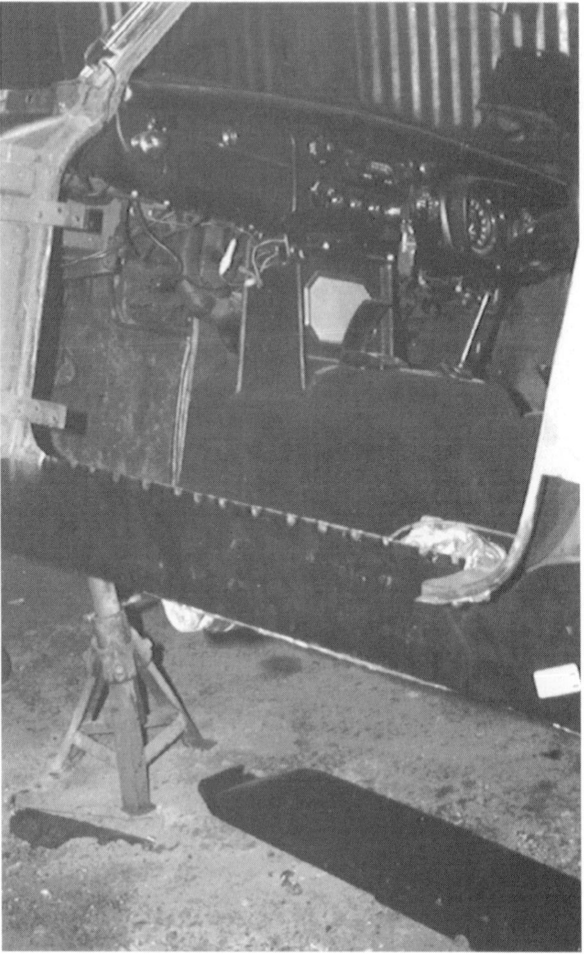

Sills

Whilst replacement of the castle rails, the inner and outer sills, the inner wings or any of the associated panels is all within the capabilities of the DIY restorer, if the inner sill step (visible inside the car) is rotten – particularly at the ends – then serious consideration should be given to stripping the car to a shell then having at least the sill/inner step replacement carried out professionally.

ABOVE LEFT *With the castle rail in position, do not forget to weld on the jacking point reinforcer!*

ABOVE *Ideally, you should remove the A-post and weld the centre sill section into position underneath. However, in this case we decided to tailor the sill around the A-post and avoid a great deal of unnecessary extra work. The results are equally strong.*

LEFT *Until the inner sill upright has been welded into position, the car is weak and distortion would be certain should one of the supports slip.*

With the sill structure including the inner step removed, there is a great danger of the body distorting unless it is really well supported, especially in the case of the Roadster. It is as well to provide cross-bracing within the door aperture when carrying out this work on a Roadster. The professional restorer should be able to spot and correct (or preferably prevent) the slightest body distortion, which might not be apparent to the DIY restorer.

The inner step can be seen from inside the car, and can be examined by merely removing carpets and mats. If the inner step has to be replaced and you wish to replace it yourself, then it is highly recommended that you begin by stripping the car to a bare shell in order to reduce weight stresses on the bodywork.

More usually, whilst the other three sill sections will have rotted, the inner step will have surface rust but it will not be rotten (and can be cleaned, patched if necessary, and rustproofed), so that the car tends to hold its shape given a reasonable amount of body support, in which case the amateur can confidently tackle the replacement of the other sill components.

Most of the restored MGBs (both DIY and professional) which have had attention to the inner step and which have been examined by the author have patches on the original inner step sections. The better of these utilise readily available profiled sections which can be welded on top of the original sections, after all traces of rust have been removed from existing metal and rust-preventative measures have been taken.

If the ends of the inner step have rotted then the repairs will be extensive and probably include the floor pan, pedal box assembly and dash side assembly, in addition to the other sill sections. The amateur is advised to strip the car to a shell as a starting point. However, it is possible to work with the car on its wheels, provided that some means is available to raise it to a comfortable working height.

If the car is stripped to a bare shell then it can be supported using a combination of axle stands and hardwood bolsters, steel box section runners and trestles. Even better, the shell could be lifted onto a frame made up from welded angle iron. This allows you to raise the body to waist level for easier access. As already recommended, however, the complete restoration of a thoroughly rotten car is probably best tackled by a professional bodyshop, which has experience and facilities to ensure that the body

remains straight and true during the rebuild.

If the work can be limited to just sill replacement (without the inner step), and adjacent panels repaired as necessary, then it is by no means impossible to carry out the work (uncomfortably) with the engine and gearbox in situ and one side of the car raised with suitable support underneath.

The first step is to strip out interior trim which could possibly catch fire during body welding, including all carpets and mats, seats and side trim panels, plus any sound deadening matting or foam rubber which might have been placed on or under the panels. Sound deadening material on the floor sections should be scraped off, and any wires or pipes in the vicinity should also be removed. The batteries must be disconnected and removed, and connections to the dynamo/alternator removed. Removal of the petrol tank and pump is recommended.

It is imperative that before any work commences the car is firmly supported so that the body cannot distort as panels are cut away. This can usually be best achieved by placing a thick hardwood runner under the front side chassis rail and supporting this on axle stands which in turn are on a crumble-proof concrete floor, and by supporting the rear spring hangers on axle stands, suitably chocked with hardwood blocks. If the engine is left in situ then the main cross-member should be well supported. Many professionals who do have access to a proper hydraulic car lift, which can obviously raise the car to a comfortable working height, simply support the car

ABOVE LEFT *The centre sill upright was spot welded first within the door aperture, then along the join with the castle rail.*

ABOVE *Before fitting the outer sill, apply as much paint protection to the inside and to the inner upright as possible. Use the appropriate welding paint along the edges to be welded. The dash side panel, A-post and sill outer, which will be covered by the front wing, can also benefit from several layers of good paint.*

RIGHT *Almost finished! The cut along the lower quarter wings needs to be cleaned up, then the jodder used to put a step into the repair panel. This was gas welded back, although with hindsight a MIG would have probably caused less panel distortion and resulted in the use of less body filler*

by its road wheels whilst replacing the sills. During the process, extra support is provided as necessary.

Leave the doors in position during chocking-up to add to the strength of the body shell and help prevent distortion. If you weld new sills on to a distorted body then the distortion will be maintained by the sills after the car has been lowered.

Sill replacement

Raise and support the car as already described to give a comfortable working height. Double-check for any signs of body distortion before commencement.

Remove underseal from adjacent areas, because this catches fire easily during welding.

Remove the front wing and the door. It is possible to cut the bottom quarter off the front wing instead of removing then replacing it: some professional 'quick turn-around' bodyshops do this although the author can see little to commend cutting up a sound wing just to save at the most a couple of hours' work.

The rear wing is welded into position and the lower quarter must be cut in order to gain access to the rear length of the sill. Replacement quarter panels are available; obtain one, offer it into position, scribe a line around it and cut the top line, allowing a 1/2in overlap, using a hacksaw and/or padsaw. An angle grinder is the best tool for cutting the leading edge in the door frame. If a jodder will be available to provide a stepped overlap in the edge of the metal, remember to leave sufficient metal for the step.

The old sills (or whatever is left of them) have to be cut away completely. This can be achieved using a sharp chisel and hammer or preferably an air chisel. Cut into the sills along the two seams which run into the door aperture. The run of spot welds along the door aperture should be drilled out, then the three (there can be more if the sill has previously been 'bodged') thicknesses of steel can be chiselled apart. The lower joint against the castle rail is similarly dealt with. Great care should be taken cutting around the door pillar flanges, because these are an essential fixing when the replacement sill is fitted. If the lower portions of the pillar flanges are corroded, then they must be made good before fitting the new sills.

Assuming that the inner step can be cleaned, repaired and rustproofed, take the opportunity to clean it and all other visible panels back to bare metal, patch if necessary and thoroughly treat with rust-retarding paint. Seams which are to be spot welded should be treated with a proper zinc welding paint. If the inner step is to be partly or wholly replaced then the car should ideally be on its wheels, raised up on a ramp, or stripped to a shell to avoid extra risk of distortion from the engine weight. The existing metal must first be cut out, taking great care not to distort the lower edge of the side dash panel and the floor. It will be necessary to provide support for the floor edge, so that it is level and at the correct height. This will ensure that the inner step is fitted at the correct attitude.

The castle rail (sill 'floor') should be replaced first. Tack weld this into position and thoroughly check for correct alignment (by offering up the inner sill panel) and for signs of distortion before final welding. The jacking point reinforcer can then be welded into position. This area can now be treated with rustproofing primer before being closed.

Next comes the centre sill upright, which should be carefully positioned using clamps or self-tapping screws, tailored around the door post, tacked, checked for alignment and distortion and finally welded into place. Ideally, the A-post should be removed, the sill section welded on to the dash side assembly then the A-post replaced. However, removal of the A-post will probably render the side dash panel useless, so that both would need replacing were this course to be followed. Tailoring the centre sill section around the bottom of the A-post is a far easier solution.

The centre top run can be spot welded for strength and neatness, and the rest MIG or gas welded. If a spot welder is unavailable, the centre top section (the flange inside the door aperture) can be stitched or MIG 'spot welded', but take care to clean the outer edge back so that the next layer, the outer sill, can fit flush.

Fitting the outer sill can 'make or break' the job from an aesthetic viewpoint because its lines must match exactly those of the door and wings. The recommended procedure is to fix it in position with a minimal number of self-tapping screws or pop rivets, temporarily to fit the door and place the front wing into position, then to adjust the position of the sill to match. Occasionally, the sill is in exactly the right position, although more usually, endless patience is required to achieve the correct lines.

If the eventual line of the outer sill section does not exactly match those of the front wing and door, it makes no difference to the strength of the shell. The car will be sound and fully roadworthy, even if it will never win a concours competition!

The outer sill can now be spot welded into position and the A-post flanges tapped down and welded. Take the opportunity to rustproof thoroughly the ends of the outer sill section which will later be covered by the wings.

At each stage, take the opportunity to paint metal that is to be enclosed. Some of the paint will burn off during welding, but much will remain to offer protection and lengthen the life of the new sills. When welding, have a charged compressor and air gun or some sort of fire extinguisher handy.

The rear wing quarter panel can now be replaced. A far neater job results from the use of a jodder to put a step into the top of the replacement panel rather than having a butt join. The join is then either made flush with filler or lead-loaded. Take care not to cause distortion of the rest of the rear wing panel through heat whilst welding; tack the new panel into position in several places before joining these up with a MIG.

Instead of replacing just the lower quarter of the rear wing, you could opt to replace a half wing (up to the chrome strip) or the full wing. The rear wing usually rots out in a line just above the wheel arch, and it is worth thoroughly examining this area for filler 'repairs' before electing to fit a new lower quarter wing only to have to scrap it when the filler falls out at some time in the future.

To reinforce the rust-preventative measures already taken, Waxoyl or a similar wax-based corrosion inhibiter can be injected into the new sill structures through 3/8in holes drilled into the top edge of the outer sill. The holes should afterwards be filled with grommets to prevent the ingress of water.

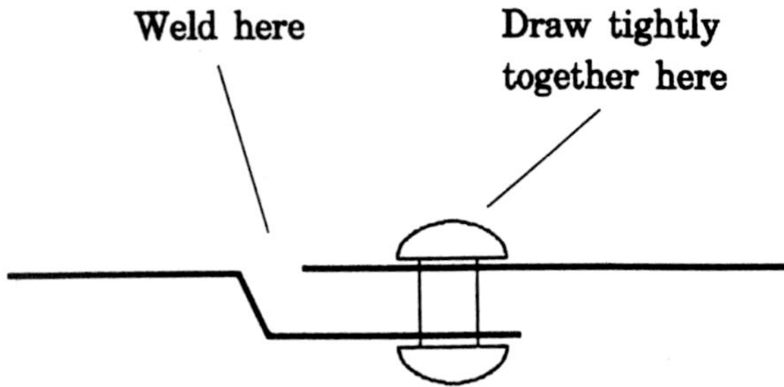

The jodder places a very shallow lip (exaggerated in this illustration) into the lower quarter wing repair section. This allows the two panels to be tightly drawn together with pop rivets for welding, and leaves the two in line, so that the job can be finished with a minimum of body filler. The author has never seen a jodder offered for hire, but the small purchase price could easily be justified in the improved results.

REAR BODYWORK REPAIRS

The availability of complete bodyshells calls into question the desirability of rebuilding a bodyshell which has deteriorated to the extent that the full rear side chassis rail sections (and therefore also the sills, inner wings, etc) require replacement. The cost of the complete shell equates to not much more than, perhaps, 120 hours (three weeks) of professional workshop time; more importantly, the difference between the cost of a new shell and that of the body panels required for a major rebuild can be very little. In fact, the cost of all the body panels likely to be needed for a major rebuild can exceed that of a complete, new shell without taking into account labour charges. Many of the MGBs on the market could more cheaply be reshelled than have a good

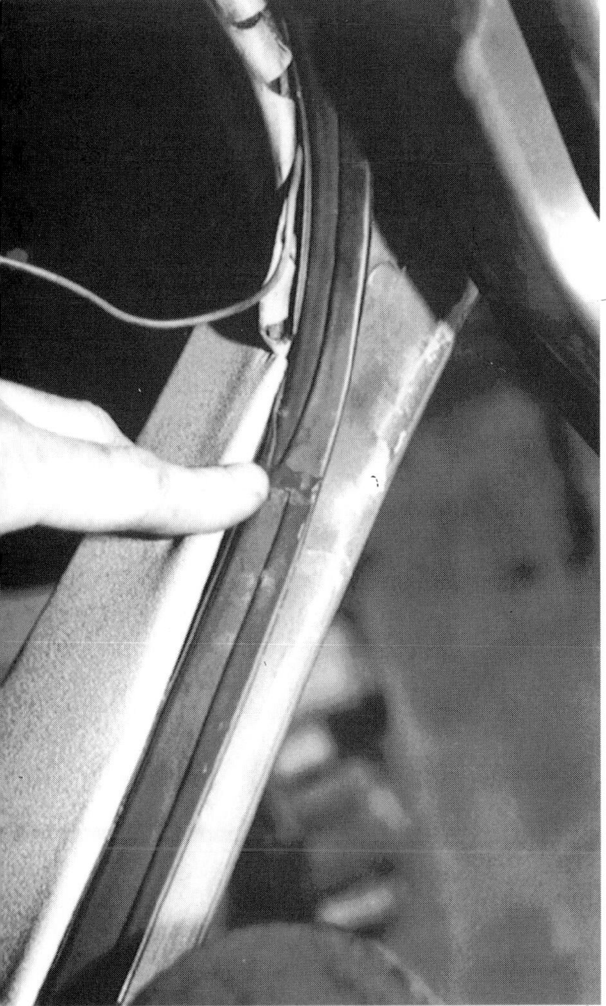

quality bodywork restoration.

Along with new shells, complete rear body sections have also become available. The cost of the component pressings alone can equate to over 80 per cent of that of the assembled body section, so that there can no longer be any justification for carrying out a complete panel by panel rebuild of either a major body section or a bodyshell complete. The welding of a new front or rear end to a bodyshell, however, does require that either the two sections be placed in a jig to ensure correct alignment, or that the work is carried out by a professional whose experience enables him to achieve perfect alignment. Either way, it is most definitely the province of the well-equipped bodyshop and not a job for the amateur. All body repair work at the rear of the car must be preceded by sill replacement if necessary.

For any body repair work which involves welding at the rear of the car, the petrol tank, fuel line and pump *must* be removed. The bumper, rear light clusters and all wiring, as well as carpeting and sound proofing material should also be removed.

First, disconnect then remove the battery or batteries. Loosen wheel nuts or spinners, jack up the rear of the car and support it on axle stands placed under the forward run of the spring hanger support brackets. Remove the road wheels. Remove the rear springs and dampers and, if necessary, the axle. See Chapter 5, Suspension & steering for full instructions.

Drain or syphon the fuel tank. The author always runs a jumper lead between the tank and the petrol receptacle in order to avoid static sparking between the two. See Chapter 5, Fuel system for a full description of fuel tank removal. Remove the fuel pump.

Remove paint, rust and dirt from panels in the vicinity. Carry out a thorough investigation of the whole area. If the boot floor, chassis side rails, inner

TOP *This is what you can find when you elect to give a car a 'quick' respray. The wheel arch is noted for rusting out, and this one had received the traditional body filler bodge-up 'repair'. Lower rear wings are not too difficult to fit, however.*

LEFT *The rear roof pillar of the GT already has a cutting line at the point of the original weld, as seen here. If you elect to follow this, then make sure that the pillar section of the replacement panel is long enough to reach! It is better, however, to cut further down, in order to avoid having to open up the old joint (and risk distorting it).*

This GT boot floor had several small rust patches which had been caused through water being allowed to lie undisturbed on the surface of the metal. This, the author's first-ever attempt at MIG welding, was unlovely, but when ground flush, it proved very strong. In fact, the author enlarged the original hole, cut a piece of steel to fit inside it, butt welded this in and then welded the plate on the top, just to be sure!

Stripping the old paint from the boot floor was accomplished very slowly, using a selection of scrapers and powered brushes. Old wood chisels are ideal for working in tight corners.

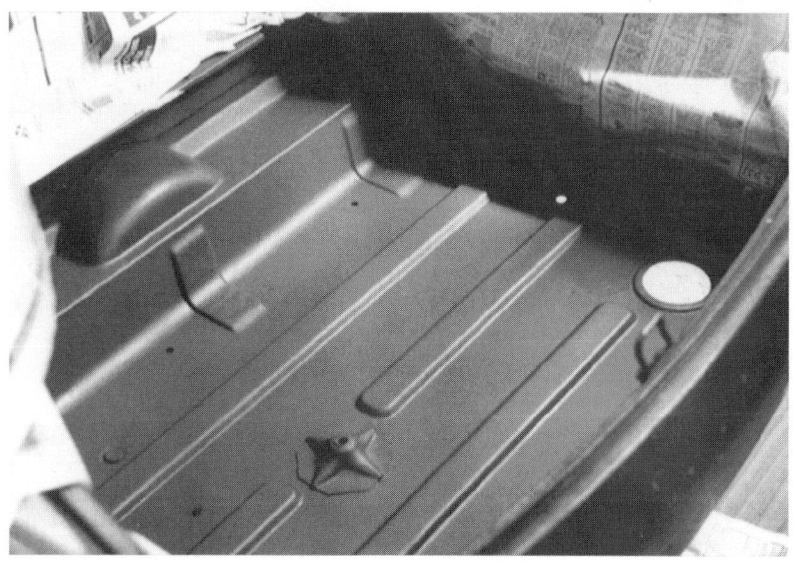

The same area primed and ready for a touch of cellulose body stopper before top-coating. An otherwise sound boot floor was thus saved, and the author was saved a rather more involved repair.

wings and valance are all in need of replacement then it might pay to have a new rear section professionally fitted, or even to opt for a complete reshell. More usually, just one or two elements require replacement whilst others can be cleaned and patched or repaired with recognized sections, such as the spring hanger portions of the side chassis rails.

If the forward run of the chassis rail (where it joins onto the sill assembly) is badly corroded then a complete chassis rail/sill rebuild is essential, and this is a doubtful prospect for the DIY restorer, because there is both a risk of the body's distorting whilst the work is carried out and, more worryingly, a risk that it has already occurred. The car should really be stripped to a bare shell and acid dipped before such work is carried out.

The rear outer wings rot around the wheel arch and also around the area which covers the sill ends. Complete wings are available, and should be used in preference to half-wings when rot is well established at the top fillet of the wing. The full rear wing repair section for the Roadster extends to include the light cluster, whilst the full wing repair panel for the GT also includes the roof pillar.

Lower half-wing replacement

If the top edge of the wing is sound then half-wing repair sections are available. Replacement entails removing the chrome strip then cutting horizontally from the light cluster up to the edge of the B-post panel (door frame side) along a line made by scribing along the edge of the replacement half-wing (plus a suitable overlap). The metal which is to be left must not be distorted, and so a Monodex-type cutter should be used. The ends are ground away from the light cluster and door frame with a mini angle grinder, and the old wing section can then be prised away.

The replacement panel is 'trial' fitted using pop rivets or self-tapping screws, followed by stitch welding. The long run of the top seam is prone to heat distortion and, thus, the use of MiG welding is recommended. The use of a jodder helps on the overlapping sections, not only to make a neater joint but also to strengthen the finished job.

Full wing replacement

Larger repair sections which cover the entire rear wing assembly including the light cluster area (Roadster) or the same plus the rear roof pillar (GT), are a more difficult prospect. Fitting the GT version is a far more complicated matter than merely replacing the lower half-wing, because the car needs reasonably rigid roof bracing whilst the old pillar is cut out and the new one fitted. Furthermore, you can not simply offer up the replacement panel and scribe cutting lines on to the existing pillars because the new wing would sit on top of the old wing's seam and behind its boat tails. It would be necessary to cut away quite a large amount of the old wing section before the new wing could sit in position for lines to be scribed.

If you clean the paint from the rear roof pillar then you should be able to find the original seam, and although you could part this seam and join on the new panel, it is not recommended. It is better to cut lower down, as this saves having to open a join with the attendant danger of distorting the metal to which you will later have to weld. By making your cut further down the panel, you can remove the old section, offer up the new and accurately make your cutting marks.

Boot side quarter replacement

The boot side trays are prime rust spots, particularly in their rear corners, but because they are not too important structurally, they may be patched. They are very difficult to cut completely out of the GT due to the very restricted access. The ideal solution in this instance is to cut the tray out whilst the outer rear wing has been removed or after the lower rear quarter of the wing has been cut away, and to fasten the replacement in position with pop rivets during the trial fitting of the rear wing, then to weld the replacements back in before fitting the new wing repair section, so that they help to preserve the lines of the replacement wing. It is then an easy matter to weld the outer seam from inside the car.

Inner wing (outer half) replacement

Replacement of the rear inner wings alone is by no means a straightforward job due to the limited access, and preferably should be carried out during outer wing replacement and with the boot floor outer quarters in good order, repaired or replaced in order

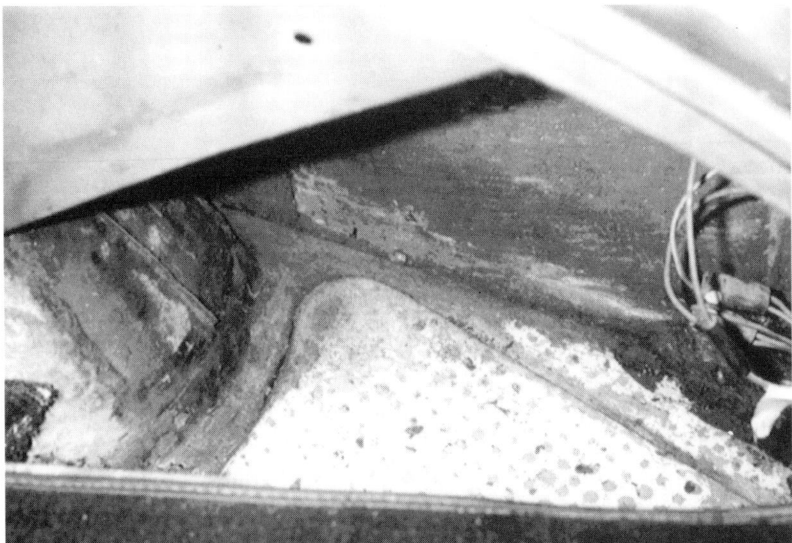

The boot trays on the author's car were basically sound and cleaned up to reveal, in the main, solid steel. There was a little rot in the rear corners. As the rear wing was not to be removed from the car, the author decided to cut out the rot then butt weld in patches, working from underneath.

The nearside of a GT photographed in Pete Harper's workshop. In this case, only a rear half-wing is to be fitted. Note the cutting line to the boat tail and light cluster back plate. First, though, the side chassis rail spring hanger section must be replaced.

With the full wing section, the boot tray and boot quarters cut away, work has started on rebuilding the rear end of this GT in Pete Harper's Bromsgrove workshop. The sills have been replaced and the side chassis rail main repair section is fitted, ready for the closing panel. After this has been fitted, the new wing will be clamped into position and checked for correct alignment, and the boot side quarter and inner wing trial-fitted and scribed. The rear wing will then be removed, and the boot quarter and inner wing welded into the correct positions. The wing can then be welded into position.

to retain the correct body lines. The recommended method is to cut away enough of the old outer wing to allow access (preferably all of it), then to remove the old inner wing section. When the new outer wing panel is secured by self-tapping screws or clamped into position during the trial fit, the inner wing section can be offered up and scribed to show its correct position. This allows the outer wing to be removed and the inner wing to be welded up in the correct position.

Working in this way, the front of the inner wing can be properly welded onto the sill end, whereas if you tackle the work after the outer wing has been welded on, there is little or no access to the sill end to carry out this essential welding. (The only reasonable method of welding an inner wing to the sill with the outer wing in situ would be to drill holes for plug welds, but this is not so satisfactory). The job must also be preceded by sill replacement since, as already stated, the inner wings have to be welded onto the rear ends of the sill sections.

Rusted inner wings can usually be cut out quite easily using an air chisel. Care must be taken when cutting around the flanges at the sill ends. Repair sections are available in one piece or in three sections (which can make refitting easier).

Boot tray replacement/repair

The boot floor should be closely examined for rust damage. Localised damage caused by water lying on top may be patch-welded or have shaped pieces of steel let in, but if rusting is widespread then the floor should be replaced.

The boot floor was originally spot welded and these joins will have to be parted using a spot weld remover or ground down and then parted with a sharp chisel, preferably an air chisel.

The metal to which the boot floor was joined will then have to be straightened up and the new floor stitched back with a gas welder or preferably 'spot welded' with a MIG.

Chassis rail repair

If the rear spring hanger sections of the chassis rails require replacement the job is more easily carried out after the boot tray has been removed.

The repair sections come in two halves, the main section which holds the guide tubes for the bumper bracket and spring hanger bolts, and a closing panel. Measure against the replacement section, then cut the old rail as cleanly and square as you are able. Clamp the replacement in position, aligning it carefully with the horizontal boot tray support panel.

Tack weld it into position then double-check alignment before welding at the front end from within the section. The 'boat tail' sections beneath the rear light clusters are prone to rotting. In most cases, repair sections can easily be fabricated from 20g steel and welded into place after all rusted metal has been cut away.

THE DOORS

The doors essentially have two major components, the shell and the outer skin. The shell usually rots out at the base, and repair sections are available for this. Door skin panels are also available and can be fitted with a great deal of care and patience. Replacement door assemblies are also available.

PREPARATION – STRIPPING THE DOOR

Remove all fittings and trim (See Chapter 6, Interior and exterior trim), then disconnect the internal fittings from the lock (these will vary according to the year of the car; early cars possessed a single link and later cars a separate link for locking and releasing). Remove the lock unit fixing screws, then the lock. Remove the lever mechanism (early cars) or the combined latch/door pull (later cars).

Remove the window runner screw and bolt, then the regulator (winder) assembly fixing screws and extension screws. Remove the regulator arc from the door glass then lift the glass and remove the regulator assembly. Lift out the door glass. The quarterlight assembly is held by two nuts on threaded studs within the top of the door, by a bolt under the front edge of the door (the hole can have a plastic plug fitted) and by bolts in the leg (which forms the front window channel). The quarterlight assembly can now be withdrawn.

An impact screwdriver is usually required to remove the door to hinge fixing set screws.

RESKINNING

To reskin a door, first cut away the fold around the edge of the old skin using an angle grinder. The two are welded together only around the quarterlight area, and this can easily be cut with a hacksaw.

Clean up the edges of the shell and examine the base and sides for rot. If this is extensive, then a new door can be obtained complete if required; otherwise, use the proper repair section for the base and patch the sides as necessary. A replacement door in reasonable condition can also be obtained from a breaker's if the door is beyond repair.

Fitting a base panel is fairly straightforward. Offer up the replacement panel and scribe a line at its edges, then scribe an inner line which allows an overlap for the join. Use a jodder if available. Pop rivet the panel into position, check that the lines are correct, then weld it into position.

Fitting the skin requires care. Lay it on a clean surface (ie with no grit or metal filings on it) and position the shell on top so that the top edge aligns correctly. Ensuring that the underside of the lip on which you are about to work is well supported, tap the flange in gently, a little at a time, working your way around the entire seam, ensuring that the area of door skin underneath is always supported by tipping the shell as you go. Finish using a block of hardwood to tighten up the seam.

The top edge which contains the quarterlight mounting holes can now be welded to the shell.

Window furniture

The window regulators fitted to cars manufactured before mid-1965 are not available new as replacement items. One major UK spares supplier catalogue carries no mention of regulators at all(!) and another lists them as no longer available. At the time of writing, regulators used in cars from mid-1965 to October 1967 also seem to be unavailable. Regulators for 4-synchromesh cars from October 1967 are widely available.

Used regulators may be sourced from breaker's yards, although these days you are probably wasting your time looking in yards other than those which specialise in the MGB. When regulators break, it is most commonly because the teeth are worn, and repair is not easy because it entails remanufacturing the faulty component. However, no component is ever completely beyond repair, and those who have a faulty pre-1967 regulator mechanism and who are prepared to spend enough time working with a hacksaw and a set of swiss files will be triumphant in the end.

The quarterlight assembly is available for all years of both the Roadster and the GT. It is, however, rather expensive, and if your otherwise serviceable quarterlight suffers just a snapped upper hinge stud (a common ailment), this can be replaced. Ease the glass part way out from the channel, then drill out the two rivets which secure the old hinge, and pull this out of the surround. It would be possible to replace the hinge and secure it with small rivets, although the author found that two short and stubby chromed, countersunk, flat headed self-tapping screws did the job admirably. Assemble the new hinge into position within the surround and with the stud located into the lower hinge hole, then secure the top hinge using the self-tapping screws.

All other door furniture is available from specialist suppliers. In common with various plastic fittings on the dashboard, these can be difficult to repair when broken. If authenticity is not too important, substitutes for some of the fittings can be taken from other cars at a breaker's.

Regulators for cars manufactured from 1967 (four-synchromesh MGBs) are being manufactured and are widely available. Those with earlier cars are best advised to contact dealers who specialise in second-hand spares, because these units are not easily repaired.

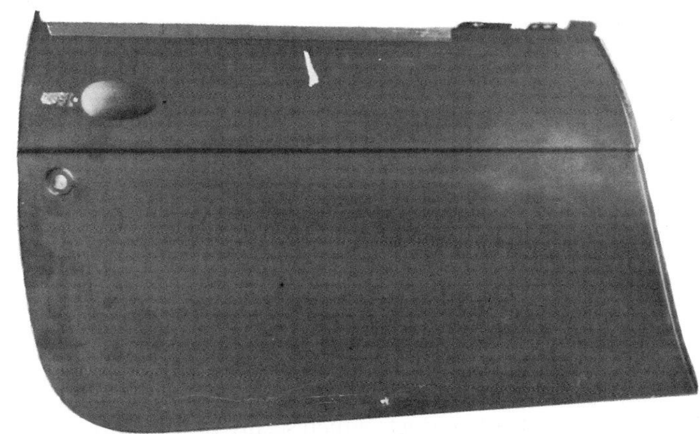

Replacement door skins are widely available and can be fitted by the DIY restorer provided that care is taken not to damage the skin whilst folding the edge. Specialist folders for this purpose are available, although expensive.

OTHER BODYWORK

The front wing

Those who have viewed a selection of MGBs whilst attempting to locate a good example to buy will be aware that many have extensive rot in those panels which are covered by the front wings. The MGB relies heavily for strength upon the complex box structure of welded panels under the front wings, and the wise buyer will have steered clear of cars with visible or suspected rot in the vicinity.

If there are signs of rot in any of the panels within the front wheel arch area, then the front wing will have to be removed so that a fuller appraisal of other, hidden, panels can be carried out. In any event, the front wing must be removed before remedial work to any of the panels can commence.

The triangular reinforcement box that joins the wheel arch panel (which forms the side of the engine bay) to the pedal box and side dash panel is a prime candidate for rust. Water kicked up by the road wheels can lie on top of the box which, unless properly protected and regularly cleaned, will rot badly. This section should be replaced if there is any sign of rot; it can rot out completely once rust has gained a toe-hold, and because its contribution to the strength of the body is considerable, patching it cures nothing. This is an inexpensive enough panel and easily fitted.

The corresponding panel in the MGC is longer and stronger – and for many years has been unobtainable. Enthusiasts had no option other than to make their own panels or to repair the existing ones. It is now available, so these days there is no excuse for not replacing these important sections complete.

When cutting out the section, take care not to distort the adjoining panels. Cut away from the seams if necessary rather than trying to part them, and then grind back as much as possible of what remains afterwards. Provided the old seams can be cleaned up you could weld the replacement section on top of them, although it is obviously better to use a spot weld remover to completely remove the old box section before welding in the new. It pays to give the new sections as much paint protection as possible.

The side dash assembly, which is hidden under the wing behind the mud splash panels, is prone to rot along its near-horizontal upper face and its lower seam (where it joins onto the sill). Rot on the top edge of this panel may be patched using 20g steel; rot along the bottom seam indicates similarly rotted forward sill sections, and both the panel (which is widely available) and the sills should ideally be replaced. Unfortunately, this entails removing the A-post, and so substantial internal bracing should be employed to ensure that the section keeps its shape. Side dash repair sections are now available, and offer a better solution than steel patching, although the lower edge could be repaired quite quickly using a strip of plain 20g sheet.

Any signs of weakness in the front side chassis rails should be treated as very serious, necessitating an engine-out complete strip-down. If these members have rotted then the chances are that all adjacent panels will be in an advanced stage of rot. In such circumstances, serious consideration should be given to reshelling the car. Although the side chassis rails are available individually as repair sections, fitting them in an otherwise rusted car is not a task for the

ABOVE *Not so long ago, an MGC with rotted-away inner wing reinforcing panels would have required specially fabricated replacements at considerable cost. Happily, they are now being manufactured and should be stock items for most MG specialists.*

LEFT *The bulkhead assembly will usually have rotted only on the very earliest of cars or on examples which have been laid up for many years. It is, however, usual to discover a thin coating of rust if you shine a torch beam through the bonnet hinge holes. This is an enclosed area which is not repairable, and serious rust can only be dealt with by replacement. This is hardly a job for the amateur, and could only be attempted during a complete base shell rebuild. Many people (including the author) spray a rust retarding primer or wax-based corrosion inhibiter through the holes in the bulkhead on a hot, dry day in the hope of at least slowing the progress of corrosion.*

ABOVE RIGHT *Never miss an opportunity to deal with rusting. Here, the author has removed the carburettors and cylinder head, allowing reasonable access to the nearside of the lower scuttle panel. Reasonably light surface rusting was dealt with using a wire cup brush in an angle grinder, and the panel treated with Bonda Prima.*

amateur. In the extremely unlikely event, however, that just the side chassis rail had rotted out and the adjoining panels were sound, there is a great chance that the far thinner adjoining panels would be severely distorted (and rendered useless) as the heavy section chassis rail was cut out.

A number of front end repair assemblies are now available. In addition to individual panels and the side chassis rail and cross-members assembly, it is possible to obtain an assembly consisting of the main centre body cross-member, side chassis rails and complete wheel arch and bonnet lock platform assembly. Such work is really the province of the professional. See the notes concerning body repair sections in Chapter 6, Rear bodywork repairs.

The front inner wheel arch/engine bay side panel is not a noted rust problem area, but if rust is allowed to do its work underneath layers of underseal within the wheel arch for any amount of time then it can spread and pose problems. Small rust areas can be patched, although the panel is structurally important and widespread rust or any rusting along welded seams should be dealt with by replacement of the entire panel; an engine-out job. Rot in the top flange of this panel (where the outer wing bolts to the inner) can, however, be dealt with using widely available repair sections and simply cutting out the affected length, letting in the new and butt welding at its ends.

After restoring the under-wing area, it is as well to apply the most thorough rust-retarding techniques. Areas which will be exposed, eg those ahead of the mud splash panel, should preferably be painted in rust-retarding primer, top-coated and then undersealed. Enclosed areas should receive rust-retarding treatment followed by as much paint as you can afford! Before refitting front wings, paint the dash side panels and sill sections with several layers of primer and paint, preferably using alternate colours for each coat of primer to ensure thorough coverage.

The compound bulkhead assembly (which contains the air intake and bonnet hinges), which is situated underneath the top shroud panel, can rust badly from the inside on the earliest cars, and is an especially difficult area for the amateur to deal with. The great problem is gaining access to this particular panel. The top shroud panel can rust along its edges, and if this is the case then it should be cut out, freshly exposed rotted metal underneath dealt with, and a repair panel fitted. The top shroud panel itself is widely available, although most of the section underneath can prove difficult to source (although it is present in Heritage bodyshells and could be available from Heritage specialist dealers) and could therefore have to be patched or replaced with a structure cut from a scrap body.

If a panel or assembly is needed which is not listed as a spare in the Heritage catalogue, the company might still be able to supply it. Those assemblies which are built up piece by piece in situ within the Heritage bodyshell will probably not be available. Assemblies which are built up on a separate jig and then built into the shell as a unit may be obtainable to special order, but only from a Heritage approved supplier. The company state that they will supply, for instance, the air box assembly.

The horizontal scuttle panel situated under the heater unit is not listed as an available spare in any of the catalogues which the author has examined, although Heritage might be willing to supply it through an approved stockist of their products. It can be patched if necessary, but the panel normally suffers surface corrosion rather than real rot, because the top face benefits from engine compartment heat which helps to evaporate moisture before it can do too much harm and because the lower face is within the passenger compartment. The heater assembly should be removed (see Chapter 5, Cooling system), in addition to the windscreen washerbottle, the brake and clutch master cylinders, and wires and pipes. Rusting of the panel (which is usually caused by brake and clutch fluid spills) can then be dealt with. The underside can of course be cleaned and repainted from within the car.

A-Post replacement

The A-post is very strongly made, and if advanced rot is found within it then the side dash panels and sills are sure to have rotted to a greater extent. In such cases it would be advisable to strip the car to a bare shell. The side will have to be stripped to such an extent (sills, probably floor, side dash assembly and A-post) that it would be wise to add substantial internal bracing in order to prevent distortion.

The A-post most commonly rots out at its base, when rot from the sill structure is left unattended for long periods of time and is allowed to spread. It is possible (although not recommended) to patch both this and the side dash panel, provided that suitably thick metal is used for each.

After any repairs to the floor pan and replacement of the sill inner step, the side dash panel could be replaced. The sill structure could then be built up and the A-post finally added.

INTERIOR AND EXTERNAL TRIM

It pays owners of pre-1974 'chrome bumper' examples of the MGB and V8 and all examples of the MGC to stick as closely to the original interior specifications and materials as possible, in order to maintain the collectors' value of their cars. More recent examples could be refitted using the modern and sometimes luxurious alternative trim which is available from many MGB specialist firms – but the time will come, no doubt, when you will wish you had left all as the manufacturer intended!

Early cars are often worth more if the aged original trim is still fitted than if reproduction trim is substituted, even if the original trim is showing its age and looking a little scruffy – there are, in any event, a number of upholstery renovation systems available. However, old leather seat covers can split, the leather itself having become as fragile and weak as thin cardboard and quite useless, often leaving the restorer with no option other than to try and source genuine replacement covers in better condition than his own or to buy and fit new reproduction covers.

The most likely source of original replacement seat covers is the car which has been dry stored but which had some degree of body rot before it was locked away; in such instances the bodywork and many components can prove quite useless and unrestorable, but the entire trim eminently salvageable. As time goes by, however, fewer and fewer such cars remain, forcing the restorer of a car with unsalvageable trim to accept reproductions.

The modern reproduction vinyl-covered trim panels for the footwell sides, on the door and rear quarter interior are usually close enough to the originals to make their use acceptable. If ordering from a mail order company do make sure that the person on the other end of the telephone appreciates exactly which colour/piping combination you require. The colour of the new panels will usually be slightly different from the originals simply due to the effects of years of sunlight which will have lightened the originals; the original vinyl seat backing panels

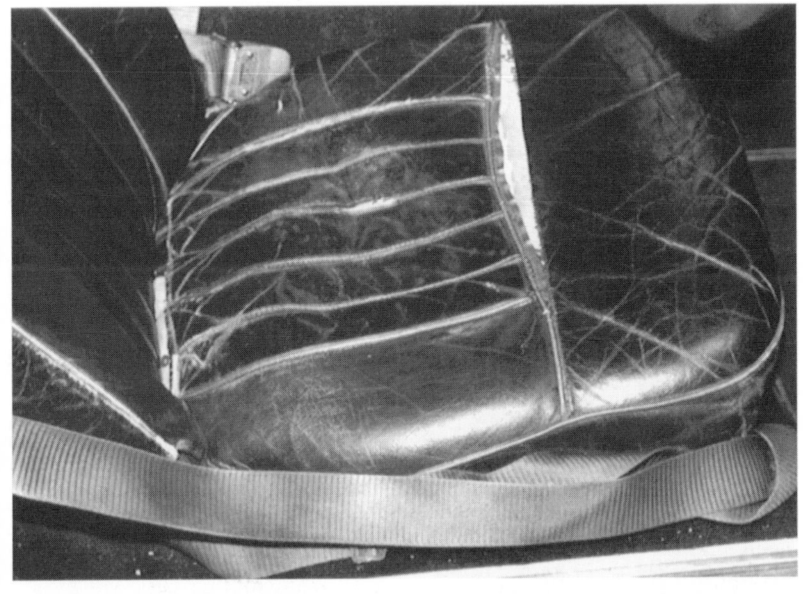

TOP *Old leather seat covers split along the seams, and can be repairable. Professional upholsterer's time is very expensive, and there is always the chance that some panels will be too brittle for repair, or that they will split again in a very short time. Replacement covers, although expensive, can be the more economical solution.*

LEFT *The door divested of fittings. Take the opportunity to deal with any surface rust at this stage.*

BELOW *Using a sharp craft knife, make small 'X' cuts through which the door handle and window winder fittings can pass. Before doing this, however, do ensure that the panels are the same size and shape as the original ones.*

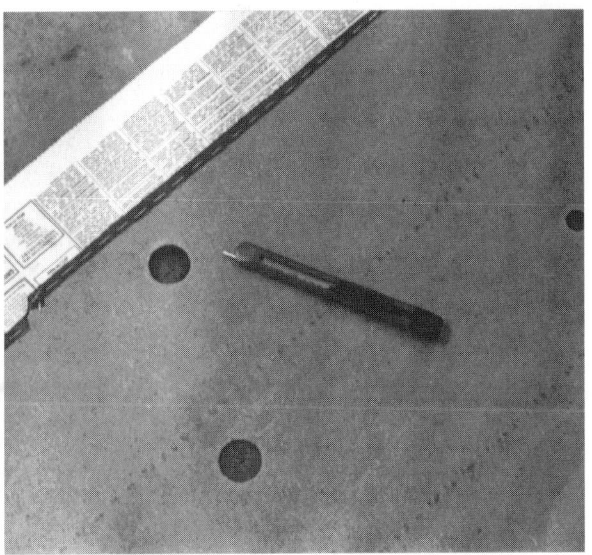

will have similarly faded, and to replace side trim but not seats may not look 'right'.

The one alternative to fitting new leather or vinyl seat covers is to try to restore the original covering. This is made possible by relatively new products. For tired and brittle old leather seat covers, kits are now available which, it is claimed, will reconstitute the leather, as are other kits which will restore the colour. Whilst the reconstituting kits certainly appear to be of use to the restorer, the problem with any colour restoring kit is in achieving a match between the leather, which can be dyed, and the other, vinyl, panels both on the seats and the side trim (plus the rear bench seat and back of GTs), which would have to be treated by another method. One product called Vinylkote seems to overcome these problems because it can be colour matched (for quantities of a litre and

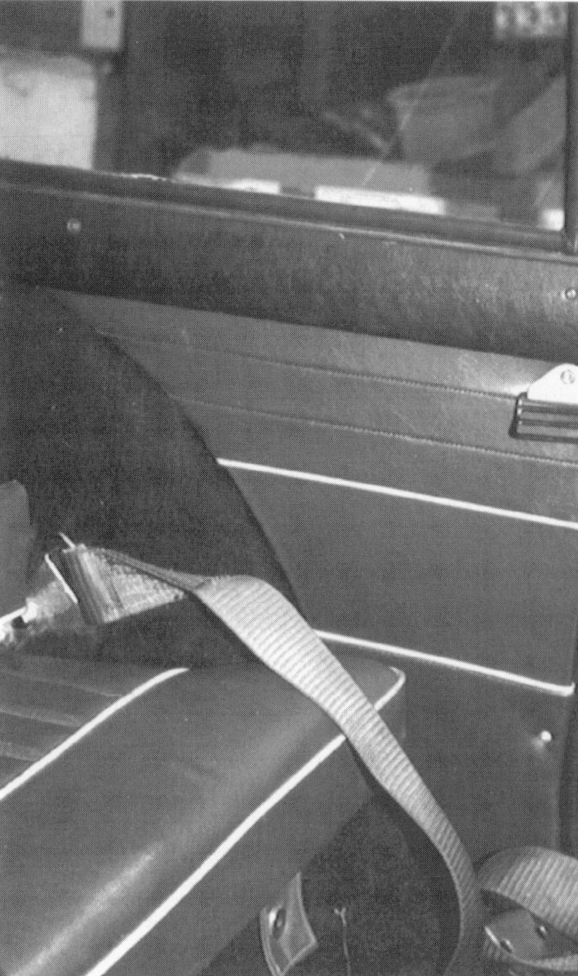

over) and is said to work equally well at penetrating vinyl and leather.

Specialist leather workers might also be able to manufacture replacement panels, dyed to the correct colour, for your existing seat covers. By a combination of reconstituting the less worn leather of the seat back and replacing badly damaged panels on the seat base, it would be possible to arrive at serviceable seat covers which are still to all intents and purposes original rather than reproduction.

Splits and tears in vinyl can be repaired using a 'welding kit', constiting of backing patches and adhesives which fuse together two torn edges. Careful use of these kits can result in virtually invisible joins.

Modern reproduction seat covers with leather facings are expensive to buy, but far preferable to the vinyl alternatives, which do not wear in the same way as leather and which become increasingly unconvincing as time passes.

When recovering a seat, it is usually advisable to replace the foam and the rubber diaphragm or canvas webbing which retains it. The rubber diaphragm is difficult to work with, being retained by steel clips which locate in the seat frames and which are under considerable tension from the stretched rubber. Removal and replacement of these is most easily and safely carried out using an easily-made special tool. Take an old screwdriver of about six to eight inches length, and cut into the centre of the blade a slot which is three hacksaw blades' width and perhaps a quarter of an inch deep. This can be achieved by making two individual cuts and then filing out the stub of metal which remains in the centre, or by strapping three hacksaw blades together at the ends with tape (the two outside ones facing in one direction, the centre in the other) and making the cut in one go.

By locating the bifurcated screwdriver blade onto a seat clip, far greater control is possible than if pliers or a self-grip wrench are used.

FAR LEFT *Hold the new panel in position using the grab handle fittings, and position the panel so that the rear and lower edges are very slightly inboard of the door edges. If you position the panel wrongly, the edge will catch on the door surround. The most worrying part of the job, making holes in the new panel with a bradawl, is about to begin. Work one hole at a time, loosely fitting each screw before making the next hole.*

LEFT *The new panels look very smart. It's a pity that they make the rear seat look so scruffy.... A good selection of self-tapping screws will come in handy when fitting the panels. Some of the original holes will be enlarged and require fatter screws, some of the original screws will have rusted and require replacement.*

BELOW *The new and old C-post panels compared. Transfer the spring fittings across, trying to keep each in the same position. Note the curvature of the old panel, which will have to be adopted by the new one in order to fit. If you begin to bend the new panel gently over your thigh until it is slightly concave, it will be much easier to fit. If you simply try to force a flat panel into position then there is a good chance that it will crack. Do not, as the author did, try this job on a hot, sticky summer's day. It would be frustrating enough in a comfortable climate.*

Re-covering seats

Remove the spring clips which fasten the seat covers to the frames. With the earliest seats, the old covers and the base foam (squab) can now be pulled from the framework. With later seats it will be necessary to remove the recliner adjustment handle and to remove the metal bezel through which the headrest stem passes. The backrest covers can now be eased off, taking care not to damage the foam underneath.

With recent seats, a hole must be cut in the new covers for the headrest bezel.

Renew seat foam if necessary, and glue thin sheet foam rubber onto the seat backs and sides. The seat back cover will be far easier to slide into place if a polythene sheet or bag is first fitted and taped into position over the back frame. Alternatively, a smooth cloth (curtain lining material is ideal and cheap) can be used either draped over the back or even sewn into a bag which fits snugly over the rubber. The new seat back cover can now be pulled down then smoothed to get rid of any wrinkles. The bottom edges can be glued before being fastened by the spring clips.

To make a hole for the recliner adjuster stud, simply tap sharply using a lightweight hammer around the hidden edge, as though cutting a gasket.

Glue the seat foam to the base. When the glue has set, the foam can be glued along its centreline

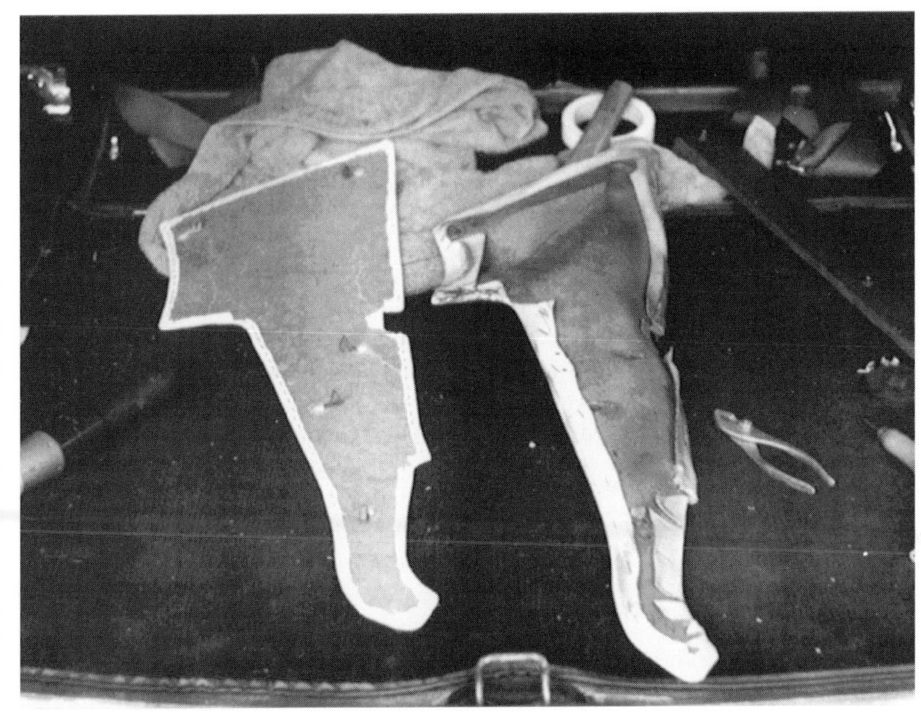

and the corresponding area of the cover (which should be turned inside out) also glued. The seat cover is positioned onto the foam and the rear flap glued and secured to the frame with spring clips, after which the cover can be drawn over the front and sides of the foam, glued and secured to the frame.

Interior vinyl trim and the headlining can often be cleaned and revitalised using various proprietary products which are widely available at motor shops, and advertised in the specialist press. If torn, however, replacement is usually advisable.

Side trim panels are fitted using self-tapping screws; it is worth buying a few dozen of these to replace the usually rusted originals. If it is possible, buy in extra screws with the same head size as the originals but slightly thicker threaded sections, for fitting into distorted holes. This should really be the very last job undertaken in the entire restoration, to avoid damaging the new panels.

Fitting panels

Remove door cappings, window winder handles, door catch handles and grab handles. Remove all fixing self-tapping screws and remove old trim from door. If the screws are to be reused and if they are not all exactly the same size, it pays to store them in the order of removal so that each can go back into its original hole.

Check the replacement panels against the old for colour, size and shape, before progressing further.

Using a very sharp craft knife or similar tool, make 'X' cuts through the holes in the backing hardboard for the door and window winder handles and the door grab handle fixing screws.

Place each panel into position and hold it temporarily using the grab handle fixings. Check that there is no overlap on the rear or lower faces of the door, and adjust the position until the panel is slightly inside these two lines. The reason for avoiding overlap here – even if it means having a slight overlap at the front edge – is that the door surround rear and bottom are tapered, so that the slightest overlap of the panel will cause it to rub on the corresponding fixed panels and wear very quickly.

Do not attempt to use the old panel as a template for positioning the screw fixing holes unless the new panel is exactly the same size as the old.

When the panel is positioned, try closing the door to ensure that nothing fouls or rubs.

Using a bradawl, make a hole through the panel for each fixing screw in turn and fit the screw loosely before moving on to the next. Take great care to make the holes in the correct places! When all fixing screws are in position, tighten them then refit the door trim.

The dash side and rear wheel arch panels are the easiest to work with. Fitting entails removal of the old panels, offering up the new and positioning correctly, then making holes with the bradawl and fitting the screws. In the case of the dash side panels, it pays to take the opportunity to examine closely for rusting, the inner sill step and underlying dash side panel, taking remedial action if necessary. Before fitting the wheel arch panels, similarly check the condition of the wheel arch fronts and the sill top/rear chassis rail.

The C-post panels on GTs are the most difficult of all to fit because replacements are merely covered hardboard panels which must be bent into a gentle curve in order to fit: furthermore, these panels are held with movable spring fittings which have to be precisely positioned before the panel is offered up. It can take many attempts to achieve success.

Offer up the bare panel and begin to bend it so that it fits properly, taking care not to bend too far and break the hardboard. Transfer the spring clips from the old panel to the new, keeping the angle of each exactly the same as on the old panel. There is no guarantee that the clips were in the correct positions on the old panels; not all might have aligned with their respective holes. Trial fit the panel until all of the spring clips align, then 'pop' them into position with a sharp but light tap.

Check the panel for correct alignment before making holes for the side window bracket fixing screws.

Carpets

Early cars did not possess carpets in the front, but moulded rubber mats (although the wheel arches, rear quarters and load platform of the GT were always carpeted). Most modern owners fit carpets throughout the interior, because they not only mask road noise through the floor panels and transmission tunnel, but also cut the amount of heat emanating from the latter.

Complete carpet sets can be inexpensive, but most are not moulded for the transmission tunnel as were original specification carpets, and are thus more difficult to fit and usually far less attractive than more expensive moulded alternatives. Some DIY restorers opt for the very lowest-cost alternative, which is to tailor their own carpets from the roll; it is difficult to obtain attractive results in this way, and, of course, it will not provide heel pads and the carpets will wear very rapidly.

To fit carpets, it is necessary to remove the seats and runners. The carpets are usually fixed with press studs – which are widely available. Carpets for the transmission tunnel – unless of the moulded variety – usually have to be fixed in position using a rubberised glue. Do not use strong adhesives for this, because the carpet will be impossible to remove subsequently without damage resulting.

Tunnel carpets, whether of the proper moulded or the cheaper variety, will have two flaps for positioning behind the radio speaker panel. On no account should these be glued down, because they cover the rubber plug which gives access to the gearbox dipstick/oil filler hole.

Other trim

The crackle-finish black paint on the dashboards of earlier cars is usually in need of attention. Replacement restored dashboards are inexpensive, but unless the dashboard is really bad and absolutely has to be removed, the amount of work involved will not justify the gains, concourse cars excepted. Black crackle-finish paint is widely available at MGB specialist spares suppliers – and many motor accessory factors – and it is possible to achieve good results simply by cleaning damaged areas and repainting them.

Many early cars will not be fitted with the large (16.5in) original steering wheel. This was the source of some criticism in early reviews of the car and many owners replaced it with one of smaller diameter and greater rim thickness (despite other criticisms that the steering was heavy even with the large original wheel). Reproduction steering wheels for early cars are available but expensive; examples from broken cars will also be expensive if bought from an MG specialist; but they can be found at reasonable prices if you are prepared to spend enough time scouring general car breakers' yards.

Reconditioned instruments can be quite expensive, but these are so important that the price charged is easily justified to obtain a guaranteed unit rather than an example from the breaker's yard. For instance, should the oil pressure gauge fail accurately to record a sudden drop in oil pressure or the temperature gauge a rise in temperature, the engine could be severely damaged in a very short period of time by the unsuspecting owner.

Little looks worse in an early car than a modern and completely out of period radio or, worse, a modern 'in-car entertainment (ICE) system' with tape deck, CD and graphic equalisers! If you wish to fit any ICE equipment in a pre-October 1967 Mk1 car, remember that it has positive earth electrics, and either switch to negative earth or completely insulate the ICE equipment from the car's metalwork. The option, of course, is to fit a reconditioned contemporary radio, available from a few specialists who advertise in the classic car press.

On rubber-bumper cars with more modern interiors the state-of-the-art ICE equipment does not look particularly out of place, and, because these vehicles already have negative earth electrics there is no impediment to fitting modern electronic equipment.

On rubber bumper cars, it should be noted that whilst, as a general rule of thumb, the value placed on authenticity is not so great as with chrome bumper models, Limited Edition and Jubilee cars have enhanced value which can be jeopardised by the fitting of almost any non-original equipment. Other examples of rubber bumper cars might be deemed more desirable in some people's eyes – and thus attract a higher value – if non-original luxury equipment is fitted!

Some MGB specialists, such as John Hill's MGB Centre, will supply complete colour co-ordinated interiors including seats, all trim and carpets. At the time of writing, options were limited to colour schemes similar to those of modern MG Metros and Maestros.

Headlining

Removal of the headlining should be avoided unless it is part of a bare shell restoration. Removal and reinstallation is a fiddly job at the best of times, requiring removal of the windscreen (see the following text).

Old headlining that has become discoloured can be washed, and treated with Vinylkote or a similar product if it is badly stained. Damaged headlining can only satisfactorily be attended to by renewal; there is no repair method to the author's knowledge.

Removal of the headlining can be made after unclipping the two top side cantrail trim sections and the front and rear header rail trims. Headlining panels and the adjacent rail capping are now available from specialist MG dealers; it is usually best to replace these as a complete set so that the colours match.

Hood and tonneau

Tears in the hood or tonneau can be dealt with simply by stitching the torn edges back together or by stitching on a patch. There is little looks worse than a smart MGB with a tatty hood, however, and most owners elect to replace a tired or damaged hood. Replacement hoods are widely available, and may be purchased without the header rail at relatively low cost or with the header rail fitted at around three or more times the price. Fitting the latter should be a straightforward swap. Taking the more economical option naturally involves you in far more work. First, the existing header rail must be removed from the hood. Remove the header seal then drill out the pop rivets from its retaining strip. The hood is secured at each end by screws. Remove these, then pull apart the glued join between the hood and the header rail.

The header rail should be cleaned and keyed for the glue, using a suitable abrasive, then refitted on the windscreen surround. It is important that the hood is fitted squarely, so mark the outer front centre using chalk. Erect the hood frame, then fix the hood at the rear, pull it forwards over the header rail keeping the chalk centre line mark in line with the windscreen centre rod whilst an assistant makes a chalk mark from the inside of the car along the line where the hood material reaches the cant rail. Ideally, one person should apply pressure to the centre and one edge of the hood, with another applying pressure to the other side. Do not pull too tightly on the material, because future shrinkage is possible, and if the hood is too tight to begin with, then the slightest amount of skrinkage will prevent it from reaching the header rail or at best will overstress it and accelerate wear.

Spread a line of glue on the hood underside ahead of the mark, and on the header rail, then, preferably with an assistant holding the front corners of the hood whilst you hold the centre, pull the hood into position, taking the greatest care to centralise it before allowing the two glued surfaces to touch. Impact adhesive is the best glue for the job, but make sure that you get the positioning absolutely right before you commit the material into position. Fold the corners and refix them with the screws and washers, then glue the front of the hood material down to the bottom of the header rail, line up the seal retainer holes and pop rivet this back into position. Cut away surplus material. Refit the seal.

The chrome finishing trim is fragile and easily damaged, yet fitting it requires great force. If you do not wish to have to buy expensive replacements and you are going to renew the glazing rubber, cut the finishing trim out rather than levering it.

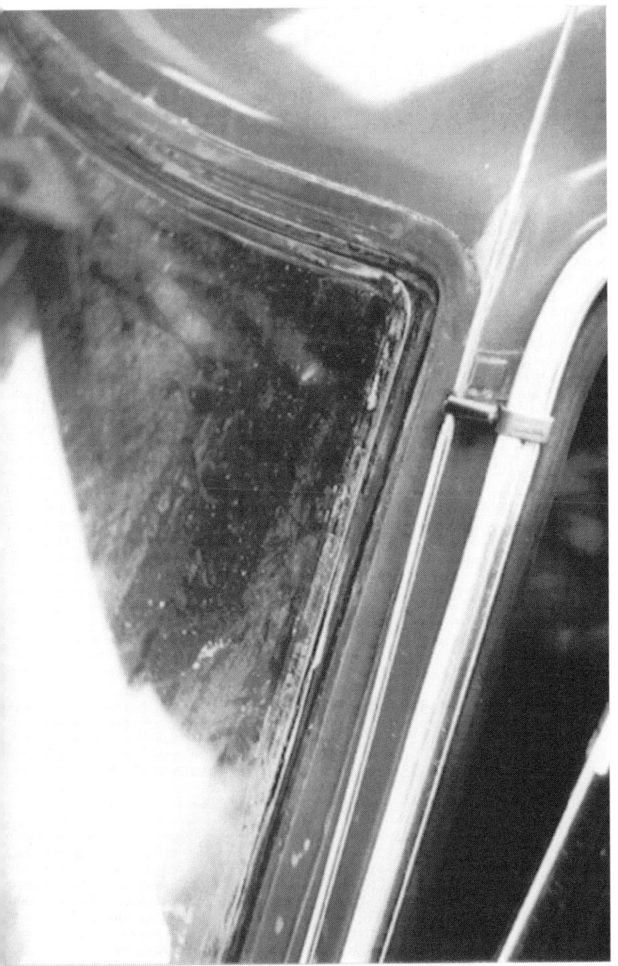

The author was given varied advice on how to remove the glass, amongst which was the brutal suggestion that he should sit inside the car and push it out with his feet! Laminated screens like the one pictured do not like that kind of treatment, and the author elected to cut away sufficient of the top and sides of the old glazing trim to allow the glass to be tilted forwards.

External trim

Chromed metalwork is not restorable by the DIY enthusiast; either he must obtain reconditioned components on an exchange basis, or he must send his old chrome fittings to a specialist company for stripping and rechroming. Neither option will be particularly cheap. It might just be possible to obtain reasonable chromeware from a general breaker's yard, although this becomes progressively less likely. Once a chrome surface is breached, even with a pin-hole, corrosion of the underlying metal begins and spreads underneath the chromium plating. The chances of discovering an unblemished bumper or light rim at a breaker's are virtually nil.

Both reproduction and reconditioned grilles for all years and Marks of MGB are widely available, as are the chromed side trim strips, quarterlight assemblies and air intake grilles. One useful tip, passed on by the Bromsgrove MG Centre, is to place a small piece of plastic tape under the riveted retainers for the side chrome trim. This helps prevent the paint from cracking whilst pressure is applied to the pop rivet and also isolates the fitting from the body, so preventing rusting.

Anything involving road wheels on the MGB range is expensive. Wire wheels were an option which originally cost per set some £30 if painted and £77 if chromed; in 1990 they were priced at that sort of money each, and the cost of converting an originally pressed-steel wheel car to accept wires almost doubled the cost of the cheaper painted wheels themselves!

The DIY restorer can send wires and pressed-steel wheels away for shot-blasting and either chroming or painting; alloys should be closely examined for damage and, if found to be good, hand-cleaned and repainted. Before sending a scruffy set of wires away for rechroming, consider whether the splines are worn and whether replacement wheels might offer a safer long-term solution.

Some early MGB 'press cars' were fitted with a single wing mirror, which was a factory option; others were photographed with a single door mirror, in both instances, on the drivers' side. Particularly for modern multi-lane trunk road and motorway driving, one or the other will make overtaking a far safer manoeuvre and is therefore recommended. Accurate reproduction mirrors are widely available through MGB specialist businesses. These come complete with fitting instructions, and so no special instructions are necessary here.

GT windscreen removal/refit

The instructions for fitting the windscreen also apply to the tailgate window. When estimating the time that might be required for this job, take into account the likelihood that the bodywork covered by the glazing strip will require attention ranging from cleaning and repainting to cutting and replacement. Parts of this job can be very difficult, and were it not for the fact that removing the windscreen at home offers the opportunity to deal with underlying rust, this is a job which would be best entrusted to a professional windscreen replacement business.

The very last stage of the job, refitting the chrome trim strips, proved so tricky that the author was forced to bring in professional assistance. The labour charge for this was a substantial proportion of that for the entire job. Arguably the best solution would be to remove the screen (which is not too difficult), deal with any rust as necessary, and then commission a mobile windscreen replacement business to come and refit the screen.

Safety is paramount during these operations. Wear leather gloves whilst handling glass. Do not place any unnecessary strain on the glass, and avoid levering against it with metal implements during refitting.

Removal of the windscreen is comparatively easy and does not take many minutes. Replacing the windscreen can be a most awkward and frustrating task, and there is vast potential for things to go wrong. If the glass is being removed prior to a respray, there is a strong case for taking it to a professional afterwards for the refitting, in order to avoid damaging the new paintwork.

To remove the windscreen, first remove the windscreen wiper blades and arms. Place some form of padding on the bonnet (a continental quilt is ideal).

Lifting the glass out. This is, in the interests of safety, really a two-man job, but the author found that the problems of working solo could largely be overcome. Have a thick protective covering, such as a continental quilt (when the lady of the house is out) on which to lay the glass. Be sure to clean the edge of the glass before refitting it.

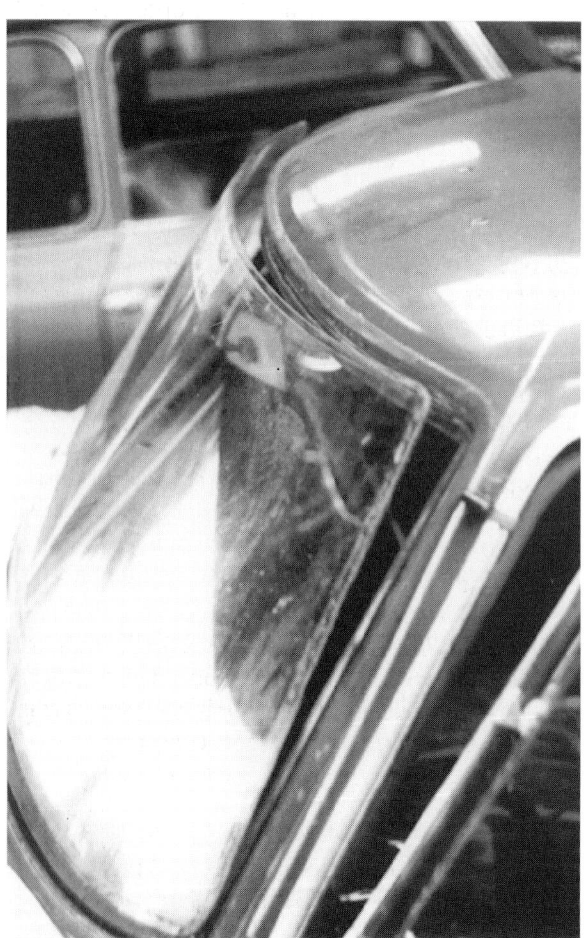

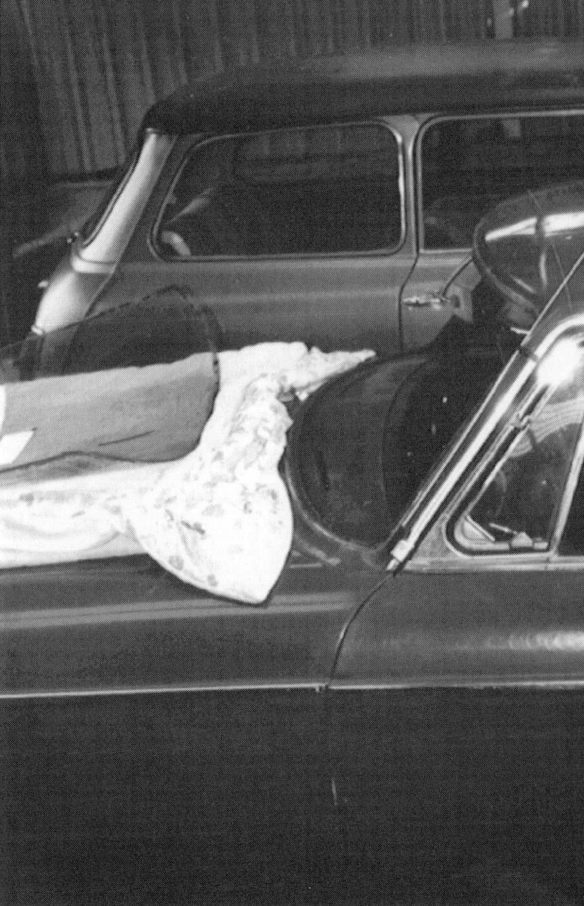

Begin removing the chromed finishing pieces. These are very prone to going out of shape and they are currently ridiculously expensive for what they are, so take care not to damage them. If the rubber surround is to be replaced, consider cutting one of the retaining lips away from the old rubber surround, which will make removal of the strips far easier and lessen the chances of their being damaged. If the screen has been removed previously, you might discover that the trim is already distorted to some extent, having undulations. Do not confuse irregular distortions with a natural and gentle bending and twisting which occurs as the fillers are removed, because this is a shape which they have adopted quite naturally as a result of being held within the glazing rubber.

If the trim is salvageable, then use it; the professional fitters at Worcester Windscreens aver that it is far easier to fit used than new trim. Trying to refit badly distorted trim, on the other hand, will increase the chance of damaging the glazing rubber, so that if the trim has more than the slightest irregular distortion, the advice must be to replace it at whatever cost.

Pull the filler strips from the glazing rubber. If either are perished then they will have to be replaced. The windscreen can now be eased out from the glazing strip, starting with one top corner, then continuing along the top edge. Either sit in the car and push while an assistant holds the other side of the glass to prevent it from suddenly popping out, or stand alongside the car with one arm each side of the roof pillar. If the glazing rubber is to be replaced then you can alternatively use a sharp craft knife to slice away part of the old rubber to reveal the screen edge.

With the windscreen removed, you may well discover rot in the newly-exposed metalwork, especially along the lower edge. Either clean and paint this or cut out the rot and weld in new metal.

To refit the screen, first fit the rubber surround, making sure that it is correctly positioned in the corners and not skewed. A soft lightweight mallet can prove of help in persuading the rubber into position.

Lubricate the glazing strip recess for the glass using soap and water (the hand cleaner, Swarfega, is also very good for this and is used by some professionals). Offer the screen into position and locate the lower edge first. Then, using a blunt screwdriver (with no sharp edges) or the end of a spoon, work your way around the glazing rubber and pull the lip over the glass.

Now for the first awkward bit! The filler strip has to be inserted. There is a special tool for this purpose but if, like the author, you do not have access to this, then try a range of implements until one can be found to do the job! An old, blunted screwdriver gave the author the best results, and was used to work a run of three inches of the inner edge into position, then to work in the outer edge. The inner edge of the strip must go quite deeply into the glazing rubber recess, and not into the top lip, which is for the finishing strip.

If the filler strip is a touch awkward to fit, the finishing trim verges on the impossible. The edges locate under a thin rubber lip and there is ample opportunity to stab your way through the glazing strip while you try to persuade it to move over the lip of the trim.

The author spent six hours trying to fit the finishing trim, yet had to eventually admit defeat. After speaking to spares dealers, professional restorers and Heritage, the division of the Rover Group that supplies the trim to the trade, the author discovered that none knew of any 'easy' way to fit the trim. Ron Hopkinson MG Parts Centre and the Bromsgrove MG Centre were, as usual, very helpful. Their advice was to find a professional window replacement business which employed a fitter who had previously carried out the work!

The author contacted Worcester Windscreens's Droitwich fitting centre and was informed that most windscreen fitters 'ran the other way' when the MGB GT was mentioned. In the end, it took two very experienced fitters (two pairs of hands) a long time to do the job. It transpired that fitting GT windscreens was probably the least popular task in their profession. The best advice is to have the entire windscreen fitting carried out professionally.

Roadster windscreen

Whilst the filler trim was being fitted to the author's GT, the fitters explained that fitting a new windscreen to the MGB Roadster was probably their *second* least favoured job! The main cause for concern is the retightening of the tie bar, and fears of what the resulting forces could do to the screen itself. Again, the author strongly advises that, although the amateur can safely strip the screen assembly to allow the metalwork to be cleaned, the glass is fitted professionally.

Remove the windscreen and surround complete (See Chapter 5a). The frame can be dismantled from around the windscreen. First, remove the tie rod from the top bracket. The frame side pieces are held by screws in the top and bottom rail (two top and bottom, each side). Remove these and then ease or gently tap the sides off. The top and bottom rails can then also be removed. The glazing rubber can then be eased from the glass.

When reassembling, clean all sealant residue from the edge of the screen then use screen sealer around the glazing rubber and along the bottom sealing rubber. A sash cramp can be of help in pulling the top and bottom rails together. Use gentle but firm pressure when fitting the rails, to allow excess sealer time to ooze out. Further reassembly is the opposite of stripping.

BELOW LEFT *And you thought that this would be a quick and easy job! Prepare yourself mentally for the shock of seeing a considerable amount of rust which has languished unseen under the leaky old glazing strip. This rust turned out to be far less entrenched as it first appeared, and was cleaned, treated to rust-retarding primer then topcoat, then left for the paint to harden. The delaminated join right in the corner was clamped then MIG welded.*

BELOW *At this stage, the glazing rubber was sealing neither the glass nor the surrounding metal. The filler strip swells the glazing rubber, pushing the two lips down tight against glass and metal. Fitting it is anything but a pleasant experience.*

PROFESSIONAL RESTORATION

Irrespective of whether you wish a professional restorer to carry out specific tasks or a full restoration, the problem remains of finding the right business for the job. Restoration businesses which will agree to undertake work on the MGB, range from the very worst examples of ill-equipped, unskilled backstreet 'cowboys' to the most highly reputable and competent craftsmen. The price of sending your car to a poor restorer may not be apparent for some months or even a year or two after the completion of the work, because it will probably take this long for the shiny new paintwork to rust through or the liberally-applied filler to drop out!

Second in importance only to avoiding 'cowboys' is to avoid general body repair companies which have no experience of the MGB. They will take longer to do a less satisfactory job than the specialist. Classic car restoration businesses which have no specific experience of restoring the MGB will also usually take longer than a specialist in the car. It is far from unknown for such companies (which might be reputable, employ skilled craftsmen and use proper techniques) to undertake an MGB restoration but to tell the owner afterwards that they would never care to repeat the exercise!

The author has seen cars which have been restored by supposedly reputable general body repair shops and which have looked absolutely stunning when returned to the owner, but which have deteriorated quite quickly in the all-important, hidden sections such as the sills. One car in particular looked so good when freshly restored by such a business that a knowledgeable MGB specialist volunteered a very high valuation for it without closely examining even the sills. Two or three years later, however, the still stunning looks of this car blind admirers to the fact that portions of the sill structures have rotted because the sills had been patched rather than replaced during the original restoration. Deal only with specialists.

Most of the reputable MGB restoration trade does not produce truly concours cars but rather sound, roadworthy cars which will not require any bodywork attention for many years. This is not because they cannot produce concours cars but, rather, because so few of their clients wish to incur the immense expense involved in rebuilding a car to 'as new' condition. Any worthy restorer will be pleased to quote for jobs ranging from basic body rebuilding to make the shell sound, to a complete concours restoration, or to provide a range of estimates for different extents of work, which allows you to pick the price structure which best suits your own abilities and pocket.

Sorting the good restorer from the cowboy is really a matter of commonsense. The very best way to find a restorer for your car is by personal recommendation from a satisfied previous customer of the business. A person whose car has been well restored will usually be only too happy to make such recommendations and will miss few opportunities to show off the car. It can be difficult, however, when looking at a newly restored car to determine whether the work was carried out by a cowboy (who was nevertheless an artist with body filler) and will require repair in the not too distant future, or whether it was the work of a competent bodyshop and will be sound for many years. This is because the worst element of the trade are highly adept at covering up their shoddy workmanship and making the car appear excellent with the application of a few pounds of body filler.

Nevertheless, the best way to judge the competence of a restoration business is by a car which was restored by them, but an example which was restored a year or preferably more ago. A competent restorer who has nothing to hide will be pleased to show you or send you to see a car which he restored even three or more years previously. Looking at a car straight from the paint booth will tell you nothing.

The owners' clubs might be able to recommend a good restorer in your area, and classic car magazines occasionally publish a list of 'approved' restorers. The author knows, however, of several very good restoration businesses in his own area which do not appear to be on any recommendation lists, so no such list should be taken as exhaustive.

You can gauge a restoration business by its workshop. A neat and tidy workshop indicates a neat and tidy approach to work, and will usually be reflected in the quality of workmanship. A scruffy workshop which has tools scattered liberally and seemingly at random is not a good recommendation, if for no other reason than because the workforce will waste a lot of time (which you will be paying for) looking for misplaced tools! Another good sign is when MGBs are the predominant (or only) car to be seen in and around the workshop. This indicates a high degree of specialisation and experience which will result in a faster and better through-put of work.

A good restoration business will use high quality tools. If you see an incomplete socket set of dubious and mixed origins then it will probably be of poor quality and it will be incomplete because the missing sockets either burst or rounded. You cannot obtain good quality results using poor quality tools. Even worse would be the discovery of rusted tools, which would indicate not only a willingness to use poor equipment, but also a damp workshop which will rust panels as they are welded onto cars! Similarly, you should be able to see a proper spray booth (although many restorers take their charges to a spraying specialist, so if you cannot see a booth ask where the cars are sprayed).

When you first visit a workshop, take a look at the work in progress. Ascertain whether short cuts such as welding a new panel onto a rusted one or cutting off the bottom quarter of a front wing rather than removing it are being taken. Gauge the extent of rustproofing techniques which are being applied. See whether areas such as the dash side panel and A-post are cleaned and repainted before being covered by the outer front wing.

Best of all, take a knowledgeable friend when you first visit a restoration business, to gain a valuable second opinion. Although not really fair to the business, turning up without an appointment will ensure that you see the business as it actually is, rather than allowing a more dubious restorer time to tidy up the workshop and remove anything which he does not wish you to see!

Before visiting a professional restorer, you should ascertain as precisely as possible the extent of work that will be necessary. This will prevent rogues from giving you a low cost estimate which suddenly rises when further rot is 'discovered' half-way through the job. It will also guard against the quick turn-around business which offers a flat rate for sill replacement, only to again 'discover' part-way through the job that far more than the sills is in need of replacement. When this happens the customer is helpless because his car, divested of a sill, cannot be removed from the premises without suffering terminal body distortion! There is no practical option to sanctioning further, unbudgeted, work at whatever huge cost the business elects.

Before visiting a restorer, therefore, you should carry out a full bodywork appraisal as described in Chapter 2, taking notes as you go. List all panels which you know need replacing, and all which you suspect will need attention. If your subsequent list includes work which the restorer fails to notice during his own appraisal, then you have good cause to suspect either his knowledge of the subject or his honesty!

The estimate

An honest restorer will provide a written estimate which lists parts and itemises labour costs throughout the job, but will always point out that there is a chance that further work may be found to be necessary. This is because some problems only come to light after adjoining metalwork has been removed. A rogue will hold back such information as a surprise for later on when the car is immobile.

A written estimate can tell you much about the business. Labour should be totalled in hours and priced, allowing you to find the hourly rate. If this appears unduly high, then either the business offers fabulous standards or they are very busy and will only take your work if you make it worth their while by paying overtime rates! If the hourly rate appears unduly low, then the probably explanation is that the business is incompetent at estimating or that it employs very low-paid and low-skilled staff. New body panels should be listed and priced, allowing you to compare the prices with those advertised widely by mail order businesses. If the prices are very high then the proprietor might be adding too great a profit margin, if the prices appear low then the business might be using panels of doubtful quality.

An estimate should give some indication of when the work might commence. A good restorer is always in demand, and will often have a waiting list ranging from two months to the best part of a year. A business which can take your car for a full restoration the next day is likely to be able to do so because it is unpopular.

It usually pays to obtain more than one, and perhaps three or more, estimates for the work, so that in assessing any of them you have comparisons which take account of current overheads and material costs.

Attitudes

A good restorer who has nothing to hide will show you around the whole work area and answer any questions you might dream up. Be warned, however, that all restorers fall victim to many time-wasting 'dreamers' who ask endless questions, frequently visit or telephone, but lack the finance for the actual work.

The good restorer will normally invite you to visit the premises at any time during the restoration to inspect the car. If a verbal invitation to visit is not forthcoming, then ask whether you will be made welcome should you 'happen to be passing' and drop in to take a look at the car. A restorer who utilises short-cuts and dubious methods will not wish to have customers visiting without appointments and consequently witnessing what goes on.

A readiness to comply with requests from customers for work which could leave a car in a dangerous condition is the hallmark of the worst rogue restorer. If your first question to a restorer is how much he would charge to weld centre sill cover sections onto your car, then the good restorer will refuse point-blank to do the job and the poor restorer will volunteer a price but offer no warning of the dangers of the practice. This might seem a little underhand, but because you will be spending a large sum of money when commissioning the restoration, it is easy to justify any attempt to establish the competence and bona fides of a restorer.

Payment

You will usually be expected to pay a proportion of the bill in advance. In the case of a good restorer, a small sum will be necessary as insurance in case you suddenly change your mind just before the job is due to start and leave him with an empty workshop and a wages bill plus other overheads; remember that the work-load will be planned ahead for many months. This deposit might also cover the costs of any components which have to be bought in prior to the commencement of the job.

An advance payment (on acceptance of the estimate and commissioning of the work) of 10 per cent of the written estimate should be sufficient in most cases. Never part with much more than this as a deposit. Rogue businessmen in all trades and callings, who realise that their business is becoming or is insolvent, sometimes try to raise as much cash as possible as quickly as possible by taking deposits and even full advance payment from customers. When the liquidator is called in by a creditor, the poor customer is at the very end of the line when it comes to getting money back!

A further sum might justifiably be payable shortly after the job has started to cover the costs of bought-in panels and other materials. Thereafter, payments at intervals might also be requested, linked to the portion of work that has been done.

One must have sympathy with the restorer whose customer becomes 'financially embarrassed' part-way through a restoration: the car might be in a state whereby it cannot be moved (with the sills off) and he might not be able to spare the workshop space to leave the car where it is until the customer's own cash-flow improves. There can be, despite this risk, no justification for charging very high deposits.

NEW BODYSHELLS

Up until 1989 many MGBs were forced off the road by advanced and widespread bodyrot and the very high costs of rectification. Despite the relatively low cost of individual MGB body panels, a complete bodyshell restoration requiring the replacement of most of the panels could easily cost far more than the resultant value of the car – even if the work was carried out on a DIY basis. By 1990 it would probably have been true to say that any MGB (the newest of which was in its tenth year) was a candidate for serious and widespread bodyrot, and it is little wonder that many cars were scrapped in the 1970s and early 1980s.

This situation began to change during the middle to late 1980s as the collector's value of MGBs soared along with those of other classic sports cars, so lessening the difference between restoration costs and the eventual worth of the car; even then it was still all too easy to spend far more than the final value of the car on its restoration. MGBs were still regularly broken down for spares or allowed to rot away in garages.

The introduction of 'Heritage' (a division of the Rover Group) bodyshells altered matters. Suddenly, even a totally rotten MGB could be rebuilt around a new bodyshell, and accordingly, the prices realised by completely rotten chrome bumper Roadsters began to reflect their new usefulness. The prices paid for rusted hulks that had valid registrations, windscreen surrounds (Roadster), plus chassis and engine numbers, came close to that paid for a 'borderline MOT failure' which merely required new sills and

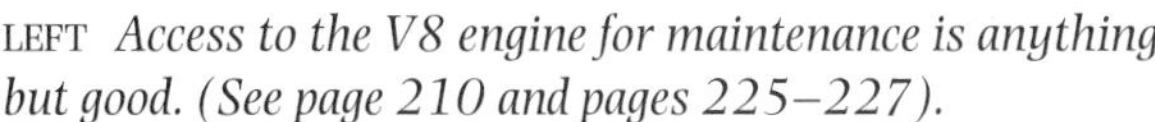

LEFT *Access to the V8 engine for maintenance is anything but good. (See page 210 and pages 225–227).*

ABOVE RIGHT *The repositioned oil filter and alternator. There is scant clearance between the new water pump pulley and the radiator.*

ABOVE *The nearside rear head clearance is minimal, as can be seen. The off-side clearance is even less. The positioning of the engine mountings is thus vital, and it would be worth having at least this portion of the job carried out by a company with a track record of successful V8 conversions.*

sundry other bodywork repairs to make it roadworthy. Some who opted for a reshell in the belief that it was a low-cost method of obtaining an 'as new' MGB, were to discover to their cost, however, that the price of the old car and new shell were but a fraction of the eventual rebuild costs.

To prove this, take a spares catalogue from any major MGB parts specialist, and total the costs of those items which will probably require replacement/ exchanging. Take into account the fact that most components from a rotten reshell candidate car will have deteriorated as much as the bodywork and need attention or replacement. For the sake of speed, ignore the hundreds of small items which cost from a few pence to a few pounds each, and you will soon discover that the ancillaries for a new bodyshell build can cost as much as a new small car – without taking the cost of the shell or the 'donor' car into account!

At the time of writing, the cost of the replacement bodyshell appears to come to approximately one quarter or one fifth of the total bill if the typically large percentage of components are exchanged or renewed.

Nevertheless, the bodyshells do give us the opportunity to build what can in effect be a brand-new MGB sports car for the same or slightly less than the cost of a modern alternative. The time needed to strip the old shell, clean, recondition or replace all the mechanical, electrical and trim components and rebuild the lot into a sparkling new MGB will be hundreds of hours for the person working alone at home, but a fraction of that for a professional restorer who will be geared up for the work and who will usually already carry many of the necessary spares within his stock.

The professional restorer who undertakes a reshell on behalf of a customer will be purchasing spares at trade prices, so that the difference between a DIY reshell and a professional one should be far less than the DIY price plus labour.

The best business to undertake such work will be the spares specialist which also possesses workshop facilities, because most of the spares needed will be in stock and will have been bought in by the business at the best bulk discount rates. The ideal business for such work would resemble the Bromsgrove MG Centre, which allies a professionally-staffed workshop to a large MG spares store. In fact, the difference between the 1990 quoted price for a professional reshell from this business, and the cost at full retail prices of the shell and all components for reconditioning or replacement (plus the cost of a decent donor car) was surprisingly little.

At the time of publication, MGB and GT shells are available only in Mk2 (1967–69) form, which means that if a shell is to be used with an earlier donor, some alteration will prove necessary. This mainly involves the transmission tunnel/air box assembly, which has to be reshaped to accept the inertia starter of the Mk1, plus the filling of certain extraneous holes and so on. In one reported instance the transmission tunnel and air box assembly were cut out of the new shell and those cut from the donor car fitted in place. Because the transmission tunnel is amongst the very last of body panels to rust, this seems a perfectly acceptable practice, although not by any stretch of the imagination can it be considered a DIY job.

In order to reshell an MGB, you will need a lot of working space and even more for storage of all the components. You will also need a donor car to provide the bulk of components for exchange or reconditioning.

Economies in the selection of a donor could easily prove to be false economies. An absolute wreck which had not run for a period of time, might be very cheap to buy but may well prove to have a predominance of useless mechanical and electrical components which would all have to be replaced at ever-mounting expense. A more expensive car which had an MOT and was a runner, on the other hand, could be used on the road for a short period before work commenced, during which time mechanical faults would, hopefully, become apparent. The problem is that many components age more quickly if not used than they do if the car is used regularly.

The ideal donor car would be one which had terminal but until-recently hidden bodyrot, on which the hapless owner has lavished large sums of money on mechanical repair and replacement. Look for 'for sale' advertisements along the lines of 'Much money spent, some body work needed for MOT' . . .

Having acquired a donor car, the first step is to strip it to the last nut and bolt, placing components into two separate stores; one for items which can be cleaned and reused, the other for components needing replacement or reconditioning. Bearing in mind the potentially huge costs of replacement and reconditioning of components, it would be as well to draw up lists of all spares and outwork which will be necessary, and to try to estimate costings before becoming too financially committed, eg before ordering a new shell.

Should the projected total transpire to be obviously beyond your means, at least you will have a garage full of saleable commodities in the form of spares from your dismantled bodyshell.

If you totally strip the car and make a comprehensive list of spares needed, then you might be able to negotiate a reasonable discount on the combined prices of the spares and the new body shell from an MGB spares supplier, due to the high total value of the order.

Do not dispose of the old bodyshell any sooner than is absolutely necessary, just in case some insignificant component emerges as essential part-way through the fitting out of the new shell. The old shell will also prove invaluable for identifying holes which have to be drilled, panels which could require some small alteration etc, before the new shell is painted.

The Heritage shells are primed using a process in which the metalwork is polarised using an electric current which attracts the paint into every nook and cranny of the shell. Unfortunately, this also attracts the paint into the threads of every captive nut. The first part of the rebuild should entail running a tap through every captive nut thread on the shell, then sealing them from your own primer and topcoat by screwing in a bolt prior to painting.

If you wish to use a Mk2 shell for a Mk1 donor rebuild, then there are a number of bodywork modifications which must be carried out prior to painting the shell. Most obviously, the two reversing light holes will each need a plate welded in if authenticity is important. This is the only 'cosmetic' alteration which offers an option to the rebuilder. The decision is whether to blank off the holes or fit slightly out-of-period, but very useful, reversing lights. Doing so would entail making up some sort of gear-activated switch for which the three-synchro gearbox has no provision, or alternatively, merely running the reversing lights off a dash-mounted switch. Other alterations are essential and will be hidden from view in the finished car.

The gear lever holes for the Mk1 and Mk2 are different shapes and are situated in different positions, so that either a section cut from the donor car's tunnel can be fitted, or a plate can be cut and shaped to fit. This is why it is so important to try and keep the old shell until the rebuild is nearly complete; if a component will not fit then you can immediately compare the two shells and discover whether there are any discrepancies.

The transmission tunnel/air box assembly cannot accommodate the bendix drive gear of the inertia starter motor. Both this and the previous difference (the gear lever hole) could be dealt with by cutting out the transmission tunnel from the new shell and welding in the one from the old. Few amateurs would be keen to undertake such work and to have it carried out professionally would be extremely expensive. More usually, the tunnel is beaten out until the starter motor drive gear will fit.

A bulge should be beaten just behind and below the existing small bulge within the transmission tunnel. Fit the gearbox into position and offer up the starter motor to this in order to gauge how deep the bulge should be. When the bulge is finished, there should still be ample room for the floor-mounted dip switch. When the starter motor can be accommodated (leave some small clearance around the bendix gear), dress the bulge whilst an assistant holds a dolly on the other side to prevent distortions.

Another fundamental difference between Mks 1 and 2 MGBs is that the latter car possesses face-level ventilation, and obviously the air vents will have to be blanked off if the Mk1 dash assembly is to be fitted. There would be little point in welding on a plate and consequently spoiling the primed finish as heat from the welding travelled through the surrounding area. It would be easier to affix a plate with bolts or self-tapping screws, remembering to use sealant.

After any necessary bodywork modifications have been carried out, the underside of the car should be given proper protection. This work will be made many times easier if the shell is raised to a comfortable working height. It might be deemed worth giving enclosed areas, such as the side dash panel sections and the tops of the sill outer panels, which are enclosed by the outer front wing, as much protection as possible at this stage; removing the mud splash panel will allow reasonable access.

The running gear can now be fitted, if desired, so that the shell can be moved around the workshop and pushed onto a car trailer if the topcoats are to be applied at a proper spray booth (which is advisable). Before the front suspension is fitted, however, take the ideal opportunity to spray the engine bay without risking getting overspray onto the front suspension. The quality of the finish within the engine bay is arguably not so important as that of the external body panels, although a mobile professional sprayer could be brought in if you doubt your own ability. An alternative method of making the shell mobile is to weld up a small trolley on castors or small wheels, which could bolt on to the chassis rails. It would be easy enough to roll this up ramps onto a trailer, so that the spray booth could handle the entire job including the engine bay. Mark and Derek Blazier made up a frame with lifting handles in order to move Mark's GT shell and Derek's Heritage Roadster shell around and to turn the GT on its side.

Before taking the shell to a spray booth, compare it minutely against the donor car shell and ensure that no extra holes have to be drilled into the new shell. Such holes could be for the fitting of wing mirrors, for a bracket, for a pipe or wire to pass through a bulkhead, for such items as boot badges and side trim. With the Roadster check that all holes necessary for the fitting of the hood are drilled. It would be ridiculous to have to drill holes in a freshly-painted shell.

The Heritage bodyshells are now not only supplied primed, but also with the front wings fitted. This raises the question of whether to remove the front wing in order to give the inside of the side dash panel and the front of the sill extra paint protection or not. With the Roadster, there is always a danger that you could refit the front wing slightly out of true, so that it pays to trial fit the screen after refitting the wing in order to check the position of the wing. Early shells were supplied without front wings, and some DIY restorers omitted the trial screen fitting, with the result that they had to reposition the front wing *after* the entire shell had been sprayed, in order to get the screen to fit! This ruined the paintwork around the top fillets and, of course, on and around the bonnet side channel bolts.

Heritage leave up to the individual owner the decision of whether to apply further primer to their shells . The primer is ready in theory for top-coating, although delivery and even manoeuvring the shell into your garage could result in scratches appearing in the primer. It is recommended that the shell is at the least carefully checked for any damage to the primer, and that any breaches of it are dealt with at the earliest opportunity.

Not everyone would risk applying the topcoat themselves: any one of a dozen things could go wrong with the process, and in some cases, this could mean stripping the paint (including the primer) and starting again from square one. If you commission a professional respray it is best to ask the company concerned to examine the primer finish and to carry out any final finishing (including further primer) they deem fit. If they recommend that further primer is applied then it is best to abide by their judgement, because they will be responsible for the final finish. It would be a crime to spoil the whole job for the sake of a few hours' labour charges!

Following the application of the topcoat, many will consider it prudent to leave the shell well alone whilst the paint hardens fully. Rebuilding the mechanicals of a car without touching soft paint is not impossible but the practice could hardly be recommended. The 'curing' times will vary according to the type of paint used. When choosing a paint type, bear in mind that although modern 2-pack paints will give a more luxuriant and probably tougher finish, they might not look entirely appropriate on an early car.

When the mechanical rebuild begins, try to think ahead and protect any areas of paintwork which could possibly be scratched. Perhaps the most obvious such precaution would be heavily padding the front wings and engine bay sides before fitting the engine/gearbox unit. Even something as seemingly insignificant as a piece of swarf on your clothing, a belt buckle, watch or a bunch of keys in your pocket could scratch that virgin paint surface.

The time required to carry out a complete donor reshelling will vary tremendously according to the facilities and experience of the individual concerned. If an extra pair of hands can be brought in then work will usually progress at more than twice the speed of a solo effort.

It appears usual to seriously underestimate the total time requirement for this undertaking. When the Heritage shells first became available, some small bodyshop owners, not fully familiar with the MGB, were attracted to the idea of building cars for customers. One of these thought that two people might complete the job in two weeks, and started trying to arrange credit facilities with major spares suppliers on that basis. Needless to say, the larger organisations were too well informed to give credit to outfits with such poor knowledge of the car and such inaccurate business plan forecasts.

A realistic, if perhaps discouraging, estimate would be between one and two years for the average person working solo during evenings and some weekends. This will vary according to circumstances. The person who lives within close proximity of a good spares supplier will obviously not have to waste much time acquiring an overlooked spare; a less fortunate person might have to obtain through mail order from a distant supplier, taking and wasting much more time.

The tempting option

The Heritage shell offers what, for many, will prove an irresistible temptation because the engine bay is shaped to accept the Rover V8 engine.

When rebuilding a new bodyshell it obviously pays not to spoil the proverbial ship by skimping on reconditioning of brake and suspension components. Those who elect to fit the V8 engine should on no account settle for anything less than 100 per cent efficiency from all elements of the braking and suspension, and these should be beefed-up where appropriate with suitable components to deal with the higher stresses from the V8 and the speeds which can be attained through its use. Read the relevant notes in Chapter 7.

Motor Fayre of Kidderminster, who have built a V8 engine into a new bodyshell, have informed the author that there are many necessary modifications in order to shoehorn the large unit into place. There is a basic decision to be made of whether to fit the engine lower down within the bay and hence avoid having to provide a bonnet bulge for carburettor clearance, or whether to fit the engine higher and to have to modify the bonnet.

Irrespective of the attitude of the engine, the old mounts must be cut out and new ones welded into place. Motor Fayre staff manufactured their own engine mounts because the correct replacement ones were not available. In practice, this meant making up three trial sets and having three trial fittings before the correct dimensions were discovered. The company will be able to supply (and fit) mounts for anyone contemplating building a V8; their address is at the end of the book.

Modifications, however, go much further than merely manufacturing new engine mounts. The V8 starter solenoid fouls the scuttle panel, the alternator has to be moved higher, the oil filter has to be repositioned, the radiator surround must be reshaped and positioned further forwards, as must the radiator. The horizontal platform immediately ahead of the radiator must be tailored to accept the radiator. The inlet manifold has to be machined and turned around to lower the carburettors. A different water pump has to be fitted.

Motor Fayre's John Shilcock described the actual fitting of the engine. The engine and gearbox unit had to be presented to the engine bay almost in a vertical attitude, and the gearbox needs to protrude some distance underneath the car before the angle of attack can be altered, so that ideally, you would use an engine hoist and have the car over a pit.

With the engine fitted, clearances between it and the bodywork are in the order of fractions of an inch, and in some places there appears to be less than 1/4 inch. Obviously, not only the dimensions but also the positioning and angle of the engine mounts is critical.

The advice for anyone who wishes to build a V8 MGB around the Heritage bodyshell must be to contact a company which, like Motor Fayre, has carried out the conversion before. At the very least, you should ask the company to carry out the necessary bodywork modifications (especially fitting new engine mounts, which must be precisely placed) and perhaps to fit the engine and gearbox; preferably, you should ask them to carry out considerably more. Motor Fayre estimate that to carry out a complete reshell restoration of a car to the highest standards and fit it with a V8 engine would cost roughly 30 per cent more than reshelling a standard MGB.

MGC LHD/RHD CONVERSION

The prices realised by MGCs in the United Kingdom during the late 1980s were far higher than the prices asked for the car in the United States. The price differential was, at one time, so great that many people reimported the cars from the USA with a view to converting them to right-hand drive either for sale or for use on the British roads.

Unlike the MGB, home and export market versions of the cars possessed differences in bodywork which make the conversion rather more difficult than in the case of the MGB. A glance within the engine bay of an exported MGC will reveal that there is no hole in the offside pedal box panel for the steering column. There is also no bracket for the fitting of the column within the cab. The bracket can easily be fabricated or cut from a scrap car, and cutting the hole for the steering column should present no problems.

Pedals and their brackets have to be moved across the car, and cables rerouted.

Another obvious difference between US and UK specification MGCs is the dashboard, which places the instrumentation on the 'wrong' side. Replacing the dashboard is not too serious a problem in itself, although it does necessitate the fitting of a new wiring loom (the recommended option) or the 'customisation' of the existing loom (not recommended).

However, the differences between UK and US versions of the dashboard extend beyond their being handed; they are actually different shapes because the top shroud panels on UK and US cars are very different from each other. The UK panel extends much further back than the US version, and the top shroud panel must be replaced. This is the starting point for the conversion.

Remove the windscreen, dashboard, loom and any trim from the vicinity. Remove the three bolts which hold each of the wing tops. The top shroud panel can now be removed. It pays to use a proper

spot weld remover in order to prevent distortion to underlying panels.

With the panel removed, an ideal opportunity arises to deal with any rusting within the normally inaccessible sections underneath. Because American cars often show less rusting than UK cars, this might extend only to cleaning and repainting.

UK specification top shroud panels are available, and are fitted in the general manner of any welded panel. First offer the new panel up to ensure that adjacent panels align correctly, then hold the panel with welding clamps or pop rivets/self-tapping screws whilst it is welded up. It is recommended that you hire a spot welder for the occasion if you do not possess one in order to obtain a top-quality finish.

Other parts of the conversion naturally include moving across the pedals and rerouting brake and clutch pipes. It is recommended that this fundamental work is carried out by a company that has a track record in such conversions, because their experience will result in a fast and high-quality conversion.

An MGC undergoing left-hand to right-hand drive conversion at Bromsgrove MG Centre. The top shroud has been welded into position, and a hole drilled in the pedal box assembly for the steering column. It is time to weld on a bracket for the column. This can be cut from a scrap car.

PAINTWORK

There is greater potential for things to go disastrously wrong when a car is being painted than at any other time during the restoration. Because of this and the not inconsiderable costs of primer, paint and thinners, it will often be better for the novice to have his car professionally sprayed than to do the work himself.

Many DIY restorers will wish to learn to spray in order that they can carry out the whole restoration themselves, or to reduce costs. In fact, the cost of buying both paint and the necessary equipment can equal that of the highest quality professional respray. The most cost-effective route to high quality results is to carry out all preparation and perhaps to spray the primer at home, then to commission a paint shop to carry out the final stages. Having said that, however, many first-rate paint jobs, some concours-winning, have been achieved by amateurs.

It is recommended that the first-time paint sprayer first reads *How to Restore Paintwork* by Miles Wilkins (published by Osprey Automotive).

Paint types

Earlier cars would have left the factory finished in a cellulose paint. Although more modern types of paint can be used to produce a finish of equal or better quality and more easily, they always look wrong – a little 'plastic' – on an older car. Each paint type has its own character, which is partly due to its lustre, partly due to its apparent depth, which is readily apparent in the finished article. The restorer must decide whether ease of use and durability is of greater importance than perfect authenticity and the capacity for retouching.

Cellulose is an expensive paint to use because the wastage is very high. In its favour are its rapid drying time, which reduce the chances of dust settling on wet paintwork, plus the fact that the thinners used will soften existing paintwork if a blow-in repair has to be carried out following future repairs, so blending the new paintwork with the old. Surface scratches and fading can be attended to by rubbing down and repolishing.

In addition to its expense, cellulose has other drawbacks. The preparation of the surface before painting must be of the highest standards, because cellulose shrinks after spraying and will show the slightest marks and scratches from underneath. Cellulose must never be sprayed onto any existing synthetic paintwork, because the powerful thinners will lift the underlying paint. Also, respraying a car in a light colour, such as white over red, will require special preparation to prevent the under-colour from 'grinning' through.

The modern alternative to cellulose most likely to be used by the DIY restorer is synthetic paint. This has a slower drying time, and so the premises must be kept dust-free for some time until the paint has air-dried. This can often prove difficult in the typical workshop-cum-spray booth. Even with the concrete floor dampened down with water, dust, leaves and flying insects can often be blown in through gaps around doors.

Synthetic paints are entirely appropriate for rubber bumper cars. They have a depth of body, however, that looks out of place on earlier examples.

Many professional paint shops today use two-pack synthetic paint.Again, the finish is more appropriate to rubber bumper cars, but it is paint of a very high performance in terms of finish and longevity. The chief drawback with most paints of this type is that, whilst uncured, they are highly toxic, inhalation being fatal in some circumstances. This is overcome by the use of respiration equipment which includes a full-face helmet fed with an external air supply at above atmospheric pressure. The equipment and safe environment that is required for use of this type of paint does not rule it out for amateur use, it merely makes its use rather impractical.

Equipment

There are essentially three types of devices for spraying paint. The most common is a compressor feeding a paint gun. Small 'airless' DIY units are available, but are better suited to small 'blow-in' repair work than complete car resprays because they invariably have a short 'duty-cycle' (you will have to allow the machine to cool down frequently during work, which can result in visible dry edges when spraying cellulose). Finally, there is the new high-volume, low-compression type of sprayer.

When choosing a compressor for spraying, you should always buy the largest and most powerful that you can afford, because smaller compressors have several drawbacks which can make achieving a good finish very difficult. First, they lack sufficient tank volume and the air pump will consequently be working almost continuously in order to maintain sufficient air pressure. Often the gun will use air more quickly than the compressor can supply it, so that frequent stops have to be made while the compressor catches up, so to speak. This leads to a phenomenon called the 'dry edge'. Basically, while you are waiting for the compressor to build up pressure, the last paint band to be applied dries, giving a visible edge which can be difficult to hide.

Because a small compressor has to work continuously, the motor and pump become very hot. The heated air which is then fed from the tank will promote drying of the paint whilst in the air and before it reaches the surface.

A compressor which has at least a 50-litre, preferably a 100-litre, tank unit with a 3hp motor will be very suitable for spraying. Smaller units with only a 25-litre tank and a 1.5hp motor will be markedly less satisfactory.

In addition to the compressor and spray gun, you will require a rubber air hose and a oil filter/water trap. When air is compressed, water droplets form in the tank, often to be expelled along with the air. The water droplets can become contaminated with oil which leaks from the pump, the two combining into a sticky, oily liquid. Such contamination is apparent on the sprayed surface as tiny dark circles with lighter circles around them. The contaminated paint will be unable to adhere to anything and will eventually cause pin-holes in the top surface. This contamination is easily seen with grey primer paint – do not spray topcoat over contaminated primer, because it will lift. The author discovered (to his cost) that a single oil/water trap in line was insufficient to prevent oil contamination; two filters proved necessary.

When using a compressor the tank must be drained at regular intervals, to allow water to escape; in damp weather a considerable quantity of water can build up in a short space of time. It is essential that the pump head bolts are checked for tightness at regular intervals; failure to do so can allow oil to escape into the tank.

The atmosphere must be kept dust and silicon-free during the spraying process, which in DIY terms usually entails sealing the spraying area. The air quickly fills with paint particles and it is vital that you use breathing apparatus. Simple dust masks are insufficient to protect against thinner fumes, and a proper spraying mask should be used. Eye protection is also needed.

Preparing to spray

The bare metal and areas of body filler must first be primed. When all repairs have been carried out, flatting down can begin. Start using 400 grade wet-or-dry used wet, progressing to 800 or even 1200 grade. The quality of the final finish will reflect the care taken during this lengthy stage, which can, if undertaken on an evenings-and-weekend basis, take weeks. Before painting, the surface should be cleaned with a tack cloth to remove dust, then finally with a spirit wipe to remove grease and oil. All traces of oil, grease and any solvent or contaminant must be removed before the primer is sprayed on.

First, stir then strain the primer. Even 'new' paint can contain impurities in the form of lumps. An old pair of tights will suffice for this. Then mix the primer with the appropriate thinner in the recommended quantity, and again stir well. Then stir again.

If using a compressor, set the pressure gauge to read 50–60psi when the gun is in use. Set both the paint and air controls to the fully open positions and make a rapid pass with the gun over a test surface. If large particles of paint are apparent, reduce the amount of paint until good atomisation is achieved. Then reduce both paint and air controls by equal amounts until the desired amount of paint emits from the gun. If the width of the spray pattern is too narrow, increase the pressure at the gauge by 5psi stages until a width of 6–8in is achieved with the gun 6–9in from the test piece.

Damp down the floor around the car to minimise the chances of dust being kicked into the air. Check that nothing is in the air such as seeds or insects. Take a deep breath and commit paint to metal.

It is advisable to 'spot' prime those areas which have been taken down to bare metal during the preparation, which have been repaired or which have been filled, in order to keep rust at bay and to keep moisture from newly-applied filler (which is porous) until the entire shell can be primed.

When the entire outer body is to be sprayed, begin with the roof (where applicable) and pillars, followed by the bonnet and boot/tailgate, then the doors, sides and wings and finally the valances.

If the entire shell is to be sprayed, then the engine bay and car interior/boot space can be sprayed separately before the exterior if desired. This will give the novice a valuable opportunity to practice on slightly less important areas before tackling the unforgiving exterior.

When the shell is primed, it will almost certainly look as though the finish will be first-class, but do not be deceived; the matt finish of primer hides all manner of blemishes which the topcoats -- particularly cellulose – will highlight. Carry out an inch by inch examination of the shell, looking for scratches and unevenness. These can be dealt with using very fine grade wet-or-dry and body stopper (cellulose putty).

The entire shell should then be flatted using the finest grade of wet-or-dry. After flatting with wet-or-dry the panel concerned should be washed down to remove all traces of paint residue. If the topcoat is to be applied professionally, then it usually pays to ask the person doing the work to make sure that your preparation is acceptable before he starts spraying. The experienced eye of the professional can find blemishes which can escape your notice.

When spraying topcoat, it is advisable first to spray on a thin coat. This will 'key' strongly to the primer and also highlight flatting marks and other blemishes which can be dealt with before a lot of valuable paint is expended prematurely, and therefore wasted.

When the job is just too difficult: a Heritage shell and the people who supply it.

7 • MODIFICATIONS

The MGB is a classic car and its value, both financial and aesthetic, as such is to a large degree dependent upon the originality of all components. There can be little argument in favour, therefore, of fitting any non-standard component which has mere 'cosmetic' value. State of the art in-car entertainment equipment, no matter how good, will detract from the value of earlier or rare examples of the car rather than enhance it. Even worse, flared wheel arches, boot spoilers and other body styling kit components are anathema to the enthusiast, the collector and the investor, and will reduce the value of the car to such potential purchasers. The 'Sebring' body styling kit from Jon Hill's could prove an exception, recreating as it does a successful competition car of the 1960s. Because, however, 1960s MGBs in original condition continue to become rarer and more sought after, there will come a time when a good standard example will be worth far more than any subsequently modified car, no matter how good.

The practical benefits of non-standard modifications which improve the car's performance or handling could be outweighed by the detrimental effect they can have on the collector's value of the car. This is particularly relevant in the case of rarer variants such as the earliest MGBs, the MGC and the factory MGB V8.

Fitting equipment from, say, a Mk2 to a Mk1 MGB or GT can reduce its value considerably, yet people unthinkingly obtain reversing lights, interior lights and other Mk2 fittings for their now-rare Mk1 cars. The greatest error of judgement appears to be carrying out such 'improvements' to a car while it is being restored, instead of aiming for the original specifications. When taken to extremes such cars often sport walnut dashboards, velour trim, centre consoles, reclining seats, stereo systems with graphic equalisers, and other extras which will increasingly be viewed as abominations by enthusiasts.

An early car given such treatment will still probably be worth a considerable amount of money (as much as a late or more common car similarly treated) but will loose the extra value it holds as a rarity.

To illustrate the above contentions one small detail will suffice. For years, MGB owners have been fitting 'pancake' air filter holders to their cars. These usually give an increase in power and are in fact widely recommended for those who wish to gain a little more power without huge expense or substantial alterations to the car. In the late 1980s, one of the fastest-selling of MGB spares was the newly manufactured original design air filter holder, sought after as owners strive to restore their cars to original specifications.

Having said all that, if the enjoyment that you get from your car comes chiefly from driving it, then there are worthwhile modifications that can be made to improve the car's performance and driveability.

In areas where modifications can take place to improve safety, few people could argue that originality takes precedence over the benefits which they offer. There are also worthwhile modifications which will enable the car to, for instance, take advantage of unleaded petrol.

The ideal modifications must be any which enable the car to be returned to standard specification in future without too much trouble. Many components will one day probably be in short supply and available in modified form on an 'exchange' only basis. In the case of an over-bored block or gas-flowed cylinder head it will not be possible to return a modified component to standard specifications, and it will be worth scouring the breaker's yards to obtain a

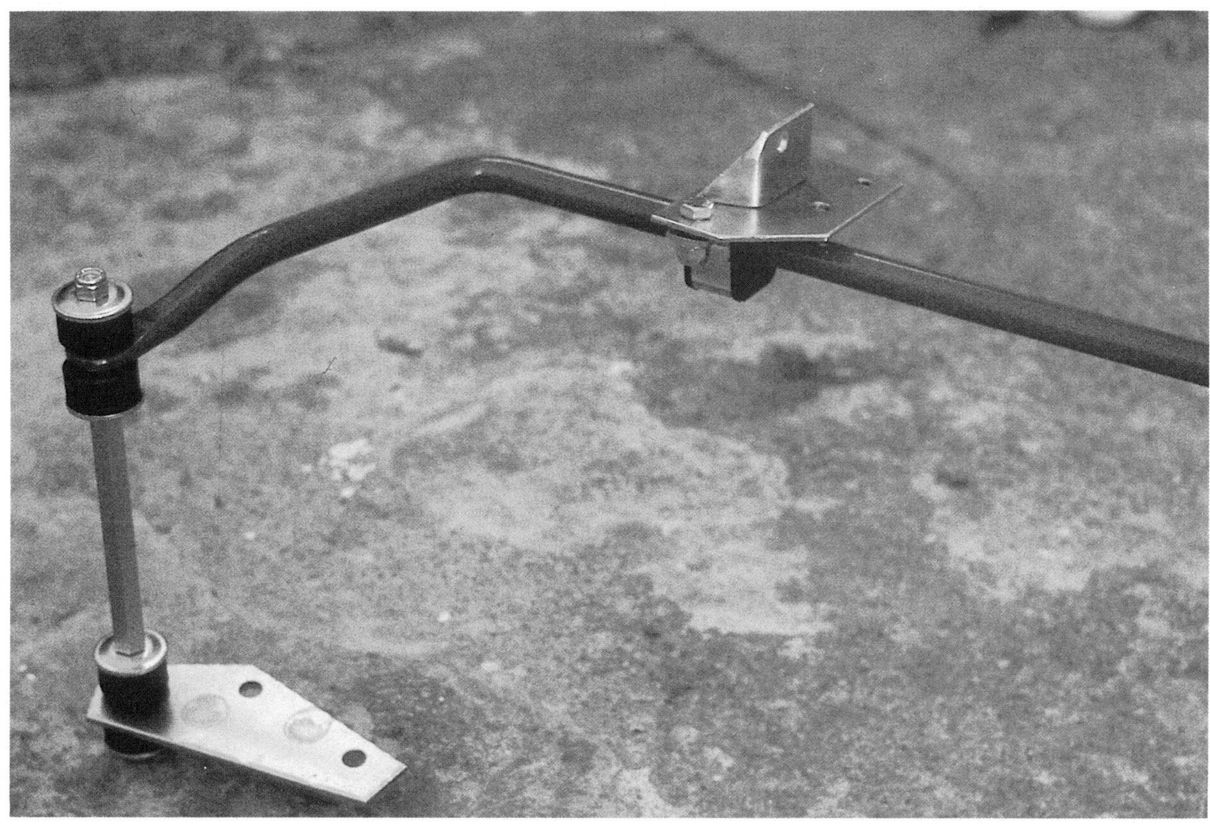

It is much easier to visualise how the rear roll bar and fittings should look by trial assembling than it is when you are laid on your back underneath the car!

standard spare before exchanging the item which was fitted to the car (or better still sending the spare away for exchange and keeping the original), just to make sure that the car can be returned to original specifications if desired.

This chapter is concerned only with those modifications which bring benefits great enough to clearly outweigh any detrimental effects they may have on the value of the car, both financial and aesthetic. There will be exceptions to this rule, however, if they are applied to a particularly historically relevant car, such as the Downton MGC, a 1962 MGB or perhaps a 1965 MGB GT.

Handling

There are many methods by which the handling of the MGB and its variants can be improved. Many alternative suspension components have been developed from the motor sport world. The MGB was a notable competition car as a works and privateer entry, not only on the track but also in rallying.

A glance at most MGB specialist's catalogues will reveal the wide availability of uprated suspension components. Simply buying and fitting, say, uprated springs will on its own do very little if anything to improve the car's handling. The various components must be chosen so as to complement each other and work as a balanced whole. The exception is the Ron Hopkinson roll bar kit. Because this is the most easily fitted MGB handling improvement aid it will be covered first.

The Ron Hopkinson MGB handling kit consists basically of two anti-roll bars plus various fittings which enable the front and rear anti-roll bars to be fitted to cars which may have previously lacked one or both. An anti-roll bar is, in essence, a device which makes the suspension unit on one side of the car, at the front or the rear, 'talk' to the opposing unit on the other side. In simple terms, if the suspension is compressed on one side of the car on a bend, the suspension on the other side will be lifting, the anti-roll bar, which connects the two, evens out the two opposing motions and, thus, cuts the amount of body roll.

The benefits in cutting down the huge amounts of body roll of which the MGB is capable when pushed around a bend are obvious. More equal traction is maintained by each set of wheels. The tremendous loading on the suspension on the outside track is eased by being shared. The centre of gravity of the rear of the car is less prone to lift and go over-centre, which precedes the potentially savage shift from understeer into oversteer and then an uncontrolled spin on the most severe cornering.

The Ron Hopkinson kit has been precisely tailored to suit the MGB. Those who have driven 'before and after' cars (the author included) will vouch for the immediate and marked improvement in the handling and safety. Of course, hindsight is a wonderful thing, but had a properly set up anti-roll bar kit been fitted as standard equipment during the 1970s, when it was so fashionable for motoring journalists to criticise the car's handling, then so much of that bad publicity would have been avoided.

Before fitting the kit it is essential to ensure that all other elements of the suspension and steering are in good order. Ineffectual dampers, worn springs, tyres or steering gear will adversely affect the benefits of the kit.

It must also be stressed that the bodywork in the vicinity of the boot must be in first-class and sound condition, because the centre section of the rear anti-roll bar is fixed here and can exert high forces.

Roadholding and Handling

Although the MGB – especially in later life – came in for a lot of press and 'bar-room expert' criticism of its handling and roadholding, had it not been for the vast improvements in these areas which were made with the 1959 launch of the front-wheel drive Mini and since copied by just about every motor manufacturer worldwide, then judged against the general standards of roadholding and handling of contemporary rear wheel drive sports cars (the Triumph Spitfire and GT6 spring immediately to mind), the MGB would have acquitted itself quite well. So let's begin by accepting that the chrome bumper MGB and GT are competent and entirely predictable in the roadholding and handling departments, and that the black bumper cars' shortcomings in these areas were greatly exaggerated! Nevertheless, there is a lot of room for improvement. It is vital to establish exactly what you require of suspension modifications before carrying out any work. Most people seek to improve the handling rather than go for ultimate levels of roadholding, and there is an important distinction to be made between the two.

RIGHT *Modern telescopic dampers are a great improvement on the original lever arm dampers fitted across the MGB range. The conversion entails fitting special brackets to the rear side chassis rails and to the axle 'U' bolts. This example is fitted to an MGC, which would have had telescopic dampers at the front but lever arm dampers at the rear. Telescopic dampers are available for all variants. Adjustable dampers are a further option which allow users to set the suspension for different circumstances, from normal road use to track use.*

Handling improvements in the main strive to affect the way the car reacts during cornering, by taming its body roll. This is usually achieved by fitting anti-roll bars, but in itself this modification's contribution to roadholding is far from a straightforward gain. In the dry and at all sensible road speeds, an otherwise standard car fitted with anti-roll bars will indeed tend to grip the road better and, more importantly, will lose some of its tendency to under and oversteer when entering and exiting bends respectively at speed. Perhaps the most apparent benefit of having anti-roll bars occurs when one sudden directional change follows another, such as when you pull out to overtake a slower vehicle and, before the suspension has fully recovered from this, pull back in again. The same thing happens on tight 'S' bends and – sadly – when you have to take sudden avoiding action if, for instance, someone pulls out of a road junction into your path. At such times the springs on one side of a car without anti-roll bars will be almost fully compressed and very quickly have to become almost fully extended, and vice versa – the car loses poise and hence traction. The flatter-cornering characteristics of cars fitted with anti-roll bars should ensure that they do not suffer such problems.

However, competition cars, which are driven flat-out in wet and dry conditions, may well be better served by other suspension modifications centred around lowering and general stiffening of the springing and damping. This has some of the beneficial effects of fitting anti-roll bars, but – especially in the wet and at high speeds – tyre

traction will inevitably be better than that of an otherwise standard car merely fitted with anti-roll bars. Lowering the car lowers the centre of gravity and makes the bodyshell far more stable, so that the tendency for the rear end to lift and cause the onset of oversteer is reduced. Stiffening the springing and damping reduces the body roll to manageable proportions, so that rapid direction changes are less likely to unsettle the suspension. Improved damping also helps to keep the rubber in contact with the tarmac irrespective of bumps in the road – the basis of roadholding. So why not on road cars?

The answer is that competition drivers usually have to accept far lower standards of ride comfort than ordinary motorists demand – and competition suspension coupled to even the better MGB seats can prove very uncomfortable indeed, which is why road cars in general are not usually fitted with full competition specification suspension. It must be said that fitting a fairly stiff anti-roll bar at the rear of the MGB or even over-compressing the bushes of a mild anti-roll bar will increase the posterior pounding of the car's occupants to a marked degree!

In truth, few MGB enthusiasts ever drive their cherished cars on the public roads at high enough speeds and in a reckless enough manner to warrant tolerating the buffeting to the posterior that competition suspension imparts and, if they did, few would manage to hang onto their driving licences (or perhaps their lives) for very long, because the sort of speeds necessary to truly warrant full competition suspension would be highly illegal on the public highway.

Instead of trying to turn their MGB into a race or rally winner, most owners are more than happy with the handling improvements which can be achieved by fitting anti-roll bars (or uprated bars on later cars which were fitted as standard with mild anti-roll bars front and rear), coupled in some cases with mild damping and springing modifications.

The Ron Hopkinson handling kit was the first of its kind and has now been joined by other bolt-on handling kits. Amongst these, the kits offered by the MG Owners' Club are especially noteworthy. The Club offers two kits. Kit One comprises a stiffer front anti-roll bar and uprated bushes; the effect of stiffening the front anti-roll bar is to keep the front end of the car more level in corners.This reduces the car's tendency to understeer (for the front end of the car to run wide) and allows the car to be steered around corners more accurately.

Kit Two includes the uprated front anti-roll bar and couples this with dual 'A' frames, which help locate the axle. On the standard car, centrifugal forces generated during hard cornering can distort the rear leaf springs and their mounting bushes, with the effect that the bodyshell tends to move in relation to the wheels, aggravating the circumstances which lead to a shift into oversteer (the rear end runs wide). The 'A' frames locate the axle far more positively than can the leaf springs, greatly reducing the possibility of the car oversteering. But the 'A' frames do more than simply locate the axle.

When power is applied to the driving wheels, some is lost as the axle twists against the force of the leaf springs. The axle will twist to a point at which the force imparted into the distorted leaf springs is great enough to overcome that delivered by the engine, and then the axle twists the other way. This process of the axle first twisting one way then the other is referred to as axle 'tramp', and the 'A' frames will reduce the tendency to tramp and so help the car deliver its power to the road surface on acceleration.The MG Owners' Club 'A' frames can be bought separately, and it should be possible to fit them in conjunction with other handling kits and modifications, but it will pay to check when ordering them that they are compatible with whatever other modifications you may have carried out to your car.

Dampers

One of the areas of the MGB's suspension which offers considerable room for improvement is the damping, because the old-fashioned lever arm dampers leave a lot to be desired.

Uprated dampers are available on an exchange basis, but should really be fitted in conjunction with suitable springing and even then only if all other aspects of the suspension and steering are in good order.

The alternative is to fit the widely-used SPAX adjustable dampers. These can be fitted in conjunction with the Ron Hopkinson handling kit. If a telescopic damper kit from another source is to be fitted to a car which already has the Hopkinson handling kit, ensure that the two may be used together.

Shock absorbers or dampers perform a vital function in damping out and controlling the forces released on the compression and rebound of the suspension springing medium. When dampers fail, a car can pitch uncontrollably after hitting even a minor bump or pothole, exerting unwanted forces on the suspension which severely compromise wheel traction. This obviously has a disastrous effect on the car's cornering ability, and also seriously affects braking and increases braking distances.

The degree to which a damper should literally 'absorb' the energy from suspension springs varies according to the application. A softer suspension will give a better and more comfortable 'ride', suitable for a car usually driven at normal touring speeds, than will a stiffer suspension, which will be more desirable on a vehicle to be driven in a more sporting manner. Adjustable dampers are the ideal option for the MGB owner who uses his car as everyday transport and also indulges in historic racing, rallying or hill climbs.

The choice of replacement dampers for the MGB generally consists of straight lever-type replacements, uprated lever-types (which should be used only in conjunction with uprated springs) and telescopic types, of which the Spax adjustable is the most widely employed on the MGB because of the conversion kit which allows its easy use.

The major factor which weighs heavily in favour of the Spax dampers is that they may be used in conjunction with the Hopkinson handling kit already covered. Because both require the fitting of an extra rear spring bottom plate it pays to fit the two at once if possible, to avoid having to undo those eight damage- and seizure-prone nuts on the axle 'U' bolts.

Braking modifications

The efficiency of disc brakes depends on the ability of the discs to dissipate heat quickly, and one common modification for competition cars is to ventilate the discs so that they can dissipate more heat by drilling holes in them. This is by no means a modification which should be contemplated by the average DIY enthusiast, although ventilated discs may be purchased from many MGB specialists and are not too expensive. Under normal road braking this modification will probably not have any apparent effects, but under very hard braking there should be a noticeable gain in braking efficiency. Competition brake pads and shoes are also available.

USING UNLEADED FUEL

The exchange cylinder head can offer increased performance over the standard item by raising the compression ratio, and by improving gas flow through the incorporation of larger exhaust valves and the shaping and smoothing of the ports and valve seats. Special conversions are also available to permit the MGB to run on unleaded petrol. A further option permits performance increases combined with the switch to unleaded petrol.

Unleaded petrol

Early motor cars ran on unleaded fuel because that was all that was available at the time. Lead was introduced into petrol to improve the anti-knock characteristic of the fuel, by making it more stable in the conditions of extreme heat and pressure experienced within the combustion chamber, so controlling its tendency to detonate. Greater knock-resistance allowed an increase in compression and allowed the ignition spark to be advanced, both of which gave a goodly increase in performance. The new wonder additive – in the form of tetra-ethyl lead – also had the added advantage of lubricating valve stem to guide bearing surface as well as helping to protect the exhaust valve seat from burning away prematurely.

With one exception all MGBs were designed to run on leaded petrol. The engines usually need the lead to prolong the life of the exhaust valve stem and its guide, but more particularly the exhaust valve seat.

The MGB 'B' series engine has a standard cylinder head which is manufactured from cast iron and which is rapidly damaged if run on unleaded fuel. The exhaust valve obviously runs very hot even with leaded petrol and far hotter with unleaded, and on each closure of the valve an instantaneous weld can occur between the valve and its seat, rapidly destroying the latter. The lead in leaded petrol forms a protective covering which prevents this from occurring. The standard cast-iron valve guide suffers rapid wear without the protection of lead.

Excessive wear of the valve stem and guide might not appear at first sight to be too important a consideration. Maintaining a good contact between the two bearing surfaces is vital because this allows the conduction of much excess heat from the valve into the head, which is then dissipated . Without a good contact area between valve and guide the valve itself will be unable to dissipate heat and will quickly become so hot that fuel mixture will be pre-heated, or even ignited by it, as it enters the cylinders, promoting pre-ignition with all its attendant long-term damage.

This, however, is not the whole story. Unleaded petrol must only be used with the ignition retarded from normal settings, otherwise the tremendous energy which is liberated on the rapid combustion literally has no way to expend itself other than as a shock wave which hits the tops of the pistons and the cylinder walls. This is audible inside the car as 'pinking', and although the noise sounds harmless enough it is actually the only manifestation of huge forces which are at work (amongst other things) literally destroying the pistons!

When unleaded fuel detonates it releases its heat too early, which means that the inlet manifold reaches far higher temperatures than is recommended, pre-heating the fuel before it reaches the cylinders and worsening the already too-rapid fuel burn rate. All in all, unleaded fuel is a virtual executioner to the standard MGB cylinder head.

At the time of writing, exchange cylinder heads capable of use with unleaded fuel have only recently become available, and finding evidence of their long-term performance is not always possible. The best way to find a good supplier is through recommendation, via the owner's clubs, your local MG specialist, and other's personal experience, etc.

It is interesting to note that from 1976, MGBs destined for the North American export market were not only able to be used with unleaded fuel, they had to use it! This was because they were also fitted with a catalytic converter, a device which cuts the emission of harmful exhaust gases and which is damaged by contamination if leaded petrol is used. Unfortunately, the North American-spec cars are *not* suitable for use with today's UK unleaded fuel because of a difference in the octane rating between it and the US unleaded fuel at the time the MGB was manufactured to utilise it.

In order for the MGB cylinder head to run on unleaded fuel, certain modifications are essential. The head will be reconditioned. The exhaust valve seats will be machined out and special hardened inserts will be pressed into place. The valve guides will be replaced with alternatives that do not require the lubrication protection of lead. The exhaust valves with be replaced with alternatives manufactured from harder material that will neither burn nor rapidly wear away. All sharp edges will be ground away from the head to prevent them from glowing red hot (or even hotter) and causing pre-ignition. In addition, specific suppliers will carry out other work.

Some exchange unleaded cylinder heads will have the compression ratio slightly lowered for petrol of lower octane ratings, which should have a very small effect in reducing the power of the engine. Some will fit larger exhaust valves to help the engine breathe, which will give a power increase if the carburation and ignition are properly adjusted. Some go so far as to profile the exhaust porting to further improve the engine's breathing and hence performance.

Leading questions

At the time of writing little is understood by the motoring public about the use of unleaded fuels in contemporary cars, let alone obsolete models like the MGB. Thus, dangerous myths have arisen, such as the belief that it is acceptable to use unleaded fuel on an occasional basis, say, one tankful to three of leaded fuel. The long-term effects of such experiments are not yet understood, and so they are best avoided. *Do not* use any unleaded petrol in the standard MGB or MGC.

Even amongst car manufacturers there appears to be little agreement about whether unleaded fuel may be used in certain engines. The author contacted three motor car manufacturers who used the Rover V8 engine and asked whether it could be used with unleaded petrol. The first replied 'definitely', the second 'definitely not' and the third 'depends'. It appears that in its low-tune Range Rover guise as fitted to factory MGB V8s, the engine may be used with unleaded petrol, but that in higher states of tune it may not. Owners of V8 MGBs should firstly ascertain the genuine origins of their car to determine the state of tune, and then obtain from the manufacturer a guarantee that the use of such fuel will not harm their engine.

The simple rule which should be applied to the question of whether an engine may be run on unleaded fuel is that if there exists the slightest element of doubt then do not use the fuel but keep filling up with leaded petrol.

Fitting an 'unleaded' cylinder head

There is more to 'going unleaded' than merely swapping the cylinder head. The engine must be in good condition, if not, it might pay to consider fitting an exchange reconditioned 'short' engine (everything up to the cylinder head) at the same time.

Instructions on removing the cylinder head can be found in Chapter 5 dealing with repairs. Before fitting the replacement head, turn the engine so that two of the pistons are at the top of their travel, and stuff clean rags into the others. The piston crowns must be cleaned of all traces of carbon which would otherwise heat up and cause pre-ignition of the following stroke. Repeat for the other pistons.

Depending on the grade of fuel to be used, the ignition can require adjustment. 'Standard' unleaded fuels have a low RON rating equivalent to the old '2 Star', and if they are used then the ignition has to be retarded in accordance with the instructions that should be given by the company who supply the replacement head. 'Super' unleaded fuels have a higher RON rating and no adjustment is necessary. If the ignition is set for Super unleaded then on no account should the standard grade be used.

If the unleaded cylinder head offers a performance increase then it is essential that all elements of the ignition and carburation be in excellent condition and that the carburation be precisely set up using a 'rolling road' dynamometer. Be aware that almost all insurance companies demand that they be informed if modifications to a car are made that increases its performance; very likely, the insurers will require that an increased premium be paid. Do not be tempted to hide any modifications from the insurers, because their subsequent discovery following an accident claim will give grounds for voiding the policy, leaving the uninsured personally liable not only for his own loss (the car) but also for third-party claims.

ENGINE MODIFICATIONS

It is a relatively straightforward matter to raise the power of the 1800cc MGB 'B' Series engine, and the procedures have long been widely established. The BMC Competitions Department laid the ground with modifications dating as far back as the early 1960s when they first campaigned the car, and many worthy companies and individuals have also contributed to the high level of understanding which exists about performance preparation for the MGB. This has not prevented certain myths from becoming widely accepted as facts, nor needless bolt-on 'performance' accessories from being sold to hapless owners.

There is no reason why the MGB owner should not implement certain DIY performance modifications or even experiment to try and find new modifications. The chances are, however, that the results of any such work will be difficult to subjectively gauge excepting those occasions when performance is markedly reduced!

Whatever the desired state of tune, the average MGB owner would be well advised to have whatever work proves necessary carried out professionally. Even getting the standard engine to perform efficiently really requires an exhaust gas analyzer, and preferably a rolling road for objective 'before and after' testing. Without some means of measuring the output of the engine the amateur can be hard pressed to gauge whether any work he carries out actually improves performance!

In the preparation of this section the author was fortunate in enlisting the help and advice of Graham Hickman from Rolling Road Auto Tune Services (RATS) of Martley. Having worked at one time for Austin Rover in the research and development of engines, Graham set up RATS for rally/competition engine development and preparation, and his depth of knowledge is thus based on a strong theoretical grounding and a wealth of practical experience.

Before deciding to try and raise the power output of the engine, a few points are worthy of consideration. First comes the question of whether the performance gain can be justified (in the case of the average road car) when it can be costly in terms of increased insurance premiums and (depending on the state of tune) fuel consumption. The person who needs a really fast road car might often be better advised to buy a more modern second vehicle which might out-accelerate the MGB, have a higher top speed than the MGB, and still be in a lower insurance group and give more miles per gallon than the MGB!

If much more than a modest power increase is desired, then, depending on the approach chosen, additional drawbacks can emerge including more difficult starting, a loss of tractability, higher and 'lumpy' tickover and increased engine wear. Furthermore, one should never loose sight of the fact that the MGB was designed to perform within certain limits and that both braking and suspension modifications should parallel any substantial increases in engine power.

The stiffness of the MGB's body only becomes an important consideration if the particular car has weak sills or if a very highly tuned or V8 'competition' conversion is attempted.

Most cars would probably show a significant power increase plus better fuel economy and tractability simply by being properly set up! No special 'performance' components are needed, no increases in insurance premiums are incurred! Quite simply, this would entail fitting new jets and needles (and renewing any worn carburettor components such as pistons, damper pistons, float chamber needle valves etc) to the carburettors, setting the ignition and then balancing the carbs and finally fine-tuning the carburation settings professionally with the engine running, using an exhaust gas analyzer and a rolling road.

This is, of course, assuming that other components are in good order and adjustment. Binding brakes will slow the car considerably, a leaking or partially blocked exhaust can have a very marked effect, and even low tyre pressures adversely affect performance.

The ignition components must also be in good working order. A seized auto advance mechanism will ruin performance, as can a weak spark caused, perhaps, by poor high tension lead insulation. Furthermore, the compression of each cylinder should be tested and ideally the cylinder head decoked and given a full overhaul, valves ground in and valve clearances reset. The object of the whole exercise is to allow the engine to make the most of the mixture in the cylinders. The gain in efficiency will not only give a worthwhile power increase in many instances but can pay for itself over a period of time in terms of lessened fuel consumption.

A properly set-up MGB will give an on-the-road performance which to all intents and purposes comes fairly close to that of many sub-2 litre cars of the late 1980s (give or take a couple of seconds in the 0-60mph times, and albeit inevitably using more fuel to do so). The attractions of forgetting all thoughts of extra performance tuning and running the car in efficient standard tune are that outlay is minimal and that the car is still in wholly original specification.

Before looking at performance modifications, it is worth stating that quoted bhp figures for the MGB are often grossly misleading. According to Graham and other authorities, the engine as fitted to production cars was not capable of the once widely accepted figure of 95bhp at the flywheel. Over the years, different methods of measuring bhp have given widely different figures; for instance, the 1962 accepted figure for the power of the engine was 95bhp, but fifteen years later this had been discredited by some authorities as inaccurate and replaced with a far more realistic figure around 84bhp.

When considering increasing the power of the car it is as well to bear in mind that some modifications can give high peak bhp, but only in a trade-off against either the range of power or the mid-range torque developed by the engine. Remembering that there is quite a large gap between second and third gears in the standard MGB gearbox, the torque of the engine which peaks at around 3000rpm is obviously quite an important factor; changing from second gear to third at 36–37mph (4500rpm in second) will drop the revs down to 2790rpm, at which level the 'pulling power' of torque is highly beneficial. It is also very useful during overtaking manoeuvres.

A mild power increase can be achieved most easily by allowing the engine to breathe more efficiently, by lessening the restrictions on mixture reaching the cylinders and possibly on exhaust gases leaving them. At its simplest, this could entail merely fitting K&N pancake air filters to achieve a small gain. Fitting a larger bore or straight-through (no baffles) exhaust system could add a little more power (although by itself this will give a hardly discernible increase and too large a bore will have the opposite effect). Such power increases as might result from these two modifications, in addition to the correct setting-up of the carburation, might give a gain of as much as 5 per cent at the flywheel, but should have no bearing on the smooth starting, smooth running and tractability of the engine. An extra 3-4bhp makes so little difference to the road performance of the car that it will hardly be noticed.

Further performance improvements will require the fitting of non-standard components and should be declared to the insurers. Furthermore, proper setting up on a rolling road becomes essential if the expense incurred is not to be totally wasted.

Probably the most popular next stage (because it can be relatively economical and does not involve removing the engine as a unit from the car) is to fit a high-performance cylinder head. This will be professionally converted and fully profiled and polished, but might also feature profiled and larger valves and seats. Again, the principle is to get more mixture into and out of the cylinders. The best of these are claimed to give an increase of around 20 per cent at the flywheel without losing power at lower revs or giving a lumpy tickover. The power at the flywheel could be 90-100bhp at this stage.

For a road (as opposed to a competition) car, in preference to an exchange performance cylinder head, Graham recommends boring the block out to 1950cc, fitting K&N pancake filters and a long centre branch exhaust manifold, then reneedling and setting up on the Rolling Road. The result, says Graham, is a car with all of the delightful characteristics of the standard MGB engine but with higher power. This approach makes even more sense if one considers that, on removal of the standard cylinder head, the bores might be found to be scored, necessitating a rebore and over-sized pistons and rings.

Further improvements can be made with a change of carburation, the use of high lift camshafts, lightened flywheels and so on. Of these, Graham recommends the mild 'modern technology' camshaft, but points out that it must be of modern design. Apparently, older high lift camshafts also increased the duration of the valve opening, and this could give lumpy running.

After the exchange cylinder head, the next most popular stage is to fit a complete exchange engine. Performance exchange engines are usually referred to as 'fast road, half race and full race' or 'Standard, Stage 11 or Stage 111' (other terminology could be encountered).

For road use the 'fast road' or 'Stage 11' engine will usually prove the most practical because it should have the widest power band; that is, the power from the engine extends throughout the engine rev range. More highly tuned engines usually suffer a progressively narrower power band.

The terms above actually tell you nothing about how the power increases are achieved. Some might begin by fitting a cylinder head which is gas flowed, having reshaped combustion chambers, raised compression ratios and larger valves; others might use an overbored block as their starting point. It is as well to find out exactly what work has been carried out on the engine you are thinking of buying, and then to match the probable characteristics to your requirements. The alternative recommended by

Graham (to start with an overbored unit in which the cylinder diameters are enlarged and oversize pistons fitted, and then to take the engine to higher states of tune as desired) gives the starting point of a smooth, tractable and powerful engine. Such engines might typically give a volume increase to 1870cc, 1900cc or 1950cc. The latter is the largest practical overbored size, because further enlarging of the cylinders would probably weaken their walls! For those who must have it, around 100 bhp (overboring and setting up) and 120–130bhp (overboring plus gas flowing, high lift cam etc) at the flywheel is available.

Much has been made in the past of polishing inlet and exhaust ports and manifolds to smooth flow, and of precisely matching manifolds to ports, as a first stage of engine tuning. Graham is dismissive of such techniques being applied except as a final stage to a comprehensive competition engine build. Similarly, Graham is a great believer in the simple efficiency of the standard SU carburettors and does not especially recommend the use of alternatives except, again, as a final stage of a high performance engine build.

MGC

It is unlikely that most owners of the MGC will wish substantially to alter this ever-more collectable car in the name of performance gains. In standard form and in good condition the 'C' series engine arguably possesses more than sufficient power in relation to the roadholding capabilities of the car (which are already adversely affected by the extra weight of this engine!). For this reason performance modifications will not be covered in this book. However, it is recognised that many people successfully campaign the MGC in 'historic' competitions, and in such instances it is usual and recommended that professional assistance be gained.

If you have an MGC and are dissatisfied with its performance, then the chances are that the engine is not operating efficiently. Overhauling the engine then setting up the carburation on a rolling road will restore the performance to quite satisfactory levels.

MGB V8

First Ken Costello and then British Leyland realised that the way to break through the 1800cc/120bhp barrier without losing tractability, smooth tickover, etc was to fit the V8 3500cc engine then used in Rover vehicles. Ken Costello used the Rover car version of the engine which gave around 150bhp at the flywheel, whereas MG opted for the version as fitted to the Range Rover, which gave 137bhp. The latter had torque increased from the 'B' series figure of 110 ft lb to 193 ft lb, which meant that the gear lever had to be used even less on longer runs!

The aluminium V8 engine was almost 40lb lighter than the old 1800cc 'B' series engine, although in order to shoehorn it into the MGB engine bay, the manufacturer had to fit certain special ancillaries. These in addition to other standard items, raised the overall weight to around that of the standard engine, although still well short of that of the MGC. This in addition to the emission equipment raised the car's weight by some 160lb, thus altering the front-to-rear weight distribution slightly. Some held the view at the time that this slight alteration gave the car poorer handling characteristics, an opinion which would doubtless be vehemently opposed today.

The V8 conversion obviously transforms the 'straight line' performance of the car, giving 0–60mph times of around 8 seconds (Costello or 150bhp engine) and 8.6 seconds ('factory' or 137bhp Range Rover engine), with the potential to go considerably faster with performance modifications.

Rubber bumper cars inherited the bodywork modifications which were necessary to give clearance to the V8 engine and ancillaries (many of which were non-standard and some of which were specially developed), and many have in fact been successfully fitted with the V8 in the past. This was possible because the cars were comparatively 'recent' and not weakened through bodyrot, whereas today any MGB is sufficiently long in the tooth to be too weak for the conversion and in need of a body rebuild first. Pre-1973 cars are the most difficult to convert, and will require several extra bodywork modifications (though growing rarity value is now 'protecting' venerable early cars from conversion). Mark 3 chrome bumper cars are suitable for conversion, although the engine bays of the 1800cc and V8 engined cars were not standardised until the introduction of the rubber bumper cars, so that the

Mk3 car requires several bodywork modifications. Whichever mark is chosen, the individual car should possess first-class bodywork.

The transmission of the MGB was not originally designed to handle 137bhp or more and so both it and the rear suspension should at the least be very sound; the rear suspension would certainly benefit from stiffer springing and improved damping. The four synchromesh gearbox may be used (the three synchromesh unit is not acceptable), and overdrive is recommended to make the most of the V8 engine's massive mid-range torque. An adaptor plate is necessary to mate the V8 engine to the standard MGB gearbox. The factory modified the gear selector overdrive switch so that overdrive was unavailable in third, because the quite massive forces of this engine under acceleration in third placed too great a strain on the overdrive unit in the lower gear.

The 'ideal' conversion for a competition car would be to fit the SD1 engine and gearbox, which requires further modifications to the transmission tunnel (letting in a 'bulge' on chrome bumper cars and some dressing on rubber bumper cars) and to the gearbox cross-member, plus modifications to the prop shaft, clutch hydraulics and speedometer cable. The fifth gear of the SD1 unit takes the place of overdriven top on the standard MGB item, and the gearbox will be found to be stronger and possess more appropriate ratios.

If a bonnet 'power bulge' is to be avoided then a special inlet manifold and carburettors will be required, although the standard SU carburettors of the Rover V8 can be used if a bulged bonnet is sourced or the standard item is adapted. The exhaust manifolds used on Rovers will not fit, so a tubular system which is widely available should be sought. Modifications will also have to be made to the electrical and cooling systems, brakes and axle.

Among the extra bodywork modifications necessary for the chrome bumper cars are new side chassis rail engine mountings, a special steering shaft, the radiator mountings moved, front pan cut-away and strengthening, and the bulkheads have to be cut back to accommodate the V8 cylinder heads.

If the V8 is in anything other than standard tune then brakes and suspension should be uprated. Ventilated discs front and rear with four-pot calipers at the front, should stop the car from the higher speeds of which it will be capable. Adjustable SPAX or similar shock absorbers will give a vast improvement in handling, and they should preferably be used in conjunction with uprated springs and new fittings all round.

Because the rear axle is located only by the leaf springs it is able to twist as the extra power is applied. Anti-tramp bars will help prevent this and are recommended if the power of the V8 is raised substantially.

Anyone wishing to undertake or commission a V8 conversion is advised to contact the V8 Conversion Company, which supplied much of the information above. The company produces a 32-page guide to the conversion which goes into great detail in describing necessary modifications, and has a long track record in undertaking conversions for clients and also produces a kit for those wishing to do the work themselves. Their address is in the directory at the back of the book.

Another company which is a mine of advice and experienced in V8 conversions is Motor Fayre of Kidderminster, run by Pete Taylor and John Shilcock. The Heritage bodyshells have the correct engine bays to accept the V8 unit, although there are many modifications which are necessary both to the shell and to the engine and ancillaries. See Chapter 6, New bodyshells for more details.

To the limit

The V8 engine possesses the potential for impressive power increases, although normally it is taken to high states of tune only in cars used for track and hill climb events rather than in road cars. The engine is often overbored for competition cars, and RATS of Martley can take this engine when overbored to 4 litres (they will take it out to 4.9 litres if required) to a maximum 360bhp (which gives a 'low' torque figure of 250 ft lb) or to a far more satisfactory 350bhp for a torque of 320 ft lb. As with the 1800cc 'B' series engine, attaining the absolute maximum bhp figure costs dearly in torque.

The basic performance preparation of the V8 engine recommended by Graham very closely follows that pertinent to the standard MGB! Again, K&N pancake air filters will help the engine to breathe and, combined with reneedling and setting up on the rolling road, this will be as far as most of road users will wish to take matters. Unlike the 1800cc recommendations, a better tubular exhaust manifold coupled with a more appropriate exhaust system will give a useful boost to power at this stage, after which,

V8 engine, an option never directly offered to American customers.

Graham again recommends the use of a higher lift (but not a longer duration) camshaft.

Amongst those MGBs which can be said to have been taken to the very limit of performance are competition V8s used in track events and hill climbs. Typical of such cars is a V8 MGB GT belonging to and campaigned (in hill climbs) by Chris Lawrence. This is one of two cars which were developed specifically for track events and then subsequently outlawed from the same!

POSTSCRIPT - A NEW DAWN

The MGR V8 is a fine car, but a disappointingly low demand showed that it was not the car which MG enthusiasts the world over had for so long been hoping and waiting for.

Throughout 1994, the motoring press began to carry a story about a 'proper' and completely new MG but, in the absence of official factory confirmation, MG enthusiasts could only drool over the (I suspect) leaked specification details and keep their fingers crossed that - this time - Rover got it right.

Then, in the spring of 1995, British car enthusiasts learned that the Rover Group had been sold to BMW. This news was generally greeted with disbelief turning quickly to horror - not least because BMW were known to be developing a small sports car which would compete directly against the new MG sports car. Surely BMW would not allow Rover to manufacture a sports car to compete against its own? There was one glimmer of hope; the Chairman of the Executive Board of Directors of BMW - Bernd Pischetsrieder - is not only the nephew of the designer of the (at the time, revolutionary) Morris Minor and Mini, the late Sir Alec Issigonis, but also a classic car enthusiast. Rover were allowed - encouraged perhaps - to go ahead with the new sports car.

As this is being written in the Summer of 1995, the motoring world has gone crazy for that new MG - the MGF. I was fortunate enough to see the MGF for myself at the Top Gear Classic and Sportscar show in Birmingham, and the car looks a real cracker - if it goes as well as it looks, the initials MG will once more adorn a worthy car. If you're wondering, ADO 21 (see page 14) was the MGD, the Rover EXE was the MGE, and therefore the new MG is the MGF - for my money, exactly the kind of MG sports car Abingdon would today be manufacturing.

And for the future? Rover Group were obviously aware of the value of the MG marque prior to the BMW take-over, because the MGF was by then at an advanced stage in the pre-production process. For many enthusiasts, a question mark will still hang over the intentions of BMW, but not for me. I have received a letter from Herr Pischetsrieder, in which he states that our motoring heritage will be treated with the greatest respect - not only for sentimental reasons but also for its great importance to the group.

It seems strange to reflect that those proud initials MG would appear to be in safer hands today than they have been at any other time in their seventy-year history!

My only minor reservation regarding the styling of the MGF is the windscreen, raked like that of a chopped saloon rather than the traditional small upright roadster screen. I could live with that, however, and the MGF does *look right with the hood erected!*

APPENDICES

CAPACITIES

	Pint	*Litre*	*US Pint*
Engine	7.5	4.26	9
+ Oil cooler	0.75	0.42	0.9
Gearbox to 18GB	4.5	2.56	5.6
18GD on	5.25	3	6
Gearbox/overdrive to 18GB	5.33	3.36	6
18GD on	6	3.4	7
Automatic transmission	10.5	6	12.7
Rear axle 3/4 floating	2.25	1.28	2.75
Semi floating	1.5	0.85	2
Cooling system (early cars)	9.5	5.4	11.4
18V (GHN5 GHD5 from 410002)	11.5	6.6	13.8
With heater (early cars)	10	5.68	12
18V (GHN5 GHD5 from 410002)	12	6.8	14.4

	Gal	*Lit*	*US Gal*
Fuel tank (early)	10	45.4	12
(later)	12	54	14

Steering/Suspension

Steering arm bolts	60–65	8.3–8.9
Steering wheel nut 9/16″ UNF	27–29	3.73–4.01
11/16″ UNF	41–43	5.66–5.94
Export cars	36–38	4.98–5.26
Steering tie rod locknut	33–37	4.6–5.2
Steering lever ball joint nut	34–35	4.7–4.8
Steering column universal joint bolt	20–22	2.8–3
Front damper bolts	43–45	5.9–6.2
Rear damper bolts	55–60	7.6–8.3
Brake disc to hub	40–45	5.5–6.2
Brake caliper bolts	40–45	5.5–6.2
Wheel bearing nut	40–70	5.5–9.7
Cross-member to body	54–56	7.5–7.7
Spark plugs	18	2.5
Road wheel nuts	60–65	8.3–9

Recommended lubricants and fluids

Engine, Gearbox/overdrive, carburettor damper – SAE 20W/50 Multigrade

Automatic transmission – fluid type F

Rear axle/steering rack – SAE 90 EP Hypoid

Grease nipples – Lithium multi-purpose grease

Dampers – Armstrong thin fluid No.624

TORQUE WRENCH SETTINGS

Engine	ft lb	kg m
Main bearings nuts	70	9.7
Big end bolts	35–40	4.8–5.5
Little end bolts (early cars)	25	3.4
Flywheel bolts	40	5.5
Clutch to flywheel bolts	25–30	3.4–4.1
Cylinder head nuts	45–50	6.2–6.9
Rocker post bolts	25	3.4
Rocker box cover nuts	4	0.56
Oil pump nuts	14	1.9
Oil pipe banjo	37	5.1
Oil release valve dome nut	43	5.9
Sump bolts	6	0.8
Crankshaft pulley nut	70	9.6
Camshaft nut	65	8.9
Timing cover 0.25in screws	6	0.8
0.31in screws	14	1.9
Front plate	20	2.8
Rear plate 0.31in screws	20	2.8
0.31in screws 18V	30	4.1
0.375in screws	30	4.1
Water pump bolts	17	2.4
Manifold nuts	15	2.1
Oil filter bolt (early cars)	15	2.1
Carburettor stud nuts to 18V	2	0.28
18V	15	2.1
Distributor clamp bolt nut (25D4)	4.1	0.57
(45D4)	2.5	0.35

SPECIALISTS' ADDRESSES

This is being written in May, 1995. The average age of an MGB today is 23.79 years - not that far off a quarter of a century! Whilst a few MGBs will have received total rebuilds, the majority will still contain many thousands of their original components, many of which, unsurprisingly, will succumb to the effects of old age and keep the massive MGB spares trade busy for many a year to come.

In my own opinion, MGB spares suppliers are the best there is. I find it easier to obtain spares for my twenty-nine year old MGB GT than for any other car I have ever owned. In addition, the prices asked for MGB spares are generally far less than the equivalents for more modern cars.

MGB spares suppliers - take a bow!

Inclusion in the following list of spares suppliers should not be taken as a recommendation, and there are many excellent companies not on the list, which has been compiled to try to cover the UK, rather than be comprehensive.

Bromsgrove MC Centre
(Proprietor Graham Pearce)
Unit 10, Sugarbrook Road, Aston Fields Industrial Estate, Bromsgrove B61 3DW
Telephone 01527 879909 *Fax.* 01527 575385
Bromsgrove MG Centre stock a comprehensive range of spares for the MGB. Graham and his staff are very knowledgeable and always very helpful. The company has a well-staffed workshop and will undertake any work on the MGB, from servicing to complete restoration work and re-shelling. The company has achieved 5-Star ratings with the MG Owner's Club as a spares supplier and for its workshop.

Ron Hopkinson MG Centre
(Proprietor Ron Hopkinson)
850 London Road, Derby DE2 8WA
Telephone 01332 756056 *Fax.* 01332 572332
Ron Hopkinson MG Centre is a long-established and large MGB spares supplier. The company possess facilities for engine and gearbox rebuilding. The staff have always proved helpful and knowledgeable. The company publishes a mail order spares catalogue.

Brown & Gammons Ltd
(Proprietor Ron Gammons)
18 High Street, Baldock, Herts SG7 6AS
Telephone 01462 490049 *Fax.* 01462 896167
Ron Gammons has enjoyed immense success in Historic rallying, with MG cars prepared by his own company taking 2nd. 3rd. and 4th. places in the 1990 Pirelli Classic (and subsequently enjoying outright victory). The company thus supplements its comprehensive range of spares with a selection of performance engine, gearbox and suspension components which in many cases have been proven in the most testing of competition work... The company publishes a mail order spares catalogue.

Pete Harper Restorations
Sugarbrook Industrial Estate, Aston Fields,
Bromsgrove B61 3DW
Pete Harper's premises are usefully situated right next door to the Bromsgrove MG Centre. Pete undertakes body repair work and all work from respraying to a complete MGB restoration.

SIP (Holdings) Ltd
Gelders Hall Road, Shepshed,
Leicestershire LE12 9HN
SIP supply an excellent range of compressors and accessories, MIG and arc welding equipment, for the home restorer. The author used a SIP Handymig gasless MIG welder during the compilation of this book and was impressed with its ease of use and the very good results which were achieved with it. The author's SIP Airmate Tornado 21025 compressor has proven to be one of the most useful tools in the workshop.

MG Owner's Club
Octagon House, Swavesey, Cambridgeshire CB4 5QZ
Telephone 01954 231125
The MG Owner's Club is reportedly the largest single-make car club in the world, with branches in all major export market countries. The club organises a huge range of events, publishes a monthly full colour magazine, runs an insurance scheme, has a large spares department and publishes a list of approved spares suppliers and restorers/workshops.

MG Car Club
Kimber House, PO BOX 251, Abingdon,
Oxford OX14 1FF
Telephone 01235 555552
The MG Car club has 65 centres outside the UK and over 100 within the UK. The club specialises in organising competitive events, including track, rally, hill climb and sprint events. Other club benefits include a magazine, insurance and social/concours events.

The V8 Conversion Company
123 High Street, Farnborough, Kent. BR6 7AZ
Telephone 01689 861211
All the help, advice and parts you need to convert your 1800 'B into a V8 - if you don't fancy doing it yourself, the company carries out full V8 conversions.

British Motor Heritage Ltd
Unipart House, Cowley, Oxford OX4 2PG
Telephone 01865 713510
We must all thank the British Motor Heritage company for the vast range of spares available for our MGBs today. The company supplies (to their own Heritage-approved trade outlets only) body shells for the MGB and GT, plus a wealth of spares.

British Motor Industry Heritage Trust
(Production records tracing service)
Heritage Motor Centre. Gaydon,
Warwickshire CV35 0BJ
Telephone 01926 641188
The BMIHT offer a service which allows MGB owners to ascertain the original specifications of their own car when manufactured, as mentioned in Chapter 2. Telephone to find the current charge for this service.

Classic Cars magazine
(Thoroughbred and Classic Cars outside UK)
King's Reach Tower, Stamford Street,
London SE1 9LS
Telephone 0171 261 5858
Excellent monthly magazine dealing with all aspects of classic car ownership.

Classic and Sportscar magazine
38-42 Hampton Road, Teddington,
Middlesex TW11 0JE
Telephone 0181 943 5995
Thriving glossy magazine.

Popular Classics
Bushfield House, Orton Centre, Peterborough PE2 5UW
Telephone 01733 237111
Lively monthly magazine dealing with all classic and sports cars, with articles on all aspects of owning and driving classic cars.

Practical Classics
Bushfield House, Orton Centre,
Peterborough PE2 5UW
Telephone 01733 237111
Sister magazine to Popular Classics. Ideal for the DIY enthusiast. Concentrates more on the practical side of restoration, repair and maintenance of classic cars.

MG International
Lord Street, Birkenhead, L41 1HT
Telephone 0151 666 1666
MG International is a large spares supplier offering a fast mail order spares service for all MGBs. The range includes special tuning equipment. The company publishes a mail order spares catalogue.

MG SPARES SPECIALISTS

MG Enthusiast Magazine
PO Box 11, Dewsbury, West Yorkshire TW9 2JX

Abbey Autos
1-2 Hill Reach, Woolwich, London SE18 4AJ
Telephone 0181 854 3890
Spares and service.

AG Motors
Church Street, Burton Pidsea, Nr. Hull HU12 9BG
Telephone 01964 671006
Spares, service.

AJ Buckle Sportscars
40 The Drive, Caldecote, Nuneaton CV10 0TW
Telephone 01203 325293
Car sales, spares, servicing, mechanical repair, body restoration.

Aldon Automotive Ltd
Telephone 0138478508
Performance modifications work and components.

Brandon MG Centre
Brandon Lane, Brandon, Co Durham CH7 8SU
Telephone 0191 378 0592
Spares, mail order service.

Britbits
Drinsey Nook, Gainsborough Road, Saxilby, Lincoln LN1 2JJ
Telephone 01522 703774
Spares, mechanical repair, body restorations.

Brooklands MG Centre
Unit 10, Barbour Gardens, Dunmurry, Belfast BT17 9AB
Telephone 01232 301430
Spares and service.

Car Craft
Alstons Court, Leslie Road, Ipswich IP3 9PL
Telephone 01473 723991
Spares, all mechanical repair and body restoration work.

Cardiff MG Centre Cardiff
Unit 10, Alexandra Industrial Estate, Wentlog Road, Cardiff CF3 8LP
Telephone 01222 777834

Cheldon Motor Services
Gatwick MG Centre, Units 5-6 Hollybush Business Centre, Shipleybridge Lane, Horley, Surrey RH6 9TL
Telephone 01342 716306

Composite Automotive Technology Ltd
Unit 6, Audnam Trading Estate, High Street, Audnam, Stourbridge DY8 4AH
Telephone 01384 442203
CAT supply MGB spares both over the counter and mail order, in addition to carrying out all mechanical repair and restoration work.

Cox & Perry
Frettenham Road, Horstead, Coltishall, Norwich NR12 7LB
Telephone 01603 737195
Spares, service.

Paul Depper MGs
The MG Centre, Stafford Road, Great Wyreley, W.Midlands WS6 6BA
Telephone 01922 711727
Spares. Mechanical repair, body restoration. Used spares specialist.

DS Classic Sports Cars
The MG Garage. Warwick Road, Blackhill, Stratford Upon Avon CV37 0PX
Telephone 01789 731739
Spares, MGB car sales.

Early BBB'S MGB Spares
Unit 5, Relkila Buildings, Ebblake Industrial Estate, Verwood, Dorset BH31 6XA
Telephone 01202 823076
Chrome bumper MGB specialist. Spares, service.

Euro MG Centre
32 Bellbrook Industrial Estate, Uckfield, East Sussex. TN22 1QL
Telephone 01825 763051
Car sales, spares, servicing, mechanical repair and body restoration.

G&H Motor Services
46 Heathcote Road, Leamington Spa. CV31 2NF
Telephone 01926 881887
Spares, servicing, mechanical repair and body restoration.

Gloucester MG Centre
Unit A, Ryeford Industrial Estate, Stonehouse, Gloucestershire GL10 2LA
Telephone 01453 825164
The company supplies all new and second-hand spares both over the counter and mail order, in addition to offering restoration and all mechanical services.

Halls Garage
Folkingham Road, Morton, Bourne, Lincs PE10 0NS
Telephone 01778 570540
Spares, service.

Jacob Engineering
Grove Court, Upton St. Leonards, Gloucester GL4 8DA.
Telephone 01452 612006
Spares, workshop, sales.

John Hill MG Centre
Arthur Street, Redditch, Worcestershire B98 8JY
Telephone 01527 520880
Spares, mail order.

Leacy MG
102 Tame Road, Witton, Birmingham B6 7EZ
Telephone 0121 328 3735
Car sales, spares, mechanical repair and restoration.

Meonstoke Garage
Alton Road, Corhampton, Hants. SO3 1ND
Telephone 01489 877823
Car sales, spares, servicing mechanical repair and body restoration.

Mercury Motors
Largo Road, Ludlin Links, Leven, Fife KY8 6DJ
Telephone 01333 320096
Car sales. Servicing, mechanical repair and body restoration.

The MGB Hive
Marshalls Bank. Parson Drive, Wisbech, Cambs PE13 4JE
Telephone 01945 700130
Spares and service.

MG Bits
Guildford, Surrey GU23 6EL
Telephone 01483 223830
Spares, mechanical repair.

MGB Spares & Service
Beech Hill Garage, Beech Hill. Nr. Reading RG27 2AU
Telephone 01734 884774
Spares & service, remarkably enough.

MG Car Clinic
Ackrill Automotive, High Street, Littlebourne, Canterbury, Kent.
Telephone 01227 720121
Spares, servicing, mechanical repair and body restoration.

MG Services
34 Fulmer Drive, Gerrards Cross, Bucks.
Telephone 01753 880267
Spares, mail order, servicing, mechanical repair and body restoration.

Moss Darlington
15 Allington Way, Yarm Road Industrial Estate, Darlington, Co. Durham DL1 4QB
Telephone 01325 281343
Huge spares business with eight UK retail showrooms (mail order address above) plus others in the USA. Special tuning equipment, free quarterley magazine to customers. The company publishes a mail order spares catalogue.

Moto-Build
328 Bath Road, Hounslow, Middlesex.
Telephone 0181 572 8733

MRP Garages
Carreg Farm. Craignant, Nr. Selattyn, Oswestry, Shrops. SY10 7NX
Telephone 01691 718476
Spares, service.

NE MG Services
3,Tunstall Road, Sunderland.
Telephone 0191 567 5751
Spares, mechanical repair and body restoration.

Nottingham MG Centre
Unit 13, Colwick Business Park, Private Road No.2, Colwick, Nottingham NG42JR
Telephone 0115 961 5283
Spares, servicing, mechanical repair and restoration.

PJM Motors
Unit 2, Bert Smith Way, Adderley Road, Market Drayton, Shropshire TF9 3SN
Telephone 01630 652873
Spares, servicing and mechanical repair, plus upholstery.

RK Autos
Unit 3, Swift Lane, Bagshot, Surrey.
Telephone 01276 452569
Spares, servicing, mechanical repair and body restoration.

Rugby MG Centre
122 Oxford Street, Rugby.
Telephone 01788 571896
Car sales, spares, mechanical repair, body restorations.

Steve McKie MG Services
Albert Street North, Whittington Moor, Chesterfield S41 8NP.
Telephone 01246 454527
Spares, servicing, Crypton tuning, mechanical repair and body restoration.

Sussex MG Parts
Unit 132 Huffwood Trading Estate, Partridge Green, Nr. Horsham, West Sussex RH13 8AU
Telephone 01403 711551
Spares. Mail order catalogue.

Tamar Valley MG Centre
Harrow Barrow, Callington, Cornwall PL17 8JQ
Telephone 01579 50542
Spares, servicing, mechanical repair and body restoration.

Welsh MG Centre
Pen-y-Bryn, Wrexham, Clwyd, North Wales.
Telephone 01978 263445
Spares, servicing, mechanical repair, body restoration and MOT testing.

US CLUB ADDRESSES

American MGB Axxociation
PO Box 11401, Chicago, Il 6061 10401

American MGC Register
PO Box 2816, Setauket, NY 11733, Connecticut

Bloomington MGB Club Unlimited
7421 N, Chester Avenue, Indianapolis, Indiana 46240

Central Jersey MG Club
14 Birchwood Road, denville, NJ 07834

Central Ohio MGB Association
318 Reber Avenue, Lancerter, Ohio 43130

MGCC DC Club
19600 Crystal Rock Drive, 24 Germantown, MD 20874

MG Club of Central Florida
309 E Alpine Street, Altamonte Springs, Florida 32701

MG Motorcar Group
9832 N Range Line Road, Mequon, Wisconsin 53092

Philadelphia MG Club
1913D Darby Road, Havertown, PA 19083

Plymouth County MG Owners Club
7 Chestnut Street, Kingston, MA 02364

Rocky Mountain MGCC
PO Box 152, Denver,Colorado 80201

San Diego MG Club
PO Box 112111, San Diego, CA 92111

Seattle MG Car Club
5204 NE 193rd Place, Seattle, WA 98155

Washington MG Car Club
Northwest Central, 12835 N E 36th Street, Belview, Washinton 98005

Willamette MG Club
2375 N 5th Street, Springfield, Oregon 97477

Windsor-Detroit MG Club
1327 Austin, Lincoln Park,Michigan 48146-2002

INDEX

Page references in *italics* refer to captions.

MILLER'S

Every two minutes someone, somewhere buys a Miller's Guide

MILLER'S COLLECTORS CARS PRICE GUIDE

For anyone interested in classic and collectors cars, this book is a must, with its extensive coverage of a huge variety of vehicles and motoring paraphernalia. The only illustrated classic car price guide available.

£19.99

MILLER'S CLASSIC MOTORCYCLES PRICE GUIDE

A comprehensive and informative survey of the classic motorcycle market over the past twelve months. Coverage ranges from manufacturer's classics to military and competition motorcycles, and "specials" are now included.

£10.99

Latest editions will be supplied, subject to availability.

Both Guides are available from all good bookshops and specialist wholesalers.
In case of difficulty please phone 01933-414000.

Miller's Publications is part of Reed International Books Limited
Registered Office: Michelin House, 81 Fulham Road, London, SW3 6RB
Registered in England No:1527729